W9-BFN-658

Contents at a Glance

Contents

Thomas Fredell

With Michael Morrison, Stephen Campbell, Ian Morrish,
and Charles Williams

SAMS
Teach Yourself

Windows
Script Host
in 21 Days

SAMS

A Division of Macmillan Computer Publishing
201 West 103rd St., Indianapolis, Indiana, 46290 USA

Sams Teach Yourself Windows Script Host in 21 Days

Copyright © 1999 by Sams Publishing

International Standard Book Number: 0-672-31374-x

Library of Congress Catalog Card Number: 98-85760

Printed in the United States of America

First Printing: July 1999

00   99   98   4   3   2   1

Trademarks

Warning and Disclaimer

ACQUISITIONS EDITOR
Dustin Sullivan

DEVELOPMENT EDITOR
Tom Dinse

MANAGING EDITOR
Lisa Wilson

PROJECT EDITOR
Sara Bosin

COPY EDITOR
Kelly Talbot

INDEXER
Becky Hornyak

PROOFREADER
Benjamin Berg

TECHNICAL EDITOR
Eric Richardson

INTERIOR DESIGN
Gary Adair

COVER DESIGN
Aren Howell

COPY WRITER
Eric Bogert

LAYOUT TECHNICIANS
Ayanna Lacey
Heather Miller

About the Authors

Thomas Fredell is the co-founder and CTO of Cambridge Technology Vision (www.cambridgevision.com), the leading provider of extranet software that assists corporations in performing mergers and acquisitions. Thomas was the first graduate with a degree in cognitive science from the University of Virginia. Since then, he's spent most of his time developing software and performing consulting to assist companies in integrating Internet technologies with their business processes. He spends his minimal free time playing with his wife Susan and dog Chloe, skiing (particularly steep mogul trails), and sailing.

If you want to reach Thomas, please send him email at t@email.com, or visit him at www.fredell.com.

Michael Morrison is a writer, developer, toy inventor, and author of a variety of books, including *Sams Teach Yourself MFC in 24 Hours*, *Complete Idiot's Guide to Java 1.2*, *Java 1.1 Unleashed*, *How To Program JavaBeans*, *Presenting JavaBeans*, *Sams Teach Yourself Internet Game Programming with Java in 21 Days*, and *Windows 95 Game Developer's Guide Using the Game SDK*. Michael is also the instructor of several Web-based courses, including DigitalThink's Introduction to Java 2 series, JavaBeans for Programmers series, and Win32 Programming series. When not glued to his computer, risking life and limb on his skateboard, or watching movies with his wife, Mahsheed, Michael enjoys hanging out by his koi pond.

Stephen Campbell, president of Marchview Consultants Ltd., considers himself a generalist in the specialized field of Information Technology. Lately, he has concentrated on architecting and implementing enterprise directory and messaging solutions for medium and large corporations using Microsoft BackOffice products. As a long-time developer, Stephen is comfortable designing and implementing sophisticated three-tier applications and Active Server Page Web sites. He saw the benefits of Windows Script Host early on, developing automated Exchange server installation and configuration scripts. Stephen can be reached by email at stephen.campbell@marchview.com.

Ian Morrish is an IT consultant in New Zealand. He specializes in BackOffice architecture and solutions and is always working with leading-edge technologies. Ian saw the potential of Windows Script Host when it was part of the IE4 beta, and soon provided the first Web site to promote this new technology: http://wsh.glazier.co.nz.

He is often heard saying "I'm not a programmer," which you might not believe, but this is just a hobby. Any excuse to use a script in a project is met with great enthusiasm. Ian does have a life outside of computers; his wife Cathy (imported from California) and two children, Joshua and Daniel, get to see him for dinner most nights.

Chuck Williams currently works at your "average" Fortune 1000 company and is responsible for all Office Systems and Internet endeavors. He co-manages an outsourced environment that consists of approximately 180 employees and a multimillion dollar budget. Prior to this position he was the corporation's Webmaster, and was responsible for developing the company's intranet and extranet. Chuck has contributed to *Windows NT Professional Reference* and *Active Server Pages Unleashed*. He earned an Oracle certification in 1995, his MSCE in 1996, and, in 1998, focused on Information Security issues. Chuck received his B.S. in computer science and interpersonal and public communication from Central Michigan University and is currently earning an M.S. in computer and information science from the University of Michigan.

Dedication

In memory of my father-in-law, George William Bishop, an inspiring man. You are greatly loved and missed.

Acknowledgments

Many thanks to the crew at Macmillan that helped to make this book a reality. In particular, Dustin Sullivan is the guy that made this book possible. He was extremely patient and understanding when work demands made it difficult to be as responsive as I'd like to have been, and he was very adept at adding superior authors to the mix to enhance the book. My thanks to the other members of the team at Sams, including the development editor, Tom Dinse, and the technical editor, Eric Richardson.

I also want to acknowledge the hard work of the other authors who helped to make this book a superb resource for the Windows Script Host. Many thanks to Michael Morrison, Stephen Campbell, Ian Morrish, and Charles Williams; your contributions were excellent! I have no doubt that our readers will appreciate the effort that went into making this book the most comprehensive and useful resource for the Windows Script Host.

Special thanks to Rob Lanni at Combe Incorporated; he provided ideas and inspiration about practical applications for scripting in a corporate environment.

On a personal note, I want to thank my wife Susan for putting up with me while I was working on the book. She was very supportive and understanding when I needed to devote my weekends and evenings to writing. Susan, you're the greatest! Many thanks to my parents, Lars and Wendy, who made this all possible by being terrific parents and by supporting my interest in computers. I couldn't have asked for better parents!

To everyone else—my family, the whole Bishop family, including Bill, Sharon, Mike, and Linda, and my friends—Thank You!

Tell Us What You Think!

As the reader of this book, *you* are our most important critic and commentator. We value your opinion and want to know what we're doing right, what we could do better, what areas you'd like to see us publish in, and any other words of wisdom you're willing to pass our way.

As an associate publisher for Sams, I welcome your comments. You can fax, email, or write me directly to let me know what you did or didn't like about this book—as well as what we can do to make our books stronger.

Please note that I cannot help you with technical problems related to the topic of this book, and that due to the high volume of mail I receive, I might not be able to reply to every message.

When you write, please be sure to include this book's title and author as well as your name and phone or fax number. I will carefully review your comments and share them with the author and editors who worked on the book.

Fax: 317.581.4770

Email: opsys@mcp.com

Mail: Associate Publisher
          Sams Publishing
          201 West 103rd Street
          Indianapolis, IN 46290 USA

Introduction

"Damn those batch files!"

"I can't stand batch files!"

If you're an experienced Microsoft DOS or Windows user, you've probably cursed batch files at one time or another. Batch files enable you to automate tasks that you perform repetitively, but they are pretty weak and relatively unstructured. It can also be difficult to debug them and get them to work correctly, and they have some strict limitations that severely limit their capabilities.

The Windows Script Host (WSH) has come to the rescue of Windows users that are held hostage by crummy batch files. The Windows platform includes a very powerful scripting solution that enables you to do everything that is possible with batch files—plus much, much more! They are incredibly useful no matter what your needs are—whether you're an administrator, a power user, or a software developer.

Note
> By the way, you'll notice that throughout this book, *Windows Script Host* is referred to as *Windows Scripting Host*. Microsoft decided to change the name while this book was being written, and although the title was changed to reflect that, we didn't go back and change every occurrence in the book.

WSH is an intrinsic part of Microsoft Windows 98, Windows 2000, and Windows NT 5.0. For earlier versions such as Windows NT 4.0 or Windows 95, you can install a free operating system add-in from Microsoft. When you have WSH running on your computer, you have the capability to run scripts that use the Microsoft VBScript or JScript languages to automate your tasks. WSH is also flexible enough to support other languages, thanks to its modular architecture. Furthermore, WSH enables you to automate practically everything in Windows because it's plugged in to the standard OLE/ActiveX capabilities.

The goal of this book is to teach you everything about WSH and all its uses. I think that we've come pretty close to the first goal, but we can't possibly reach the second because WSH is so flexible it can do almost anything! Instead, we decided lay out a ton of information about WSH, and then discuss ways that you can use it to automate a wide variety of tasks—everything from working with files to administering Microsoft SQL server and the Microsoft IIS Web server. Hopefully, when you've finished this book, you'll have the capability to see how WSH technology can be applied creatively to solve your unique challenges.

How to Use This Book

This book is intended to be a standalone, comprehensive guide for the Windows Script Host technology. It lays a foundation for understanding WSH by discussing the roots of the technology and by looking at some basic examples. Then it provides a reference for the objects and languages that are part of WSH. Finally, it moves into very detailed examples of how you can use WSH for many different tasks. Along the way, we also discuss the tools that you can use to build WSH scripts, techniques for debugging WSH scripts, and steps for deploying the scripts that you write.

In short, if you want one comprehensive guide to learning and using WSH, this book is it! It covers WSH from soup to nuts, and lays a strong foundation so that you can leverage WSH for your own needs. It also provides standard functions for many tasks that will make it easier for you to quickly leverage WSH.

This book is a great book no matter what type of user you are; if you're an administrator, you'll be intrigued by the ways that we use WSH to script user logins and to perform server administration for software such as Microsoft IIS and SQL Server. If you're a power user, you'll find that it is a useful tutorial and reference for software, and that you can use it to make your life easier by automating many of the tasks that you do manually. Finally, if you're a developer, you'll love the detailed descriptions and examples of how you can build your own components to integrate with WSH.

How This Book Is Organized

Sams Teach Yourself Windows Script Host in 21 Days covers the Windows Scripting Host technology in depth. For each of the 21 days, there's a corresponding chapter. Following is a rough breakdown of the chapters and the categories into which they fit.

Introduction to WSH

Day 1, "Introduction to the Windows Script Host (WSH)," is WSH 101. You learn about the types of technologies that have been used for automation, such as batch files, and how WSH fits in to the picture. You also get an overview of the components that are used with WSH.

Day 2, "Writing a Simple Script Using WSH," jumps right in and shows you how you can begin to create WSH scripts. It describes the tools that are used to write scripts, from the Windows Notepad to more powerful editors, and gives you a step-by-step process with a detailed example that shows you how to create your scripts.

Day 3, "The Scripting Object Model," provides a comprehensive reference, with examples, for the objects that are provided by the scripting engine that is used by WSH.

Day 4, "The WSH Object Model," gives you a comprehensive reference, with examples, for the objects that are provided by WSH.

Day 5, "Using Microsoft VBScript with WSH," gives you a reference for the VBScript language that can be used with WSH.

Day 6, "Using Microsoft JScript with WSH," gives you a reference for the JScript language that can be used with WSH.

Running and Debugging WSH Scripts

Day 7, "Running and Scheduling Scripts," shows you how you can run and schedule scripts to automate repetitive tasks.

Day 8, "Testing and Debugging WSH Scripts," shows you practical techniques that you can use to test and debug your scripts to ensure that they run correctly.

Performing Administrative Tasks Using WSH

Day 9, "Handling WSH Script Arguments and Reading/Writing Files," gives you some standard techniques that you can use over and over again in your scripts.

Day 10, "Replacing Batch Files with WSH," shows you how you can begin to eliminate your batch files and replace them with more robust WSH scripts.

Day 11, "Administering User Logins, Program Settings, Folders, and File Shortcuts Using WSH," will help you to understand how you can use WSH to control users, programs, folders, and files.

Day 12, "Automating Microsoft SQL Server Administration Using WSH Scripts," shows you how you can leverage the SQL Server Distributed Management Objects to automate your SQL Server administration.

Day 13, "Automating Microsoft IIS Administration Using WSH Scripts," will help you to create scripts that enable you to quickly and easily administer the Microsoft IIS Web server.

Scripting Applications and Accessing Databases Using WSH

Day 14, "Overview of WSH and Application Scripting Capabilities," describes how you can use WSH to script any application that provides interfaces through OLE Automation/ActiveX.

Day 15, "Scripting the Microsoft Office Suite," shows you how you can use WSH scripts to control and automate Microsoft Office applications such as Word and Excel.

Day 16, "Using WSH to Access Databases Through Microsoft Active Data Objects (ADO)," offers an introduction to the Microsoft Active Data Objects and a reference that will help you to use ADOs to access databases from your WSH scripts.

Day 17, "Using ADO for WSH Scripting Tasks," shows you how to use ADO objects to integrate databases with your WSH scripts.

Day 18, "Using WSH to Manipulate the Microsoft Active Directory," will help you use WSH scripts to control the Microsoft Active Directory.

Extending and Deploying WSH Scripts

Day 19, "Using Scripting for Messaging," touches on using Active Directory to manage Microsoft Exchange server and goes into more depth on Collaborative Data Objects (CDO), which are Microsoft's objects for accessing any messaging system.

Day 20, "Using WSH with Custom VB and Java Objects," shows you how to create new objects, using Visual Basic and Java, that you can use to enhance your WSH scripts.

Day 21, "Deploying Script Solutions," will help you transfer your scripts to other work-stations or servers so that you can leverage the scripts you write throughout your organization.

Special Features in This Book

This book has some special features that are designed to help you get the information you need—fast. These features are described in this section.

SIDEBARS CONTAIN INTERESTING NUGGETS OF INFORMATION

Sidebars are detours from the main text. They usually provide background or interesting information that is relevant, but not essential reading. You might find information that's a bit more technical than the surrounding text, or you might find a brief diversion into the historical aspects of the text.

Note

Notes provide additional information that is related to the text. They provide you with useful tidbits of information.

Cautions alert you to problems that you might encounter when you are using parts of the technology.

Conventions

In addition to the special features that help you find what you need, this book uses some special conventions that make it easier to understand. The following sections describe the keyboard, mouse, typographical, and other conventions found in this book.

Keyboard

The keyboard conventions that are listed here help you to better understand what the instructions are telling you to do. For example, they help you understand the key combinations and menu commands that you are type or choose:

Element	Convention
Hot keys	Hot keys are underlined in this book, just as they appear on Windows menus. For example, the F in File is a hot key. To use a hot key, press Alt and the underlined letter to make that menu appear.
Key combinations	Key combinations are separated by plus signs. For example, "Press Ctrl+Alt+D" means that you press and hold down the Ctrl and Alt keys simultaneously and then press and release the D key. Always press and release, rather than hold down, the last key in a key combination.
Menu commands	A comma is used to separate the parts of a pull-down menu command. For example, if you are told to "Choose File, New," you need to open the File menu and select the New option.

In most cases, special-purpose keys are referred to by the text that actually appears on them on a standard 101-key keyboard. For example, you'll see "Press Esc," "Press F1," or "Press Enter." However, some of the keys on your keyboard don't have words on them. Following are the conventions that are used for those keys:

Backspace key
Up-, down-, left-, or right-arrow key

Mouse

In this book, the following phrases tell you how to operate the mouse within Windows:

Click
Double-click
Drag
Drop

Typeface

This book uses some special typeface conventions that make it easier to read:

Element	Convention
Italic	Italic indicates new terms. It also indicates place-holders (words that stand for what you actually type) in commands, addresses, and code listings.
Bold	Bold is used for menu commands and options that appear in dialog boxes, as well as for URLs.
`Computer font`	`Computer font` is used for text you see onscreen, code listings, and any text you're asked to type.

Other

When a line of code is too long to fit on one line of this book, it is broken at a convenient place and continued to the next line. The continuation of the line is preceded by a code continuation character (➥).

WEEK 1

DAY 1

Introduction to the Windows Script Host (WSH)

The Windows Scripting Host (WSH) is an incredible enhancement to the Microsoft Windows series of operating systems. Finally, Windows users have equivalent scripting functionality to what UNIX users have had for years!

On the first day of your journey to become an expert WSH user, you'll do the following:

- Get an introduction to the new Microsoft scripting technology
- Learn about how WSH relates to other scripting technologies
- Learn about the major components of WSH

Introduction to the Windows Script Host (WSH)

Microsoft has finally fixed a problem that has plagued the MS-DOS and Windows operating systems for years. Until recently, neither MS-DOS nor Windows has included a powerful scripting tool. Anyone who has tried to automate standard tasks on a PC running Windows or MS-DOS knows that it isn't easy. At best, you can throw together a couple of commands in a DOS batch file, but you don't have any real control over what happens: There's no looping, poor variable support, painfully simple logical statements, and limited error-handling support. UNIX users have been thumbing their noses about this issue for years!

The solution to the problem is the Microsoft Windows Scripting Host (WSH). WSH leverages technologies that Microsoft developed to perform scripting on the Web; you'll learn more about how it relates to other Microsoft Internet technologies later in this chapter. WSH provides the capability to develop scripts using the Microsoft scripting languages VBScript and JScript (which is very similar to the popular JavaScript language). Like DOS batch files, you can run them from the command line. Unlike DOS batch files, they have all the power of the programming language that you choose; for example, if you're using VBScript, you have the capability to define variables, use loops, and do anything that you would expect from a robust language. Additionally, you have the capability to access and control ActiveX objects. That means that the capabilities of WSH for automation are almost limitless! Figure 1.1 shows you the output from the simple WSH script in Listing 1.1.

FIGURE 1.1

The output from a simple WSH script.

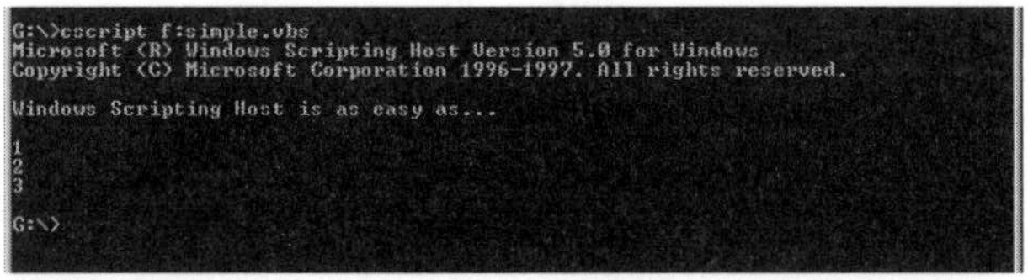

```
G:\>cscript f:simple.vbs
Microsoft (R) Windows Scripting Host Version 5.0 for Windows
Copyright (C) Microsoft Corporation 1996-1997. All rights reserved.

Windows Scripting Host is as easy as...

1
2
3

G:\>
```

LISTING 1.1   A SIMPLE WSH SCRIPT

```
Dim count

Wscript.Echo "Windows Scripting Host is as easy as..."
Wscript.Echo ""

For count = 1 to 3
    Wscript.Echo count
Next
```

> **Note**
>
> You will have trouble running this script from the command line if you don't already have the WSH components installed. If you have Windows 98 or are running Windows NT 4.0 with the NT option pack, you already have WSH. Otherwise, you need to install the WSH components. You can get them off of the Microsoft Scripting Web site at http://www.microsoft.com/scripting.

In this book, you'll learn about the underpinnings of the Windows Scripting Host. You'll find out how it works, you'll learn about the VBScript and JScript languages that can be used with it, and you'll see useful examples that you can leverage to automate tasks that you might need to accomplish as a user, programmer, or system administrator.

Background: Automating Tasks

The moment that you type the same command twice at the command line, or heaven forbid, a string of commands, you realize that it would be great to be able to capture the commands that you entered so that you can run them again without having to retype all of them. You record your commands in some type of command or script file. If you use a word processor such as Microsoft Word or a spreadsheet a la Excel, you might have automated some of your common tasks using macros. Macros are conceptually similar to scripts; the difference is that they run within an application environment such as Word or Excel.

After you've done that, you might find that the commands are good, but a little inflexible. Sometimes you might want them to do things a little differently; for example, you might not want to hard-code the name of a file that your commands process. Instead, you might prefer to be able to tell the script what file to process. You implement parameters for your script.

If you're an experienced computer user, this probably sounds like an experience that you might have had first-hand. If you haven't had this experience, you have a lot to gain from this book because it will show you how you can begin to automate things that you might be doing repetitively today.

Your capability to automate tasks and to create command or script files depends to some degree on the type of operating system that you're running. If you're a Windows user, you have the option of using DOS batch files or WSH scripts. If you're a UNIX or Linux user, you can use common UNIX scripting languages such as Perl or TCL. To put these scripting solutions into context, and so that you understand the background for WSH, a little description of each is given in the following sections.

DOS Batch Files

DOS batch files were the original command scripting tools for the MS-DOS operating system. As the Windows shell emerged, DOS batch files were carried forward as the inherent scripting technology. Even with the version of Windows that finally left DOS behind, Microsoft Windows NT, batch files remained the only scripting choice provided by the operating system.

Batch files are extremely simple text files that contain sets of commands. Some commands are inherent in the batch language; for example, the IF command is used for logical processing. From a batch file, you can also call or use any other program in the system. For example, you can use the sort program to sort the contents of a file alphabetically. (The sort program is a standard DOS-style utility that is provided with Microsoft Windows.) Figure 1.2 shows a sample batch file that takes a text file as input and displays the contents sorted alphabetically.

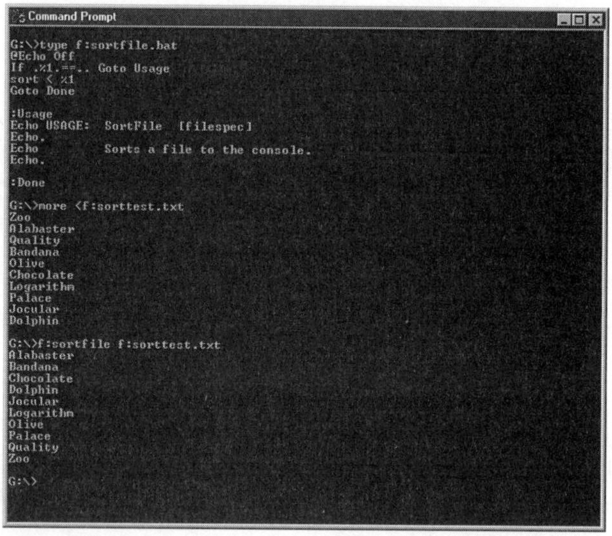

FIGURE 1.2

An example of a DOS batch file.

The benefit of DOS batch files is that they provide a simple, easily understandable language for command scripting. At the most basic level of functionality, it doesn't take a whole lot of knowledge to slap together a few commands in a single file. However, there are a lot of problems with batch files.

1

If you need to do an iterative process, batch files can be extremely difficult to use. Why? Because they have no intrinsic looping mechanism. About the best that you can do is have the batch file call itself, and use some flags to make sure that you break out of the call-loop at some point. And if you want to do a specific number of iterations, such as performing some task *x* times, forget about it! There might be a way to kludge that type of functionality in a batch file, but if there is, it would be complex enough that no one would want to maintain it!

DOS batch files are a simple method of command scripting, but they suffer from a number of serious limitations. Looping is one of the easiest limitations to point out, but there are many others as well (such as limited variable handling, no inherent regular expression tools, and no capability to create self-contained functions or procedures). Certainly, compared to UNIX scripting languages, batch files are a weak, kludgey solution to a common problem. Thankfully, they've been supplemented by the Windows Scripting Host, which you'll read about later in this chapter!

UNIX Scripting

The various flavors of the UNIX operating system provide robust scripting capabilities. The UNIX system shell, which is basically the equivalent of the command prompt in Windows, enables you to define shell scripts that automate tasks. Several languages are available for scripting; two of the most popular are Perl and TCL. Unlike DOS batch files, Perl and TCL are languages that include all the functionality that you would expect from a full programming language. Using variables, implementing loops, and creating functions or procedures are simple using either language.

With either Perl or TCL (often pronounced "Tickle"), you have full capabilities to create variables and to perform iteration and looping. You also have some really useful capabilities, such as Perl associative arrays and support for regular expressions. Associative arrays, which are supported by WSH and which you'll read about later in this book, enable you to create arrays that are indexed by strings rather than by numbers. Regular expressions are expressions that provide a matching syntax. You might be familiar with the * notation in DOS. That's an example of simple regular expression syntax. The * acts as a wildcard, so if you type del *.doc in the DOS or NT command line, all the files in the current directory with the .doc extension will be deleted. That's a very simple example of the type of wildcard capabilities that are possible with regular expressions; they can be extremely complex. Support for regular expressions provided by WSH will be discussed later in this book.

Note

> One "problem" with Perl is that Perl code can become very difficult to
> understand. As a matter of fact, there are contests where the explicit goal is
> to develop the most complex Perl expression in the shortest number of lines
> that performs the most interesting task. People can get extremely creative in
> the contest! It's truly amazing what can be done using just a paragraph's
> worth of Perl code. The only problem is that the code looks like junk! If you
> take a quick look at it, it looks like the contents of a corrupted file! One of
> the dangers with Perl is that it's easy to develop code that will be literally
> not maintainable.

Knowledgeable DOS power users have envied the scripting capabilities of UNIX for
years! There simply hasn't been a built-in solution for powerful scripting on the
Windows platform until the introduction of WSH. Granted, there are other third-party
solutions, and there are Perl interpreters for the Windows platform, but they don't provide the robust ActiveX support that is intrinsic to WSH.

Microsoft's New Solution: WSH

The Windows Scripting Host (WSH) is a new solution to the problem of command
scripting for the Windows operating systems. WSH enables you to develop command
scripts using a scripting engine. It provides two scripting engines: the Microsoft
VBScript and JScript scripting engines. VBScript is a language that's very similar to
Microsoft Visual Basic, and JScript is very similar to the JavaScript language, which has
become popular for client-side Web browser scripting. You might also be familiar with
either language if you've used the Microsoft Active Server Pages (ASP) technology for
server-side scripting in the IIS environment.

You might wonder why VBScript and JScript are referred to as scripting engines. The
reason is that Microsoft has defined a very powerful concept for the interface between
the scripting language and the scripting environment. With WSH, you can plug in new
scripting engines that provide different language capabilities. For example, you could
plug a version of Perl into WSH if you prefer to use the Perl language as your scripting
language. More of the conceptual model of WSH is covered a little later in this chapter.
Also, if you're unfamiliar with the VBScript or JScript languages, don't worry because
you get a primer in Chapter 5, "Using Microsoft VBScript with WSH," and Chapter 6,
"Using Microsoft JScript with WSH."

In a nutshell, WSH provides much more robust scripting capabilities than DOS batch
files. When you write WSH scripts, you can take full advantage of the features of the
language that you decide to use. For example, if you choose VBScript, you can create
variables, make iterative FOR or WHILE loops, or do anything else that is a standard

capability of the language. It is much, much more powerful than DOS batch files. It's very comparable to the UNIX scripting languages, but it's even more powerful in one respect: With WSH, you can leverage any of the massive number of OLE automation or ActiveX components that have been developed for the Windows platform. You'll read more about that later, and you'll see some examples of the power of WSH to leverage OLE and ActiveX components.

Note

It's important to point out that various script interpreters are available for the Windows environment. For example, there are several Perl interpreters that are available for Windows. So, before WSH, you could use a script interpreter if you wanted a more powerful solution than DOS batch files. However, there are two major benefits of WSH over that alternative: (1) WSH enables you to leverage any ActiveX object or component; (2) unlike add-on script interpreters, WSH is becoming an integral part of the Microsoft Windows operating system, so you'll eventually be able to use it immediately in any Windows environment.

WSH Overview

The Windows Scripting Host (WSH) enables you to execute scripts directly from the Windows desktop or the command prompt. WSH uses the same scripting engines that are used by Microsoft Internet Explorer for client-side scripts running in the Web browser and by Microsoft Internet Information server for client-side scripts that are embedded in Active Server Pages. The difference is that WSH provides a low-memory requirement environment to execute scripts that you develop.

When you use WSH, you can use any scripting language that provides a scripting engine for WSH. VBScript and JScript are provided "out of the box", but third-party vendors might provide support for other languages such as Perl, TCL, REXX, and others. This capability of WSH makes it an incredibly flexible tool! If you come from a UNIX background, it gives you the capability to stay with a scripting language that you already use, assuming that a Windows scripting engine exists for the language. One of the major benefits of WSH is that scripting engines, assuming that they successfully implement all the interfaces required by WSH, should all be able to leverage the same ActiveX components! (See Figure 1.3) That's incredibly powerful because that means that irrespective of the language you use, you can still leverage all the capabilities of the ActiveX components on your system. For example, if you want to write a script that uses Microsoft Excel to dynamically generate a chart and spreadsheet, you can use any WSH language—even Perl—to do it.

FIGURE **1.3**

The WSH architecture with scripting engines and ActiveX component access.

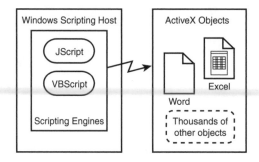

Right now, WSH is provided as an add-on component for Microsoft Windows 95 and NT 4.0, but it is an integrated component of Windows 98 and will be an integrated component of Windows NT 2000. It's very worthwhile to learn WSH. It will rapidly become the standard for scripting in the Windows environment. Microsoft is already leveraging it for the installation of some of their technologies; for example, the Windows NT 4.0 option pack, which includes the Microsoft Transaction Server, includes VBScript script files to install or uninstall MTS examples.

WSH and Scripting Engines

WSH scripting engines are COM components that support the IActiveScriptParse COM interface. Because Microsoft has defined the interface between the scripting engine and the scripting environment using the COM interface conventions (see Figure 1.4), new scripting engines can be added as easily as new COM components are added to a system.

Note

For those of you who are unfamiliar with COM, here's a quick explanation. COM stands for the Component Object Model. It is the object technology that Microsoft has used for the Windows operating system. It's the underlying technology used by OLE (Object Linking and Embedding), which enables you to embed documents, such as spreadsheets, in other documents, such as word processing files. Fairly recently, Microsoft has begun to refer to almost all these technologies under the ActiveX umbrella. Throughout this book, any COM/OLE capabilities of WSH are referred to as ActiveX capabilities.

When WSH runs a script, it first instantiates the scripting engine by creating the COM component that implements the scripting language. Then, it passes the text of the script to the scripting engine by calling the IActiveScriptParse::ParseScriptText() method. The scripting engine is responsible for parsing and executing the text of the script.

FIGURE 1.4

*A diagram of the WSH
script interface.*

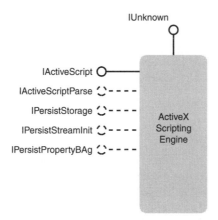

There are two ways for you to run a script using WSH: You can either use the command-line `cscript` program or the Windows-interface `wscript` program. When you use either, it finds the appropriate scripting engine to interpret your script by examining the Windows Registry. The following steps are performed by WSH to find and instantiate the appropriate scripting engine component:

1. It searches the `HKEY_CLASSES_ROOT` Registry key to find an entry that corresponds to the extension of the scripting file. For example, if you are executing a VBScript script, the file extension of the script is `.vbs`.

2. The default value of the file extension entry in the Registry points to a different Registry entry. For the `.vbs` file, it has the value `VBSFile`. WSH opens the entry under `HKEY_CLASSES_ROOT` with the key `VBSFile` to retrieve the scripting engine identifier, which is stored in the `ScriptEngine` value. The `ScriptEngine` value is, appropriately enough, `VBScript` for the VBScript language.

3. WSH uses the `ScriptEngine` value to find the CLSID for the implementation of the scripting engine. The CLSID is, of course, stored in the Registry. It is the default value of the `HKEY_CLASSES_ROOT\VBScript` key.

4. WSH instantiates the scripting engine component by calling the Windows COM API `CoCreateInstance()` function. The API call causes the Windows ActiveX libraries to instantiate an instance of the scripting object. The result of `CoCreateInstance()`, assuming that the call is successful, is a pointer to the `IUnknown` interface of the scripting engine.

5. Finally, WSH retrieves a pointer to the `IActiveScriptParse` interface of the scripting engine by calling `IUnknown::QueryInterface()` with the CLSID of the interface. Assuming that `QueryInterface()` succeeds, the scripting host can now interact with the scripting engine.

Running Scripts Using WSH

As indicated in the previous section, you have two options to use WSH to run a script. You can either run a script using the command-line or console WSH scripting utility (cscript), or using the Windows interface version of the utility (wscript).

The cscript utility uses the following syntax:

```
cscript scriptname.extension [options] [arguments]
```

Note

> The cscript command options control the way that WSH executes scripts. You'll notice that all the options include two slashes (//) in front of the option name. If you have used command-line utilities before, you might find that strange because typically, command options are prepended either with a single slash or with a dash. You must make sure to use two slashes! This is because cscript uses the double slashes to differentiate the cscript options from the arguments for your script.

The options for cscript are the following:

//B	Runs the script in batch mode. In batch mode, script errors and prompts are prevented from displaying.
//H:Cscript	Changes the default scripting host to the cscript.exe program.
//H:Wscript	Changes the default scripting host to the wscript.exe program. wscript.exe is typically the default option.
//I	Runs the script in interactive mode. Interactive mode is the opposite of batch mode; both script errors and prompts are displayed to the end user.
//Logo	Causes the scripting host to output a logo that indicates the version of the scripting host and the Microsoft copyright information.
//NoLogo	Prevents the scripting host from displaying its logo banner when it runs a script.
//S	Saves the current command-line options for this user. This can be used to ensure, for example, that all scripts are run in batch mode and that the logo is never displayed.
//T:nn	Sets the time out in seconds for the script. This is maximum time that a script is permitted to run before it is automatically terminated. This can ensure that scripts with errors such as infinite loops are shut down.
//?	Displays usage information for the cscript program.

When you want to pass arguments to your script, you include them after any options that you pass to `cscript`. Make sure that you don't use double-slashes in front of arguments to your script! If you use double-slashes, `cscript` will interpret the arguments as arguments to `cscript`, not arguments to your script. This might cause `cscript` to fail if an invalid option is specified, or might cause unexpected behavior if your script argument has the same initial letter as a `cscript` option.

You can also execute scripts using the `wscript` program. When you run `wscript`, it provides you with a dialog box that enables you to set execution options as illustrated in Figure 1.5.

FIGURE 1.5

The wscript *options dialog box.*

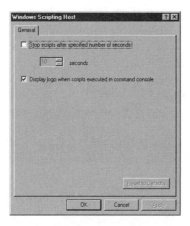

The `wscript` program is associated by default with the extensions of the script files for which you have scripting engines. For a standard WSH scripting installation, this means that `wscript` is associated with the `.vbs`, for VBScript, and `.js`, for JScript, file extensions.

The file association enables you to execute scripts by opening them from the Windows Explorer. You can make use of this capability to list scripts on your desktop or Start menu that you can launch with a mouse click.

One of the major differences between `cscript` and `wscript` is that `cscript` echoes output to the console, whereas `wscript` displays output in a pop-up message box. There are some advantages to having the console output; it makes it much easier to look at a large set of information. With `wscript`, the dialog boxes can quickly become tedious.

In Chapter 7, "Running and Scheduling Scripts," you'll see some examples using `cscript` and `wscript`, and you'll learn how you can customize the options for a script using a `.wsh` file.

Languages Provided with WSH

The Windows Scripting Host provides standard support for the Microsoft VBScript and
JScript languages. VBScript is a language with a syntax very similar to Microsoft Visual
Basic. Later in this book, you'll get an overview of the VBScript language and helpful
syntax examples. VBScript is actually quite similar to the Microsoft Visual Basic for
Applications (VBA) scripting language, which is embedded in the Microsoft Office
Suite. For the most part, the syntax of VBScript and VBA is identical. VBScript doesn't
have all the syntax elements of VBA, but it provides some objects and functions that
aren't part of VBA.

Microsoft JScript is Microsoft's version of the JavaScript language. Like JavaScript, it has
a syntax that is similar to the Java language. It doesn't enable you to specify data types for
variables, which is similar to VBScript, for which all variables are variants. It does have
some syntactic nuances that are different from JavaScript. You'll cover those in Chapter 6,
which will also provide you with an overview and tutorial of the JScript syntax.

Objects that Can Be Used from WSH

The Windows Scripting Host provides two types of objects: inherent objects provided by
the scripting engine and objects that are implemented and provided by the Windows
Scripting Host. The capabilities of the objects should be independent of the specific language, and it is important to point out that the capabilities of the scripting language
varies depending on the syntax and intrinsic functionality of the language. One capability
that should be provided by any of the scripting engines used with WSH is the capability
to manipulate ActiveX objects. Both VBScript and JScript can use ActiveX objects.

WSH provides a substantial number of objects that can be used within your WSH scripts.
There are two simple objects, the `Dictionary` and `FileSystemObject`, that are documented as VBScript and JScript language features, and there are a number of other
objects that are provided as part of the WSH scripting package. This chapter provides
you with a basic overview of the WSH objects, but you'll cover them in great depth in
Chapter 4, "The WSH Object Model." You need to be familiar with these objects because
they will provide you with the power you need to perform many standard administrative
or programming tasks.

Overview of Simple WSH Objects: `Dictionary` and `FileSystemObject`

Two WSH objects that are documented by Microsoft as VBScript and JScript language
features are the `Dictionary` object and the `FileSystemObject`. The `Dictionary` object
implements an *associative array*. If you're not familiar with an associative array, it's an
array that enables you to associate a string with an array element rather than just a

numeric array position. If you've used `Collections` in Microsoft Visual Basic, you'll already be familiar with the concept. `Dictionary` objects are very flexible and enable you to add new elements without worrying about how many elements you've already stored. If you've programmed using arrays in the past, you know that it can be tricky to handle data items if you're not sure how many you will have when you begin. With the `Dictionary` object, you don't need to be concerned about the number of data items that you store.

The `FileSystemObject` gives you access to, appropriately enough, the file system of the computer that is executing the script. The object is extremely powerful. Using it, you can copy, create, delete, and move files; you can copy, create, delete, and move folders; you can open text files and read from them or write to them; you can also retrieve information about files or folders.

It's very likely that the `Dictionary` and `FileSystemObject` will be two of the most common objects that you use when you create WSH scripts. The `FileSystemObject` alone provides much of the functionality that you might need for writing scripts. You'll learn much more about the objects in Chapter 3, "The Scripting Object Model."

Overview of Other Standard WSH Objects

WSH provides a substantial set of objects that enable scripts to manipulate the Windows environment that they run in. Here's a brief listing and description of the WSH objects:

`Wscript`	Provides information about the current script and its arguments and has the capability to create ActiveX objects.
`WshArguments`	Enables a script to get access to its script arguments.
`WshShell`	Provides access to the current system environment settings and to Windows shell folders such as the Windows desktop, the Start menu folder, and the personal document folder. It also enables you to create shortcuts and manipulate the Windows Registry.
`WshNetwork`	Enables you to access the network that the computer running the script resides on. It provides the capability to map or remove mappings to printers and network drives.
`WshCollection`	Is used by other WSH objects to provide lists of items.
`WshShortcut`	Provides parameters for a new Windows shortcut.
`WshUrlShortcut`	Provides parameters for a new Windows Internet or URL shortcut.
`WshEnvironment`	Provides the capability to retrieve a list of environment variables and to delete environment variables.
`WshSpecialFolders`	Enables you to manipulate special Windows folders such as the desktop, Start menu, or the personal document folder.

These WSH objects provide you with lots of control over the Windows environment. Using these objects, you can create, edit, and delete shortcuts on the desktop or Start menu, you can create instances of ActiveX objects, you can edit the Windows Registry, and you can create or remove network connections. The objects are extremely powerful, and you will certainly have reason to put them to use if you develop WSH scripts. In Chapter 4, you can read more about the WSH objects, and you can see examples of how the objects can be used.

WSH and OLE Automation/ActiveX

One of the most powerful capabilities of the Windows Scripting Host is its capability to access ActiveX components. The language capabilities of WSH alone are very powerful, but coupled with the capability to access ActiveX components, the potential uses for WSH scripts are limitless. You can use WSH scripts to access any OLE Automation-enabled COM component! That means that scripts can leverage all the power of COM-enabled applications, such as Microsoft Word or Excel. In Chapter 15, "Scripting the Microsoft Office Suite," you'll see how you can use WSH to script the Microsoft Office suite.

The entire foundation of the Windows Scripting Host is based on ActiveX technology. The Windows Scripting Host defines interfaces that are implemented by scripting engines. Consequently, the same scripting engine can be used in any application that can use the scripting interface the way that WSH uses it. If you need a scripting solution for your application, you might want to consider the use of VBScript or JScript through the scripting interface. Adding support for a scripting engine to your application involves substantial complexity, so this book's not going to cover that topic.

Because WSH leverages ActiveX technology throughout, as mentioned previously, it provides very easy capabilities that enable you to access and manipulate ActiveX objects. If you use WSH, you will certainly make use of this capability. You will probably use it to access objects that are intrinsic to WSH, such as the aforementioned standard WSH objects, but you will also use it to access other ActiveX objects. You might use it to access objects such as those provided by the Microsoft Office suite; that was hinted earlier in this chapter, and you can read much more about it later in this book.

If you've scripted the Microsoft Office suite before, you might wonder why you would need to use the WSH scripting capabilities. After all, Visual Basic for Applications (VBA), which is a part of all the Microsoft Office applications, provides very robust automation. Here's one specific reason why you might want to use it: How do you launch your Microsoft Office VBA scripts? If you're using something such as Microsoft Word, you can run them as auto launch macros. That still leaves you with a problem: How do you actually launch the Microsoft Word application to get your VBA scripts started? That's where WSH can be applied. You can use WSH as your entry point to

Microsoft Word. If you wanted to, you could use it to completely script the Word environment because it can use all the automation objects exposed by Word, which are the same objects that you leverage in your VBA scripts. That would have the benefit of enabling you to develop scripts that control Word that are not as tightly tied-in to the environment as macros that are embedded in documents. Alternatively, you could simply use it to instantiate Word and to kick off embedded VBA macros. This would enable you to preserve VBA code that you've already developed and would give you the opportunity to provide additional error checking, as appropriate, within your WSH script.

WSH isn't only applicable to large-scale objects like the objects exposed by the Microsoft Office suite. You can also use it with smaller objects such as the Microsoft Active Data Objects (ADO). Microsoft ADO provides a fast, easy-to-use interface to relational database systems. Using ADO, you can read and write to databases, execute stored procedures, manipulate the database schema, and do basically anything that you would want to do with a SQL-compliant data source. Some examples and a tutorial of using ADO with the Windows Scripting Host are in Chapter 16, "Using WSH to Access Databases Through Microsoft Active Data Objects (ADO)."

Furthermore, you can use WSH to script objects that you might develop in other languages. For example, if you use Borland Delphi, Microsoft Visual Basic, or any other language that is capable of generating ActiveX objects, to create business objects, you can use WSH to script those objects. There are some pretty interesting capabilities that this gives you; you can use WSH as a simple, easy-to-maintain scripting language that provides high-level control that you don't need to maintain in your low-level components. Alternatively, you could use WSH as a scripting language to test your components. Say that you're building a large system that utilizes custom ActiveX components developed using Microsoft Visual Basic. You will no doubt have plenty of interaction with those objects embedded in your VB code; you might have, for example, an `employee` object that interacts with the `benefits` object or perhaps a `trade` object that interacts with a `stock` object. Whatever the situation is, you might be able to leverage scripts developed using WSH as a simple test harness for object components. You'll see how you can use WSH with custom objects in Chapter 20, "Using WSH with Custom VB and Java Objects."

WSH and Internet Scripting

The same scripting engines that are used by WSH are also used with other Microsoft Internet technologies (see Figure 1.6). The scripting engines are used heavily for Web server scripting. On the Web server, Microsoft uses Active Server Pages to provide dynamic Web-page generation on their Microsoft Internet Information Server (IIS). Active Server Pages enable you to embed scripting code alongside HTML code. When the Web server reads a page that contains the embedded scripting code, it runs the script. The embedded scripts can do anything, including reading and writing from a database and dynamically generating HTML that is sent to the client Web browser.

FIGURE 1.6

The relationship of WSH and the scripting engines to Microsoft Internet technologies

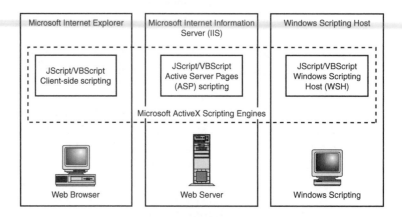

The technology that executes the embedded script is the same technology that's used by the Windows Scripting Host to run command scripts. Consequently, you can use VBScript, JScript, or any other language for which there is an implementation of the correct type of scripting engine. This is an excellent example of a situation in which Microsoft has created a great, flexible framework technology that can be leveraged in many different situations. As a matter of fact, the same scripting technology can also be leveraged on the Web browser client side!

That's right; the underlying scripting engine technology is also leveraged by the Microsoft Internet Explorer to execute client-side scripts. With client-side scripts, VBScript or JScript code can be embedded within an HTML page. When a Web browser reads the page, it interprets the HTML to display the page, and it runs the embedded scripting code as appropriate. Some scripting code might not run until the user interacts with the page because some of the code might be activated by events that occur as the user enters text in textboxes or makes selections from drop-down menus.

The capability of the scripting engines to run in multiple different environments is very interesting for several reasons. First of all, it's impressive that Microsoft has developed a technology that they've apparently easily and robustly leveraged in several extremely different solution environments (Web client vs. Web server vs. command line). Secondly, the model that underlies the scripting engine is impressive because it provides the same capabilities across the hosting environment and across languages. It's great that the scripting engines, wherever they are running, can leverage pre-existing ActiveX components. From a practical perspective, that's really useful because that enables you to leverage a tremendous amount of code that's already been developed! For example, you can leverage the Microsoft Excel objects to generate spreadsheets without having to implement your own objects to perform the same task. Not to mention, there are literally thousands of other software vendors that provide ActiveX components that encapsulate useful functionality.

It's also very cool that the scripting engines can leverage the same object capabilities across scripting languages. As long as the language has some convention for handling object instances and accessing object methods or properties, the language can be used to access ActiveX objects with a framework that is partially provided by the scripting host architecture. Microsoft has a great, free tool that demonstrates this capability. The tool is the ActiveX Control Pad (see Figure 1.7). The ActiveX Control Pad is intended to simplify the process of developing scripts that run within the Internet Explorer Web browser.

FIGURE 1.7

Using the ActiveX Control Pad to add script to browser objects

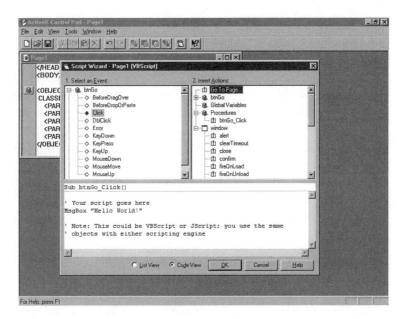

When you use the ActiveX Control Pad, you can choose the scripting language that you want to use on the client side. Your two choices are VBScript and JScript. With either language, you select objects from an object browser. The object browser displays both "intrinsic" objects that are always available, such as the current window and document, and objects that you add to the control pad.

The capability of switching between languages and maintaining exactly the same development UI for accessing objects is really great. Some of the magic that makes it work is certainly provided by the control pad application software; for example, if you develop scripting code for an object event, it generates function headers for you that are appropriate to the language that you are using. However, some of the magic is also provided by the underlying infrastructure—the scripting host model that enables scripting engines to be treated as components.

To summarize, the underlying technology for the Windows Scripting Host is leveraged throughout the Microsoft Internet products. It appears to offer a pretty ubiquitous scripting model that is clearly extraordinarily flexible and that is not tightly bound to a single application. As a user of the scripting technologies, one of the side benefits of this technology ubiquity is that knowledge and experience that you gain in one area can be seamlessly transferred to other very useful situations.

Summary

The Windows Scripting Host is an exceptionally powerful solution for command scripting in the Microsoft Windows environment. No longer are Windows users neglected when it comes to automation control over the Windows environment. Relative to other operating systems with powerful scripting capabilities, Microsoft has made up lots of ground with the introduction of the Windows Scripting Host. Windows users are no longer stuck with DOS files that provide only the most rudimentary command scripting. Microsoft has raised the bar with regard to scripting capabilities. The WSH solution has some unique characteristics, such as its ability to support multiple scripting engines using an object-oriented engine interface that is based on standardized ActiveX scripting interfaces. Also, WSH can leverage a wealth of ActiveX objects that already exist. Finally, the scripting technology that is used by WSH is also used for Internet scripting on both the client and server side, so the knowledge that you gain from working with WSH can also be leveraged if you are developing or maintaining scripted Internet applications.

The goal of this book is to provide you with a deep understanding of the Windows Scripting Host. Initially, basic information about the background of WSH and its capabilities is covered, and later in the book specific uses of WSH for administrative and development purposes are discussed. So read on, learn, and enjoy!

Q&A

Q The Windows Scripting Host isn't installed on my system. Where can I find the files for WSH?

A You can find the files for the Windows Scripting Host on the Microsoft Web site—www.microsoft.com. You can download the files and then run the installation program to install WSH on your system.

DAY 2

Writing a Simple Script Using WSH

At this point, you should have a reasonable understanding of the technology that underlies the Windows Scripting Host. During Day 1, "Introduction to the Windows Scripting Host (WSH)," you learned how the Windows Scripting Host works and what it can do for you to automate tasks. Today you're going to put your new knowledge into practice. By the end of today, you'll know how to develop your own WSH script. Here's what you'll do:

- Find out what tools you need to develop WSH scripts (from Notepad to more full-featured tools)
- Learn how to define an algorithm and plan your coding
- Code your algorithm and run your new script

Tools You Need to Get Started

At the most basic level, you don't really need any tools to get started with WSH script-ing. Naturally, you have to have WSH installed on your machine, but that's about it. The script files that you develop are, like batch files, simply text files that contain instructions in one of the scripting languages. In this case, you're looking at the two standard WSH scripting languages—VBScript and JScript.

So, to create script files, you need to have some type of text editor. Your options range from ultra-simple editors, such as Notepad, to more fully functional editors, such as Microsoft Visual InterDev. I'll discuss the editors a little later in this chapter. That will handle the mechanics of creating the scripts, and coupled with the Microsoft help refer-ence and this book, you'll have everything that you need to begin developing your scripts.

That's only half of what you'll eventually need, however. You also need to have some type of debugging tool that will assist you to work out the kinks in your scripts. There are basically two approaches to debugging; one is to write code embedded in your script that assists in the debugging process, and the second is to use a debugging tool that enables you to step through your scripting code as it executes. Both approaches can be used synergistically, and both have some advantages and disadvantages. I'll discuss debugging in more detail later in this chapter, and you can also read about it in Day 7, "Running and Scheduling Scripts."

So the two basic tools that you need to develop scripts are a script editor and a script debugger. If you develop scripts that integrate with other technologies, you might also need to use other tools. For example, if you develop a script that accesses databases, you might make use of a query generator to help you with SQL syntax. That's one example of many; later in this book, you'll see examples of integrating scripting with the Microsoft Office suite, databases, and custom components developed using Visual Basic and Java. However, fundamentally, all you need is a text editor and debugger. Read on to learn more about various types of editors and script debugging.

Text Editors—from Notepad to Microsoft Visual InterDev

You can edit script files using any text editor. Notepad does a pretty good job; see Figure 2.1 for an example of a WSH script in Notepad. Granted, it's a really minimal text editor. All that it provides is a few functions that enable you to edit or replace text; it doesn't include any real development-oriented functions.

FIGURE 2.1

*You can use Notepad
to edit a WSH script.*

```
dirscan.vbs - Notepad
File  Edit  Search  Help
' FILE: dirscan.vbs
' DESC: Given a root directory, this script will scan for
'       subdirectories and will output the size of each
'       subdirectory.
' AUTH: Thomas L. Fredell

On Error Resume Next

Dim RootDir, FileSystem, RootFolder, SubFolders, Folder
Dim FolderSize, Tmp

' 1. Get the root directory parameter
' IF no parameter is specified, quit and show the usage of the script
If Wscript.Arguments.Count <> 1 Then
        ' Show the usage
        Wscript.Echo "USAGE: dirscan.vbs  [root directory]"
        Wscript.Echo ""
        Wscript.Echo "       Given a root directory, dirscan will scan"
        Wscript.Echo "       all subdirectories and output the size of"
        Wscript.Echo "       each subdirectory."

        ' And quit
        Wscript.Quit 0
Else
        RootDir = Wscript.Arguments(0)
        Wscript.Echo "Root directory is: " & RootDir
        Wscript.Echo ""
End If

' 2. Open the root directory
' First we need to instantiate a FileSystemObject
Set FileSystem = CreateObject("Scripting.FileSystemObject")
Set RootFolder = FileSystem.GetFolder(RootDir)
If Err.Number <> 0 Then
        ' Display the error that occurred
        Wscript.Echo "(" & Err.Number & ") " & Err.Description
        Wscript.Echo ""
```

The advantage of Notepad is that, heck, everyone has it! Because Notepad is a standard
Windows program, you can be assured that you have it on your computer. The problem
with Notepad is that it certainly isn't the most productive environment for developing
WSH scripts. That's for several reasons: One, it provides only the most simple search
and replace capabilities; two, it has no integrated facility to link with help for WSH
scripts; and three, it doesn't provide any mechanism to develop macros that can automate
standard editing tasks.

Conversely, the Microsoft Visual Studio environment provides a very robust, fully-
functional script editor with links to online help and the capability to define useful editor
macros. Figure 2.2 shows the Visual Studio environment as it is used to edit one of the
examples from Day 2.

Visual Studio is an excellent environment for editing your scripts. You might have
already used it if you've used Microsoft Visual C++, J++, or Visual InterDev. It's become
the common editing and development interface for Microsoft's programming tools. The
following sections highlight the capabilities of three of the most powerful features of
Visual Studio: regular expression support, online help titles, and editor macros.

*You can use Microsoft
Visual Studio to edit a
WSH script.*

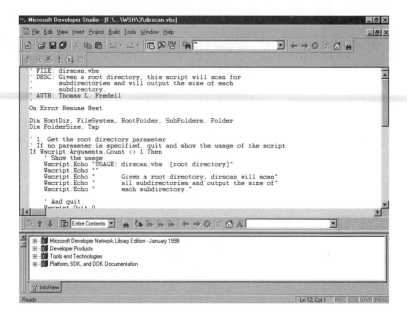

Visual Studio Regular Expressions

With Visual Studio, you have sophisticated capabilities for searching and replacing program text. For example, you can use regular expressions to perform wildcard search and replacement. Regular expressions are extremely powerful; as illustrated in Figure 2.3, you can use them to do such things as commenting or uncommenting a section of code.

Tip

If you're not an experienced developer, you might wonder why you would want to have the capability to quickly comment or uncomment a section of code. It can be extremely useful when you're testing and debugging your script. You can comment out sections of code selectively to try to understand the runtime behavior of your script. Also, you can comment out portions of your code that might be useful in the future but are currently unused. That way, you keep the skeleton code around, and you don't lose the ideas that prompted you to begin the initial implementation.

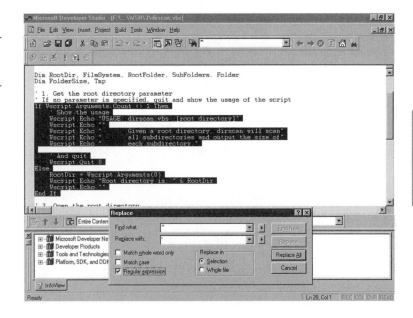

FIGURE 2.3

You can use a regular expression in Visual Studio to comment a section of script code.

2

That's just one very simple example; regular expressions can be used for many, many search and replacement tasks. If you would want to find out more about the capabilities of regular expressions, review the online help provided with Visual Studio.

Visual Studio Online Help

On the subject of online help, Visual Studio provides really excellent, integrated help titles that give you a quick, searchable reference. The help titles are also seamlessly integrated with the development environment, so you don't have to switch from one application to a different application for help. Figure 2.4 illustrates the help titles within Visual Studio. Notice that the screen is split into roughly two areas; at the top of the screen you see reference information about the WScript object, and at the bottom of the screen you see a tree view that displays a table of contents-style view of the help information.

Note

The configuration that I use for help browsing in Visual Studio is a little bit different from the traditional layout. When you first run Visual Studio, it puts the tree view on the left side of the screen and the help information on the right side. I find that layout to be a pain in the neck; as you expand the tree on the left side, the expanded titles are truncated because the window is too narrow. With the window at the bottom, the titles are never truncated. The disadvantage is that I see less code or help text at any given time, but that really doesn't bother me.

FIGURE 2.4

You can view online help titles in Visual Studio.

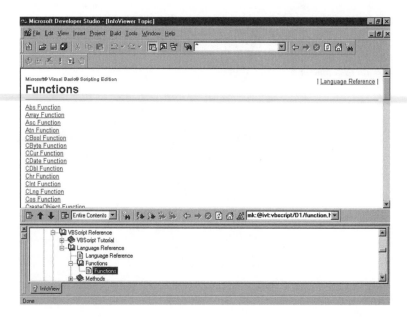

From the example, it is obvious that Microsoft includes some detailed help files for WSH scripting. I recommend that you refer to the help files as you run into issues when you're developing scripts. Of course, you can also refer to this book if you want more detailed examples or step-by-step instructions for accomplishing scripting tasks. One of the benefits of an online reference is that you can perform searches to quickly find information on specific topics. Figure 2.5 illustrates the results of a search using the text **WScript.Arguments**.

You can do two types of searches with the Visual Studio help; you can search using a text query, or you can search using an index of all the keywords in the titles installed on your system. You can also refine the scope of your search by restricting the search to a specific subset of the help titles on your system. For example, you might want to define a search subset that includes only the Windows Scripting Host, VBScript, and JScript help titles. Figure 2.6 illustrates how you can define a search subset.

In Figure 2.6, I use the Define Subsets dialog box to select a group of titles that I lump in a subset called WSH Information. Any time I want to find something related to WSH, I can use that as my searching subset to quickly find information without lots of extraneous information from unrelated topics.

FIGURE 2.5

You can search within the Microsoft Visual Studio help titles.

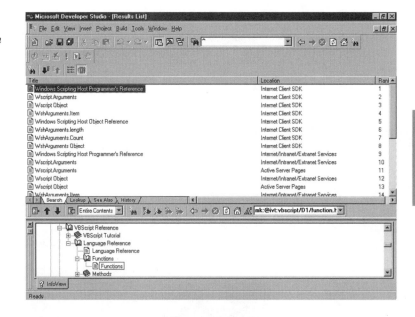

FIGURE 2.6

You can define a search subset for only WSH-related information.

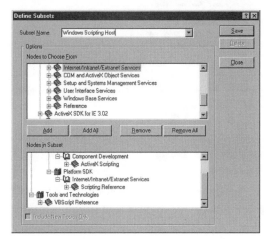

Visual Studio Editor Macros

One of the most powerful capabilities of Visual Studio is the capability to define editor macros. Visual Studio includes robust support for—surprise!—VBScript. Clearly, Microsoft views VBScript as the ubiquitous scripting solution across its product line.

You can create macros to perform any task that you perform using the Visual Studio interface. You can also do more: You can create loops with logical branches that perform steps several times until a condition has been satisfied.

Creating a basic macro with Visual Studio is really easy. As an example, take the regular expression I used earlier and turn it into a macro that can be used to comment out VBScript code. To create the macro, first select the text that you want to comment out. Don't record that as part of the macro because you want the macro to use whatever text is currently selected. Next, select the Tools | Macro menu option to show the Macro dialog box illustrated in Figure 2.7.

FIGURE 2.7

You can define a new macro.

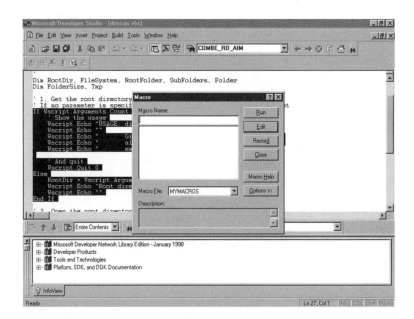

For your new macro, enter the name **CommentVBScript** in the Macro Name edit box. Next, click the Record button. Before the macro recording begins, you're prompted to enter a descriptive comment for the macro, after which the macro recording session begins. You can tell that you are in the macro recording mode because the cursor displays as an arrow with a small cassette and a macro recording toolbar is displayed. After the macro recording begins, all your keystrokes or menu selections are captured as part of the macro. Consequently, you need to be careful about the keys you hit or the actions you perform to ensure that you record only the actions you want. For the comment macro, select Edit | Replace. For the Find What field enter the *beginning of line* character, or

"^". For the Replace With field, enter the *comment* character, or "'". Next ensure that the Regular Expression checkbox is checked and that neither of the other checkboxes is checked. Also ensure that Replace In is set to Selection. If you want to see a screenshot of the settings, refer to Figure 2.3. Then, click the Replace All button to perform the search and replace; on the screen you can see that the selected text has been commented. Next, click the Close button, and click the square Stop icon on the macro recorder control panel.

After you click the Stop icon, you are brought to the code that was recorded for your CommentVBScript macro. The code is illustrated in Figure 2.8. You can see that Visual Studio has added a number of comments to the macro code; the macro description that you entered earlier is included as a comment line, and you can see that the search and replace that you recorded is bracketed by Begin Recording and End Recording comments. For this simple macro, the source code is only a single line! If you wanted to, you can add additional functionality by directly editing the generated VBScript code.

FIGURE 2.8

Macro code is generated when recording a macro.

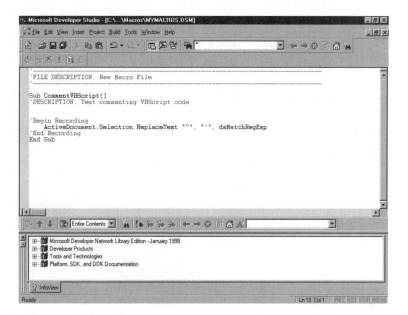

To make the new macro really easy to access and use, you can create a toolbar for the macro. The new toolbar integrates with the Visual Studio environment as seamlessly as the other standard Visual Studio toolbars. To create the toolbar, select Tools | Customize from the main menu. The Customize dialog box appears; switch to the Toolbars section to edit the current toolbar settings. The dialog box is shown in Figure 2.9.

FIGURE 2.9

You can create a new toolbar.

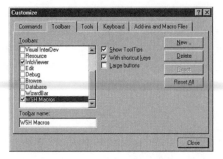

Click the New button to create a new toolbar. You're prompted to enter a name; for my examples, I enter the name "WSH Macros". After you enter the name and click OK, you see a new blank toolbar. Next, you need to add the icon for the CommentVBScript macro to the toolbar. To do so, switch to the Commands tab on the Customize dialog box. Select Macros for the Category. You can see the CommentVBScript macro listed. Select CommentVBScript by clicking it, and then click and drag the name of the macro to your new toolbar. The mouse cursor turns into an arrow with a small button and a plus sign. Release the mouse button when the new toolbar is highlighted. You're prompted to select an image, text, or a combination for the toolbar button. Figure 2.10 shows the results after I add the button with an image and text. To run the CommentVBScript macro, all you need to do is select the text you want to comment, and click the toolbar button.

FIGURE 2.10

You can add icons for the custom editor macros to the toolbar.

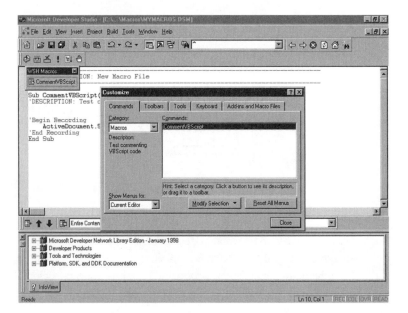

WSH Installation Components

If your corporate environment is entirely based on Windows 98, you don't need to worry about installing WSH. Your machine and the other desktops already have WSH installed. However, if you're using Windows 95 or Windows NT, you need to install the WSH software. If you need to get the installation software for WSH or any of the accompanying components, such as the Microsoft Script Debugger, check out the www.microsoft.com/scripting site. Microsoft has aggregated their scripting-related tools at that Web site, which provides numerous downloads for documentation, examples, and scripting tools.

WSH Debugging Tools

One of the most essential tools that you need when you're developing WSH scripts is a good debugging tool. Luckily, Microsoft provides an excellent debugging tool, the Microsoft Script Debugger, which can debug WSH script files, Active Server Pages, embedded script-like JavaScript or VBScript on Web pages, and Java code. It's a very powerful, very useful tool that you need to have if you intend to get serious about writing WSH scripts. Figure 2.11 shows the Microsoft Script Debugger with a WSH JScript file.

FIGURE 2.11

The Microsoft Script Debugger can debug a WSH script.

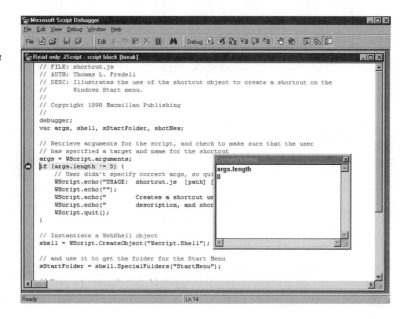

For those of you who might not be familiar with the purpose of debuggers, a debugger is a tool that enables you to monitor the execution of your programs. Typical debuggers enable you to perform the following functions:

- **Trace the flow of execution of your code**   Debugging tools typically enable you to step through your code as it executes so that you can see the effect of your branches or looping logic.

- **Set breakpoints within your code**   Debuggers enable you to set breakpoints within your code so that you can jump in and examine the execution process. Simple breakpoints tell the debugger to pause execution at a specific point in the code; complex breakpoints enable you to specify conditions for a breakpoint to occur, such as a variable having a specific value.

- **Examine variables during execution**   With a debugger, you can see the values stored in variables while your program is executing. This can help you to track down errors by enabling you to examine the specific state of your program while it's running.

The Microsoft Script Debugger provides all the aforementioned capabilities. It does have some unique features, however. Most debuggers typically support only one language. For example, a C compiler likely is included with a debugger that enables you to debug C code. However, that debugger doesn't enable you to debug Visual Basic or Java code. The Microsoft script debugger doesn't enable you to debug Visual Basic code either, but it does enable you to debug code in JScript, VBScript, or Java! That's a very flexible tool.

 Caution   One problem with the Microsoft Script Debugger version 1.0 is that it isn't specifically designed for use with the Windows Scripting Host. It appears to have been originally intended for use with server side scripts embedded in Active Server Pages or client side scripts embedded in HTML pages. However, that notwithstanding, it functions as an excellent debugger for Windows Scripting Host scripts. It is a little clunky to start the debugging process, but when it's going, the debugger works very well.

Notice that if you attempt to open a file through the Script Debugger, there's no option to open a WSH scripting file. Unfortunately, you can't open a WSH script directly from the debugger and just start debugging. Instead, you need to embed a command that launches the debugger. For the VBScript language, the command to launch the debugger is Stop. For the JScript language, the command to launch the debugger is, appropriately enough, debugger. As your script executes, the moment that the debugging statement is encountered, your script stops and the Microsoft Script Debugger takes control. At that point, you can use the Script Debugger to step through your code or to examine your variables. You can also set a breakpoint later in your code if you want to run up to a specific point.

Later in this chapter, you'll see how the Script Debugger can be used in practice. At that point, you'll get into more of the features and details of the script debugger.

Creating a Simple Script

Now you've reached an important milestone; the creation of your first WSH script. You're going to put together some of the tools that you learned about to create a simple script. At this point, I haven't discussed the languages used for scripting or the objects provided by the scripting languages. If you want to get a preview, you can skip ahead to Days 3, 4, 5, or 6. Otherwise, continue through this chapter and see the full development of a basic script.

The steps in developing a script are illustrated in Figure 2.12. When you develop a script, first you need to understand exactly what the script needs to accomplish—the requirements for the script. After you define the requirements, you can design the script. Designing the script might involve putting together pseudocode that serves as an outline for the scripting code that you develop. Next, you write the scripting code, and then you test and debug your new script. When your script appears to run successfully, you're done; hopefully you have ironed out any bugs in your script during the testing and debugging process.

FIGURE 2.12

There are four basic steps involved in creating a script.

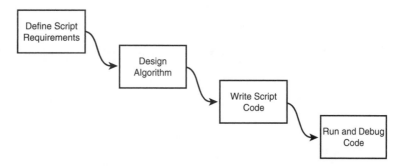

The rest of this chapter is spent developing a new WSH script. For your example, you develop a script that returns the size of all the subdirectories of a root directory that is specified as a command parameter.

Define the Requirements for Your Script

The requirements for the script are the functions that the script must perform stated at a high level without design or coding details. For your sample script, the requirements are relatively simple. The script must provide the user with the capability to specify a root directory. When the script runs, it must output a size listing for all the subdirectories of the root directory. The listing must be output as standard text that can be redirected to a text file if necessary.

Design the Algorithm You Want to Implement

The design of the script is the blueprint for the script coding. In this situation, the algorithm is the key concept that you need to define before you begin coding. The algorithm specifies the sequence of steps that the script executes as it performs its function.

When you first state the algorithm, you state it as pseudocode. Psuedocode is a description of the steps for the algorithm. When you write psuedocode, you don't need to worry about exactly how you state your algorithm; the idea is that you state it in a simple, easily understandable manner that helps you when you write code. Here's the psuedocode for the script example:

```
1. Get the root directory parameter; if no parameter is specified, quit
   ➡and show the usage of the script
2. Open the root directory
3. Find all of the sub-folders of the root directory
4. For each sub-folder,
      4.1. Determine the folder size
      4.2. Print the folder size
```

This is a simple example; consequently, the pseudocode is also simple. The next step is to use the pseudocode as a template for the script code that you develop.

Defining a Basic Script with Descriptive Comments

Now that you know the requirements and the design for your script, you can begin coding it. When you begin your script, it's important that you include a descriptive header and comments that provide information about who wrote the script and what it does. That way, if you distribute the script, people are able to understand how the script functions internally. You're going to develop your example using the VBScript language, so here's an example of a scripting header with appropriate details:

```
' FILE: dirscan.vbs
' DESC: Given a root directory, this script will scan for
'       subdirectories and will output the size of each
'       subdirectory.
' AUTH: TY WSH in 21 days
'
```

If you actually begin to write your script, you can run Notepad and type the aforementioned script header comments in your file. In the next step, you develop the instructions for the algorithm that does the work for the script.

> **Caution**
>
> If you use Notepad to write your script, be careful how you save the script. By default, Notepad always appends the .txt extension to files when you save them. To ensure that your script is saved with the .vbs extension, which is the standard for VBScript scripting files, select File I Save As. For the filename, type in the full name including the file extension. In your example that's dirscan.vbs. If you don't include the file extension, Notepad saves the file as dirscan.txt.

Coding the Algorithm

Now you can begin to code the algorithm for your script. For each step in your algorithm, you can define code that implements the step. Begin with Step 1: Get the root directory parameter or show usage. To store the root directory, you need to define a variable. Underneath your script header, add the following line:

```
Dim RootDir
```

The RootDir variable provides storage for the root directory name. If you want to learn more about the VBScript language, see Day 5, "Using Microsoft VBScript with WSH."

Next, you add code that checks to ensure that a parameter is specified on the command line. If no parameter is specified, you output a message that lets the user know how the script is intended to be used, and then you quit. Here's the code that implements that step:

```
' 1. Get the root directory parameter
' If no parameter is specified, quit and show the usage of the script
If Wscript.Arguments.Count <> 1 Then
    Show the usage
    Wscript.Echo "USAGE: dirscan.vbs  [root directory]"
    Wscript.Echo ""
    Wscript.Echo "        Given a root directory, dirscan will scan"
    Wscript.Echo "        all subdirectories and output the size of"
    Wscript.Echo "        each subdirectory."

    ' And quit
    Wscript.Quit 0
Else
    RootDir = Wscript.Arguments(0)
    Wscript.Echo "Root directory is: " & RootDir
    Wscript.Echo ""
End If
```

Note

You're seeing the development of the script code in bits and pieces. If you're confused about how the script is put together, you can skip ahead in this chapter to see the finished script.

Caution

When you run WSH scripts from this book, I suggest that you use cscript to run them. If you run the scripts using wscript, every Wscript.Echo will cause a message box to appear. Using csript, Wscript.Echo just sends another line to the console—just like the Echo statement in a batch file.

Observe a couple of things in the code that checks for the script arguments. First, it includes the pseudocode as a comment that describes the code that checks for the arguments. Next, you'll see that there's a logical branch; if exactly one argument isn't specified, the script displays the usage information and quits. If an argument is specified, its value is stored in the RootDir variable. You might be wondering about the Wscript object that is referenced in the code. You'll describe the Wscript object and other objects provided by the Windows Scripting Host on Day 3, "The Scripting Object Model," and Day 4, "The WSH Object Model."

For Step 2, you need to develop code that opens the root directory. The Windows Scripting Host provides a really useful object, the FileSystemObject, that enables you to manipulate directories and files. First, you need to create an instance of the object, and then you can use it to get the folder that corresponds to the root directory. Here's the code that you use to do that:

```
' 2. Open the root directory
' First we need to instantiate a FileSystemObject
Set FileSystem = CreateObject("Scripting.FileSystemObject")
Set RootFolder = FileSystem.GetFolder(RootDir)
```

In the code example, you use two new variables—FileSystemObject and RootFolder. You need to add those two variables to the Dim statement at the beginning of the script as follows:

```
Dim RootDir, FileSystem, RootFolder
```

Now you need to perform Step 3 of the algorithm: Find all subfolders of the root directory. Thankfully, the Folder object that is stored in the RootFolder variable has a SubFolders property that returns all the subfolders of the folder. That's just one of the properties that Folder objects have; another is the Size property. You use the Size property for Step 4.1 of your algorithm. On Day 3, "The Scripting Object Model," you'll learn all about the FileSystemObject, the Folder object, and other WSH scripting objects. Here's the code that retrieves the subfolders of the root folder:

```
' 3. Find all of the sub-folders of the root directory
Set SubFolders = RootFolder.SubFolders
```

For Step 4, you need to go through each subfolder and retrieve and display size information. You can use the convenient `For...Each` loop to iterate through each subfolder. `For...Each` enables you to perform steps for each item in a collection. A collection is just a list of some type of item. The `SubFolders` property of the `Folder` object returns a collection of subfolders. For Step 3, you stored the collection of subfolders in a variable that you called `SubFolders`. A `For...Each` loop is used in the following code for Step 4:

2

```
' 4. For each sub-folder,
For Each Folder In SubFolders
    ' 4.1. Determine the folder size
    ' 4.2. Print the folder size
Next
```

Now, all you need to do is add the code to get the folder size and the code to print the size. To get the folder size, you simply access the `Size` property of the folder object. Here's Step 4.1:

```
    ' 4.1. Determine the folder size
    FolderSize = Folder.Size
```

Then, you need to print the folder size. You can format it before you print it using the `FormatNumber()` VBScript function and then pad it out so that you can display output in neat columns. Here's the formatting and output code for Step 4.2:

```
    ' 4.2. Print the folder size
    Tmp = FormatNumber(FolderSize, 0, 0, 0, -1)
    Tmp = Right(Space(20) & Tmp, 20)
    Wscript.Echo Tmp & " " & Folder.Path
```

First, you format the size to include commas using the `FormatNumber()` function. The resulting string is stored in a temporary variable that you name `Tmp`. Next, you append 20 spaces to the front of the size and then strip off the right 20 characters. That ensures that the result is a number that's at least 20 characters long and padded at the front with spaces. Padding the numbers this way limits you to folder sizes that are fewer than 20 digits long, including commas.

You've examined the code to implement the algorithm in little bits and pieces. Here's the full code for the example so that you can see everything when it's assembled together:

LISTING 2.1   SCRIPT THAT RETURNS THE SIZE OF ALL THE SUBDIRECTORIES OF A ROOT DIRECTORY

```
' FILE: dirscan.vbs
' DESC: Given a root directory, this script will scan for
'       subdirectories and will output the size of each
```

continues

LISTING 2.1   CONTINUED

```
'        subdirectory.
' AUTH: Thomas L. Fredell
'

Dim RootDir, FileSystem, RootFolder, SubFolders, Folder
Dim FolderSize, Tmp

' 1. Get the root directory parameter
' If no parameter is specified, quit and show the usage of the script
If Wscript.Arguments.Count <> 1 Then
    ' Show the usage
    Wscript.Echo "USAGE: dirscan.vbs  [root directory]"
    Wscript.Echo ""
    Wscript.Echo "       Given a root directory, dirscan will scan"
    Wscript.Echo "       all subdirectories and output the size of"
    Wscript.Echo "       each subdirectory."

    ' And quit
    Wscript.Quit 0
Else
    RootDir = Wscript.Arguments(0)
    Wscript.Echo "Root directory is: " & RootDir
    Wscript.Echo ""
End If

' 2. Open the root directory
' First we need to instantiate a FileSystemObject
Set FileSystem = CreateObject("Scripting.FileSystemObject")
Set RootFolder = FileSystem.GetFolder(RootDir)

' 3. Find all of the sub-folders of the root directory
Set SubFolders = RootFolder.SubFolders

' 4. For each sub-folder,
For Each Folder In SubFolders
    ' 4.1. Determine the folder size
    FolderSize = Folder.Size

    ' 4.2. Print the folder size
    Tmp = FormatNumber(FolderSize, 0, 0, 0, -1)
    Tmp = Right(Space(20) & Tmp, 20)
    Wscript.Echo Tmp & " " & Folder.Path
Next
```

That's all there is to it! This is not a very complicated script example. The code is also a little longer than it needs to be because you used variables where you could simply access the properties of objects. For example, you did the following:

```
Set SubFolders = RootFolder.SubFolders
...
For Each Folder In SubFolders
```

Instead, you can just do this:

```
For Each Folder In RootFolder.SubFolders
```

Either way of accessing the properties works. Use your preference; the first approach that you used is very clear, but it's a little less efficient than the second approach because you used another variable, which consumes additional memory.

Next, you'll run the script and demonstrate a problem with it! That's right; there's a problem in the scripting code that you defined. Specifically, what happens if the root directory doesn't exist? Read on to see the result and the techniques that are used to ensure that the script runs correctly.

Running and Debugging Your Code

To run the script that you've created, you can use the `cscript` command. On my machine I have several hard disks. I'm going to use the script to display the size of all the subfolders on the E: drive. Here's the command line that I'll use:

```
cscript dirscan.vbs E:
```

When I run the `dirscan` command, I see the results that are illustrated in Figure 2.13. The output tells me the version of Windows Scripting Host that's running, the root directory that is being scanned, and the sizes and names of all the subfolders.

FIGURE 2.13

The output of running the dirscan.vbs script can provide useful information.

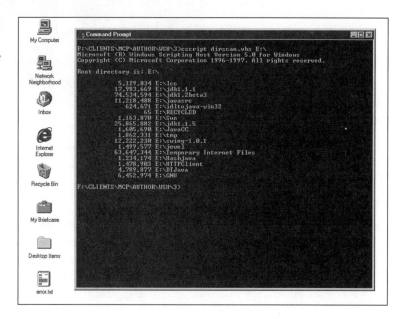

As I alluded earlier, there is a problem with the script that you've developed. It fails if you specify a root directory that doesn't exist. This type of problem is very common; many times software developers create software without considering the fact that people might enter invalid parameters. The following command causes the script to fail on my machine:

```
cscript dirscan.vbs NOTADRIVE:\JUNK
```

When I run the aforementioned command, my script quits with an error. Figure 2.14 shows what happens when I run the script with the invalid parameter. The error message indicates that a runtime error occurred; the path was not found.

FIGURE 2.14

An error occurs with the dirscan.vbs *script.*

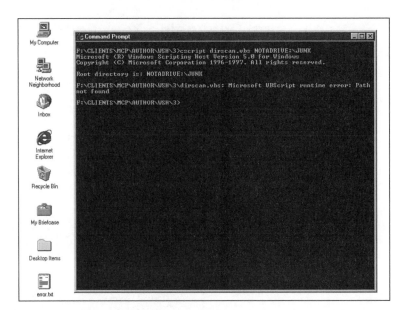

If you run the script using the wscript interpreter instead of cscript, your results are slightly different. Wscript.exe displays the error in a pop-up window rather than through the standard console. The error displayed when running wscript dirscan.vbs NOTADRIVE:\JUNK is illustrated in Figure 2.15.

How do you figure out where the error is occurring? You can use the debugger to run your script. To cause the debugger to break in immediately when the script begins executing, add Stop to the very first line in the file; it is a new line above the first comment line. Next, run the script again. When the script begins running, it launches the script debugger. Figure 2.16 shows the script debugger with the dirscan.vbs script.

FIGURE 2.15

The dirscan.vbs run-time error is displayed by wscript.

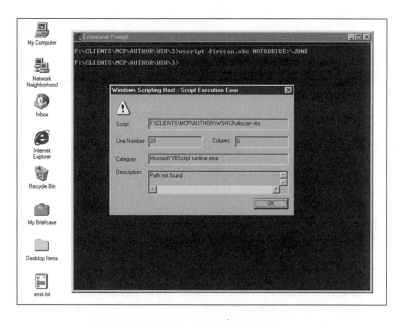

FIGURE 2.16

You can debug the dirscan.vbs script.

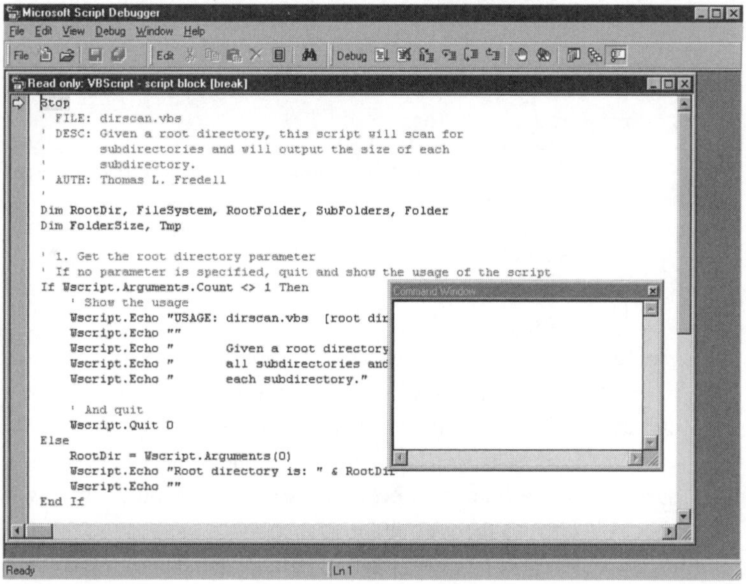

The first line in the script, Stop, is highlighted in yellow to indicate that it is the current line. You can now step through the code to see on what line the error occurs. There are a number of ways to step through the code. For now, you're going to use the simplest way:

You step through the code statement by statement. For detailed information about the script debugger and its usage, refer to Day 8, "Testing and Debugging WSH Scripts." To step through on a statement by statement basis, press the F8 key. As you step into the code, the display highlights the current line of code with a yellow background. Keep stepping through until the debugger stops. The debugger stops on the following line of code:

```
Set RootFolder = FileSystem.GetFolder(RootDir)
```

This is the line of code that fails when an invalid directory is used as a parameter for dirscan.vbs. How do you prevent an error from terminating the script if that line fails? You can set up error handling for your script.

NEW TERM *Error handling* is code that is specifically designed to handle error conditions that can occur at runtime when code is executing. It's extremely important that you add error handling to your scripts. Error handling helps you to ensure that your scripts function successfully and nondestructively even if the execution environment or parameters are incorrect. To add error handling, add the following line to your script before the first Dim statement:

```
On Error Resume Next
```

Next, add the following code after Set RootFolder = FileSystem.GetFolder(RootDir):

```
If Err.Number <> 0 Then
    ' Display the error that occurred
    Wscript.Echo "(" & Err.Number & ") " & Err.Description
    Wscript.Echo ""
    Wscript.Echo "The path that you entered is invalid, please " & _
        "select a different path."
    Wscript.Quit Err.Number
End If
```

The first code that you added sets up error handling so that the code continues to execute if an error occurs, which enables you to provide your own error handling logic. The second code snippet is your error handling for the invalid path. It checks the Err.Number value to see if an error occurred. If the value of Err.Number isn't 0, an error occurred during runtime. If an error occurred, your error handler simply outputs the information about the error to the user and then displays a message indicating that the path was invalid. It doesn't do much, but it's better than enabling the user to see the default, raw, unintelligible error message. When I run dirscan.vbs with the new code but the same invalid argument, I see the output depicted in Figure 2.17.

FIGURE 2.17

Adding error handling changes the output.

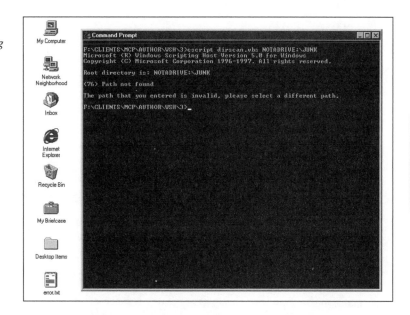

In this example, you provide very simple, very minimal error handling. Basically you're filtering the message to provide the user with what is hopefully an easy-to-understand error message. You can also provide more extensive error handling; for example, if the path isn't found, you can prompt the user to enter a new path. When you develop your script, use your judgement to determine the most appropriate way to handle runtime errors when they occur. As a rule of thumb, I recommend that you try to enable the user to recover from the error first, and then, if recovery isn't possible, terminate gracefully without causing side-effects.

The final source code for your first script is listed in the following example. It includes the modifications that support error handling:

LISTING 2.1   SCRIPT THAT INCORPORATES ERROR HANDLING

```
' FILE: dirscan.vbs
' DESC: Given a root directory, this script will scan for
'       subdirectories and will output the size of each
'       subdirectory.
' AUTH: Thomas L. Fredell
'
On Error Resume Next
```

continues

LISTING 2.1   CONTINUED

```
Dim RootDir, FileSystem, RootFolder, SubFolders, Folder
Dim FolderSize, Tmp

' 1. Get the root directory parameter
' If no parameter is specified, quit and show the usage of the script
If Wscript.Arguments.Count <> 1 Then
    ' Show the usage
    Wscript.Echo "USAGE: dirscan.vbs  [root directory]"
    Wscript.Echo ""
    Wscript.Echo "        Given a root directory, dirscan will scan"
    Wscript.Echo "        all subdirectories and output the size of"
    Wscript.Echo "        each subdirectory."

    ' And quit
    Wscript.Quit 0
Else
    RootDir = Wscript.Arguments(0)
    Wscript.Echo "Root directory is: " & RootDir
    Wscript.Echo ""
End If

' 2. Open the root directory
' First we need to instantiate a FileSystemObject
Set FileSystem = CreateObject("Scripting.FileSystemObject")
Set RootFolder = FileSystem.GetFolder(RootDir)
If Err.Number <> 0 Then
    ' Display the error that occurred
    Wscript.Echo "(" & Err.Number & ") " & Err.Description
    Wscript.Echo ""
    Wscript.Echo "The path that you entered is invalid, please " & _
        "select a different path."
    Wscript.Quit Err.Number
End If

' 3. Find all of the sub-folders of the root directory
Set SubFolders = RootFolder.SubFolders

' 4. For each sub-folder,
For Each Folder In SubFolders
    ' 4.1. Determine the folder size
    FolderSize = Folder.Size

    ' 4.2. Print the folder size
    Tmp = FormatNumber(FolderSize, 0, 0, 0, -1)
    Tmp = Right(Space(20) & Tmp, 20)
    Wscript.Echo Tmp & " " & Folder.Path
Next
```

Summary

In this chapter, you've seen everything that you need to begin developing WSH scripts. First you covered the tools that you need to develop scripts. The fundamental tool is the text editor; without it, you'd have a really hard time writing code! For a very basic text editor, you can use the Notepad program that comes with Microsoft Windows. If you want a more enhanced editor, you can move up to the Microsoft Visual Studio environment. Visual Studio provides support for complex search and replace expressions, online help, and user-defined macros using the VBScript language. The editor helps you to write the code for your script; when you need to run your script, you have to have the WSH components installed. WSH comes with Windows 98, but you need to install it if you're running Windows 95 or Windows NT. If you want to find the WSH installation components, check the Microsoft Web site at www.microsoft.com/scripting. When you run into a problem with your code, you need a debugger to help you to isolate and fix the problem. Microsoft provides the Microsoft Script Debugger, which helps you to debug JScript, VBScript, or Java code.

When you go through the process of developing your script, first you define the requirements for the script. The requirements are a high-level statement that describes what the script needs to do. Next, you define the design for your script, which includes the algorithm that your script implements. You use the design as a blueprint when you develop the code for your script. After you develop the code, you run and debug your script. If your script encounters runtime errors, you can add error handling to perform recovery or to fail gracefully.

That's all the steps that are involved with writing WSH scripts; in the next few chapters, you'll cover some additional topics that will help you to write powerful, robust scripts. Next, you'll learn about the Scripting object model and the WSH object model, both of which provide numerous objects that help you to perform many tasks. After you've learned the objects, you'll read about the languages that you'll use—VBScript and JScript.

Q&A

Q If I use Microsoft Visual Studio as my text editor, can I modify macros that I record?

A You can modify any macros that you record. Recording a macro initially can be a useful technique to get your macro started; after you record it, you can modify it any way you want and add loops or other logic. You can also make use of the many objects exposed by the Visual Studio editor.

Q Do you have any suggestions concerning defining the requirements for a script?

A Defining the requirements for a script depends a lot on your situation. If you're developing a script that will be used by many other users, you should check with the users to analyze their requirements and to verify that you have the correct requirements for the script. If you're simply developing a script for your own use, you can skip the formal requirements analysis.

Q Why wouldn't you add the On Error Resume Next statement from the very beginning when implementing your script?

A You certainly could add the On Error Resume Next statement when you begin writing your script code. However, because VBScript has relatively limited error handling capabilities, you might miss errors that affect your script. Why? Because one error might ripple through and cause multiple errors which will be hidden if you just use the On Error Resume Next statement. Initially, you might find it easier to omit some error handling to help you isolate the bugs in your script code.

Workshop

The following section helps you test your comprehension of the material presented in this chapter and put what you've learned into practice. You'll find the answers to the quiz and exercises in Appendix A.

Quiz

1. How do you launch the debugger from VBScript or JScript code?
2. What are the steps involved in creating a script?
3. What languages can the debugger be used to debug?

Exercises

1. Extend the dirscan.vbs example to include additional error checking. For example, incorporate code that handles an error if a subfolder is deleted while the script is executing.
2. Change the dirscan.vbs example to output the subfolders listed in order from smallest to largest. Include a command line parameter that controls the sort order.
3. Go through the full development process for your own script. First, define the requirements and design your algorithm. Next, code, run, and debug your script. You might want to skip ahead a few chapters to read about the objects and languages to help you to develop the code for your script.

WEEK 1

DAY 3

The Scripting Object Model

One of the most useful aspects of the Windows Scripting Host is the scripting objects. The scripting objects are components that are provided by Microsoft as components of the core scripting engine. Today, you'll learn about the scripting objects, and you'll find out how they provide you with the capability to use associative arrays and to access disk drives, folders, and files.

On the third day of your introduction to WSH, you'll do the following:

- Get an overview of the scripting object model
- Read detailed information about standard scripting objects
- See full examples that illustrate the use of each scripting object

Introduction to the Scripting Object Model

By now you know that the Windows Scripting Host is an exciting new technology that can help to provide more robust command scripting capabilities on the Windows platform. You've only begun to scratch the surface; there's a lot more that WSH provides than just language capabilities that are far superior to MS-DOS batch files.

Some of the most powerful capabilities of WSH are provided by the scripting objects. WSH includes a variety of objects that enable you to perform numerous tasks with your system. Using the WSH scripting objects, you can open and read files; create, copy, or delete folders; check file attributes; and maintain an associative array with an arbitrary number of elements. That's just for starters!

In this chapter, you'll cover all the standard scripting objects with reference information describing their properties and methods, and you'll see examples of how each object can be used. This chapter is intended simply to give you a basic familiarity with all the objects; later in the book, you'll see examples that use combinations of these components to perform really useful administrative and programming tasks.

Standard Scripting Objects

The standard scripting objects are WSH objects that are typically referred to as language components. The two primary objects are the Dictionary object and FileSystemObject. They are very important objects. You can use the Dictionary to store an array of any length that can be indexed using a string rather than just a standard numeric position. The FileSystemObject enables you to get access to a computer's file system. From the FileSystemObject, you can also access the Drive, Drives, File, Files, Folder, Folders, and TextStream objects, all of which provide some file system functionality. Figure 3.1 provides a diagram illustrating the relationships between the objects in the standard scripting object model.

The standard scripting objects are useful for many different tasks. Any time you want to store a varying number of items, I highly recommend using the Dictionary object! Also, the associative array capabilities can be extremely useful if you need to store items indexed by a string.

This section of the chapter provides full descriptions of the standard scripting classes with some illustrative examples to help you to use them in your WSH scripts.

FIGURE 3.1

The scripting object model.

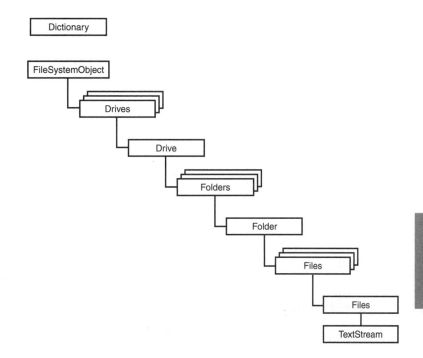

> **Note**
>
> It's important to emphasize that the standard scripting objects are available from any of the scripting languages that adhere to the WSH scripting engine standard. So if you learn how to use the objects in VBScript, your knowledge also transfers to the JScript language. For the standard scripting examples, you'll be using the JScript language, but on Day 4, "The WSH Object Model," you'll use the VBScript language extensively. Hopefully that will help you to get used to the similarities and differences of the two languages.

Dictionary Object

The Dictionary object provides very flexible associative array capabilities for your WSH scripts. Figure 3.2 illustrates the difference between standard array indexing and associative array indexing using a dictionary. Dictionaries are very powerful objects; learn how to use them because you'll find them extremely useful as you develop your own WSH scripts.

FIGURE 3.2
Indexing using an associative array vs. indexing using a standard array

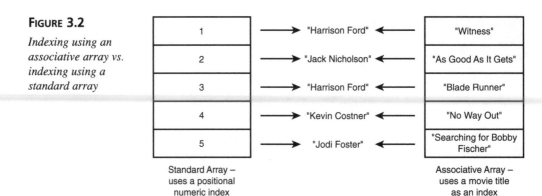

Standard Array – uses a positional numeric index

Associative Array – uses a movie title as an index

To create an instance of a Dictionary object, you need to use the full name, or PROGID, of the Dictionary object, which is Scripting.Dictionary. Look for the section "Dictionary Object Code Sample" later in this chapter for more details about creating and using Dictionary objects.

Dictionary Properties

TABLE 3.1   Dictionary OBJECT PROPERTIES

Property Name	Description
CompareMode	This returns or sets the comparison mode that is used to compare strings used as item keys in the Dictionary object. Valid options for CompareMode are: 0—binary comparison; 1—text comparison; and 2—database comparison. You can use values greater than 2 to refer to a comparison using a specific Locale ID.
Count	This returns the number of items that are currently stored in the Dictionary object.
Item	The Item property sets or returns the value of an item stored in a Dictionary object using the item's key.
Key	This sets or returns a key to an item within a Dictionary object.

Dictionary Object Methods

TABLE 3.2   Dictionary OBJECT METHODS

Method Name	Description
Add(*key*, *item*)	This adds a new item to the dictionary. The key is the identifier for the item in the dictionary; keys must be unique within a dictionary: You can't add two items to the dictionary with the same key.
Exists(*key*)	This checks the dictionary to see if the specified key exists and returns true if it does or false if it doesn't.
Items()	This returns an array that contains all the item values from the dictionary.
Keys()	This returns an array that contains all the key values from the dictionary.
Remove(*key*)	This removes a key and its corresponding item from the dictionary.
RemoveAll()	This removes all the keys and items from the dictionary.

Note   When I refer to methods of an object, I mean functions that the object enables you to call. You can't call the methods until you've instantiated the object. When you call them, you use the object.method(*argument1*, *argument2*, ...) syntax. For example, to call the Dictionary.Add() method, you must first instantiate a Dictionary object, and then you can call its Add() method. For more details, review the examples in this chapter.

Dictionary Object Code Sample

Here's an example of how you can use a Dictionary object to relate user names to their home pages:

LISTING 3.1   dictex.vbs   THE DICTIONARY OBJECT

```
' FILE: dictex.vbs
' AUTH: Thomas L. Fredell
' DESC: Shows how you can use the Dictionary object to store
'       information about a group of users.
'
' Copyright 1998 Macmillan Publishing.
'
```

continues

LISTING 3.1 CONTINUED

```
' Create a variable to store a dictionary object; note that the
' name of our object is dicHomePage. We call it that because we're
' going to use it to maintain a listing of home pages keyed by
' a person's name.
Dim dicHomePage

' Instantiate the dictionary object
Set dicHomePage = Wscript.CreateObject("Scripting.Dictionary")

' Now add user home pages to the dictionary object that contains
' home page references
dicHomePage.Add "Jack Handy", "http://users.org/jackhandy.htm"
dicHomePage.Add "Sandy Davis", "http://users.org/sandydavis.htm"

' Now display all of the home pages in the dictionaries by
' looping through them
Dim iPage, asPages

Wscript.Echo "Dumping the contents of the Home Page dictionary..."
asPages = dicHomePage.Items
For iPage = 0 to dicHomePage.count - 1
    Wscript.Echo "Page #" & iPage & ", URL=" & asPages(iPage)
Next

' Now display a specific dictionary entry using the
' associative capabilities; we're going to display the information
' for Jack Handy
Wscript.Echo ""
Wscript.Echo "Retrieving from a Dictionary using a string index..."
Wscript.Echo "The URL for Jack Handy's Home Page is: "
➥& dicHomePage("Jack Handy")
```

In the code example, first you create an instance of a `Dictionary` object using the `Wscript.CreateObject()` function, and you add a few entries to the dictionary using the `Add()` method. Next, you dump the contents of the dictionary to the screen by looping through an array of the items stored in the dictionary. Finally, you demonstrate the associative capabilities of the dictionary by retrieving the specific home page for a user via his name. The output of the script is depicted in Figure 3.3.

 Note

> One important thing to bear in mind as you look at these examples are some of the syntax differences between VBScript and Jscript. All of the objects in this chapter have the same capabilities in each language, but bear in mind that the way you use them may be slightly different. For example, when you access an array in Jscript, you'll use the name of the array with the index in square brackets, like Array[10]. In VBScript, you use standard parentheses like Array(10).

FIGURE 3.3

The results of running the dictex.vbs script.

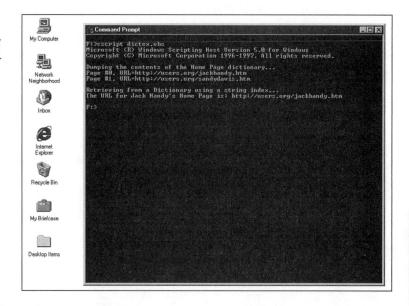

FileSystemObject

The FileSystemObject is the object that you use to manipulate your file system. It's extremely powerful; it has only one property, but it has many methods that perform useful file functions. Its methods enable you to copy or move files and folders, create or open text files, check for the existence of files or folders, and retrieve information about files and folders. It encapsulates a lot of functionality in an easy-to-use package!

Like the other objects, you must create an instance of the FileSystemObject using the Wscript.CreateObject() method before you an use its methods.

Note

If you review the language specifications for JScript and VBScript, you'll notice that there's more than one way to instantiate objects. You can use the WScript.CreateObject() method, or with JScript, you can create an object using new ActiveXObject("ObjectProgID"). For example, you can create a FileSystemObject using the following code: myFSO = new ActiveXObject("Scripting.FileSystemObject"); If you're using VBScript, you can use either the VBScript CreateObject() function or the WScript.CreateObject() method.

What's the difference between the two ways of creating an object? Well, the WScript.CreateObject() method provides more functionality than the other methods. It enables you to hook up an object that you create with methods that handle events from the object. So, if you want to handle

3

> events that an object uses, you should make sure to use
> `WScript.CreateObject()`. For more details, review the section "WScript
> Object" in Day 4, "The WSH Object Model."

FileSystemObject Properties

TABLE 3.3 FileSystemObject PROPERTIES

Property Name	Description
Drives	This returns a collection of all the drives available on the machine that is executing the script.

FileSystemObject Methods

 Note When you use the methods for the FileSystemObject, bear in mind that you may be affected by security issues, such as NTFS restrictions. Your code should include error handling in the event that you attempt an operation without sufficient access.

TABLE 3.4 FileSystemObject METHODS

Method Name	Description
BuildPath(*path*, *name*)	This appends a file or folder name to a file path. It inserts a \ if necessary.
CopyFile(*source*, *dest*, *overwrite*)	This copies the source file to the specified destination. If the optional *overwrite* argument is true and the destination file already exists, it overwrites the existing file. Wildcards can be used for the *source* parameter to copy multiple files in one function call.
CopyFolder(*source*, *dest*, *overwrite*)	This recursively copies a source directory to a destination directory. If the optional *overwrite* argument is true and a destination file or folder already exists, it is overwritten.
CreateTextFile(*file*, *overwrite*, *unicode*)	This enables you to create an object that you can use to read or write to a file. If you specify true for the *overwrite* parameter, this method overwrites an existing file. If you specify true for the *unicode* parameter, it creates a unicode text file instead of an ASCII text file.

Method Name	Description
DeleteFile(*filespec*, *force*)	This enables you to delete a file or a set of files if you use a wildcard. If the *force* argument is true, it deletes files that are marked with the read-only attribute.
DeleteFolder(*folderspec*, *force*)	This deletes a folder and all files or folders that it contains. If the *force* argument is true, it deletes folders that are marked with the read-only attribute.
DriveExists(*drivespec*)	This returns true if a drive exists or false if it doesn't.
FileExists(*filespec*)	This returns true if a file exists or false if it doesn't.
FolderExists(*folderspec*)	This returns true if a folder exists or false if it doesn't.
GetAbsolutePathName(*pathspec*)	This returns the full, unambiguous path name for a specified path. For example, assuming that the current directory is c:\test\foo and you pass a subdirectory, subtest, to this method, the resulting value is c:\test\foo\subtest.
GetBaseName(*path*)	This returns the base name of a file or folder when given its path.
GetDrive(*drivespec*)	This returns a Drive object when given a specified drive designation, such as C:.
GetDriveName(*path*)	This returns the drive name when given a path to a folder or file.
GetExtensionName(*path*)	This returns the extension of a file or folder when given its path.
GetFile(*filespec*)	This returns a File object when given a path to a file.
GetFileName(*pathspec*)	This returns a file name from a path.
GetFolder(*folderspec*)	This returns a Folder object when given a path to a folder.
GetParentFolderName(*path*)	This returns the name of the parent folder for a path to a file or folder.
GetSpecialFolder(*specialfolder*)	This returns a Folder object for a special system folder. The following constants can be used to get special folder objects: WindowsFolder—this returns a

continues

TABLE **3.4**   CONTINUED

Method Name	Description
	folder object for the Windows directory; SystemFolder—this returns a Folder object for the system folder, which contains device drivers and so on; TemporaryFolder—this returns a Folder object for the system temporary folder.
GetTempName()	This returns a randomly generated temporary file or folder name.
MoveFile(*source*, *dest*)	This moves a file from its current location to the destination location.
MoveFolder(*source*, *dest*)	This moves a folder from its current location to the destination location.
OpenTextFile(*file*, *iomode*, *create*, *format*)	This opens a specified file and returns a TextStream object. The *iomode* flag can be either ForReading, indicating that the file is open for reading, or ForAppending, indicating that the file is open for writing or appending. The *create* flag can be true or false; if it is true, it creates a file even if it doesn't exist already, or if it's false, it doesn't create the file. The *format* flag indicates the format used to open the file. It can be: TristateTrue—the file should be opened as unicode; TristateFalse—the file should be opened as ASCII; or TristateDefault—the file should be opened using the system default.

Caution

If an error occurs with the Copy...(), Delete...(), or Move...() functions, none of the changes made up to the occurrence of the error are rolled back. So be careful when you use these functions! Conceivably, you could miss copying, moving, or deleting some files or folders. Make sure you verify the results of the commands in your script.

FileSystemObject Code Sample

The FileSystemObject is chock-full of useful methods that you'll frequently use if you need to create or manipulate files or folders. Here's a simple example that uses the FileSystemObject to create a text file and output some information about the disk drives on the current system:

Tip

Notice in the JScript sample code that all the methods or properties of the `FileSystemObject` are referenced with an initial lowercase letter, rather than the initial uppercase letter that's in the preceding method list. This is because the convention for the JScript language is an initial lowercase letter, then uppercase for the first letter of each subsequent word that comprises a property or method name. It actually doesn't matter too much because either uppercase or lowercase works for the object methods or properties.

LISTING **3.2**   `testfso.js`—SCRIPT TO CREATE A TEXT FILE AND OUTPUT

```
// FILE: testfso.js
// DESC: Provides an example of the use of the FileSystemObject
//       in JScript.
// AUTH: Thomas L. Fredell
//
// Copyright 1998 Macmillan Publishing
//

var fso, tsOut, collDrvs, drv, iDrv;

// First create an instance of a FileSystemObject (FSO)
fso = WScript.createObject("Scripting.FileSystemObject");

// Now we can use the FSO to create a text file for output
// Note that the createTextFile() method returns a TextStream
// object, hence the "ts" prefix on the "tsOut" variable
WScript.echo("Writing drive information to 'drives.log'...");
tsOut = fso.createTextFile("drives.log", true);
tsOut.writeLine("DRIVE LOG");
tsOut.writeLine("---------");

// Now retrieve information about the drives on the current system
collDrvs = fso.Drives;
tsOut.writeLine("There were " + collDrvs.Count + " drives found on
➥this system.");
tsOut.WriteBlankLines(1);

// Iterate through the drives and output information about each drive
var enumDrvs;
enumDrvs = new Enumerator(collDrvs);
while (!enumDrvs.atEnd()) {
    drv = enumDrvs.item();
    tsOut.write("Drive " + drv.driveLetter + "; ");
    if (!drv.isReady) {
        tsOut.writeLine(" drive is not ready.");
    } else {
```

continues

3

Listing 3.2 CONTINUED

```
            tsOut.write("filesystem = " + drv.fileSystem + ", ");
            tsOut.writeLine("available = " + drv.availableSpace);
        }
        enumDrvs.moveNext();
    }

// Now close the text file that we used for logging
tsOut.Close();

// And output a "done" message.
WScript.echo("Finished writing drive information.");
WScript.echo("");
```

> **Caution**
>
> If you look at the Microsoft JScript documentation, you can see an example that uses the for(... in ...) syntax to iterate through a Drives collection. In practice, that doesn't appear to work. However, you can use an Enumerator object as a workaround, as you do in the FileSystemObject example.

This script uses the FileSystemObject fairly extensively. First it's used to open a text file using the FileSystemObject.createTextFile() method. Next it's used to display information about all the current drives in the system using the Drives collection. The output from the script is a text file called drives.log; you can see the results of running the script in Figure 3.4.

Figure 3.4

The results of running the testfso.js script.

Drive

The Drive object represents a disk drive or network share. To use a Drive object, you must reference it from an instance of the FileSystemObject. You can't instantiate it directly using CreateObject(). This also holds true for the Drives, Files, File, Folders, Folder, and TextStream objects. In the example for the Drive object, you see how to get it from the FileSystemObject and then use it to output information about the C: drive.

Unlike the Dictionary and FileSystemObject, the Drive object has no methods. You can, however, use some of its properties to change the characteristics of drives on your system (specifically the Volume label).

Drive Object Properties

TABLE 3.5 Drive Object Properties

Property Name	Description
AvailableSpace	This returns the amount of space that is available to a user on a local drive or on a network share.
DriveLetter	This returns the drive letter of a local drive or a network share. It might return "" if the drive is a network share that hasn't been mapped to a drive letter.
DriveType	This returns a string that indicates the type of a drive.
FileSystem	This returns a string that indicates the file system of a drive. The types that can be returned are FAT, NTFS, or CDFS.
FreeSpace	This returns the amount of free space that is available on a local drive or network share. This might be different from the amount of available space if the drive is on a system that supports disk quotas.
IsReady	This indicates whether the drive is ready. If you access a drive that represents a floppy disk and no disk is in the drive, this returns false.
Path	This returns the path to the drive (for example, C:).
RootFolder	This returns a Folder object that represents the root folder of a drive.
SerialNumber	This returns the decimal serial number that is used to uniquely identify a disk volume.
ShareName	This returns the network share name for a drive. If the drive is a local drive, it returns "".
TotalSize	This returns the total space in bytes of a local or network drive.
VolumeName	This enables you to retrieve or set the volume name of a drive.

3

> **Tip**
>
> Make sure to use the IsReady() method in your JScript code before you attempt to access the properties of a drive. The current version of JScript suffers from a lack of good error handling capabilities, so if an error occurs when you attempt to access a drive, your JScript code just bombs out with an error. Support for enhanced error handling will be available in an upcoming JScript version release from Microsoft.

Drive Object Methods

The Drive object has no methods.

Drive Object Code Sample

The Drive object enables you to retrieve all the details for a drive. Here's an example that illustrates how you can use it:

LISTING 3.3   drive.js—Obtaining Drive Details

```
// FILE: drive.js
// AUTH: Thomas L. Fredell
// DESC: Illustrates the use of the Drive object to display information
// about a local or network drive.
//
// Copyright 1998 Macmillan Publishing
//

var args, fso, drv;

// Retrieve arguments for the script, and check to make sure that the
// user has specified a drive letter.
args = WScript.arguments;
if (args.length != 1) {
    // User didn't specify arguments, so quit and display usage
    WScript.echo("USAGE:  drive.js  [driveletter]");
    WScript.echo("");
    WScript.echo("        Displays the information about a drive.");
    WScript.quit();
}

// Now instantiate a FileSystemObject and use it to get the Drive object
fso = WScript.CreateObject("Scripting.FileSystemObject");
drv = fso.Drives(args(0));

// Check to make sure that the drive is ready and quit if it isn't
if (!drv.isReady) {
    WScript.echo("Drive " + args(0) + " is not ready.");
```

```
    WScript.quit();
}

// The drive is ready, so we should be able to display all of the
// drive details
WScript.echo("Drive " + args(0) + " details:");
WScript.echo("");
WScript.echo("availableSpace = " + drv.availableSpace);
WScript.echo("driveLetter = " + drv.driveLetter);
WScript.echo("driveType = " + drv.driveType);
WScript.echo("fileSystem = " + drv.fileSystem);
WScript.echo("freeSpace = " + drv.freeSpace);
WScript.echo("isReady = " + drv.isReady);
WScript.echo("path = " + drv.path);
WScript.echo("rootFolder = " + drv.rootFolder);
WScript.echo("serialNumber = " + drv.serialNumber);
WScript.echo("shareName = " + drv.shareName);
WScript.echo("totalSize = " + drv.totalSize);
WScript.echo("volumeName = " + drv.volumeName);
```

The drive.js script uses a FileSystemObject to get access to the drives property, which is the Drives collection. The Drives collection can be indexed using a string much like the Dictionary. You use this capability to get a Drive object that corresponds to the argument that the user passed on the command line. Next, you output all the information about the Drive by echoing its properties to the screen. You can see the results of running the drive.js script in Figure 3.5.

FIGURE 3.5

The results of running the drive.js script.

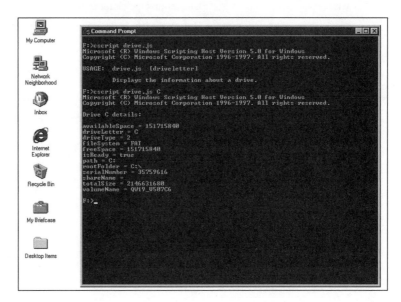

File Object

The File object represents a file stored on a local or network disk. Using a File object, you can retrieve all the properties of a file, you can open it to read or write as text, and you can copy, move, or delete the file. You can get an instance of a File object from either a FileSystemObject or Folder object.

File Object Properties

TABLE 3.6   File OBJECT PROPERTIES

Property Name	Description
Attributes	This enables you to set or get the attributes of a file. It is a numeric value that uses a logical combination of the following values: 0—Normal; 1—ReadOnly; 2—Hidden; 4—System; 8—Disk drive Volume label; 16—Directory; 32—Archive; 64—Alias (like a link or shortcut); and 128—Compressed.
DateCreated	This returns the date and time that the file was created.
DateLastAccessed	This returns the date and time that the file was last accessed.
DateLastModified	This returns the date and time that the file was last modified.
Drive	This returns the drive letter where the file resides.
Name	This can be used to either change or retrieve the name of a file.
ParentFolder	This returns the Folder object for the parent of the file.
Path	This returns the path for the file.
ShortName	This returns the name of the file under the short DOS 8.3 naming convention.
ShortPath	This returns the path to the file using the old DOS 8.3 naming convention.
Size	This returns the size of the file in bytes.
Type	This returns the type of the file based on the Windows association for the file's extension.

File Object Methods

TABLE 3.7   File OBJECT METHODS

Method Name	Description
Copy(*dest, overwrite*)	This copies the file to a different location. If another file with the same name already exists at the destination, it is not overwritten unless the *overwrite* flag is specified as true. The *overwrite* flag is false by default.
Delete(*force*)	This deletes the file; the deletion fails if the file is read-only unless the *force* flag is specified as true.
Move(*dest*)	This moves the file to a different destination. If a file already exists at the destination, an error occurs.
OpenAsTextStream (*iomode, format*)	This enables you to open the file for reading or writing. The *iomode* specifies the mode to open the file in; it can be one of the following: ForReading—opens the file for reading only; ForWriting—opens a file for writing; ForAppending—opens a file and enables you to write to the end of the file. The *format* flag can be one of the following: TristateUseDefault—indicates that the file should be opened using the system default; TristateTrue—indicates that the file should be opened as Unicode; TristateFalse—indicates that the file should be opened as ASCII.

File Object Code Sample

The File object enables you to retrieve all the details for a file; here's an example that illustrates how you can use it:

LISTING 3.4   file.js—OBTAINING FILE DETAILS

```
// FILE: file.js
// AUTH: Thomas L. Fredell
// DESC: Illustrates the use of the file object to display information
// about a file.
//
// Copyright 1998 Macmillan Publishing
//

var args, fso, fil;

// Retrieve arguments for the script, and check to make sure that the
// user has specified a file.
```

continues

LISTING 3.4   CONTINUED

```
args = WScript.arguments;
if (args.length != 1) {
    // User didn't specify arguments, so quit and display usage
    WScript.echo("USAGE:  file.js  [filespec]");
    WScript.echo("");
    WScript.echo("          Displays the information about a file.");
    WScript.quit();
}

// Now instantiate a FileSystemObject and use it to get the File object
fso = WScript.createObject("Scripting.FileSystemObject");
fil = fso.getFile(args(0));

// Display the file details
WScript.echo("File " + args(0) + " details:");
WScript.echo("");
WScript.echo("dateCreated = " + fil.dateCreated);
WScript.echo("dateLastAccessed = " + fil.dateLastAccessed);
WScript.echo("dateLastModified = " + fil.dateLastModified);
WScript.echo("drive = " + fil.drive);
WScript.echo("name = " + fil.name);
WScript.echo("parentFolder = " + fil.parentFolder);
WScript.echo("path = " + fil.path);
WScript.echo("shortName = " + fil.shortName);
WScript.echo("shortPath = " + fil.shortPath);
WScript.echo("size = " + fil.size);
WScript.echo("type = " + fil.type);

// Now call a function that outputs a listing of the
// file's attributes
WScript.echo("");
ShowFileAttributes(fil);
```

The first part of the example displays all of the information that we can gather from the properties of a file object. You'll notice that we use a custom function, ShowFileAttributes(), to decode and display the information about the file attributes. The body of ShowfileAttributes() is listed below.

```
//---------------------------------------------------
// FUNC: ShowFileAttributes(fil)
// DESC: Decodes and shows the attributes for the
//       specified file object.
//---------------------------------------------------
function ShowFileAttributes(fil) {
    var nAttribs;

    nAttribs = fil.Attributes;
    WScript.echo("File Attributes:");
    if (nAttribs == 0) {
        WScript.echo("Normal");
```

```
        return;
    }

    if (nAttribs & 1)
        WScript.echo("ReadOnly");
    if (nAttribs & 2)
        WScript.echo("Hidden");
    if (nAttribs & 4)
        WScript.echo("System");
    if (nAttribs & 8)
        WScript.echo("Volume");
    if (nAttribs & 16)
        WScript.echo("Directory");
    if (nAttribs & 32)
        WScript.echo("Archive");
    if (nAttribs & 64)
        WScript.echo("Alias");
    if (nAttribs & 128)
        WScript.echo("Compressed");
}
```

This very simple script displays all the available information about a file, including its size, name, attributes, and more. First you instantiate a FileSystemObject; you use it to call the FileSystemObject.getFile() method, which returns a File object. Then you simply echo all the properties of the File object to the screen. Notice that, for simplicity's sake, you've split out the code that checks the file attributes into a separate function called ShowFileAttributes(). The results of the script are illustrated in Figure 3.6.

FIGURE 3.6

The results of running the file.js script.

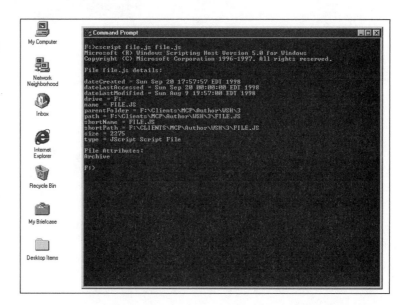

Folder Object

The Folder object represents a folder (or directory) on a local or network disk. Using a Folder object, you can retrieve all the properties of a folder, you can retrieve a collection of the files or folders within it, and you can copy, move, or delete the folder. You can get an instance of a Folder object from either a FileSystemObject or Drive object.

Folder Object Properties

TABLE 3.8   Folder OBJECT PROPERTIES

Property Name	Description
Attributes	This enables you to set or get the attributes of a folder. It is a numeric value that uses a logical combination of the following values: 0—Normal; 1—ReadOnly; 2—Hidden; 4—System; 8—Disk drive Volume label; 16—Directory; 32—Archive; 64—Alias (like a link or shortcut); and 128—Compressed.
DateCreated	This returns the date and time that the folder was created.
DateLastAccessed	This returns the date and time that the folder was last accessed.
DateLastModified	This returns the date and time that the folder was last modified.
Drive	This returns the drive letter where the folder resides.
Files	This returns a collection that lists the files stored in the folder.
RootFolder	This returns true if the folder is the root folder for a drive, otherwise it returns false.
Name	This can be used to either change or retrieve the name of a folder.
ParentFolder	This returns the folder object for the folder that contains the current folder.
Path	This returns the path for the folder.
ShortName	This returns the name of the folder under the short DOS 8.3 naming convention.
ShortPath	This returns the path to the folder using the old DOS 8.3 naming convention.
Size	This returns the size, in bytes, of all the files or subfolders of the folder.
SubFolders	This returns a collection of the folders that are contained within the folder.

Folder Object Methods

TABLE 3.9 Folder OBJECT METHODS

Method Name	Description
Copy(*dest, overwrite*)	This copies the folder to a different location. If another folder with the same name already exists at the destination, it is not overwritten unless the *overwrite* flag is specified as true. The *overwrite* flag is false by default.
Delete(*force*)	This deletes the folder and all files or subfolders that it contains; the deletion fails if the folder is read-only unless the *force* flag is specified as true.
Move(*dest*)	This moves the folder to a different destination. If a folder already exists at the destination, an error occurs.

3

Folder Object Code Sample

The Folder object enables you to retrieve all the details for a folder; here's an example that illustrates how you can use it:

LISTING 3.5 folder.js—OBTAINING FOLDER DETAILS

```
// FILE: folder.js
// AUTH: Thomas L. Fredell
// DESC: Illustrates the use of the folder object to display information
// about a folder.
//
// Copyright 1998 Macmillan Publishing
//

var args, fso, fldr;

// Retrieve arguments for the script, and check to make sure that the
// user has specified a folder.
args = WScript.arguments;
if (args.length != 1) {
    // User didn't specify arguments, so quit and display usage
    WScript.echo("USAGE:  folder.js [folderspec]");
    WScript.echo("");
    WScript.echo("        Displays the information about a folder.");
    WScript.quit();
}
```

continues

LISTING 3.5   CONTINUED

```
// Now instantiate a FileSystemObject and use it to get the Folder object
fso = WScript.createObject("Scripting.FileSystemObject");
fldr = fso.getFolder(args(0));

// Display the folder details-we just dump each file property to
// the screen; for information about each property, refer to the
// property reference for the Folder object in chapter 3
WScript.echo("Folder " + args(0) + " details:");
WScript.echo("");
WScript.echo("dateCreated = " + fldr.dateCreated);
WScript.echo("dateLastAccessed = " + fldr.dateLastAccessed);
WScript.echo("dateLastModified = " + fldr.dateLastModified);
WScript.echo("drive = " + fldr.drive);
WScript.echo("count of files = " + fldr.files.count);
WScript.echo("isRootFolder = " + fldr.isRootFolder);
WScript.echo("name = " + fldr.name);
WScript.echo("parentFolder = " + fldr.parentFolder);
WScript.echo("path = " + fldr.path);
WScript.echo("shortName = " + fldr.shortName);
WScript.echo("shortPath = " + fldr.shortPath);
WScript.echo("size = " + fldr.size);
WScript.echo("count of subFolders = " + fldr.subFolders.count);

// Now call a function that outputs a listing of the
// folder's attributes
WScript.echo("");
ShowFolderAttributes(fldr);


//-------------------------------------------------
// FUNC: ShowFolderAttributes(fldr)
// DESC: Decodes and shows the attributes for the
//       specified folder object.
//-------------------------------------------------
function ShowFolderAttributes(fldr) {
    var nAttribs;

    nAttribs = fldr.Attributes;
    WScript.echo("Folder Attributes:");
    if (nAttribs == 0) {
        WScript.echo("Normal");
        return;
    }
// We check the file attributes by
// using a bitwise AND operation to
// determine which attributes are set
    if (nAttribs & 1)
        WScript.echo("ReadOnly");
    if (nAttribs & 2)
        WScript.echo("Hidden");
    if (nAttribs & 4)
```

```
        WScript.echo("System");
    if (nAttribs & 8)
        WScript.echo("Volume");
    if (nAttribs & 16)
        WScript.echo("Directory");
    if (nAttribs & 32)
        WScript.echo("Archive");
    if (nAttribs & 64)
        WScript.echo("Alias");
    if (nAttribs & 128)
        WScript.echo("Compressed");
}
```

In this sample script, first you instantiate a FileSystemObject, and then you get a Folder object by calling the FileSystemObject.getFolder() method. At that point, you simply echo folder properties to the screen. The output of the folder.js script is displayed in Figure 3.7.

FIGURE 3.7

The results of running the folder.js script.

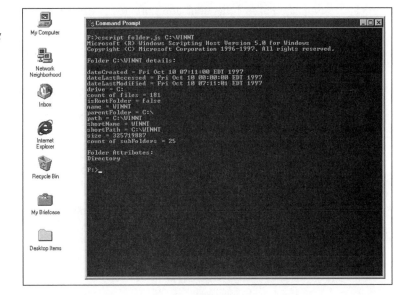

Collections (Drives, Files, and Folders)

Earlier in this chapter, you learned about the various objects that you can access through the FileSystemObject. For each object, there is a collection object that holds a group of objects. For example, many Drive objects can be in a Drives collection. These collections are used simply to represent a group of file system components. If you want to find out how to access these collections, review the FileSystemObject and its methods and properties.

All the collections have the same basic capabilities; they can return a count of entries and enable the user to access individual entries. Consequently, you're not going to look at each one separately because they are so similar. There is one exception to the rule; the Folders collection has a method that enables you to add a folder whereas the Drives and Files collections do not. In any case, after you learn how to use one collection, it is easy to use any of the others.

Collection Properties

TABLE 3.10   COLLECTION PROPERTIES

Property Name	Description
Count	This returns the number of items in the collection.
Item	This returns a specific item within a collection given the item's key.

Collection Methods

The Drives and Files collections don't provide any methods. The Folders collection provides the following method:

TABLE 3.11   Folders COLLECTION METHODS

Method Name	Description
AddFolders(foldername)	This adds a new Folder to the Folders collection.

Collections Code Sample

Here's an example that shows you how you can use the various collections to display information about a drive and its files and folders:

LISTING 3.6   coll.js—USING COLLECTIONS TO OBTAIN DRIVE, FILE, AND FOLDER INFORMATION

```
// FILE: colls.js
// AUTH: Thomas L. Fredell
// DESC: Displays information about drives, files, and folders using the
//       various collections objects.
//
// Copyright 1998 Macmillan Publishing
//

var args, fso, drv, drvs, fil, fils, fldr, fldrs, enumObj;

// Check to make sure the user specified a drive.
args = WScript.arguments;
```

```
if (args.length != 1) {
    // User didn't specify drive, so quit and display usage
    WScript.echo("USAGE:  colls.js  [drive]");
    WScript.echo("");
    WScript.echo("        Uses collections to display information
➥about");
    WScript.echo("        a drive.");
    WScript.quit();
}

// Now instantiate a FileSystemObject and use it to get the Drives
// collection which will be used to get the specific drive
fso = WScript.createObject("Scripting.FileSystemObject");
drvs = fso.Drives;
drv = drvs(args(0));
WScript.echo("Scanning drive " + drv + "...");
if (!drv.isReady) {
    // The drive isn't ready, so print error message and quit
    WScript.echo("");
    WScript.echo("The drive isn't ready.");
    WScript.quit();
}

// Now use the drive to retrieve the root folder
fldr = drv.rootFolder;

// From the root folder of the drive, display information about the
// sub-folders by using the subFolders collection
fldrs = fldr.subFolders;
WScript.echo("");
WScript.echo("Folders:");
WScript.echo("--------");
enumObj = new Enumerator(fldrs);
while (!enumObj.atEnd()) {
    fldr = enumObj.item();
    WScript.echo(fldr.name);
    enumObj.moveNext();
}

// Now display information about the files in the root of the selected
➥drive
fils = drv.rootFolder.files;
WScript.echo("");
WScript.echo("Files:");
WScript.echo("------");
enumObj = new Enumerator(fils);
while (!enumObj.atEnd()) {
    fil = enumObj.item();
    WScript.echo(fil.name);
    enumObj.moveNext();
}
```

3

For this example, you use the various collection objects to display information about a disk drive. First, you instantiate a FileSystemObject so that you can access the Drives collection. Next, you get the specific drive that you want by using the argument as the index into the Drives collection, and then you check the state of the drive using the isReady property. It's important to check the isReady property; if you don't check it, your script might experience errors if the drive is, for example, a CD-ROM drive that doesn't currently contain a CD-ROM disk. You get the root folder of the drive using the rootFolder property and display all the subfolders of the rootFolder by iterating through the subFolders property. Finally, you display all the files in the root folder of the drive by iterating through the rootFolder.files collection. Figure 3.8 shows the output from the colls.js script.

FIGURE 3.8

The results of running the colls.js script.

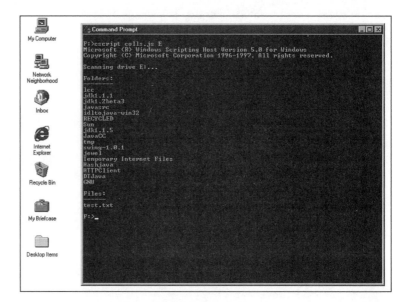

TextStream

The TextStream object makes it easy to perform sequential access functions with a text file. You can use it to read or skip through a file, to write to a file, and to track your position within a file. Like many of the other objects, you can't instantiate it directly. Instead, you have to use either a FileSystemObject or a File object to create a TextStream.

TextStream Object Properties

TABLE 3.11   TextStream OBJECT PROPERTIES

Property Name	Description
AtEndOfLine	This indicates whether the file pointer is positioned immediately before the end-of-line marker.
AtEndOfStream	This indicates whether the file pointer is positioned at the end of a file.
Column	This returns the column number of the current file pointer position in a file.
Line	This returns the current line number of the file pointer in a text file.

TextStream Object Methods

TABLE 3.12   TextStream OBJECT METHODS

Method Name	Description
Close()	This closes an open file.
Read(characters)	This returns a specific number of characters from an open text file.
ReadAll()	This returns the entire contents of a file as a string.
ReadLine()	This reads an entire line from an open text file.
Skip(characters)	This skips a specified number of characters within the open text file.
SkipLine()	This skips the next line when reading through a text file.
Write(string)	This writes a string to an open text file.
WriteBlankLines(lines)	This writes a specific number of newline characters to the open text file.
WriteLine(string)	This writes a string to an open text file and then writes a newline.

TextStream Object Code Sample

Here's an example that uses the FileSystemObject to instantiate a TextStream object that's used to output a file to the console with line numbers:

LISTING 3.7   textstrm.js—INSTANTIATING A TEXTSTREAM OBJECT

```
// FILE: textstrm.js
// AUTH: Thomas L. Fredell
// DESC: Echoes the contents of a text file to the console with line
// numbers.
//
// Copyright 1998 Macmillan Publishing
//

var args, fso, tstrm, nLine, sLine;

// Check to make sure the user specified a file
args = WScript.arguments;
if (args.length != 1) {
    // User didn't specify file, so quit and display usage
    WScript.echo("USAGE:  textstrm.js  [file]");
    WScript.echo("");
    WScript.echo("          Echoes the contents of a text file to");
    WScript.echo("          the console with line numbers.");
    WScript.quit();
}

// Now instantiate a FileSystemObject and use it to open the specified
➥file
fso = WScript.createObject("Scripting.FileSystemObject");
tstrm = fso.openTextFile(args(0), 1, false);

// Read through the file line-by-line
while (!tstrm.atEndOfStream) {
    nLine = tstrm.line;
    sLine = tstrm.readLine();
    WScript.echo(nLine + ": " + sLine);
}
```

This example uses an instance of the FileSystemObject to create a TextStream object by calling FileSystemObject.openTextFile(). The openTextFile() method returns a new TextStream object, and then a loop reads lines from the TextStream until you reach the end of it, at which point the TextStream.atEndOfStream property returns True. Figure 3.9 shows the output of the textstrm.js script.

FIGURE 3.9

The results of running the `textstrm.js` *script.*

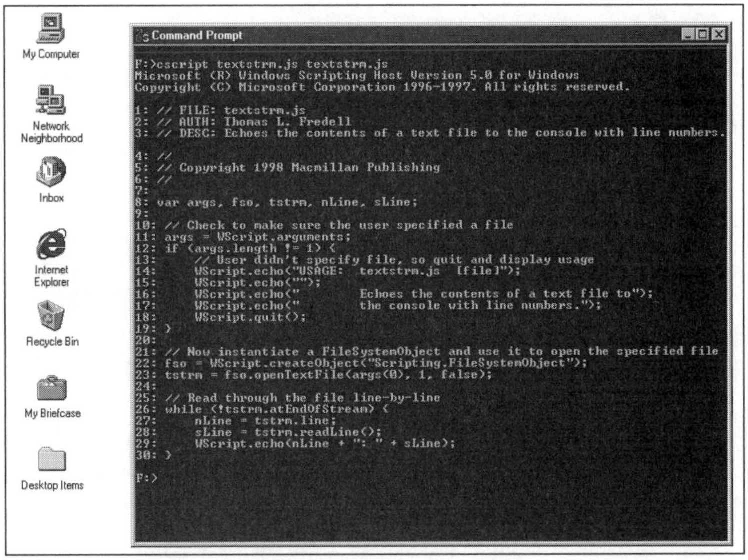
My Computer
Network Neighborhood
Inbox
Internet Explorer
Recycle Bin
My Briefcase
Desktop Items
Command Prompt
F:>cscript textstrm.js textstrm.js
Microsoft (R) Windows Scripting Host Version 5.0 for Windows
Copyright (C) Microsoft Corporation 1996-1997. All rights reserved.
1: // FILE: textstrm.js
2: // AUTH: Thomas L. Fredell
3: // DESC: Echoes the contents of a text file to the console with line numbers.
4: //
5: // Copyright 1998 Macmillan Publishing
6: //
7:
8: var args, fso, tstrm, nLine, sLine;
9:
10: // Check to make sure the user specified a file
11: args = WScript.arguments;
12: if (args.length != 1) {
13: // User didn't specify file, so quit and display usage
14: WScript.echo("USAGE: textstrm.js [file]");
15: WScript.echo("");
16: WScript.echo(" Echoes the contents of a text file to");
17: WScript.echo(" the console with line numbers.");
18: WScript.quit();
19: }
20:
21: // Now instantiate a FileSystemObject and use it to open the specified file
22: fso = WScript.createObject("Scripting.FileSystemObject");
23: tstrm = fso.openTextFile(args(0), 1, false);
24:
25: // Read through the file line-by-line
26: while (!tstrm.atEndOfStream) {
27: nLine = tstrm.line;
28: sLine = tstrm.readLine();
29: WScript.echo(nLine + ": " + sLine);
30: }
F:>

3

Summary

This chapter has given you an overview of the standard scripting objects provided by the Windows Scripting Host. This is one half of the objects provided by WSH; the other half is discussed in Day 4.

You can use the reference material for these objects as you write your own scripts, and the sample code will provide you with a solid start for your own efforts. It should be obvious from the examples and the reference descriptions that the objects are extremely useful; with them, you can read and modify drives, folders, and files. Read on to find out about the other WSH objects, then stick with me, and I'll give you some examples of how you can use all the objects together in the following chapters.

Q&A

Q **The scripting object model appears to be a fairly deeply nested hierarchy. Do I need to walk through each object in the hierarchy to get an instance of a low-level object? In other words, to get a `Folder` object do I first need to instantiate a `FileSystemObject`, `Drives`, `Drive`, `Folders`, and then `Folder` object?**

A No. Thankfully, the scripting object model provides shortcuts that enable you to get direct access to a `Folder` object (or any of the other objects). You can navigate through the object hierarchy if you want to, but if you just want to get a specific folder with a specific path, you can use the `FileSystemObject.GetFolder()` method.

Q **Using VBScript, it's possible to dynamically resize an array by using the `ReDim Preserve` statement. Why would I want to use the `Dictionary` instead of an array that I dynamically resize?**

A You certainly can make an array resize dynamically using the `ReDim` statement. However, it's very inefficient because every element in the array is affected by `ReDim`. The `Dictionary` object is implemented differently; consequently, it's more efficient to use when you need a dynamically resizable array of elements.

Q **Why do the collections have both `Count` and `length` properties? They seem redundant.**

A The properties are indeed redundant; the collections include the `length` property to adhere to JavaScript standards.

Workshop

The following section will help you test your comprehension of the material presented in this chapter and put what you've learned into practice. You'll find the answers to the quiz and exercises in Appendix A.

Quiz

1. What object would you use to open a file?

2. After you've opened a file, how do you read from it?

3. How can you determine if a `Dictionary` object contains a specific element?

Exercises

1. Use the associative array capabilities of the Dictionary object to store information that you retrieve using a string rather than a numeric index.

2. Use the FileSystemObject to write a script that takes a filename and echoes it to the screen with a break after every 25 lines.

3. Write a script that takes a folder name as input and writes a list of the files in the folder to a nicely formatted text file. For an advanced exercise, modify the program to go through the subfolders of the folder while outputting file information to a text file.

3

DAY 4

The WSH Object Model

The Windows Scripting Host provides two types of standard objects; there are objects that are part of the scripting engine, and there are objects that are specifically provided by the Windows Scripting Host. In this chapter, you'll learn about the Windows Scripting Host objects, which can be used to change network drive mappings, manipulate the Windows registry, create shortcuts, and more.

On the fourth day of your introduction to WSH, you'll do the following:

- Get an overview of the WSH object model
- Read detailed information about WSH objects
- See full examples that illustrate the use of each WSH object

Introduction to the WSH Object Model

The Windows Scripting Host scripting environment provides basically two sets of objects: objects that are included with the scripting engine and WSH-specific objects. You learned about the scripting objects on Day 3, "The Scripting Object Model," and in this chapter you'll learn about the WSH scripting objects.

Note

> This chapter assumes basic familiarity with Microsoft OLE and ActiveX. OLE is the standard for embedding objects inside of applications; you may have used it to put a a spreadsheet excerpt inside a document. ActiveX (or the Component Object Model [COM]) is essentially the object standard that underlines OLE—it provides the fundamental capabilities to instantiate and use objects. If you'd like more information, refer to the Microsoft web site (www.microsoft.com).

Like the scripting objects, the WSH objects provide very powerful tools that enable you to access and change the Windows environment. For example, they enable you to change network drive mappings and read or modify the Windows registry. In this chapter, you'll cover all the WSH scripting objects; you'll see reference information describing their properties and methods and examples using each object. Like Day 3, this chapter is intended to give you a basic familiarity with the objects. In subsequent chapters, you'll develop examples that use WSH objects combined with standard scripting objects.

WSH Objects

The WSH objects are provided by the Windows Scripting Host environment. They are extremely powerful and provide you with the capabilities that you need to perform many standard tasks. The standard objects include `Wscript`, `WshArguments`, `WshShell`, `WshNetwork`, `WshShortcut`, `WshUrlShortcut`, `WshCollection`, `WshEnvironment`, and `WshSpecialFolders`. The WSH objects are depicted in Figure 4.1.

The name of the object corresponds to the functionality provided by the object. For example, the `WshShell` object enables you to manipulate the Windows shell. The `WshNetwork` object enables you to change connections to the network. The purposes of the others should be fairly self-explanatory given the naming convention. Later you'll find more specifics about each of the objects, and you'll see code examples that illustrate the use of each object. Bear in mind that later in the book you'll have more complete examples that show you how you can use groups of these objects together to perform really useful tasks.

FIGURE 4.1

The WSH object model.

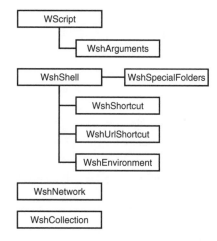

Wscript Object

The root WSH object is the Wscript object. It's always available when a script is running in the scripting host, so you don't have to create an instance of the object. It's not really a root object from an inheritance perspective, but it's easy to think of it as such because it plays a central role for WSH scripts. The Wscript object provides the capability to retrieve information about a the script's runtime environment and arguments. It also provides the capability to create objects or retrieve them from files. Finally, it provides the capability to echo information to the screen and to quit with an exit code. You will almost certainly use the Wscript object, if only to create objects or echo information to the screen!

When you access the object, you use the object name Wscript. Unlike the other objects that are described in this chapter, you don't have to initialize a new object instance for it. The Wscript or cscript program takes care of those details for you.

Wscript Object Properties

TABLE 4.1 Wscript OBJECT PROPERTIES

Property Name	Description
Application	This returns the IDispatch interface for the WSH scripting host.
Arguments	This returns a collection that contains the parameters for the script.
FullName	This returns the full path to the host executable, including the name of the scripting host program (cscript.exe or Wscript.exe).

continues

TABLE 4.1 CONTINUED

Property Name	Description
Name	This returns the "friendly" name of the scripting host program (Windows Scripting Host).
Path	This returns the directory in which the scripting host program resides.
ScriptFullName	This returns the full path to the script that is currently running. This includes the filename of the script and the path where the script resides.
ScriptName	This returns the filename of the currently executing script.
Version	This returns the version of the WSH scripting host program.

Wscript Object Methods

TABLE 4.2 Wscript OBJECT METHODS

Method Name	Description
CreateObject(progid, evtprefix)	This enables you to create an ActiveX object that supports the IDispatch interface. It also hooks up event handling for the object that you create. You must specify the PROGID of the object to create it, such as Excel.Application, and you can optionally specify the prefix of event-handling methods that you implement.
DisconnectObject(object)	This enables you to disconnect event handling from an object that you connected using the CreateObject() or GetObject() methods.
GetObject(path, progid, evtprefix)	This enables you to retrieve an ActiveX object from a file. You must specify the path to the object, and you can optionally specify the PROGID and event handler prefix for the object.
Echo(arg1, arg2, ...)	This enables you to echo information to the screen. If Wscript is executing the script, the output pops up in a dialog box. If cscript is executing the script, the output is echoed to the screen, such as the DOS ECHO batch file command.
Quit(errorcode)	This enables you to terminate the execution of your script with a specific error code.

Wscript Object Code Sample

The Wscript object is a very powerful object that you use all the time in your WSH scripts. Here's an example using WSH that shows how you can create and manipulate ActiveX objects exposed by Microsoft Excel to programmatically create a spreadsheet:

LISTING 4.1 Vscript.vbs—SCRIPT TO CREATE AND MANIPULATE ACTIVEX OBJECTS

```
' FILE: Wscript.vbs
' AUTH: Thomas L. Fredell
' DESC: Demonstrates the ability of the Wscript object to create an
'       ActiveX object.
'
' Copyright 1998 Macmillan Publishing
'

' Create an instance of the Excel.Application object
Dim oXL
Set oXL = Wscript.CreateObject("Excel.Application")

' Ensure that its visible to the end-user
oXL.Visible = TRUE

' Add a workbook
oXL.WorkBooks.Add

' And add some data to the spreadsheet
oXL.Cells(1,1).Value = "Using"
oXL.Cells(2,1).Value = "WSH"
oXL.Cells(3,1).Value = "with"
oXL.Cells(4,1).Value = "Excel"
oXL.Cells(5,1).Value = "is"
oXL.Cells(6,1).Value = "easy!"
```

4

In this script, you're using the ever present Wscript object to create an instance of the Excel.Application object. Most people recognize that Excel is the popular spreadsheet provided by Microsoft as part of their Office Suite. However, many people are unaware that Excel provides a very powerful OLE automation interface that enables you to develop external programs that control Excel. Basically, any external program that can use OLE automation objects can use Excel programmatically. You can do it from Visual Basic, Delphi, or C++. In your example, you're controlling it from a WSH script implemented using the VBScript language. You could also do it using the JScript language in a WSH script; any WSH scripting engine should be able to access OLE automation objects such as the objects provided by Excel.

You begin with the Excel.Application object, and then you call a few methods and change some Excel properties. For more information about the Excel object model, refer to the programming information provided by Microsoft. The results of running the script using cscript Wscript.vbs from the command line are illustrated in Figure 4.2.

FIGURE 4.2

*The results of running
the* Wscript.vbs
script.

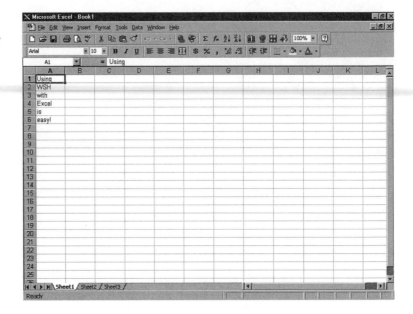

WshArguments Object

The WshArguments object provides you with a collection of the arguments for the current
script. You can use arguments to customize the execution of your script at runtime. For
example, you might define a script that runs a special backup routine. For the backup
script, you might want to define source and destination device arguments. That's one
simple example; when you are creating your script, keep in mind the portions of your
script for which you want to use arguments. That helps you to create scripts that you can
write once and reuse over and over without any modification.

To access the WshArguments object, you don't need to create an instance using
CreateObject(). It's immediately available to a running script from the
Wscript.Arguments property.

WshArguments Object Properties

TABLE 4.3   WshArguments OBJECT PROPERTIES

Property Name	Description
Item	This array contains the parameters for the script. You can access members of the array using a numeric index. This is also the default property for the WshArguments object.
Count	This returns the number of command-line parameters that were passed to the script.

Property Name	Description
length	This provides the same functionality as the Count property; it returns the number of command-line parameters. This property is provided to comply with JScript standards, which use the standard .length property for arrays.

WshArguments Object Code Sample

The WshArguments object is very easy to use. The following code example shows how you can use it to display the list of arguments for your script:

LISTING 4.2   showparams.vbs—LISTING SCRIPT ARGUMENTS

```
' FILE: showparams.vbs
' AUTH: Thomas L. Fredell
' DESC: Shows the arguments for the script
'
' Copyright 1998 Macmillan Publishing
'
Dim iArg, args

Wscript.Echo Wscript.ScriptName & ": Showing command line arguments"

' Get an instance of the Arguments object
Set args = Wscript.Arguments

' Loop through the arguments and echo them back to the user
For iArg = 0 to args.Count - 1
    Wscript.Echo "Argument #" & CStr(iArg) & ": " & args(iArg)
Next
Wscript.Echo Wscript.ScriptName & " done."
```

In the preceding showparams.vbs script, you begin by setting the variable args to the Wscript.Arguments property. The Wscript.Arguments property returns a WshArguments object. Next, you loop through the arguments with a standard For loop; begin at the first index, which is 0, and continue through the last argument (Count - 1). Figure 4.3 shows the results of running the script with some additional command-line arguments.

4

FIGURE 4.3

FIGURE 4.3

The results of running the showparams.vbs *script.*

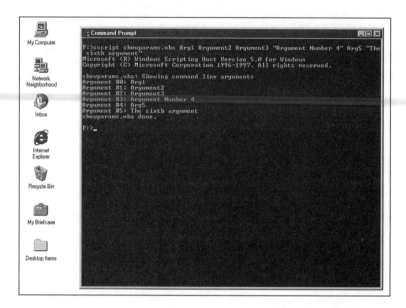

WshShell Object

The WshShell object is a very powerful object that provides access to the Windows shell and Registry. Using the WshShell object, you can access any system environment variables. You can access special system folders including the Windows desktop, Start menu, and personal documents folder. You can use it to create shortcuts in a Windows folder. You can use it to display information to the user in a pop-up window and to capture a simple button click (such as Retry or Ignore). You can also use WshShell to access and manipulate the Windows Registry and to run other programs.

To create an instance of the WshShell object, you can call CreateObject("Wscript.Shell"). Notice that the PROGID, Wscript.Shell, drops the initial Wsh from WshShell. That is intentional and is consistent throughout the Wsh objects.

WshShell Object Properties

TABLE 4.4   WshShell OBJECT PROPERTIES

Property Name	Description
Environment	This property returns the WshEnvironment object, which contains the current environment variable settings.
SpecialFolders	This property returns the WshSpecialFolders object, which provides access to the various special system folders.

WshShell Object Methods

TABLE 4.5　WshShell Object Methods

Method Name	Description
CreateShortCut(*path*)	This creates a new WshShortcut object and returns it to the caller of the method. If the title of the shortcut ends with .url, a WshURLShortcut object is created.
ExpandEnvironmentStrings (*string*)	This method returns the environment values that correspond to the environment variable names embedded within % in a string. For example, if the input is %TEMP%, it returns something like C:\WINDOWS\TEMP.
Popup(*text, seconds, title, type*)	This method displays a pop-up window to the end user. The *text* argument specifies the text that shows up in the body of the window. The *seconds* argument determines how long the pop-up window stays on the screen to wait for user input. The *title* argument specifies the title for the window. Finally, the *type* argument specifies the type of pop-up window that you create. The type can be a combination of a button type and an icon type. The valid button types are as follows: 0—show OK button; 1—show OK and Cancel buttons; 2—show Abort, Retry, and Ignore buttons; 3—show Yes, No, and Cancel buttons; 4—show Yes and No buttons; and 5—show Retry and Cancel buttons. The valid icon types are the following: 16—show stop icon; 32—show question mark icon; 48—show exclamation point icon; and 68—show information icon.
RegDelete(*key*)	This method enables you to delete a Registry key or value. You must specify the full name of the key, including preceding key hive (such as HKEY_CURRENT_USER or HKEY_CLASSES_ROOT).
RegRead(*key*)	This method enables you to read a Registry key or value. You can only retrieve values with the data types REG_SZ, REG_EXPAND_SZ, REG_DWORD, REG_BINARY, and REG_MULTI_SZ.
RegWrite(*key, value, type*)	This method can be used to set a Registry key or value. RegWrite() can set a key using the REG_SZ, REG_EXPAND_SZ, REG_DWORD, and REG_BINARY data types.

continues

4

TABLE 4.5 CONTINUED

Method Name	Description
Run(*command*, *style*, *wait*)	This method can be used to run a program from the current script. You can use it to spawn the program with command line parameters, you can control the window state when the program launches, and you can indicate whether you want to wait for the program to return. The valid parameters for the style can be found in the Windows 32 API documentation for the ShowWindow() function.

WshShell Object Code Sample

The WshShell object is an extremely versatile and powerful object. In the following code example we'll see how it can be used to find the current TEMP directory. The example illustrates just one simple use of the object, but you'll see it used throughout the book to perform numerous functions:

LISTING 4.3 shell.vbs—USING THE WshShell OBJECT

```
' FILE: shell.vbs
' AUTH: Thomas L. Fredell
' DESC: Demonstrates the use of the WshShell object.
'
' Copyright 1998 Macmillan Publishing
'

Option Explicit

Dim shell, sTmp

' Create an instance of a WshShell object
Set shell = Wscript.CreateObject("Wscript.Shell")

' Use the shell object to retrieve the value of an
' environment variable
sTmp = shell.ExpandEnvironmentStrings("%TEMP%")

' Now display the value of the TEMP environment
' variable to the user with a Prompt
shell.Popup "Value of TEMP=" & sTmp, 0, "TEMP Variable", 0 & 48
```

This script uses the WshShell object for a very simple purpose—to retrieve the value of the TEMP environment variable. This is very useful; you might use it in a WSH script to determine the temporary directory so that you can store temporary files created by your script code. In the script, you create an instance of the WshShell object by calling the standard `Wscript.CreateObject()` method. Next, you retrieve the value of the `TEMP` variable by passing a string to the `shell.ExpandEnvironmentStrings()` method. `ExpandEnvironmentStrings()` recognizes environment variables using % delimiters and replaces them with the value of the variable. Finally, you display the value of the variable using a pop-up window. The results of running the script are shown in Figure 4.4.

FIGURE 4.4

The results of running the shell.vbs script.

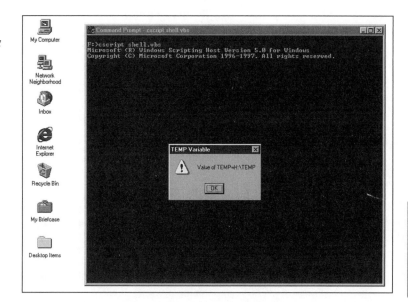

WshShortcut Object

NEW TERM   The `WshShortcut` object represents a Windows shortcut. A shortcut is a link to a file, folder, or URL that resides anywhere on your local machine or on the network that your machine is connected to. To launch a shortcut, you typically click or double-click on it. It's transparent to you whether the shortcut is located locally or on the network.

You can use the `WshShell` object to create shortcuts. You can't instantiate the `WshShortcut` object directly; you must use the `WshShell.CreateShortcut()` method to create the shortcut.

4

WshShortcut Object Properties

TABLE **4.6** WshShortcut OBJECT PROPERTIES

Property Name	Description
Arguments	These are the arguments, as a string, for the shortcut. You can use this to pass parameters to program.
Description	This is the description for the shortcut object.
FullName	This is the full path for the file that represents the shortcut.
HotKey	This is the hotkey that you want to establish for the shortcut. You can set a hotkey using literally any keystroke combination; you use an encoded string that represents the combination of key modifiers, such as CTRL and ALT, with the key name, such as K. You can only specify hotkeys for shortcuts located on the Windows desktop or Start menu.
IconLocation	This specifies the location of the icon for the shortcut object. This is in the form Path,index, where Path refers to a valid DLL or executable file.
TargetPath	This specifies the target path of the shortcut object. This can refer to a file or folder.
WindowStyle	This specifies the style with which the window for the shortcut target is to be launched. This can be any of the window style constants.
WorkingDirectory	This specifies the working directory for the target of the shortcut.

WshShortcut Object Methods

TABLE **4.7** WshShortcut OBJECT METHODS

Method Name	Description
Save()	This saves the shortcut to the location specified by the FullName property.

WshShortcut Object Code Sample

Here's an example where the WshShortcut object is used to create a shortcut on the Start menu:

LISTING 4.4   `shortcut.js`—CREATING A SHORTCUT ON THE START MENU

```
// FILE: shortcut.js
// AUTH: Thomas L. Fredell
// DESC: Illustrates the use of the shortcut object to create a shortcut
//       on the Windows Start menu.
//
// Copyright 1998 Macmillan Publishing
//

var args, shell, sStartFolder, shctNew;

// Retrieve arguments for the script, and check to make sure that the
// user has specified a target and name for the shortcut
args = Wscript.arguments;
if (args.length != 3) {
    // User didn't specify correct args, so quit and display usage
    Wscript.echo("USAGE:  shortcut.js  [path] [desc] [name]");
    Wscript.echo("");
    Wscript.echo("          Creates a shortcut using the specified path");
    Wscript.echo("          description, and shortcut filename.");
    Wscript.quit();
}

// Instantiate a WshShell object
shell = Wscript.CreateObject("Wscript.Shell");

// and use it to get the folder for the Start Menu
sStartFolder = shell.SpecialFolders("StartMenu");

// Now create a new shortcut object
shctNew = shell.CreateShortcut(sStartFolder + "\\" + args(2));

// Set remaining shortcut properties
shctNew.TargetPath = args(0);
shctNew.Description = args(1);

// And save it
shctNew.Save();
```

4

In this script example, you first check to ensure that you have sufficient arguments. If you don't, you quit with a usage message. If you do, you instantiate a WshShell object. You use the SpecialFolders property to get access to the folder that contains the Windows Start menu for the current user. Next, you create a shortcut using the WshShell.CreateShortcut() method, which returns a new WshShortcut object. You set the target path and description for the shortcut using the TargetPath and Description properties respectively. Finally, you save the shortcut using the Save() method. You can see the results of running the script in Figure 4.5; the Windows Start menu contains a new shortcut created by the shortcut.js script.

FIGURE 4.5

*The results of running
the* shortcut.js
script.

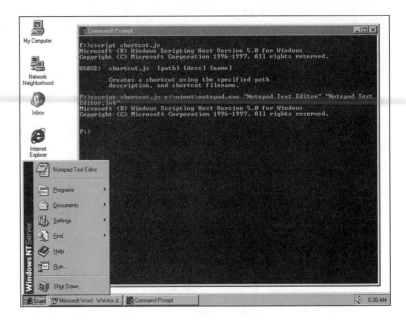

WshUrlShortcut **Object**

The WshUrlShortcut object represents a link to an Internet URL. Like the WshShortcut object, the location of the link target is transparent to the user of the link. A user simply clicks on the link, and the operating system takes care of the details of accessing the resource represented by the shortcut. The URL can point to a location anywhere, on your local machine, on a remote server on the Internet, or on a server on your corporate intranet.

The URL link shows up on your Windows desktop just like a standard icon. The difference with the URL shortcut is that clicking on it will launch your Web browser instead of lauching an application. It works like a bookmark that it separated from your Web browser, and as a matter of fact URL links are actually used to implement the bookmarks in the Microsoft Internet Explorer browser.

You can use the WshShell object to create URL shortcuts as well as file or folder shortcuts. You can't instantiate the WshUrlShortcut object directly. You must use the WshShell.CreateShortcut() method to create the shortcut.

WshUrlShortcut **Object Properties**

TABLE 4.8   WshUrlShortcut OBJECT PROPERTIES

Property Name	Description
FullName	This is the full path of the URL shortcut object.
TargetPath	This is the full path of the target of the URL shortcut object.

WshUrlShortcut Object Methods

TABLE 4.9 WshUrlShortcut OBJECT METHODS

Method Name	Description
Save()	This saves the shortcut to the location specified by the FullName property.

WshUrlShortcut Object Code Sample

Here's an example where the WshUrlShortcut object is used to create a new shortcut on the user's desktop:

LISTING 4.5   urllink.vbs—CREATING URL SHROTCUTS

```
' FILE: urllink.vbs
' AUTH: Thomas L. Fredell
' DESC: Illustrates the use of the shortcut object to create a URL
'       shortcut on the Windows desktop.
'
' Copyright 1998 Macmillan Publishing
'

Dim args, shell, sDtopFolder, sShctFile, shctNew

' Retrieve arguments for the script - and check argument validity
Set args = Wscript.arguments
If args.Count <> 3 Then
    ' Show usage for this script
    Wscript.Echo "USAGE:  urllink.vbs  [URL] [DESC] [NAME]"
    Wscript.Echo ""
    Wscript.Echo "       Creates a URL shortcut using the specified"
    Wscript.Echo "       URL, description, and shortcut filename."
    Wscript.Quit
End If
Stop
' Instantiate a WshShell object
Set shell = Wscript.CreateObject("Wscript.Shell")

' and use it to get the folder for the Start Menu
sDtopFolder = shell.SpecialFolders("Desktop")

' Determine the full path for the URL shortcut file
sShctFile = args(2) & ".url"
sShctFile = sDtopFolder & "\" & sShctFile
' Now create the URL shortcut object
```

continues

LISTING 4.5   CONTINUED

```
Set shctNew = shell.CreateShortcut(sShctFile)

' Set remaining shortcut properties...
shctNew.TargetPath = args(0)

' ...and save it
shctNew.Save
```

The `urllink.vbs` script listed in the preceding code follows the standard pattern for your sample scripts; first you check arguments, and then you perform the work if sufficient arguments were specified. This example is very similar to the `shortcut.js` example; the primary difference is that it's implemented using the VBScript language instead of the JScript language. Also, the file extension of the name passed to the `CreateShortcut()` method is different. Here you're using the `.url` extension. Consequently, the object that is returned by `CreateShortcut()` isn't a `WshShortcut`; it's a `WshUrlShortcut` object. Figure 4.6 shows the results of running the script; notice the new Internet link to the Microsoft home page on the desktop.

FIGURE 4.6

The results of running the urllink.vbs script.

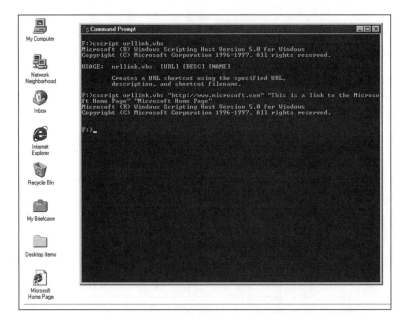

WshNetwork Object

The WshNetwork object provides the capability to create network connections to shared folders or network printers and to enumerate current network connections. You can use it to determine if a user currently has a specific network connection, and if he or she doesn't, you can take action to map a network directory. You're not limited to just directories; you can also check for printer mappings and map or remove mappings to specific printers.

With WshNetwork, you can easily perform basic networking functions. When you combine this object with other WSH objects, you can perform very powerful functions, such as checking a database, before you perform a user login. Obviously, you can't do that with DOS batch files, and you generally can't do that easily with most other scripting languages.

To use the WshNetwork object, you need to instantiate an instance of the object using the Wscript.Network PROGID. Your two basic options for doing so are to call either CreateObject("Wscript.Network") or Wscript.CreateObject("Wscript.Network"). Property and method listings and examples follow to help you make use of the WshNetwork object in your scripts.

WshNetwork Object Properties

TABLE **4.10**   WshNetwork OBJECT PROPERTIES

Property Name	Description
ComputerName	This returns a string listing the current computer's name.
UserDomain	This returns the name of the user's domain as a string.
UserName	This returns the name of the user as a string.

Note

In the context of the WshNetwork object, the UserDomain property refers to the Windows NT domain of the user. That's different from the Internet domain of the user. Windows NT domains are used to group users and computers as units that can be centrally administered by a network administrator. Internet domains are typically used to represent the presence of a corporation on the Web—like acme.com. There is no link between the two different types of domains.

WshNetwork Object Methods

Table 4.11 WshNetwork *Object Methods*

Method Name	Description
AddPrinterConnection(*LocalName*, *RemoteName*, *UpdateProfile*, *User*, *Password*)	This maps a remote printer as a local resource. *LocalName* specifies the local name for the printer. *RemoteName* specifies the remote name of the printer. If *UpdateProfile* is true, the printer mapping is added to the current user's profile. The *User* and *Password* arguments can be specified to use different user access rights to map the printer.
EnumNetworkDrives()	This returns a collection that contains all the current drive mappings.
EnumPrinterConnections()	This returns a collection that contains all the current printer mappings.
MapNetworkDrive(*LocalDrive*, *RemoteDrive*, *UpdateProfile*, *User*, *Password*)	This maps a remote drive as a local drive. *LocalDrive* specifies the local name for the drive. *RemoteDrive* specifies the remote name of the network share. If *UpdateProfile* is true, the drive mapping is added to the current user's profile. The *User* and *Password* arguments can be specified if different user access rights are to be used to map the drive.
RemoveNetworkDrive(*Name*, *Force*, *UpdateProfile*)	This removes a drive mapping. If the network share is mapped to a local drive, *Name* must be the drive name, otherwise it must the remote name of the share. If *Force* is true, the connection is removed even if the resource is currently in use. If *UpdateProfile* is true, the drive mapping is removed from the current user's profile.
RemovePrinterConnection(*Name*, *Force*, *UpdateProfile*)	This removes a printer mapping. If the printer is mapped to a local port, *Name* must be the port name (in the manner of LPT1), otherwise it must be the remote name of the printer. If *Force* is true, the connection is removed even if the printer is currently in use. If *UpdateProfile* is true, the printer mapping is removed from the current user's profile.
SetDefaultPrinter(*PrinterName*)	This sets the default printer to the remote printer specified by *PrinterName*.

WshNetwork Object Code Sample

The following example shows how you can use the WshNetwork object to retrieve information about the current network login and connections:

LISTING 4.6   `network.vbs`—RETRIEVING CURRENT NETWORK LOGIN AND CONNECTION INFORMATION

```
' FILE: network.vbs
' AUTH: Thomas L. Fredell
' DESC: Illustrates the use of the network object to enumerate
'       connections.
'
' Copyright 1998 Macmillan Publishing
'

Dim net, coll, i

' Instantiate a WshNetwork object
Set net = Wscript.CreateObject("Wscript.Network")

Wscript.Echo "Current network settings..."
Wscript.Echo ""

' Now print information about the current computer, domain, and user
Wscript.Echo "Computer: " & net.ComputerName
Wscript.Echo "Domain:   " & net.UserDomain
Wscript.Echo "User:     " & net.UserName

' List the network drive mappings
Wscript.Echo ""
Wscript.Echo "Network drive mappings:"
Set coll = net.EnumNetworkDrives()
For i = 0 to coll.Count - 1
    Wscript.Echo coll(i)
Next

' List the printer mappings
Wscript.Echo ""
Wscript.Echo "Printer mappings:"
Set coll = net.EnumPrinterConnections()
For i = 0 to coll.Count - 1
    Wscript.Echo coll(i)
Next
```

This script begins by creating an instance of the WshNetwork object using the
Wscript.CreateObject("Wscript.Network") method call. Next, the script outputs the
computer, domain, and current usernames using various properties of the WshNetwork
object. The script then displays all the current drive and printer mappings. For each of
the network mappings, the script retrieves a WshCollection object that contains the mappings using first the EnumNetworkDrives() method and then the
EnumPrinterConnections() method. The contents of the collection are displayed on
the screen using a standard For loop. You can see the results of running the script in
Figure 4.7.

Figure 4.7

*The results of running
the network.vbs
script.*

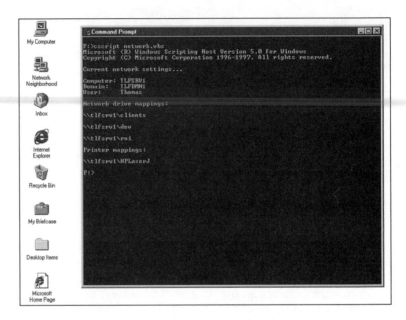

WshCollection Object

The WshCollection object is one of the true workhorses of the WSH objects. It performs
a simple function: It maintains an array of items. You can't use the WshCollection object
directly in your scripts, but you use it when you access other WSH objects, such as the
WshNetwork object. If you use the WshNetwork.EnumNetworkDrives() or
WshNetwork.EnumPrinterConnections() methods, the return value is a collection that
contains the list of network drives or printer connections respectively. The
WshCollection object provides you with the capability to retrieve the count of items in
the collection and to retrieve items using their numeric positional index.

WshCollection Object Properties

Table 4.12 WshCollection Object Properties

Property Name	Description
Item	This enables you to retrieve an item from the collection by specifying an index.
Count	This provides the number of items in the collection.
length	Like the Count property, this also returns the number of items in the collection. This is provided for compatibility with JScript conventions.

WshCollection Object Methods

The WshCollection object does not provide any methods. It is simply used as a repository for information that is returned by methods from other objects.

WshCollection Object Code Sample

The WshCollection object is illustrated in the previous code sample for the WshNetwork object. Refer back to that sample, and pay attention to the use of the coll variable. It's a collection variable that's used to retrieve information about drive and printer mappings.

WshEnvironment Object

The WshEnvironment object provides access to Windows environment variables. Typical environment variables include the current PATH, which is the set of directories that Windows searches to run a program that is invoked either from the Start | Run menu or from the command prompt. There are many other environment variables; some are standard Windows variables such as PATH, whereas others are defined by applications.

You can use the WshEnvironment object to add, read, modify, and delete environment variables. You can't create an instance of the WshEnvironment object directly; you need to use the WshShell.Environment property to access an instance of the object. The following methods show you the various capabilities that you have through the WshEnvironment object.

WshEnvironment Object Properties

TABLE 4.13 WshEnvironment OBJECT PROPERTIES

Property Name	Description
Item	This enables you to read, change, or add an environment variable.
Count	This is the number of current environment variables.
length	This is the number of current environment variables. This is provided for compatibility with JavaScript standards.

WshEnvironment Object Methods

TABLE 4.14 WshEnvironment OBJECT METHODS

Method Name	Description
Remove(Name)	This removes the environment variable specified by Name.

WshEnvironment Object Code Sample

The following example shows how you get an instance of the WshEnvironment object, scan the environment variables, and access specific settings:

LISTING 4.7   environ.js—INSTANTIATING THE WSHENVIRONMENT OBJECT

```
// FILE: environ.js
// DESC: Illustrates the use of the WshEnvironment object.
// AUTH: Thomas L. Fredell
//
// Copyright 1998 Macmillan Publishing
//

var shell, env, enumVars;

// First create an instance of the WshShell object
shell = Wscript.createObject("Wscript.Shell");

// Then use that instance to get the current environment
env = shell.environment;

// Display some specific environment variables
Wscript.echo("Showing specific environment variables...");
Wscript.echo("");
Wscript.echo("PATH=" + env("PATH"));
Wscript.echo("windir=" + env("windir"));

// Now display all of the environment variables
Wscript.echo("");
Wscript.echo("");
Wscript.echo("Showing all environment variables...");
Wscript.echo("");
enumVars = new Enumerator(env);
while (!enumVars.atEnd()) {
    Wscript.echo(enumVars.item());
    enumVars.moveNext();
}
```

This sample script shows how you can use the WshEnvironment object to access specific environment variables or to scan all the environment variables. First, the script instantiates a WshShell object. Next, it sets the value of the env variable to the WshShell.Environment property, which returns a WshEnvironment object. It displays the value of the PATH and windir environment variables by using the variable name as an index to the WshEnvironment object. Finally, it displays all the environment variables by enumerating through the environment variable collection. Figure 4.8 illustrates the results of running the script.

FIGURE 4.8

The results of running the environ.js script.

WshSpecialFolders Object

The WshSpecialFolders object holds a collection of special system folders. Using a descriptive string index, you can retrieve the file system path to a specific folder that you want to access or modify. For example, say you want to access the current user's desktop folder. You can use the WshSpecialFolders object to determine what physical on-disk folder represents the user's desktop. The example later in this section shows you can find folder paths using the WshSpecialFolder object.

You can't instantiate a WshSpecialFolder object directly; you have to access it via the SpecialFolders property of the WshShell object.

WshSpecialFolders Object Properties

TABLE 4.15   WshSpecialFolders OBJECT PROPERTIES

Property Name	Description
Item	This contains the full paths of special folders. You can specify a string index for this property as in Item("Desktop"). The list of special folders includes the following: AllUsersDesktop; AllUsersStartMenu; AllUsersPrograms; AllUsersStartup; Desktop; Favorites; Fonts; MyDocuments; NetHood; PrintHood; Programs; Recent; SendTo; StartMenu; Startup; and Templates.

continues

TABLE 4.15 CONTINUED

Property Name	Description
Count	This returns the number of folders in the special folders collection.
length	This returns the number of folders in the special folders collection.

WshSpecialFolders Object Methods

The WshSpecialFolders object provides no methods.

WshSpecialFolders Object Code Sample

The following code example shows how you can use the WshSpecialFolders object to find specific Windows folders:

LISTING 4.8 specfldr.vbs—LOCATING SPECIFIC FOLDERS

```
' FILE: specfldr.vbs
' DESC: Provides an example of the use of the WshSpecialFolders
'       object
' AUTH: Thomas L. Fredell
'
' Copyright 1998 Macmillan Publishing
'

Dim shell, fldrs, fldr

' First get a WshShell object
Set shell = Wscript.CreateObject("Wscript.Shell")

' And use the shell to get the WshSpecialFolders
Set fldrs = shell.SpecialFolders

' Use it to display some selected special folders
Wscript.Echo "Specific 'special folders'..."
Wscript.Echo ""
Wscript.Echo "Desktop=" & fldrs("Desktop")
Wscript.Echo "Favorites=" & fldrs("Favorites")
Wscript.Echo "Programs=" & fldrs("Programs")

' And dump all of the special folders to the screen
Wscript.Echo ""
Wscript.Echo ""
Wscript.Echo "Dumping list of all special folders..."
Wscript.Echo ""
```

```
For Each fldr In fldrs
    Wscript.Echo fldr
Next
```

The `specfldr.vbs` script shows how you can retrieve the physical paths for special Windows folders. First the script instantiates a `WshShell` object so that it can access the `SpecialFolders` property. You store the value of the `SpecialFolders` property, which is a `WshSpecialFolders` object, in the `fldr` variable. Next, you use several strings to index to the `fldr` object and retrieve paths for the `Desktop`, `Favorites`, and `Programs` folders. Finally, you display all the special folders using a standard `For Each...Next` loop. The output from the `specfldr.vbs` script is illustrated in Figure 4.9.

FIGURE 4.9

The results of running the `specfldr.vbs` *script.*

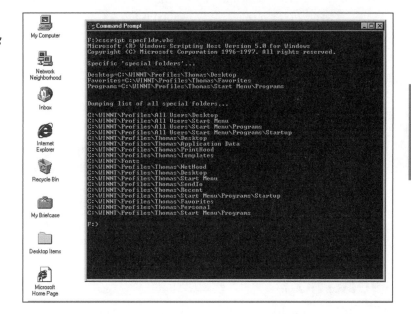

4

Summary

In this chapter you've learned about the objects provided by the Windows Scripting Host. They are extremely useful objects, and the examples for each object illustrate how you can use them. When you're writing your own WSH scripts, use this chapter as a reference for WSH objects and their properties and methods. The same holds true for the previous chapter; it provides a similar reference for the very useful standard scripting objects.

At this point, you've only scratched the surface possibilities for the Windows Scripting Host and the objects it provides. The examples illustrate object usage well, but they are fairly trivial. As you continue through this book, you'll encounter code that shows how the WSH objects can be used in conjunction with the standard scripting objects and other OLE automation objects to perform sophisticated administrative and application tasks.

Q&A

Q Is there any reason why I would want to use the `Wscript.CreateObject()` method to create instances of objects instead of the `CreateObject()` function in the VBScript language?

A If you want to include support for handling events from objects that you use, the `Wscript.CreateObject()` method is the way to go because the `CreateObject()` function doesn't provide that capability.

Q What are the ways that I can get access to the value of an environment variable using the WSH objects?

A You can get environment variable values using either the `Environment` property of the `WshShell` object or by calling the `WshShell.ExpandEnvironmentStrings()` method.

Q Both the `WshShortcut` and `WshUrlShortcut` objects are created using the `WshShell.CreateShortcut()` method. How do you ensure that a URL shortcut is created rather than a standard shortcut?

A The type of shortcut that is created depends on the extension of the shortcut file. To create a `WshShortcut` object, use the extension `.lnk` for the shortcut filename. To create a `WshUrlShortcut`, use the extension `.url`.

Workshop

The following section will help you test your comprehension of the material presented in this chapter and put what you've learned into practice. You'll find the answers to the quiz and exercises in Appendix A.

Quiz

1. What would you use to check for a network drive mapping and then to remove the network drive mapping?
2. How do you check the number of arguments that are passed to a script?
3. Can you instantiate the `WshSpecialFolders` object directly?

Exercises

1. Write a script that takes a different script as an argument and then creates a link to that script on the Start menu. This is a useful convenience utility to install scripts for yourself or other users.

2. Write a script that checks for specific printer and drive connections. If a printer or drive connection doesn't exist, map the printer or the network drive. Remove any unexpected drive or printer mappings.

3. Write a script that displays a list of all the files in the user's temporary directory. (Hint: Use the WshEnvironment class to find the value of the TEMP environment variable.)

4

WEEK 1

DAY 5

Using Microsoft VBScript with WSH

By Ian D. Morrish

As you have seen in the previous chapters, the Windows Scripting Host provides a mechanism for executing the script language of your choice. But which one? Your background will dictate your choice. If, like me, you are an NT administrator, VBScript might be the most logical choice. Experienced VB or VBA programmers will also feel right at home with VBScript.

In this chapter you will take a look at the features of VBScript and see some practical examples of how you can use the language in your scripts.

On the fifth day of your introduction to WSH, you'll do the following:

- Get an introduction to VBScript
- Learn the language syntax
- Understand how to use VBScript features through sample code

Introduction to VBScript

VBScript is the scripting version of Visual Basic. This helps to explain the subset of VB features that are supported by the VBScript interpreter.

If you are not a programmer by trade, VBScript is a good language to start learning with because it has a simple syntax, and you will be writing your own scripts before you know it. When you have mastered VBScript, you will be able to expand into Visual Basic for Applications (VBA), which is used in all MS Office applications, and into full-blown Visual Basic programming.

VBScript Background

VBScript is an interpreted language, which means it cannot be compiled into an executable. The interpreter reads in the script file, checks some basic syntax requirements, and then executes the commands and functions in the script. It was first used in Internet Explorer so that Web page authors could run code dynamically on the remote user's PC. Microsoft took a subset of functions from Visual Basic for Applications, which in itself is a subset of Visual Basic, that meet the functionality required while maintaining performance and keeping the interpreter as small as possible.

Because VBScript was first used in a browser, it had to be safe, which means that there can be no access to the operating system or file system. The only interaction with the system is via the msgbox() function for displaying a message and the inputbox() function for requesting user input.

The VBScript interpreter is available to any application via the ActiveX Scripting standard. Active Server Pages (ASP) and WSH are examples of applications that host the Microsoft Scripting languages to enable their functions to be used.

VBScript Syntax Overview

The syntax for VBScript is very simple. There are no special requirements for braces or start and end of code identification. The language is not case sensitive, and you don't have to declare variable types. This means that you can write ad hoc code that won't produce runtime errors, although it is advisable to properly structure production scripts.

VBScript uses parentheses () to control the order in which a complex combination of expressions is evaluated. Expressions are evaluated from the inner most parentheses outward.

The comment symbol, ' (apostrophe), tells the interpreter to ignore any following text. It can be placed at the beginning of a line or at the end of an executable line but not on a continued line. For example:

```
'
'This is a comment Line
Dim strUser ' Name of currently logged on user
' strUser = "Guest"  this whole line is ignored
'
```

The line continuation character, _ (underscore), is useful for breaking up long lines for readability, as in the following example:

```
' I prefer this
Wscript.Echo "Welcome to the XYZ Corporation " & vbLF &_
       "Logon Script." & vbLF & vbLF &_
       "Please remember to logoff" & vbLF &_
       "when you are finished"
' To this
Wscript.Echo "Welcome to the XYZ Corporation " & vbLF & "Logon Script."
& vbLF & vbLF & "Please remember to logoff" & vbLF & "when you are
finished"
```

Similarities to Visual Basic

VBScript shares a lot of functions with Visual Basic and Visual Basic for Applications. However, there are some notable differences to be aware of:

- Error handling   There is no `On Error Goto` statement.
- Data Types   Only the `Variant` type is available.
- Objects   You can't use the `Dim` object `As New Object`.
- Functions   There are no financial, Dynamic Data Exchange, or file I/O functions.
- Compiler directives   There is no support for include files or type libraries.

The last item above should be available in the next version of WSH.

Standard VBScript Syntax

VBScript code consists of variables, constants, operators, conditional statements, and functions. For each of these areas, you will cover the essential features and see some examples.

5

Declaring and Using Variables

Variables are placeholders for information that you want to operate on. Most scripts make heavy use of variables. They are used to store command-line options, user input, and the results of mathematical and string functions. Each variable name identifies an address in memory where the actual data is stored.

You can give your variables any name, providing the following conditions are met:

- There can be no more than 255 characters in the name.
- The name must start with an alphabetic letter.
- It must not contain a space, full stop, or mathematical symbols (!, +, -, /).
- It cannot be the same name as built-in VBScript function names.

Variable naming conventions are covered in the section "Naming Conventions" later in this chapter.

To define a variable's name and allocate storage space in memory, VBScript provides the DIM statement:

```
DIM strFileName
```

The DIM statement can be used in the main part of a script, which makes it a global variable, or in a procedure (function or sub), which limits the variable's availability to only the procedure in which it is created.

You do not have to dimension a variable in order to use it. VBScript does this automatically if it encounters a variable name in the script that has not been dimensioned. You can prevent this behavior by including the Option Explicit statement at the beginning of your code. This causes a runtime error if an undimensioned variable is encountered.

Arrays are also created with the DIM statement. Array elements are numbered from zero, so the statement DIM myFiles(9) creates an array of 10 items. An array can be dynamic by having no value in the parentheses.

If you have used or seen VB code before, you will have noticed the statement DIM *variable* AS .... In VBScript, all variables are of one type, so you don't have to define the type of data that will be stored in the variable. This variable type is called a variant, and you generally don't have to worry how VBScript stores your data except to remember that numbers and strings are operated on differently.

VBScript stores a value in the most appropriate format, and you can mix value types in some operations:

```
a=21
b=15
c="My age is: "
d=a+b ' =36
e=c&d ' = "My age is: 36"
f=c+d ' = Error: Type Mismatch
```

You can force numbers to be stored as strings by enclosing them in quotes ("). Time and date information can be enclosed in hashes (#):

```
StartDate = #1-Apr-1999#
```

VBScript stores the date according to the regional settings on your PC.

VBScript Constants

VBScript includes a number of built-in constants. A constant is used like a variable except that its value is fixed. You can also define your own constants, which can be used to make code more readable. This example shows script using a constant to add a line feed character in a message box:

```
Wscript.Echo "First line" & vbLF & "Second line"
```

Some of the more useful constants provided in VBScript are VbCR, vbLF, vbTab, vbBinaryCompare, vbTextCompare, vbTrue, and vbFalse.

This example shows how to define a constant and use it in your code:

```
Const ForWriting = 2
Set objFS = CreateObject("Scripting. FileSystemObject")
Set objFile = objFS.OpenTextFile("c:\myfile.txt", ForWriting)
```

You can also create string constants by enclosing the value in quotes ("). Dates and times can be enclosed in pound symbols (#):

```
Const StartDate = #1-Apr-1999#
```

The use of constants makes your code more maintainable because if you use a particular string in many places and you need to change it, you only have to do it in one place.

Operators

VBScript supports basic mathematical operations such as addition, subtraction, division, and multiplication using the +, -, /, and * symbols. Some of the other operators that you will find useful include the following:

5

- Concatenation (&)—used to combine two expressions into a string.
- Modulus (Mod)—Returns the remainder after dividing two expressions. If you have a loop and want to display a message box each time you have incremented a counter by 10, you can use the following code:

```
For I = 1 to 100
x = I Mod 10
If x = 0 Then
    Wscript.Echo I
End If
Next
```

- or—Expression 1 and/or Expression 2 must be true for the result to be true. Under some circumstances if one of the expressions is null, the result can be null:

```
a=vbTrue
b=vbFalse
result = a or b
Wscript.Echo result
```

Note

Note: True = -1, False = 0, and Null = 1

- And—Expression 1 and Expression 2 must be true for the result to be true:

```
a=4
b=3
If a=2 And b=3 Then
    Wscript.Echo "Condition is True"
Else
    Wscript.Echo "Condition is False"
End If
```

Conditional Statements

Most programs need to test the condition or state of something and perform actions based on the result of the test. VBScript provides the If and Case statements to execute conditional code.

The syntax for If is the following:

```
If Expression Then
    Code to executeElseIF Expression Then
    Code to execute
Else
    no previous expression is true
     so execute this code
End If
```

The expression can be a simple assignment or the result of a function:

```
' see if a=2
If a = 2 then
    .
    .
End If
' see if we have a full name or just part
If Instr(Ltrim(strName), " ", vbTextCompare) = 0 Then
    .
    .
End If
```

The last example might look complicated, but all it does is use some built-in VBScript functions (covered later in this chapter) to remove any leading spaces in the value for strName and then return the character position of the space character. If this character is not found in the string, 0 is returned.

If your Then code is a single line, you can include it on the If line without the need for an End If statement:

```
If Cancel = True then Wscript.Quit()
```

The ElseIf statement can be used to test many expressions, but if you only have one expression that has a number of possible values to test, the Select Case statement is more efficient because it only evaluates the expression once:

```
Select Case strUser
    Case "FJONES"
        msgbox "Hi Fred Jones"
        .
        .
    Case "JSMITH"
        msgbox "Hi John Smith"
        .
        .
    Case Else
        msgbox "User unknown"
        .
        .
End Select
```

5

You can have many lines of code between each Case statement. However, this might make the code hard to read. It might be more appropriate to call a subroutine or function:

```
Select Case strUser
    Case "FJONES"
        Call Fjones()
    Case "JSMITH"
        .
```

```
       .
Sub Fjones()
    msgbox "Hi Fred Jones"
       .

       .
End Sub
```

Looping Constructs

Everyone, regardless of computing background, should be familiar with the most common method of looping:

```
For I = 1 To 10
    Print I
Next I
```

This is still commonly used when you have a known, fixed number of repetitive tasks to perform. This section will cover each of the looping methods available in VBScript and examples showing when and how you can use them.

For Next

The full syntax for this command is the following:

```
For counter = start To end [Step]
Next
```

You can terminate the loop at any time with the Exit For statement. The increment constant (default = 1) can be set by adding Step = x on the end of the For line.

If you want to loop through each item in an array but you don't know the size of the array, you can use the Ubound function to get the highest index number:

```
Dim MyArray()
...
For I = 0 To Ubound(MyArray) Step 2
    If MyArray(I) = "Bad Data" Then
        Exit For
    End If
Next
```

If you have nested For Next loops, it helps to put a comment after the Next showing the name of the counter for readability:

```
For I = 1 To 10
    For J = 1 to 20

        .

        .
    Next 'J

    .

    .
Next 'I
```

For Each

The For Each statement repeats the code between the For and Next statements for each element in an array or collection:

```
Set objFS = CreateObject("Scripting.FileSystemObject")
Set objFolder = objFS.GetFolder("C:\")
Set objFiles = objFolder.Files
For Each file in objFiles
    Wscript.Echo file.name
Next
```

The word file in this example is arbitrary and could be anything.

This is often used when a collection object doesn't support an absolute reference to the items within it:

```
ObjFiles(1).name
```

This is used most often with objects that contain a collection of items such as the File System Object or an Outlook Folder/Item Collection.

You can exit the For Each loop at any time with the Exit For statement.

Do Loop

The Do Loop executes a statement repeatedly until a condition is true or while a condition is true. The While or Until condition can be set with the Do or Loop command, but you normally see it used in conjunction with the Do command:

```
Do Until count = 5
    count = count + 1
Loop
Status = True
Do While Status = True
    count = count + 1
    If count = 10 Then
        Statue = False
    End If
Loop
```

5

You can use this method if you are testing each value with a function and want to find the first value that meets a certain condition.

While Wend

This is similar to the Do Loop, except the condition is not checked until the code gets to the Wend statement. If the condition is not met, execution starts over from the While statement:

```
While count <10
    count = count + 1
    msgbox count
Wend
```

This method of looping is not very common.

VBScript Functions

There are a large number of functions provided by VBScript. They assist with conversions, string manipulation, formatting expressions, date/time functions, mathematical functions, and user input/output.

In this section, you will look at examples of the more common functions that you are likely to use in WSH scripts.

Conversions

Probably the most commonly used conversion function is Chr(), which returns the character for a given ANSI character code. The ANSI code for printable characters starts at 33. An example of using the Chr() function follows:

```
for i= 65 to 75
    strMsg = strMsg & i & " = " & chr(i) & vbLF
Next
Wscript.echo strMsg
```

Because VBScript stores expressions automatically in the most suitable variant subtype, you might need to pass a variable to a function or COM object as a known type. These are some of the common conversion types:

- Cdate(strDate) converts a recognizable date string to a date. An example of when you would use this is when your source date is in a long format and you want to add x days to it.

- Cint(number) removes any decimal point value and returns an Integer.

For example:

```
strBirthDate = "September 20, 1962"

Wscript.echo "I am " & Cint((Date - Cdate(strBirthDate)) / 365) & " years
►old"
```

In the preceding example, Cdate(strBirthDate) returns 20/09/62. This is based on my OS system local settings. Subtracting this from today's date results in 13283 days. Dividing this by 365 gives 36.3917808219178 years (approximately). Finally, Cint returns 36.

If you experience type mismatch errors, you will probably need to use one of the conversion functions to solve the problem.

If you want to find out how VBScript is storing your variable, there is a VarType function, which returns an Integer indicating the variant sub type:

```
IType = VarType(veriable)
Select Case Itype
    Case 0 ' Empty
    Case 1 ' Null
    Case 2 ' Integer
    Case 3 ' Long Integer
    Case 4 ' Single-precision floating-point number
    Case 5 ' Double-precision floating-point number
    Case 6 ' Currency
    Case 7 ' Date
    Case 8 ' String
    Case 9 ' Object
    Case 17 ' Byte
End Select
```

There is also a simple test you can perform to detect if a variable is a number or text. IsNumeric() returns true if the variable or expression can be evaluated as a number.

String Manipulation

If you were to tell a programmer that VBScript can do cool things with strings, they would laugh and tell you to look at Perl because it has regular expression support. If you have ever seen one of those expressions, it probably didn't make any sense at first, and fortunately, this is the VBScript chapter so I don't have to explain it to you. VBScript has enough string manipulation functions to perform fairly complicated manipulations.

You will cover these functions:

- Instr   Returns the position of the first occurrence of one string within another
- InstrRev   Returns the position from the end of the string where the required string is found
- Len   Returns the number of characters in a string
- Ucase   Returns a string that has been converted to uppercase
- Left   Returns a specified number of characters from the left side of a string
- Mid   Returns a specified number of characters from a string
- Right   Returns a specified number of characters from the right side of a string
- Replace   Replaces part of a string with another string

5

The in string function is useful for checking that a string contains a required sub string or for finding the starting position for one of the other string functions.

The syntax for this function is as follows:

```
InStr([start, ]string1, string2[, compare])
```

The square brackets ([ ]) indicate optional values.

An example is checking to see if an entered Internet email address is valid. If the @ symbol is not found in the string, the function returns 0. If there is an @, you check that there is at least one dot in the domain name as follows:

```
strAddress = InputBox ("Please enter e-mail address")
iATposition = Instr(StrAddress,"@")
If iATposition <> 0 Then
    If Instr(iATposition, strAddress, ".") <> 0 Then
        Wscript.Echo strAddress & " is a valid address"
    Else
        Wscript.Echo "Invalid domain in " & strAddress
    End If
Else
    Wscript.Echo "Internet address must contain an @ symbol"
End If
```

You will notice that the second If statement started looking for the dot character after the @ symbol because it is valid to have a dot in the username. Note that this is not an exhaustive test of valid Internet email addresses.

The Left and Right functions are useful for returning parts of a string. For example, to get the extension of a filename, use the following:

```
path = Right(path, InstrRev(path, "."))
```

To get the path of a UNC filename, use this:

```
path = Left(path, InstrRev(path, "\"))
```

To find the filename without an extension requires removing the drive/path prefix and extension, which can be done with the Mid function:

```
FileStart = InstrRev(path, "\")
FileLength = InstrRev(path, ".") - InstrRev(path, "\")
FileName = Mid(path, FileStart, FileLength)
```

This can also be done with one line:

```
FileName = Mid(path, InstrRev(path, "\"), InstrRev(path, ".") -
➥InstrRev(path, "\"))
```

Probably the most powerful string function is Replace. The full syntax is as follows:

```
Replace(expression, find, replacewith[, start[, count[, compare]]])
```

To demonstrate how useful this function is, imagine you have to convert a UNC path name to a URL. Assuming you have removed the Drive: and added http:// to the string, here is how you change the \ to / for every occurrence of the backslash.

```
URL = Replace(path, "\", "/", 1, -1)
```

By setting the count argument to -1, the function replaces all occurrences of the backslash.

Object Assignment

This is one of the more complex features that you will use extensively in scripts. The Set command assigns an object reference to a variable. An object in this case is a Component Object Model (COM) compliant DLL (or OCX) or a program that supports OLE automation, such as the Microsoft Office suite of applications.

Wscript is a COM object that exposes practical functions for you to use. These functions have what are called methods and properties, which you can access (or automate) after you have assigned your own variable to the object you want to automate:

```
Set WshNetwork = Wscript.CreateObject("Wscript.WshNetwork")
```

Note   OLE and COM are covered further in Chapter 14, "Overview of WSH and Application Scripting Capabilities."

5

Error Handling

There are two ways of dealing with errors in VBScript. You can either ignore them, which will cause your script to terminate and display an error message when an error is encountered, or you can use the On Error statement.

Placing On Error Resume Next in your script will result in any line causing a runtime error to be skipped and execution to continue on the next line. This can cause the next line to produce unexpected results, so you need to check the Err object at critical places in your script to see if there has been an error. Err.Number is 0 if there has not been an error. If Err.Number is not 0, Err.Description might contain a useful description of the error for display or logging purposes.

Here is an example that shows how to trap any problems with opening a file:

```
On Error Resume Next
Const ForReading = 1
Set objFS = CreateObject("Scripting.FileSystemObject")
Set ts = objFS.OpenTextFile("c:\testfile.txt", ForReading)
If Err.Number <> 0 Then
    Wscript.Echo "Error: " & Err.Number & "-" & Err.Description
Else
    ' Main code here
End If
```

If c:\testfile.txt does not exist, you get the following message:

```
Error: 53-File Not Found
```

If you want to trap an error for logging but also want to continue with the rest of the script, you can reset the error object with the following command:

```
Err.Clear
```

 Note   See Chapter 8, "Testing and Debugging WSH Scripts," for more information on debugging scripts.

Script Design

Now you are ready to start writing your own scripts, but try to remember a few good coding habits:

- Use plenty of comments in your code.
- Indent logical sections of code.
- Place repeated code into a function or subroutine.
- Use naming conventions.

You can consider a task to be sequential, starting at the top and ending at the bottom, or you can think of it as modular. For simple scripts, the sequential method is okay, but for more complicated scripts, you will want to design reusable pieces of code that you can call when required.

Consider this skeleton script design:

```
' My Script Template
'
' Global Variables
'
```

```
Option Explicit
Dim x, y, z
'
' Create Global Objects
'
Set WshShell = Wscript.CreateObject("Wscript.Shell")
'
Call Main()
'
Wscript.Quit
'
' ------------------------------------------------
' Subroutine: Main
'
Sub Main()
    'Perform main program loop
    Mode = CheckParams(option)
    Select Case Mode
        Case 1
            Call library1()
        Case 2
            Call library2()
    End Select
End Sub
'
Sub library1()
End Sub
'
Sub library2
End Sub
'
Function CheckParams(TestOption)
    Dim CheckParams
    CheckParams = 1
End Function
' End of File
```

I will now describe the two main elements of this skeleton script: Sub procedures and
functions.

Sub Procedures

A Sub procedure performs some actions but does not return any results. You can pass
arguments to the Sub procedure by placing the constants, variables, and expressions in
the parentheses on the call.

```
Call LogError("Failed to open file")
Sub LogError(description)
    objLogFile.WriteLine "Error: " & description
    If DebugInteractive = True Then
```

```
        Wscript.Echo "Error: " & description
    End If
End Sub
```

You can also call a function without the `Call` statement:

```
LogError "Failed to open file"
```

You can pass a value, variable, or reference to an object to the subroutine or function. When passing a global variable to a function, you might want to ensure that the value cannot be changed by the code in the function. You can do this with the `ByValue` argument:

```
Sub GetGroup(ByVal strUser)
```

The default is `ByRef`, which means that a pointer to the storage location of the variable is passed to the subroutine or function.

You can also pass multiple values by separating them with a comma. You must place them in the order that the subroutine expects to use them:

```
Call LogError("Failed to open file", Wscript.ScriptName)
    .
    .
Sub LogError(description, file)
    objLogFile.WriteLine "Error in " &_
            file & ": " & description
    If DebugInteractive = True Then
        Wscript.Echo "Error: " & description
    End If
End Sub
```

Functions

A function is similar to a `Sub` procedure except that it can return a result:

```
Wscript.Echo "I am " & GetYears("20/09/62") & " years old"
    .
    .
Function GetYears(birthDate)
    GetYears = Cint((Date - BirthDate) / 365)
End Function
```

The value returned is passed in the variable, which must be named the same as the function name.

Variables used in a `Sub` or function that have not been dimensioned at the top level of the script are local to that section of code.

Error trapping must also be defined for each subroutine or function if required because the On Error statement is local to the script level in which it is invoked.

Naming Conventions

Everyone likes standards, and they will help the maintainability of your code. Remember that someone else might have to figure out how your code works in the future. I have taken some of the relevant conventions for constants and variables from the Microsoft guidelines and presented them in Table 5.1.

TABLE 5.1 CONVENTIONS FOR CONSTANTS AND VARIABLES

Subtype	Prefix	Example
Byte	byt	bytDTR
Date (time)	dtm	dtmStartFinYear
Error	err	errStdMsg
Integer	int	intQuantity
Object	obj	objExcel
String	str	strUserName

Common VBScript Usage Scenarios

In this section you will look at some sample scripts that assist with tasks that can be quickly performed and save you time.

Reading an IIS Log File and Counting a Type of Request

Your boss has asked you to report on how many times the company profile has been downloaded from your Web site. You start looking inside the IIS log file with notepad using the find function. You say to yourself, "This is hopeless, there must be a better way," and you are right.

You decide to use WSH with the file system object and some VBScript string functions. This is what you come up with:

```
' FILE: VBSlogrpt.vbs
' AUTH: Ian Morrish
' DESC: search all log files for a string and output to a report file the
➥number of
'      matches per day
'
```

5

```
On Error Resume Next
'
' Define Constants
'
Const Log_File_Path = "c:\winnt\system32\logs\"
Const Log_File_Extension = ".LOG"
Const Report_File = "C:\temp\report.csv"
Const Search_String = "Component.asp"
Const ForWriting = 2
'
Dim strFileName, strLine, strLogDate
Dim iCount
'
' Get directory object
'
set objFS1 = Wscript.CreateObject ("Scripting.FileSystemObject")
Set objLogFolder = objFS1.GetFolder(Log_File_Path)
If Err.Number <> 0 Then
    Wscript.Echo "Logfile path not found"
    Wscript.Quit
End If
'
' Open report file
'
set objFS2 = Wscript.CreateObject ("Scripting.FileSystemObject")
Set objReport = objFS2.OpenTextFile(Report_File, ForWriting, True)
If Err.Number <> 0 Then
    Wscript.Echo "Error creating report file"
    Wscript.Quit
End If
objReport.WriteLine "Date,Downloads"
'
' Check logfiles for valid name
'
Set objFiles = objLogFolder.Files
For each file in objFiles
    '
    ' Get the file name and see if the extension is correct
    ' there may be other file types in this directory
    strFileName = Ucase(file.Name)
    ' Next line is for debugging & shows when we forget the
    ' trailing \ on the logfile extension constant
    ' Wscript.Echo Log_File_Path & strFileName
    If Instr(strFileName, Log_File_Extension) <> 0 Then
        'We have a log file, open it.
        set objFileContents = objFS1.OpenTextFile
➥(Log_File_Path & strFileName)
        If Err.Number <> 0 Then
            'File might be in use by IIS so skip it
            Wscript.Echo "Can't open file" & strFileName
            Exit For
```

```
        End If
        '
        ' Reset counter for each day
        '
        iCount = 0
        '
        '3rd line contains date eg #Date: 1999-01-29 00:31:21
        ' Use the Instr and Mid functions to get the year-month-date
        '
        objFileContents.ReadLine
        objFileContents.ReadLine
        strLogDate = objFileContents.ReadLine
        strLogDate = Mid(strLogDate, Instr(strLogDate, " ") + 1, 10)
        '
        ' Now read in each line looging for the file name
        '
        do while objFileContents.AtEndOfStream <> True
            strLine = objFileContents.ReadLine
            If Instr(strLine, Search_String) <> 0 Then
                iCount = iCount + 1
            End If
        Loop
        '
        ' Write daily download count to report file
        '
        objReport.WriteLine strLogDate & "," & iCount
    End If
Next 'file
```

Now you can use Excel to quickly produce a trend graph, and your boss is happy.

Using Command-Line Arguments

WSH provides the capability to access the command-line arguments that might be present when the script is run. The following script is a skeleton that you can use in your own application:

```
' FILE: VBSparams.vbs
' AUTH: Ian Morrish
' DESC: Extract command line parameters
'       matches per day
'
On Error Resume Next

if WScript.Arguments.Count = 0 then
    Call About()
    Wscript.Quit()
End If
'
' Not every Wscript argument is an argument for our application,
```

5

```vbscript
' some may be parameters for an application argument.
'
Do While i < wscript.arguments.count
    '
    ' See if we must recurse sub folders
    '
    If Ucase(WScript.Arguments(i)) = "/S" or Ucase(WScript.Arguments(i))
 = "-S" Then
        search = vbTrue


    '
    ' Get folder name
    '
    ElseIf Ucase(WScript.Arguments(i)) = "/F" or
 Ucase(WScript.Arguments(i)) = "-F" then
        '
        ' The next Wscript argument is the path so increment i
        '
        i = i+1
        strFolder = WScript.Arguments(i)
    '
    ' Is user asking for help
    '
    ElseIf WScript.Arguments(i) = "/?" or WScript.Arguments(i) = "-?"
 Then
        Call About()
        Wscript.Quit()
    '
    ' Unrecognized parameter
    '
    Else
        Call About()
        Wscript.Quit()
    End If
    '
    ' Increment the argument pointer
    '
    i = i+1
Loop
'
' Check that we got a folder name
'
If strFolder = "" Then
    Call About()
    Wscript.Quit()
End If
'
' Main code here
'
strMsg = "Path = " & strFolder
If search = vbtrue Then
```

```
        strMsg = strMsg & vbLF & "Search sub folders also."
End If
Wscript.Echo strMsg
'
' End of script
'
Sub About
    WScript.Echo "My application" & vbLF & _
        "It does something, trust me." & vbLF & vbLF & _
        "Usage:    params.vbs /f folderName /r [/?]" & vbLF & vbLF & _
        "    /f   -    The folder in which to search" & vbLF & _
        "    /s   -    search all subfolders" & vbLF & _
        "    /?   -    This message"
End Sub
```

You can test this script by placing the following commands in the Start menu's Run box:

```
Script_path\VBSparams.vbs /f c:\temp /r
Script_path\VBSparams.vbs -f c:\temp /x
```

Summary

In this chapter, you've learned the basics of the VBScript language and have seen how to use some of the built-in functions. If you do choose VBScript as your primary scripting language, there are many resources for sample scripts on the Web. You can learn a lot from looking at existing script files.

Two specific WSH sites are the following:

WSH FAQ   `http://wsh.glazier.co.nz`

Win32 Scripting   `http://cwashington.netreach.net`

Don't forget about the WSH samples installed in the `\windows\samples\wsh` directory. There are also very active newsgroups where you can get peer support.

The relevant Microsoft newsgroups are on the `msnews.Microsoft.com` server and include the following:

```
Microsoft.public.scripting.vbscript
Microsoft.public.scripting.wsh
```

5

Q&A

Q Why do I get an error "Subscript out of range"?

A This usually means you are trying to reference an item in an array that does not exist. An example of this is when you have a collection of Outlook Items and try to refer to item(0), as Outlook collections start from 1.

Q Why do I sometimes get the error "Cannot use parentheses when calling a Sub"?

A If you omit the Call command and just use the sub procedure name, you must drop the parentheses. For example:

```
Call LogEvent("Could not open file " & strFileName)
LogEvent "Could not open file " & strFileName
```

Q How can I detect which version of VBScript is installed?

A The following sample code can be used to determine the version:

```
Wscript.Echo GetVersion
Function GetVersion
  s = ScriptEngine & " Version "
  s = s & ScriptEngineMajorVersion & "."
  s = s & ScriptEngineMinorVersion & "."
  s = s & ScriptEngineBuildVersion
  GetVersion = s
End Function
```

WEEK 1

DAY 6

Using Microsoft JScript with WSH

By Michael Morrison

Yesterday you learned about the VBScript scripting language and how it is used to create scripts that run under the Windows Scripting Host. Today you'll learn about JScript, the other scripting language supported by WSH. The JScript scripting language is based on the popular Java programming language. JScript is functionally equivalent to VBScript, which means that you can write scripts in JScript that perform the same tasks as scripts written in VBScript. Using JScript or VBScript with WSH is primarily a personal preference that relates to your prior programming experience and whether you're more comfortable with a scripting language based on BASIC or one based on Java.

Today you'll learn the following:

- The basics of the JScript scripting language
- The ins and outs of the JScript language syntax
- How to create JScript scripts that run under WSH

Introduction to JScript

JScript is Microsoft's implementation of the JavaScript scripting language that was originally developed by Netscape Communications. Although JScript is similar in many ways to JavaScript, JScript includes Microsoft extensions, a broader object model, and integration with Microsoft technologies. Like VBScript, JScript is an interpreted, object-based language that is very useful for developing programs where a full-blown programming language such as Java or C++ is overkill.

JScript Background

Because the origin of JScript lies in JavaScript, let's first examine how JavaScript came to be. JavaScript began at Netscape Communications as a scripting language named LiveScript. When the Java programming language took off, Netscape and Sun Microsystems combined their efforts to revamp LiveScript. The end result was JavaScript, which used some elements of Java in the context of a scripting environment. The main purpose of JavaScript was to provide Web developers with a means of injecting interactivity into Web pages without having to build full-blown Java applets.

 Note

Although Java and JavaScript are similar in terms of their syntax, they were originally developed independently of each other. They also continue to evolve independently.

Microsoft entered the JavaScript picture with their Internet Explorer Web browser, which supported early versions of JavaScript in order to compete with Netscape Navigator. It didn't take long for Microsoft to extend their implementation of JavaScript in Internet Explorer. Thus, JScript was born. At its core, JScript is still the same scripting language as JavaScript. However, newer technologies, such as WSH, have widened the scope of JScript to encompass general scripting solutions, not just Web-based solutions.

You might see JScript sometimes referred to as an implementation of the ECMA-262 language specification. In order to help standardize both JavaScript and JScript, the European Computer Manufacturers Association (ECMA) created a scripting language specification based on joint submissions from Microsoft and Netscape. ECMA-262 is the name of the specification, which now forms the foundation for both JScript and JavaScript.

JScript Syntax Overview

With the origins of JScript now firmly entrenched in your mind, move on to the language itself. JScript scripts are created as text code including statements that follow a structure and syntax somewhat similar to Java. This means that if you have experience with C, C++, or Java, you will find JScript very easy to learn. You learn about the similarities and differences between JScript and Java in the next section. The JScript language syntax can be broken down into the following major elements:

- Statements
- Variables
- Expressions
- Comments
- Functions
- Objects

Statements

JScript statements are interpreted on a line by line basis. A statement typically consists of a combination of JScript language keywords, immediate data, variables, and operators. Although a new line indicates a new statement, it's generally considered a good JScript programming style to explicitly terminate statements with a semicolon (;). Following is an example:

```
var myName = "Michael";
```

Variables

Variables are used in JScript to store data. In the previous line of code, the var keyword is used to declare a variable named myName that contains my first name. JScript supports a variety of data types such as text strings, numbers, and Boolean true/false values. JScript is a loosely typed language, which means that you don't have to explicitly declare the data type of a variable before using the variable. JScript enables you to use different data types with variables and takes on the task of automatically converting between different types when necessary.

6

Expressions

Expressions are sort of like programming equations in that they enable you to perform mathematical operations. Expressions aren't limited to mathematical operations, however; you can also add strings together, for example. Following is an example of a JScript expression:

```
var area = length * width;
```

This expression calculates an area by multiplying the contents of the variable `length` by the contents of the variable `width`. The result is stored in the variable `area`. The multiplication operator (`*`) is used to multiply the numbers, whereas the assignment operator (`=`) indicates that the result is to be stored in the `area` variable. Following is an example of an expression that adds strings together to form a message:

```
var msg = "Hello, " + myName + "!";
```

Using the `myName` variable from earlier, the resulting value of the `msg` variable in this example is `"Hello, Michael!"`. Notice that the addition operator (`+`) is used to add the strings together.

Comments

You can include notes and descriptions in JScript code by using comments, which help to explain how a section of code works. There are two types of comments supported by JScript: single-line and multiline. A single-line comment begins with a pair of forward slashes (`//`) and indicates that the remainder of the line is a comment. Following is an example of a single-line comment:

```
var area = length * width;   // calculate the area
```

You can also place a single-line comment on a line by itself, like this:

```
// Calculate the area
var area = length * width;
```

Unlike a single-line comment, a multiline comment can continue over multiple lines. A multiline comment begins with a forward slash and an asterisk (`/*`) and ends with an asterisk and a forward slash (`*/`). Everything appearing between the `/*` and the `*/` in a multiline comment is considered part of the comment. All comments are ignored when a JScript program is run. Following is an example of a multiline comment:

```
/* Calculate the area using
   the length and the width
   variables, and store the
   result in the area variable. */
var area = length * width;
```

Functions

A function is a group of JScript statements organized together separately from the rest of a JScript program. A function performs a certain action and often returns a result. JScript programs call functions to delegate work, which has the beneficial side effect of better program organization. JScript provides a few standard functions that you can call. You can also create functions of your own to perform common tasks. An example of a standard JScript function is `eval()`, which evaluates a string expression. You pass the `eval()` function a string expression by placing the expression between opening and closing parantheses (`()`). Following is an example of how to use the `eval()` function:

```
var expression = "length * width";
var area = eval(expression);
```

In this example, the string expression stored in the `expression` variable is evaluated by passing it to the `eval()` function. The result of the expression is stored in the `area` variable.

Objects

JScript fully supports objects, which are special data structures consisting of properties and methods. Properties make up the data portion of an object, whereas methods are very much like functions. A good example of a JScript object is the `Date` object, which represents a date and time. You can get specific information about a `Date` object by calling methods on the object. The following example gets the year associated with a `Date` object that holds the current date and time:

```
var date = new Date();
var year = date.getFullYear();
```

Notice that a `Date` object must first be created before you can call the `getFullYear()` method on it. This is accomplished with the `new` operator, which is used to create objects. In this case, the new `Date` object represents the current date and time. The `getFullYear()` method then obtains the full year, which is a four- digit number, such as 1999.

JScript's Relationship to Java

Before digging any further into JScript, it's worth addressing its relationship to Java. There has been a lot of confusion among those new to both Java and JScript regarding the proper role of each language. The primary difference between the two languages is that Java is a full-blown object-oriented programming language that is designed to create standalone programs. Although some JScript programs could be considered standalone, they aren't really comparable to Java applets and applications.

JScript is significantly simpler than Java and therefore much easier to use. On the other hand, Java is much more powerful than JScript. JScript is more suitable to performing support tasks, whereas Java is geared toward building complete solutions. As an example, you might use JScript to reorganize the data in a Microsoft Excel spreadsheet or create a shortcut on the Windows desktop. You could use Java to create a spreadsheet application of your own or to create an object that graphs spreadsheet information.

6

JScript programs are entered as text files with a .js filename extension and then interpreted directly using the WSH. Java programs are entered as text files with a .java
filename extension and must be compiled using a Java compiler before they can be
executed. Compiled Java programs are stored in a special format called bytecode that
must be executed within a Java interpreter such as the one provided with the Java
Development Kit (JDK). In the case of Java applets, an interpreter is integrated with
Java-enabled Web browsers. WSH serves as the interpreter for JScript programs.

Standard JScript Syntax

You now understand the very basics of the JScript scripting language, but to be able to
use JScript effectively you need to have a more solid grasp on the JScript language syntax. The next few sections highlight the main areas of JScript language syntax with practical examples.

Declaring and Using Variables

You use variables in JScript programs to store information. A variable acts as a named
storage container for data; you access variables using their name. Generally speaking,
you aren't required to declare a variable before using it in a script, but it is a good idea to
do so. You learned how to declare variables using the var keyword a little earlier in the
lesson. Variable declaration is only required for variables that are local to a function.
Following are some examples of variable declarations:

```
var msg = "Barney Rubble, what an actor!";
var countDown = 10;
var PI = 3.14;
var hungry = true;
```

Note   Although I've defined a variable representing the value of PI, 3.14, JScript
includes this value as a property of the Math object. To use the value in an
expression, you refer to it as Math.PI.

This code demonstrates some of the different data types you can use in JScript.
Following is a breakdown of the data types of the variables:

- msg   String
- countDown, PI   numeric
- hungry   Boolean (true or false)

You might be wondering if you can name a JScript variable anything you want. JScript doesn't give you quite that much freedom, but you do have plenty of room to give variables meaningful names. JScript is a case-sensitive language, which means that the variable names pi and PI are different. JScript variables can be of any length, but they must conform to the following rules:

- The first character must be a letter, an underscore (_), or a dollar sign ($).
- Characters beyond the first character must be letters, numbers, underscores (_), or dollar signs ($).
- The variable name can't be a reserved word.

Note The JScript language uses certain reserved words that you aren't enabled to use as variable names. These reserved words are used as names for standard parts of the JScript language, such as object and function names. Reserved words also include JScript language keywords, such as true, false, and var.

Following are some potential variable names:

- interestRate
- %InterestRate
- principal&interest
- _total
- TOTAL
- 12Monkeys
- continue
- number9
- $MyMoney

Can you guess which names are valid and which are invalid? Focus on the invalid names. Following are the invalid variable names from this list:

- %InterestRate   Variable names cannot start with anything other than a letter, an underscore, or a dollar sign.
- principal&interest   Variable names cannot include anything other than letters, numbers, underscores, or dollar signs.

6

- `continue` Variable names cannot be the same name as a JScript reserved word; `continue` is a keyword, which therefore makes it reserved (refer to the JScript documentation for a complete list of JScript keywords).
- `12Monkeys` Variable names cannot start with anything other than a letter, an underscore, or a dollar sign.

Although you often initialize a variable with a value when you declare it, initialization isn't required. Uninitialized variables are considered undefined and shouldn't be used on the right side of expressions. You can also assign a value of `null` to a variable in situations where you don't know what its initial value should be. For numeric data types, a value of `null` is equivalent to `0`.

Speaking of data types, it is sometimes necessary to convert data from one type to another. Fortunately, JScript handles most data type conversion automatically. Check out the following example:

```
var PI = 3.14;
var radius = 10;
var circumference = 2 * PI * radius;
var results = "The circumference is " + circumference + ".";
```

This example shows how the numeric data type stored in the `circumference` variable is automatically converted to a string when concatenated into the `results` string data type. Although this conversion is automatic when going from numbers to strings, the opposite isn't true. Converting strings to numbers requires you to manually make the conversion. To accomplish this conversion, you use the standard `parseInt()` and `parseFloat()` functions. Following is an example:

```
var PI = "3.14";
var radius = "10";
var circumference = 2 * parseFloat(PI) * parseInt(radius);
var results = "The circumference is " + circumference + ".";
```

In this example, the `PI` and `radius` variables are initialized with strings. Even though the strings contain numbers, they are still strings. So, to use the variables in a numeric calculation, it is necessary to convert them using the `parseFloat()` and `parseInt()` functions.

Developing Program Logic

As exciting as variables might be, they aren't incredibly useful in and of themselves. JScript programming gets much more interesting when you inject logic into your scripts. Program logic is what enables a script to take different actions based on the value of a variable or expression. For example, you might input the name of a user and display different information based on the user's identification.

JScript program logic is based on Boolean tests, which always evaluate to either `true` or `false`. Not surprisingly, this type of program logic is known as Boolean logic. Although the result of a Boolean test is a Boolean value, you can use any data type as a part of the test. The main Boolean test used in JScript is the `if-else` statement. The `if-else` statement is used to conditionally execute one section of code or another. Following is the syntax for the `if-else` statement, which helps you understand how it works:

```
if (Condition)
  Statement1
else
  Statement2
```

If the Boolean `Condition` is true, `Statement1` is executed; otherwise `Statement2` is executed. Following is a simple example:

```
if (hungry)
  timeToEat = true;
else
  timeToEat = false;
```

If the Boolean variable `hungry` is `true`, the first statement is executed, and `timeToEat` is set to `true`. Otherwise, the second statement is executed, and `timeToEat` is set to `false`.

If you have only a single statement that you want to execute conditionally, you can leave off the `else` part of the `if-else` statement, like this:

```
if (isThirsty)
  pourADrink = true;
```

On the other hand, what happens if you have more than two branches you want to conditionally choose between? In situations like this, you can string together a series of `if-else` statements to get the net effect of multiple conditions. Check out the following code:

```
if (age < 13)
  person = "child";
else if (age < 18)
  person = "teenager";
else if (age < 65)
  person = "adult";
else
  person = "retiree";
```

6

This code can take one of a number of different conditions based on the value of the age variable. Keep in mind that the conditional evaluations are performed in order, so if you arrive at the test age < 65, you already know that age is at least 18 or greater. Otherwise, the previous `if` conditional would have evaluated to `true`. Also, remember that only one of the conditional statements is executed.

There is one other aspect of the `if-else` statement worth mentioning, and that is the issue of compound statements. A compound statement is a block of code surrounded by curly braces (`{}`). The significance of compound statements is that they appear to an `if-else` statement as a single statement. The following sample code demonstrates:

```
if (needSysInfo) {
  processor = "Pentium II";
  speed = 450;   // Megahertz
  memory = 128;  // Megabytes
}
```

This example shows how multiple statements can be executed within a single `if` statement by enclosing them in curly braces. Placing the opening curly brace (`{`) at the end of the line with the `if` conditional is a pretty standard JScript convention, along with placing the closing curly (`}`) brace on a new line following the compound statements.

Note

In addition to demonstrating the usefulness of conditional and compound statements, the previous example also shows how comments can be used to clarify the meaning of numbers. This is a good habit to develop when using numbers in situations where something about their meaning might not be totally apparent. It is beneficial if someone else ever needs to modify or reference your code or if you ever come back to the code and can't immediately remember all the details.

For simple Boolean tests that don't require quite the flexibility of the `if-else` statement, you have another option. JScript supports a conditional operator that works very much like a shorthand `if-else` statement. The conditional operator (`?:`) evaluates a test expression and conditionally evaluates another expression based on the test. Look at an example to help clarify:

```
var maybe = true;
var x = maybe ? 4 : 11;
```

When using the conditional operator, if the Boolean test is `true`, the expression to the left of the colon (`:`) is evaluated; otherwise the expression to the right of the colon is evaluated. In this example, the test (`maybe`) is `true`, so the line of code effectively becomes the following:

```
var x = 4;
```

Although it illustrates how the conditional operator works, this example really doesn't demonstrate the power of the conditional operator. Look at an example that's a little more interesting:

```
var age = 17;
var nickname = (x < 30) ? "young fella" : "oldtimer";
```

In this example, a less-than operator (<) is used to see if the age variable is less than 30. If so, the nickname variable is set to "young fella"; otherwise nickname is set to "oldtimer". In this case the age variable is set to 17, so the conditional operator results in the nickname variable being set to "young fella".

As you can probably tell, the conditional operator is somewhat of a shorthand version of the if-else branch. Consider the following if-else sample code you looked at a little earlier:

```
if (hungry)
  timeToEat = true;
else
  timeToEat = false;
```

The previous example can be shortened using the conditional operator like this:

```
timeToEat = hungry ? true : false;
```

Actually, if you want to get down and dirty, you can shorten the code to this:

```
timeToEat = hungry;
```

Think about it. The original example is perhaps a poor usage of the if-else statement because it could be simplified so easily, but its simplicity hopefully helps you to more easily understand how the branch works.

Note

I mentioned that the conditional operator is somewhat of a shorthand version of the if-else statement. I used the word "somewhat" because the two things aren't always equivalent. The conditional operator can only be used to conditionally execute one expression or another. The if-else statement, on the other hand, is capable of executing entire sections of code that can include multiple expressions. So the conditional operator is only a shorthand version of the if-else statement in the most simple of examples.

6

I used the less-than operator (<) in an earlier example to demonstrate the conditional operator. The less-than operator is a Boolean operator, which means that it is used to form an expression with a Boolean result (true or false). Following is a list of the Boolean operators available for use in JScript:

- AND (&&)
- OR (¦¦)
- Negation (!)
- Equal-to (==)
- Not-equal-to (!=)

The AND operator (&&) compares two values and only returns true if they are both true. The OR (¦¦) operator compares two values and returns true if either of the values is true. The negation operator (!) flips the state of a value; if a value is true, it becomes false, and if it is false, it becomes true. The equal-to (==) and not-equal-to (!=) operators check to see if two values are equal or not equal, respectively.

Looping Constructs

A loop is a programming construct that enables you to repeat a section of code over and over. Loops are very valuable in JScript because they enable you to control repetitive sections of code. The most commonly used JScript loop is the for loop, which repeats a section of code a fixed number of times. Following is the syntax for the for loop:

```
for (InitializationExpression; LoopCondition; StepExpression)
  Statement
```

The for loop repeats the Statement a number of times as determined by the InitializationExpression, LoopCondition, and StepExpression:

- The InitializationExpression is used to initialize a loop control variable.
- The LoopCondition compares the loop control variable to some limit value.
- The StepExpression specifies how the loop control variable should be modified before the next iteration of the loop.

The following example uses a for loop to count down from 10 to 1:

```
for (var i = 10; i > 0; i--)
  countMsg = "Countdown = " + i;
```

In this code the InitializationExpression is var i = 10, which is evaluated initially before the loop begins. This is the code you use to prime the loop and get it ready. The LoopCondition is i > 0, which is a Boolean test that is performed before each iteration of the loop. If the Boolean test result is `true`, the `Statement` is executed, which in this case prints the current value of `i`. After each iteration, the `StepExpression` is evaluated, which is `i--`. This serves to decrement `i` after each iteration and ultimately provides the countdown.

The loop continues to iterate and print numbers as `i` counts down to `0`. When `i` reaches `0`, the `LoopCondition` test fails (`i > 0`), so the loop bails out. To help you visualize the looping process, take a look at Figure 6.1.

FIGURE 6.1

A JScript program executing with a loop.

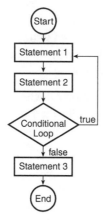

Notice in the figure that `Statement1` and `Statement2` are repeatedly executed as long as the loop condition is `true`. When the loop condition is `false`, the program falls out of the loop and executes `Statement3`.

The previous figure alludes to the fact that a loop can execute multiple statements. Loops can execute as many statements as they want, provided that curly braces (`{}`) enclose the statements. If you recall, this grouping of statements is known as a compound statement and was used earlier in the day with the `if-else` statement. Following is an example of a `for` loop with a compound statement:

```
var nums = new Array[10];
for (var i = 0; i < 10; i++) {
  nums[i] = i * i;
  nums[i] /= 2;
}
```

This code calculates the squares of the numbers `0` through `9`, stores them in an array named `nums` and then divides each number by 2. The loop counter (`i`) is used as the index to the `nums` array. This is a very common way of handling arrays. Notice that the array is created using the standard `Array` object and specifying how many elements the array contains.

6

JScript also supports a variation of the `for` loop called the `for-in` loop. This loop is specifically designed for iterating through the properties of an object. This illuminates an interesting fact about JScript arrays: Elements of a JScript array are really just properties of an `Array` object. Following is a different version of the previous example implemented with a `for-in` loop:

```
var nums = new Array[10];
for (i in nums) {
  nums[i] = i * i;
  nums[i] /= 2;
}
```

In this example, the index variable `i` is automatically set to the next property, which is the next element in the `nums` array. Although this example illustrates using the `for-in` loop with an array, you can use it with any JScript object.

The last type of loop used in JScript is the `while` loop, which has a loop condition that controls the number of times a loop is repeated. Unlike the `for` loop, the `while` loop has no initialization or step expression. Following is the syntax for the `while` loop, which should make its usage a little more clear:

```
while (LoopCondition)
    Statement
```

If the Boolean `LoopCondition` evaluates to `true`, the `Statement` is executed. When the `Statement` finishes executing, the `LoopCondition` is tested again, and the process repeats itself. This continues until the `LoopCondition` evaluates to `false`, in which case the loop immediately exits. Because the `while` loop has no step expression, it is important to make sure that the `Statement` somehow impacts the `LoopCondition`. Otherwise, it is possible for the loop to infinitely repeat, which is usually a bad thing. Following is a simple example of an infinite `while` loop:

```
while (true)
    num++;  // num is incremented forever
```

Because the loop condition in this example is permanently set to `true`, the loop repeats infinitely or at least until you manually terminate the program. Incidentally, you can think of the `while` loop as a more general `for` loop. To understand what I mean by this, check out the following example:

```
var i = 10;
while (i > 0) {
  countMsg = "Countdown = " + i;
  i--;
}
```

This is the same countdown from earlier implemented using a while loop instead of a for loop. Because while loops don't have initialization expressions, the initialization of the counter variable i has to be performed before the loop. Likewise, the step expression i-- has to be performed within the Statement part of the loop. Regardless of the structural differences, this while loop is functionally equivalent to the for loop you saw earlier in the day.

There is one last topic to cover before you're finished with looping constructs. I'm referring to the break and continue statements, which are used to exit and short circuit loops. The break statement immediately quits a loop regardless of the loop condition. The continue statement, on the other hand, immediately goes to the next iteration of a loop. Following is an example of circumventing an infinite loop with a break statement:

```
var i = 0;
while (true) {
  if (++i > 99)
    break;
}
```

Without the assistance of the break statement, this while loop would continue on forever thanks to the permanent true loop condition. The break statement sidesteps this problem by breaking out of the loop after one hundred iterations (0-99). Of course, it is rare that you purposely create an infinite loop and then use a break statement to bail out of it. However, the break statement can be very useful in some tricky loops when you need to exit at an otherwise inconvenient time.

The continue statement is a close relative of the break statement. The following example shows how a continue statement can be used to determine only the even numbers between 1 and 100:

```
var evenNums = "";
for (var i = 1; i <= 100; i++) {
  if ((i % 2) != 0)
    continue;
  evenNums += i + "...";
}
```

This example uses the modulus operator (%), which returns the remainder of a division. Because a division by 2 always yields a remainder of 0, you can determine even numbers using the modulus operator. The sample code exploits this characteristic of even and odd numbers to skip to the next iteration of the loop when it encounters an odd number. The resulting value of evenNums is of the form "2...4...6...8...".

6

Creating and Using Functions

You learned earlier in the day that a function is a section of code organized to perform a particular action. In addition to carrying out important tasks, functions can also perform calculations and return results. To create your own functions, you use the function keyword. Following is an example of a function that calculates the square of a number and returns the result:

```
function square(num) {
  return (num * num);
}
```

The name of this function is square, and it accepts one parameter named num. The return keyword is used to return a value from a function. In this example, the num parameter is multiplied by itself to calculate the square, which is returned from the function. Following is another function that uses the square() function to calculate the area of a circle:

```
function circleArea(radius) {
  result = square(radius) * Math.PI;
  return result;
}
```

The circleArea() function calls the square() function to calculate the square of a circle's radius. This number is then multiplied by the constant Math.PI to finish the area calculation. Finally, the result is returned from the function using the return keyword.

Working with Objects

You've already learned a decent amount about JScript objects, but I want to clarify exactly how they work. To recap, objects are collections of properties (data) and methods that perform actions, usually based upon the properties. A method is no more than a function that is associated with an object. JScript supports a variety of standard objects that you can use to do lots of interesting things such as access system resources.

An object's properties and methods are referred to as members of the object. You can reference object members either by name or by index. To reference an object member by name, you use the object name followed by a period followed by the member name. For example, the PI property in the Math object is referenced as Math.PI. To reference an object member by index, you use the index of the property in square brackets ([ ]) following the object name. This approach is more commonly used when accessing array elements. A twist on the indexed approach to accessing object members is using the string name of a property in square brackets. Following is an example of equivalent object member access:

```
var msg = "Welcome home!";
var len1 = msg.length;
var len2 = msg["length"];
```

In this example, `length` is a property of the `String` object. The `length` property is accessed first by name and then by using a string index of the property name.

Note

> If you recall from earlier in the lesson, arrays are actually objects. Therefore, you access the elements of an array the same way that you access properties of an object.

Common JScript Usage Scenarios

Now that you have a basic understanding of how the JScript language works, it's time to examine a few practical applications of it. The next few sections lead you through the development of some scripts that I think you'll find interesting. You start off with something very simple to get you comfortable with creating scripts in JScript.

Displaying Information

Displaying information to the user is a very common task in any scripting language, and JScript is no exception. It's easy to display information using the `Echo()` method defined in the `WScript` object. Following is an example of how this method is used:

```
WScript.Echo("Howdy!");
```

You simply pass a string to the `Echo()` method, which in turn displays the string in a message box. Figure 6.2 shows what this message box looks like.

FIGURE 6.2

The Howdy script demonstrating how to use a message box to display information to the user.

6

Obtaining System Information

Another common task performed with scripting languages is querying the system for its properties. One such property of interest is the space available on a hard disk drive. You can use a series of standard JScript objects to calculate the free space available on a hard drive. Listing 6.1 contains the JScript code for a script named `FreeSpace` that calculates the free space on the local C drive.

LISTING 6.1   FreeSpace Script JScript Code

```
WScript.Echo(GetFreeSpace("c:\\"));

function GetFreeSpace(drivePath) {
  var fso, drive, freeSpace;

  fso = new ActiveXObject("Scripting.FileSystemObject");
  drive = fso.GetDrive(fso.GetDriveName(drivePath));
  freeSpace = "Free Space on drive " + drivePath + " : " +
    Math.round(drive.FreeSpace / 1048576) + " MB";
  return freeSpace;
}
```

This code defines a function named GetFreeSpace() that accepts a drive path as its only parameter and returns a string containing the free space on the drive formatted for display purposes. A FileSystemObject is used to locate the drive, which is then used to determine the free space by calling the FreeSpace() method. Notice that the free space is converted to megabytes (MB) by dividing by the number 1048576, and the result is then rounded to an integer. The free space is then displayed to the user using the Echo() method and the WScript object.

Figure 6.3 shows the FreeSpace script in action.

FIGURE 6.3

The FreeSpace script obtains the amount of free space on a hard disk drive.

Working with Files

One last area of interest in terms of applying JScript has to do with files. JScript happens to be well suited for reading and writing files, as you'll soon see. I've always had fun tinkering with programs that display a random quote or fortune read from a text file. In fact, I typically implement such a program when learning a new language. Listing 6.2 contains a JScript program named Fortune that reads a series of fortunes from a text file named Fortunes.txt and then displays a randomly selected one.

LISTING 6.2   Fortune Script JScript Code

```javascript
// Global variables
var fortunes = new String();
var numFortunes = 0;

LoadFortunes();
ShowFortune();

function LoadFortunes() {
  var ForReading = 1, ForWriting = 2, ForAppending = 3;
  var TristateUseDefault = -2, TristateTrue = -1, TristateFalse = 0;
  var fso, file, fileStream;

  // Open the file
  fso = new ActiveXObject("Scripting.FileSystemObject");
  file = fso.GetFile("Fortunes.txt");
  fileStream = file.OpenAsTextStream(ForReading, TristateUseDefault);

  // Read the fortunes from the file into the fortunes array
  while (!fileStream.atEndOfStream) {
    fortunes[numFortunes] = fileStream.ReadLine();
    numFortunes++;
  }
  fileStream.Close();
}

function ShowFortune() {
  randFortune = Math.round(Math.random() * (numFortunes - 1));
  WScript.Echo(fortunes[randFortune]);
}
```

That might be a little more code than you're accustomed to seeing, but don't get discouraged. This is really a very straightforward script. First off, a couple of global variables are defined to hold the array of fortune strings and the total number of fortunes. Two functions are then created to handle the loading of fortunes from a text file and the displaying of a random fortune. The LoadFortunes() function obtains a TextStream object for the open file and uses it to read the fortunes one line at a time. Each fortune is added to the fortunes array, after which the numFortunes variable is incremented. Finally, a fortune is selected at random in the ShowFortune() function and displayed using the Echo() method and the WScript object.

Figure 6.4 shows the Fortune script displaying a random fortune.

6

FIGURE 6.4

The Fortune script displays a random fortune that was read from a text file.

Summary

Today you learned about the JScript scripting language and what it has to offer you as a scripting alternative to VBScript. You learned that JScript evolved as a scripting counterpart to the Java programming language. You then dug into the nuts and bolts of the JScript language and studied its syntax. This included a close examination of how to declare and use variables, how to develop program logic, how to repeat code with loops, how to create and use functions, and how to work with objects. You then finished the lesson by working through some practical JScript applications.

Q&A

Q I'm a little confused about when to use the var keyword. What's the deal?

A The var keyword is only required when declaring variables within a function. However, it's a good habit to go ahead and declare all variables using the var keyword so that you don't forget when you declare variables in functions.

Q If a for loop can do everything a while loop can and in a more organized way, then why would I ever use a while loop?

A Because there is a time and a place for everything, and in many situations you have no need for initialization and step expressions. A for loop is overkill in situations such as this. Perhaps even more important is the fact that a while loop is much more readable than a for loop when you have no need for initialization and step expressions.

Q Will learning how to create scripts using JScript help if I ever decide to learn Java?

A Absolutely. Although there certainly are differences between JScript and Java, JScript code looks a lot like Java code because of similarities in language syntax. So a JScript background gives you a sense of familiarity if you ever decide to try your hand at Java programming.

Workshop

The following section will help you test your comprehension of the material presented in this lesson and put what you've learned into practice. You'll find the answers to the quiz and exercises in Appendix A.

Quiz

1. What is the relationship between JScript, Java, JavaScript, and the ECMA-262 language specification?
2. What three things are valid as the first character of a JScript variable name?
3. How does the conditional operator (?:) work?

Exercises

1. Add some fortunes of your own to the Fortunes.txt file and test the Fortunes script to see your new fortunes. Keep in mind that you might have to run the script a few times before you see one of your fortunes because the fortunes are selected at random.
2. Write a function named CalcLiquidVolume() that calculates and returns the volume of liquid in a container in gallons, given the length, width, and height of the container in feet. Hint: To convert cubic feet to gallons, multiply by 7.5.
3. Write a script named FileCopy that copies a file. Hint: The File object has a method named Copy() that uses the method parameter as the name of the new file; it makes a copy of the file represented by the File object.

6

DAY 7

Running and Scheduling Scripts

By Charles Williams

This lesson discusses how to utilize one of the three available environments that support the execution of the various scripting languages supported by the Windows operating system. You will learn how to execute scripts using the two available "non-Web" applications supplied by Microsoft: cscript.exe and wscript.exe. You will also examine how file associations can link your scripts to your favorite script engine and how script execution can be controlled using .WSH files. Finally, you will examine the integrated components that enable you to schedule the execution of your scripts.

Standard WSH Scripting Utilities

As you are probably painfully aware, Microsoft's client-side scripting services have a history of being extremely inadequate. Until recently, the only available tool to automate activities at the client level has been batch files. The Microsoft batch file implementation has been around for eons (well, okay, a few decades) and shows its age. Typically, batch files have been incapable of providing the power and flexibility necessary in today's operating environment.

This lack of capability has prompted the creation of various third-party utilities to fill the performance gap. Many enterprise administrators have found themselves relying on third-party utilities such as KiXtart to provide the necessary functionality for activities such as login scripting.

Often, one of the most troubling aspects of a Novell-to-Windows NT server migration involves the conversion, or "dumbing down," of a Novell login script so that it works in a Windows NT batch-file environment. Thankfully, Microsoft has now implemented technology to fill the gap, providing a significantly improved client-side scripting environment to address this need and the needs dictated by many other scenarios.

Microsoft has extended the scripting environment available in Microsoft Internet Explorer (IE) and Internet Information Server (IIS) so that it is now available on the client workstation. With the advent of ActiveX technologies such as VBScript and JScript, Microsoft can provide powerful scripting capability in both client-side and server-side Web environments. As a Web programmer, I can vouch for the value of Microsoft's Web implementation and am eager to explain to you how it has been extended to the desktop.

Microsoft has provided two applications that enable scripts to be run directly from the Windows operating environment—without the intervention of Microsoft Internet Explorer or Microsoft IIS. These two applications, `cscript.exe` and `wscript.exe`, provide exceptional flexibility and functionality when automating tasks in the Windows environment. With these applications, it is now possible to run scripts on the desktop and interact with components of the operating systems; previously, that was not possible.

Note

By default, Windows 95 and Windows NT 4.0 do not include support for WSH. To install WSH desktop support for these operating systems, you must ensure that two updates have been added. First, Internet Explorer 3.0 or higher must be installed to provide support for VBScript-based and JScript-based scripts. IE 3.0 installs the scripting engines that will enable the scripts to be interpreted by the operating system. Although IE 3.0 is the minimum requirement to enable VBScript and JScript support, I highly recommend that you install the latest version of Internet Explorer. This provides you with the patches and updates that have been implemented since IE 3.0's debut in 1996. You can download Internet Explorer from `http://www.microsoft.com/ie/`.

The second update that must be installed is the WSH update itself. It contains the `cscript.exe` and `wscript.exe` applications, supplemental dynamic link libraries (DLLs), and some sample scripts. This update is operating system specific and can be downloaded from `http://msdn.microsoft.com/scripting/default.htm?/scripting/windowshost/`. Windows 2000 will provide integrated support for WSH.

Running Scripts the Old Way

Unlike scripting implementations within Internet Explorer and IIS, WSH scripts do not have to be embedded between delimiters or "tags" in order for them to function. To better understand the differences, you will look at the same script embedded in the three environments.

A client-side script used in Microsoft Internet Explorer must be surrounded by the `<SCRIPT>...</SCRIPT>` tags in order to function. These tags serve to differentiate the script code from the other components located in the Web page (HTML, for example). Using a simple `"Hello World"` script, you can see in Listing 7.1 how the `<script>` tags are used to separate the script code from the Web page's other contents.

LISTING 7.1   USING <SCRIPT> TAGS TO IDENTIFY SCRIPT IN A WEB PAGE

```
<!DOCTYPE HTML PUBLIC "-//W3C//DTD HTML 3.2 Final//EN">

<HTML>
<HEAD>
    <TITLE>WSH Sample Web Page</TITLE>
</HEAD>

<BODY>
<H3>This page illustrates the use of the script tag in a Web page.</H3>
```

continues

7

LISTING 7.1   CONTINUED

```
<SCRIPT Language="VBSCRIPT">
'This script creates a simple dialog box
Msgbox("Hello World")
</SCRIPT>

</BODY>
</HTML>
```

Figure 7.1 shows the result of this page.

FIGURE 7.1

Internet Explorer's
Hello World *the right*
way.

Figure 7.2 shows what happens if the `<SCRIPT>...</SCRIPT>` tags are not included in this page.

Notice that the VBScript was not executed by the VBScript engine, but was interpreted by the browser as simple HTML.

Now take a moment to examine how IIS interprets VBScript. Through the use of Active Server Pages, IIS is able to execute VBScript at the server and provide "active" content to the client browser accordingly. As you saw in the preceding example using an HTML page, the VBScript in an Active Server Page must also be surrounded by special tags, for the same reason as in Internet Explorer. For IIS to understand where a script begins and ends, you must encapsulate the script, using the `<%...%>` tag.

FIGURE 7.2

Internet Explorer's Hello World *the wrong way.*

Take a look at Listing 7.2, which illustrates how these tags work. Unfortunately, I can't use the Hello World example to illustrate how Active Server Pages operate, so I use another simple example that involves gathering a remote user's IP address and displaying it back through the browser.

LISTING 7.2   USING THE <%...%> TAG TO IDENTIFY A SCRIPT IN AN ACTIVE SERVER PAGE

```
<!DOCTYPE HTML PUBLIC "-//W3C//DTD HTML 3.2 Final//EN">

<HTML>
<HEAD>
    <TITLE>WSH Sample Web Page</TITLE>
</HEAD>

<BODY>
<H3>This page illustrates the use of tags in an Active Server Page.</H3>

<P>Hello User! I see you are originating from:</P>

<%
Response.Write(Request.Servervariables("REMOTE_ADDR"))
%>

<P>Nice to see you!</P>

</BODY>
</HTML>
```

7

Figure 7.3 shows the output the user sees when this page is run.

FIGURE 7.3

An Active Server Page example the right way.

If the <%...%> tag is not present, the user will see a page that looks like Figure 7.4.

FIGURE 7.4

An Active Server Page example the wrong way.

The preceding examples show you how important it is to properly delimit scripts. A misplaced tag in a Web page can mean the difference between success and catastrophic failure.

> **Note** In the desktop environment, a script can exist without the surrounding tags described here. The script is contained in a file located on the client system or on the client's server, if they interact in a client/server environment (used in a login script, for example).

Running Scripts Using CSCRIPT

CSCRIPT is one controller of ActiveX scripting engines provided by Microsoft. It operates in a command prompt (or MS-DOS prompt) environment. This provides an excellent mechanism to perform lightweight, noninteractive scripting tasks such as login scripting, frequent administrative tasks, and so on.

The CSCRIPT application provides flexibility to control how scripts are run. This flexibility is implemented through the application's supporting syntax, which includes support for arguments and switches. Arguments are passed directly to the script and can be used to provide input data to the script in a noninteractive manner. Arguments are always preceded by a single slash (/). The available host options provide flexibility in enabling or disabling the various WSH options. Host options are always preceded by a double slash (//). The syntax for CSCRIPT version 5.0 is

```
cscript scriptname.extension [options...] [arguments...]
```

The available scripting options are as follows:

Parameter	Description
//I:	Enables interactive mode, which is the default setting. Interactive mode enables the real-time submission of user input through the command-prompt interface.
//B	Enables batch mode. All noncommand UI is requested from the script. This setting will disable user input through the command-prompt interface. This option is useful when user interaction is not required.
//T:nn	Defines the script timeout (in seconds). The default is no timeout. This option can be used to prevent damage occurring from scripts caught in an infinite loop. Use of this option is recommended.
//Logo	Displays an execution banner at execution time. This is the default setting for wscript and cscript.

7

continues

Parameter	Description
//NoLogo	Suppresses the display of the following banner at execution time:
	`Microsoft® Windows Scripting Host Version 5.0 for Windows`
	`Copyright© Microsoft Corporation 1996-1997. All rights reserved.`
//H:cscript	Makes cscript.exe the default application for running scripts.
//H:wscript	Makes wscript.exe the default application for running scripts.
//S	Saves the current command-line options on a per user basis.
//?	Show the cscript command usage.

Version 5.0 of cscript.exe is included in the Windows 95 and NT 4.0 distributions of WSH, which are available from Microsoft's Web site. The latest beta version of Windows 2000, however, includes version 5.1 of cscript.exe, which provides a few more options than version 5.0. The following are the options additionally available for CSCRIPT version 5.1:

Parameter	Description
//D	Enables active script debugging
//e:engine	Allows you to specify the engine for running the script
//job:xxx	Allows you to execute a WSC job
//X	Executes the script in the debugger when active debugging is enabled

It is important to use only those options that are supported for the version of CSCRIPT that will exist on the client computers executing the script. Attempting to use an unsupported option on the older version of CSCRIPT or WSCRIPT results in a compilation error such as that shown in Figure 7.5.

FIGURE 7.5

A CSCRIPT "invalid option" error.

Running Scripts Using WSCRIPT

The second available controller of ActiveX scripting engines is the Windows-based wscript.exe. WSCRIPT allows you to execute WSH scripts directly on the Windows desktop by simply double-clicking a file containing the script.

By default, WSCRIPT is used whenever you execute a file with a .vbs or .js extension. These defaults can be modified—making CSCRIPT.EXE the default scripting controller—by executing the following command at a command prompt:

```
CSCRIPT //H:CSCRIPT
```

Doing so will provide the feedback shown in Figure 7.6.

FIGURE 7.6

Setting CSCRIPT as the default scripting host.

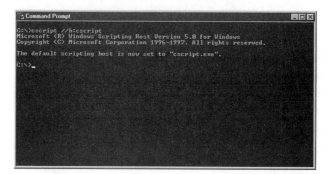

Just like CSCRIPT, WSCRIPT has several host options that can be modified through the command-prompt interface. You can also pass arguments to the script via the command-prompt interface. The available WSCRIPT options can be reviewed by typing **WSCRIPT //?**. Doing so will generate the dialog box shown in Figure 7.7.

7

FIGURE 7.7

WSCRIPT's available options.

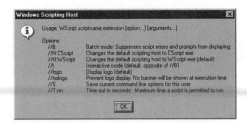

It is also possible to modify a subset of these options through the WSCRIPT property page. Typing **WSCRIPT** at a command prompt will display the property page, which looks like Figure 7.8.

FIGURE 7.8

WSCRIPT's options dialog.

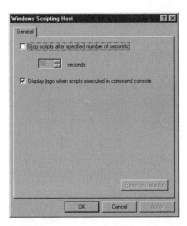

The two host options listed on the General tab can be customized at the individual script level through the use of a .WSH file. These files are described in the following paragraphs.

About .WSH Files

.WSH files are script-specific preference files that are used by WSCRIPT to control how the script is executed. These files are similar to the .PIF files that exist in current Microsoft Windows products. In this section, you will learn how to create these script-specific files and delve deeply into their contents to better understand how they operate.

Creating a custom .WSH file is quite simple. Simply right-click on .vbs or .js script file, and click Properties. You should see a properties tab that contains something you may not have seen before—a Script tab, shown in Figure 7.9.

FIGURE 7.9

The property page's Script tab.

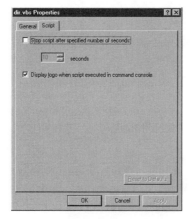

You may change any of the desired options. For this example, you will change the script timeout to 50 seconds. Go ahead and make the change, and then click OK. Now, look closely in the directory that contains the script file you just modified. You should notice that the operating system has created a file with the same name as the script you were working with, but with a file extension of .WSH, as shown in Figure 7.10.

FIGURE 7.10

A sample directory listing.

This .WSH file contains the custom settings you have just set. You can execute the script and use the custom settings you specified by double-clicking on its associated .WSH file.

Later, you will explore how the .WSH file and its associated script file are linked. Now, you will investigate their interaction a bit further. As already mentioned, you can execute a script file by double-clicking on its .WSH counterpart. You have significant flexibility regarding where the .WSH file resides; that is, it does not have to reside in the same directory as the script file itself. You must, however, keep the script file in its original location, or the .WSH file will not be able to find it. Figure 7.11 depicts the error you will receive when a .WSH file cannot find its associated script.

7

FIGURE 7.11

A "script not found" error.

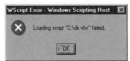

Although it might seem mysterious, magically created with minimal user influence, the .WSH file is nothing more than a simple text file containing information about the preferences you have set. Its content is very similar to the .INI files used predominantly during the days of Windows 3.x.

Open the .WSH file created from the preceding exercise, using Notepad or another text editor. In Figure 7.12, you will notice that the contents of this file are divided into two sections: the [ScriptFile] section and [Options] section.

FIGURE 7.12

A .WSH file's contents.

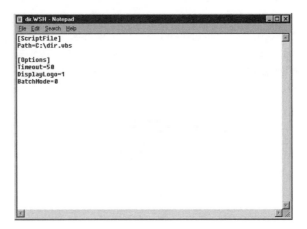

The [ScriptFile] section contains information about where the associated script file is located. Ah ha! Now it is all coming together. You now see how the .WSH file keeps track of its counterpart. If the associated script file ever has to be moved, you now know how to adjust the .WSH file so that it points to the script's new location. As an aside, it would be just as easy to delete the old .WSH file and re-create a new one that references the script's new location.

The [Options] section contains information about how the script should be run. The Timeout option defines how long the script should execute, in seconds, before timing out. A setting of zero means that no timeout exists. The DisplayLogo option defines whether the execution banner will display at execution time. The available settings for this option are 0 and 1. A setting of 0 means that no execution banner will be displayed, and a setting of 1 enables banner display. The BatchMode option defines whether the script will allow user input while the script is being executed. A setting of 0 disables batch mode, which means that user input will be allowed. A setting of 1 enables batch mode, meaning that user input will be disabled.

Adding File Associations for Scripts

As Microsoft and other companies develop ActiveX WSH engines for other scripting languages, you will also be able to execute these scripts with CSCRIPT and WSCRIPT. Like VBScript-based scripts, scripts created in these programming languages will have to be identified to the Windows operating system. The method used to identify these file types today involves, among other things, the use of file extensions.

You will notice that the sample scripts included with the WSH distribution have the extensions .vbs and .js. These identify VBScript scripts and JScript scripts, respectively. As I am sure you can imagine, these file extensions are very important. Without them, the WSH engines cannot properly identify which scripting language is being utilized and, therefore, which engine to use when parsing the script.

To illustrate this point, take one of the scripts included with the WSH distribution, and change its file extension. Before you go any further, change the default script controller back to WSCRIPT by typing **CSCRIPT //H:WSCRIPT** at a command prompt. After you've done that, locate the script named DIR.VBS. For the sake of example, execute the script, either by using cscript in a command prompt or by double-clicking on it. This VBScript script is straightforward and simply displays all the files located in the directory C:\TEMP. Now that you have tested the script and know that it operates correctly, change the script's name from DIR.VBS to DIR.JS. You will notice that the script's icon changes slightly after the name has been changed. Now try executing the script again. You will receive an error resembling that shown in Figure 7.13.

FIGURE 7.13

A JScript syntax error.

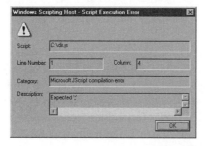

The error you received originated from the JScript engine because it did not find the required ; that is part of the JScript syntax. You now can see how the file extension and script engine are inexorably linked.

7

Caution

> Simply associating a certain file extension with WSCRIPT is not sufficient to enable WSCRIPT support for that particular language. A WSH engine must be installed, also. Otherwise, WSH will not be able to direct the code to an appropriate script engine for interpretation.

Scheduling WSH Scripts

Here you will learn how to schedule WSH scripts in both the Windows 95 and Windows NT environments. Windows NT provides integrated task scheduling functionality through the use of the Scheduler service and the AT command. Windows 95, however, does not contain integrated support for task scheduling. This functionality is available by installing Internet Explorer 4.0 or higher and specifying Task Scheduler as one of the optional components that should be installed.

Determining Whether Task Scheduler Is Installed in Windows 95

Before you run off, happily planning the automation of your mundane tasks, make sure that your Windows 95 installation has the proper components to support this initiative. There are several ways to verify that the Task Scheduler add-on has been installed, and they are discussed in the following paragraphs.

The Task Scheduler manifests itself in several areas on the Windows 95 desktop. The first place you should look is in the System Tray. An icon may exist there that looks like the one shown in Figure 7.14.

FIGURE 7.14

The Task Scheduler icon in the System Tray.

Task Scheduler icon

Didn't see it there? Okay, check in another location. Double-click on the My Computer icon located on the desktop. Inside the window that pops up (shown in Figure 7.15), you should find a folder named Scheduled Tasks. This folder looks like the other folders in Windows 95, but has a special insignia located on it.

FIGURE 7.15

The Scheduled Tasks folder.

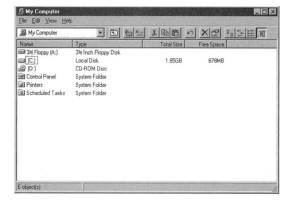

If you didn't find the references identified in the preceding paragraph, you will have to install the Task Scheduler by downloading it from Microsoft's Web site. It is an available option to Internet Explorer 4.0 and, as of this writing, is available through Microsoft's Windows Update Web page.

Using the Windows 95 Task Scheduler

The Task Scheduler is easy to use. The interface is straightforward, and managing tasks is a breeze. Now you will take a brief look at how the Task Scheduler system integrates with Windows 95 and how you can take advantage of this integration for maximum operability.

The primary interface to the Task Scheduler is the Scheduled Tasks folder located in My Computer. Double-clicking on this folder will "open" it, just like any other folder on your computer. After the folder is open, however, you will begin to notice some slight differences between this folder and the other folders on your system that are used to store files. For example, some of the menus are different; the displayed file details are different; a permanent Add Scheduled Task icon exists there; and finally, for those of you curious enough to try, you cannot move or delete the folder.

First, You Need a Task

Establishing a task entry is simple. Microsoft has included a task wizard that walks you through the necessary steps. You will run through these steps in the following paragraphs.

Before you move ahead, take a moment to arm yourself with a useful script I developed. It is quite simple and will delete all the .TMP files that exist in your computer's TEMP directory. The code appears in Listing 7.3.

7

LISTING 7.3   SCRIPT TO DELETE .TMP FILES FROM THE COMPUTER'S TEMP DIRECTORY

```
Set WSHShell = WScript.CreateObject("WScript.Shell")
Set objFileSystem = Wscript.CreateObject("Scripting.FileSystemObject")
'
'The following line points to your temp directory.
'
Set objFolder = objFileSystem.GetSpecialFolder(2)

Set colFiles = objFolder.Files
wscript.echo ("deleting temp files from ")
wscript.echo (objFolder)
On Error Resume Next
For Each FileObj in colFiles
    strFileName = FileObj.Name
    If UCASE(objFileSystem.GetExtensionName(FileObj.Path)) = "TMP" Then
        TempName = FileObj.Name
        FileObj.Delete
        If Err.Number = 0 Then
            wscript.echo(TempName)
        Else
            Err.Number=0
        End if
    End if
Next
wscript.echo("file deletion complete")
```

I will describe what this script does. As you might know, not all computers are the same. Some computers have Windows 95 installed in the C:\WINDOWS directory; others (such as yours truly) have it installed in another location. The Set objFolder = objFileSystem.GetSpecialFolder(2) code snippet examines your computer and determines where your TEMP directory is located.

Let me provide a little background about the TEMP directory. Windows 95 uses what are called *environment variables* to help the operating system manage itself. You can use a variety of environment variables, depending on your particular situation, but a common one is TEMP. This variable points to a directory somewhere on your computer, and Windows 95 uses that directory to store (you guessed it) temporary files. The aforementioned piece of code allows this script to be run on a number of computers without any customization because it automatically finds the directory that Windows has selected as TEMP.

After this directory has been located, the script outputs a brief indicator declaring what it is going to do. I use the wscript.echo to achieve this. If you are using CSCRIPT to run this script, the output will be sent to the Command Prompt window. If WSCRIPT is used, the output will be displayed in a dialog box.

The `On Error Resume Next` snippet informs the script that if an error is encountered, it should just ignore the error, continue on, and finish the task at hand. What could go wrong, you ask? Well, several things. A common error that occurs when deleting temp files involves the attempted deletion of files that are being used by the computer. You see, to prevent the untimely deletion of `TEMP` files, and the unwanted consequences of such an activity, the operating system will "lock" these files and prevent them from being touched by any outside entity. As you can imagine, the script would be slightly disgruntled by this and would *abend* (end abnormally) without finishing. Therefore, you protect the script from this potential occurrence with `On Error Resume Next`. I recommend the liberal use of `On Error Resume Next`.

The next piece of code begins the loop that will traverse through all the files that exist in the `TEMP` directory. Using what's called a collection, you can group together a number of objects (files, directories, and so on) and manipulate them one by one using a `For Each` loop. After you enter the loop, you should see whether the files in your collection meet your requirements for deletion.

To refresh your memory, you want to delete only files with the `.TMP` file extension. The `If UCASE(objFileSystem.GetExtensionName(FileObj.Path)) = "TMP" Then` checks to make sure that the file you are targeting does, in fact, have a `.TMP` extension. If it meets that criterion, you have satisfied your condition and will execute the commands located within the `If` statement.

After the if condition has been satisfied, the script begins to do several things. First, it assigns the name of the file that is being worked on to a temporary variable for later use. Next, it tries to delete the file, using the `FileObj.Delete` method. Here's where `On Error Resume Next` becomes critical. If the file that has been targeted is in use, the script will not be able to delete it and will halt unceremoniously.

This brings us to another interesting snippet: the `Err.Number` property. `Err.Number` provides feedback on the script's status. If all is well, the error code will be 0. If a problem exists, it will be described through one of several custom error codes defined by Microsoft. I am using this feature to moderate which filenames are echoed to the screen using the `wscript.echo` command discussed earlier. If an error occurs, you do not want to output the name of the file because you didn't successfully delete it. I also recommend liberal use of `Err.Number` in conjunction with `On Error Resume Next` because of the insight it can provide in error identification.

The next significant line of code sets `Err.Number` back to 0. The script does not want to affect future iterations in the `For Each` loop with data from previously erred operations.

7

The rest of the code includes the closing delimiters of your conditional and loop statements. Finally, the script wraps up with an echo to the screen, declaring the process officially complete.

Now that you have your script, how can you schedule its execution? Furthermore, do you want to save the output of this script for later review? I will discuss some of the options available to you.

Using the Task Scheduler, you can execute this script in several ways. First, you can call the script itself, which will be executed using whichever script controller (CSCRIPT or WSCRIPT) is set as the default. You can also specify which script controller to use, by including reference to it in your scheduled task. Finally, you can create a batch file that contains the command to execute the script and can then schedule the batch file for execution. The choice is yours, and your selection will depend on your objectives. Because variety is the spice of life, first you will schedule a task that calls the script directly. Then I'll show you how to modify the task after it has been scheduled, to specify which script controller to use.

Establishing a Task Entry

The first step in scheduling a task is easy: Double-click the Add Scheduled Task icon. You will see a dialog like that in Figure 7.16.

FIGURE 7.16

The Scheduled Task Wizard introductory dialog.

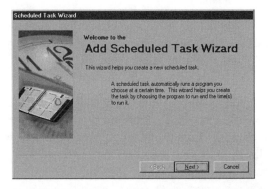

Click the Next button and select the application you would like to schedule. You should notice that neither the script nor the applications that run your script (wscript and cscript) currently exist in this list. Does this mean that you can't schedule these items? Of course not. This list includes only those applications that exist in the computer's Start menu. The list should not be considered in any way comprehensive.

Adding the desired application is simple: Just click on the Browse button, and find where your script file, CSCRIPT or WSCRIPT, exists on your computer. For this example, I selected the script file itself, shown in Figure 7.17. This script just happens to reside in the root of my C:\, so you track it down there, select it, and click the Open button.

FIGURE 7.17

Selecting the object to schedule.

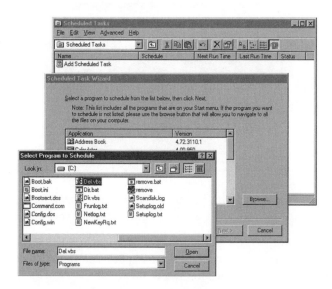

After clicking Open, you are returned to the Scheduled Task Wizard and presented with a page (shown in Figure 7.18) inquiring when the script should be run. For the purpose of this example, select Daily and click Next.

FIGURE 7.18

Choosing the schedule interval.

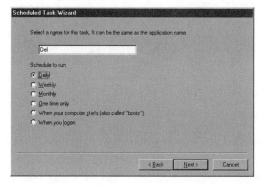

Now you will be presented with a screen (shown in Figure 7.19) that asks when the task should be executed. Note that the options on this screen depend on when you scheduled

7

the task to run (Daily, Weekly, One Time Only, and so on). It would be a good idea to go back and forth between this screen and the preceding one, changing settings as you go, to get a feel for the options that are available for each timing "cycle."

FIGURE 7.19

Configuring the time options.

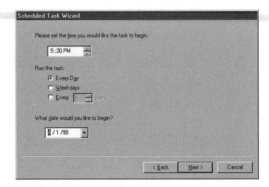

Because you selected Daily, you must specify what time the task should begin; whether you want it to run every day, weekdays only, or once every X number of days; and finally, the date the task should begin to run.

Clicking Next takes you to the summation page, shown in Figure 7.20, where all the selections made are detailed for review.

FIGURE 7.20

The Task Scheduler completion page.

Note the Open Advanced Properties of the Task check box at the bottom. Checking this will provide you with the opportunity to fine-tune the task before it is scheduled. For now, do not check this box. You will investigate the advanced options later when I explain how to modify tasks that have already been scheduled. Click the Finish button, and you will see that the task you just scheduled has been added to the folder.

Modifying a Task Entry

Now you will delve into the advanced options I spoke about earlier and investigate how to change a scheduled task. Right-click on the task you just created, and click Properties. A window with three property tabs on top will appear, shown in Figure 7.21.

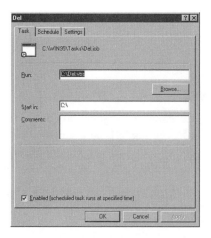

The Task tab includes information about the actual command that will be executed when the task is run, where the command you specified will be run from, and any comments that exist about the task, as well as a check box that allows you to enable or disable the task.

Now things are getting interesting! Remember that in the preceding section I said that you would change a task after it had been scheduled? Well, here's your chance. Notice that in the Run text box there is a reference to the script you created. To explicitly define CSCRIPT as the controller of this script, all you have to do is prefix the contents of that text box with the controller's name. After you make the change, the text box should contain the following text:

```
CSCRIPT C:\DEL.VBS
```

Simple, eh? Now you will see what other options are available to play with.

Click on the Schedule tab. You will notice options there that look similar to the timing options available when you first scheduled this task. Because the task you created is particularly useful when users first log on, change the Scheduled Task frequency to At Logon. Notice how the available options change as you scroll through the timing frequency options.

7

After you make that change, click on the Settings tab. Ay Caramba! Talk about advanced settings! This is one of the most useful areas of the task properties dialog. You have a high degree of control over when the task is run, even so far as to define whether to execute the task if the computer is idle. Good stuff here. Review it for future reference; you won't make any changes in this example.

Click the OK button. The dialog box will close, and the changes you have made will be reflected in the Scheduled Tasks window.

Why not reboot your computer to test the task you just scheduled?

Using the Windows NT AT Command

Now I will switch gears and talk about my personal favorite operating system, Windows NT. Windows NT supports the scheduling of tasks using the AT command and the Scheduler service. AT is an application that provides an interface to the schedule service, enabling users to control the execution of tasks with a fine level of granularity.

Tip

> To completely affect AT's task list, you must have Administrator privileges on the local or remote computer you are modifying.

The AT application has a complex syntax and can control tasks on local and remote computers. A summary of the AT command syntax is as follows:

```
at [\\computername] [[id] [/delete [/yes]]
at [\\computername] time [/interactive] [/every:date[,...] ¦
➥/next:date[,...]] "command"
```

Here are the supported parameters:

Parameter	Description
\\computername	Specifies a remote computer. Commands are scheduled on the local computer if this parameter is omitted.
id	Is an identification number assigned to a scheduled command.
/delete	Cancels a scheduled command. If id is omitted, all the scheduled commands on the computer are canceled.

/yes	Used with the Cancel All Jobs command when no further confirmation is desired.
time	Specifies the time when a command is to run.
/interactive	Allows the job to interact with the desktop of the user who is logged on at the time the job runs.
/every:*date*[,...]	Runs the command on each specified day(s) of the week or month. If *date* is omitted, the current day of the month is assumed.
/next:*date*[,...]	Runs the specified command on the next occurrence of the day (for example, next Thursday). If *date* is omitted, the current day of the month is assumed.
"*command*"	Is the Windows NT command or the batch program to be run.

Did you get that? It's okay if you didn't, because I will discuss these options at length, providing you with complete examples.

Typing **AT** at a command prompt will provide you with a listing of all the currently scheduled activities. The output you receive includes five columns, describing the task's status, task ID, the day(s) of the week the task will be run, the time the task will be run, and finally, the command that will be executed. Figure 7.22 gives an example of the AT command output.

FIGURE 7.22

The AT command output in a console window.

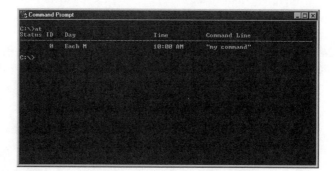

7

Now let's discuss AT's available arguments and switches. You can schedule tasks in several ways. The first argument, *computername*, is optional and provides flexibility regarding which computer will received the scheduled command. Omitting this argument will schedule the task at the local computer.

The Task ID argument is used with AT to identify the specific attributes of a scheduled task. For example, when I type **AT x** at a command prompt, I will receive a detailed description of the scheduled task with the task id of x. A sample output of this command appears in Figure 7.23. I used it to display the contents of a task with an ID of 0.

FIGURE 7.23

A detailed listing of an AT *scheduled task.*

Please note that these task IDs are automatically assigned by the system. The Task ID argument is also used to delete specific tasks. Typing **AT /DELETE** will delete all scheduled tasks on the local computer, but typing **AT 0 /DELETE** will delete only the task with an ID of 0.

As I am sure you can imagine, typing **AT /DELETE** can have serious, unwanted consequences. To prevent unintended data loss, AT asks you to verify the deletion of all scheduled tasks. Figure 7.24 displays AT's delete all confirmation.

FIGURE 7.24

AT's "are you sure?" prompt.

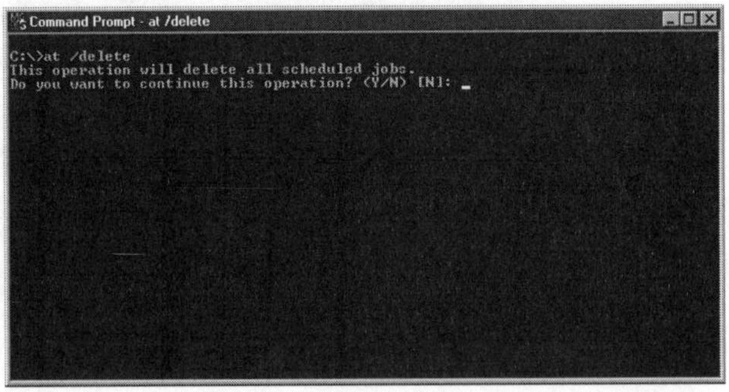

The /YES switch can be used when you want to force the deletion of all scheduled tasks by suppressing the "are you sure" prompt. You will receive no feedback when you type **AT /DELETE /YES** and press Enter—you have passed the point of no return. As a general rule, it is better to be safe than sorry. Therefore, the use of the /YES switch should be avoided. For those of you who like to walk on the wild side and don't like to waste a keystroke, you can abbreviate the command by typing **AT /DEL /Y**.

The /INTERACTIVE switch allows the scheduled job to interact with the desktop of the user who is logged on when the job runs. This is useful if input is required by the user to specify script arguments. An example of this would be a script that deletes all files with a certain file extension. This switch would allow the user to type in the file extension of the files that should be deleted by the script.

Now you are ready to schedule the execution of scripts. AT provides a significant amount of flexibility in this regard. Commands can be scheduled at any time during the day or night, on a specific day or for a recurring set of specific days.

When specifying an execution time, AT supports the use of both a.m. and p.m. identifiers, as well as times detailed using 24-hour notation. If you wanted to schedule the "my command here" task at 11:30 p.m., you would type

```
AT 23:30 "my command here"
```

AT will create a task entry that will run once: today if the current time is before 11:30 and tomorrow if you're working late and the time is after 11:30. In Figure 7.25, I illustrate this by displaying the system time and then scheduling a task that occurs earlier in the day. You will see in the output that the task is scheduled to run tomorrow evening.

FIGURE 7.25

A scheduled command occurring earlier in the day.

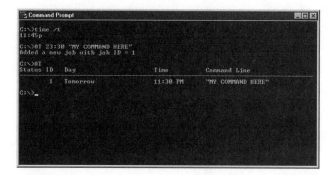

AT can also schedule tasks according to the day of the week or day of the month. For example, you can schedule a task that occurs next Wednesday or a task that occurs on the 15th or the 15th, 18th, and 22nd, and so on. The syntax for scheduling tasks in this

manner is simple. If you want to schedule a task that occurs at 11:30 this Wednesday and Friday, you would type

```
AT 23:30 /NEXT:W,F "MY COMMAND"
```

Assuming that it is before 11:30 p.m. on Wednesday when you schedule this task, the task will be executed two times this week: Wednesday and Friday. If you schedule the task on, say, Thursday, the task will occur this Friday and next Wednesday. The days of the week are represented by the following abbreviations:

Abbreviation	Day of the Week
M	Monday
T	Tuesday
W	Wednesday
Th	Thursday
F	Friday
S	Saturday
Su	Sunday

You can also schedule tasks by the day of the month. Assuming today is the third day of the month, if you type

```
AT 23:30 /NEXT:5,10,15,20,25,30 "MY COMMAND"
```

you will schedule the "MY COMMAND" task to occur on the 5th, 10th, 15th, and so on. If the current month does not have 30 days, the task will execute in the next month that has 30 days in it.

Now you are ready to begin scheduling recurring tasks. Recurring tasks follow the same basic rules as the one-time tasks just discussed. To schedule a task that occurs every Wednesday, you would type

```
AT 23:30 /EVERY:W "MY COMMAND"
```

To schedule a task that occurs the 10th and 20th of each month, you would type

```
AT 23:30 /EVERY:10,20 "MY COMMAND"
```

As you can see, the syntax is fundamentally the same, except that you must replace the word NEXT with the word EVERY.

Tip

You cannot combine the /NEXT and /EVERY switches in a single AT task entry. Don't believe me? Try it. To achieve this schedule, you would have to create two entries: one defining the task that runs on Wednesday, for example, and another task that is scheduled to run Weekly.

Now it's time to discuss the reason you're involved with the AT command: the task you want to schedule. One way to schedule these scripts is to embed them in a .bat or .cmd file and schedule the batch file with AT. The command portion of AT can exist with or without surrounding quotation marks. I prefer to include surrounding quotes to avoid any possible problems.

As an example, I have slightly modified the dir.vbs script that comes with the WSH distribution. For those of you who have not yet used it, the script simply reads the contents of the C:\TEMP directory on your computer and displays the results in a series of dialog boxes (one dialog box per file found). Rather than have the script display several dialog boxes, each containing a filename, I used the wscript.echo command to display the output at the console. The modified script looks like this:

```
Set WSHShell = WScript.CreateObject("WScript.Shell")
Set objFileSystem = Wscript.CreateObject("Scripting.FileSystemObject")
Set objFolder = objFileSystem.GetFolder("C:\temp")
Set colFiles = objFolder.Files

For Each FileObj in colFiles
    strFileName = FileObj.Name
    wscript.echo strFileName
Next
```

Using this modified script, you will create a batch file that contains the necessary command to invoke the script and log the contents to a text file. In this example, the text file is named C:\DIR.TXT. If you haven't done so already, move the modified DIR.VBS file to the root of your C:\ drive. You can store the script file anywhere; the location I specified is used simply to make this example easier.

Now you create the batch file that will run the script. Using a simple text editor, such as Notepad, create a document that contains the following command:

```
C:\WINNT\SYSETM32\CSCRIPT.EXE C:\DIR.VBS > C:\DIR.TXT
```

Save the document in the root of your C:\ drive, and name it DIR.BAT.

Let me dissect the command that is contained in the batch file. The first part of the command, C:\WINNT\SYSTEM32\CSCRIPT.EXE, describes the location of the CSCRIPT executable on my computer. If you have Windows NT loaded in a different directory than

7

C:\WINNT, obviously the command should be modified to reflect this. It is important to provide a fully qualified path to the executable to eliminate the risk that the Scheduler service will not be able to find CSCRIPT.EXE.

The second part of the batch command is simply the call to the script file, DIR.VBS. This, too, should be identified with the script's fully qualified path to prevent a FILE NOT FOUND error.

Finally, the > C:\DIR.TXT tells the computer to output the results of the script to a file named DIR.TXT.

To recap, you have the modified script file located in the root of C:\, and it is named DIR.VBS. You have created a batch file named DIR.BAT and have also placed that file in the root of C:\. Ready? It's time to schedule the task.

Schedule the task so that it occurs every Thursday at 5:00 p.m. Open a Command Prompt window and type

```
AT 17:00 /EVERY:W "CMD /C C:\DIR.BAT"
```

You should receive a response from AT that is similar to the one shown in Figure 7.26.

FIGURE 7.26

A successful task entry submission using AT.

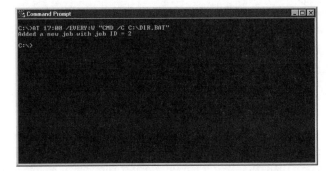

Now, every Wednesday at 5:00 p.m., the script will run and output a list of files that exist in C:\TEMP to a file named DIR.TXT. This is a straightforward example, but it effectively relates the potential that exists to automate "real life" activities. You could, for example, schedule a script to run a weekly CHKDSK and save the results to a text file.

Tip

> Tasks executed using AT run in the context of the Scheduler service. This means that the scripts you schedule will be executed using the permissions and privileges available to the Scheduler service. If you have trouble running a scheduled task, it is a good idea to see whether the problem stems from a lack of permissions to perform what is being requested.

Summary

Well, folks, you made it. By now, you have successfully scheduled WSH tasks on both the Windows 95 and NT 4.0 environments. You have also learned about .WSH files and their purpose; CSCRIPT and WSCRIPT, and their options; and a smattering of how these WSH scripts compare with their Web-based cousins. I've been watching you, and you have paid attention marvelously. You all get an A.

Q&A

Q CSCRIPT is the default application chosen by Microsoft. Why would I want to change it?

A Feature differences aside, you might want to run your script without the nagging Command Prompt window appearing and disappearing every time a script is run. From a functionality standpoint, the two applications are generally the same.

Q I'm creating a script for a mixed-client base, both Windows 95/98 and NT. What precautions should I take to make sure that the script will run in all environments?

A Aside from the obvious differences in how scripts are scheduled, most scripts should operate effectively in both environments. This advice is provided with the caveat that scripts should be tested in all environments in which they will be deployed—it's a very prudent programming practice.

Q I've created a script and tested it thoroughly. When I deploy it, my Windows NT clients cannot execute it. What's wrong?

A Well, there can be a number of reasons why, but I would first check the permissions. If your Windows NT client's hard disk is using the NTFS file system, it's possible that the file level permissions are getting in the way and preventing the script from being run in the user's context.

7

DAY **8**

Testing and Debugging WSH Scripts

By Michael Morrison

Day 8: Chapter Overview

For most programmers new to scripting, the testing phase of script development is often the most fun. Who can argue the thrill of seeing the results of your hard work? Unfortunately, scripts often don't behave as you would like them to, especially in early tests. As much as we might think we're conscientious and thorough enough to never make mistakes when developing scripts, the reality is that scripting is just another facet of programming, and programming is an inherently error-prone process. Bugs in scripts are no less insidious than bugs in full-fledged programming languages such as C++ and Java.

Today you'll learn the following:

- Types of errors that can occur in script code
- How to perform simple debugging using message box windows
- How to use the Microsoft Script Debugger
- How to deal with bugs in JScript and VBScript code
- Common script bugs and how to avoid them

Script Debugging Basics

A bug is simply a coding error that results in some unwanted action that takes place in a program. Any bug-free program became that way through thorough testing and debugging. The main difference between good programmers and great programmers is the degree to which they actively set out to uncover bugs as they are developing and testing a program. This brings me to the first rule of debugging, which is to assume that your code has bugs and that it is your responsibility to hunt them down and fix them to the best of your ability.

For the purposes of debugging scripts, it is helpful to classify different types of bugs, or errors. Following are the three main types of errors that you'll encounter when creating scripts:

- Syntax errors
- Runtime errors
- Logic errors

Syntax Errors

Syntax errors are errors that occur because a script violates the fundamental syntax of the JScript or VBScript languages. For example, misspelling a keyword and forgetting to close a block statement are good examples of syntax errors. Syntax errors are also known as load-time errors because they reveal themselves when you first load a script; the script interpreter will catch the error, display an error message, and refuse to run the script.

Note
Syntax errors are also sometimes referred to as pre-processor errors, compilation errors, or compile-time errors, even though scripts technically are never compiled.

Fortunately, syntax errors are the easiest errors to find and fix because you are always notified of them. Besides, syntax errors are usually the result of accidental oversights or typographical errors as opposed to serious script design errors. Following is an example of a common syntax error:

```
function howdy() {
  alert("Howdy!")
```

Notice that the closing curly brace (}) is missing in this example. Windows Scripting Host is quick to point out such syntax errors when it first loads a script. Figure 8.1 shows what happens if you forget an enclosing curly brace as was done in this sample code.

FIGURE 8.1

A syntax error displayed in Windows Scripting Host as a result of forgetting an enclosing curly brace in a JScript program.

As you can see in the figure, WSH provides you with some information to help track down the error. More specifically, you are given the line number in the script where the error occurred, along with the type of error (compilation error) and a brief description of the error. Keep in mind that WSH isn't always accurate in pointing out syntax errors. Depending on the specific error, WSH might incorrectly point out the line number. Even so, you should still be able to home in on the error.

Runtime Errors

The second type of error encountered in script programming is the runtime error. A runtime error is an error that is only revealed when a script is executing, or running. Runtime errors don't violate script syntax, which is why it isn't possible for WSH to detect them on first loading a script. Whereas syntax errors are generally caused by violations of script syntax, runtime errors typically involve improper use of commands. For example, a common runtime error is referencing a variable that hasn't been initialized. Consider the following example:

```
circumference = 2 * 3.14 * radius;
```

In this case, the radius variable is uninitialized, so it is impossible to perform the calculation. Unfortunately, runtime errors are not automatically caught and displayed by WSH. Typically, a script containing a runtime error will simply stop running and do nothing. This makes it significantly more difficult to track down runtime errors without using outside help. Outside help in this case is a special program called a debugger that helps you hunt down bugs. You learn how to use a debugger later in this lesson.

Note

> Runtime errors aren't all created equal. In fact, VBScript and JScript differ in terms of what they each consider runtime errors. For example, attempting to divide by zero results in a runtime error in VBScript, but not in JScript.

Logic Errors

The last of the three scripting types is the logic error, which is a functional error that doesn't disrupt the actual operation of a script. A logic error is caused when code executes without syntax or runtime errors, but the results are not what you intended. Generally speaking, logic errors are a result of the programmer not properly implementing an algorithm. For example, you might have a calculation that is dependent on a user-entered value. However, no matter what the user enters, the result is always the same. After closer inspection, the code reveals that the calculation had a hard-coded constant instead of the variable holding the user entry.

You can think of a logic error as an error caused by an inconsistency between your intentions and the actual code implementation. We're all capable of creating logic errors even after fully thinking through a solution. I'm guilty of committing the error in the sample scenario I just presented.

Logic errors are perhaps the most insidious of the three error types because there is no way to absolutely pinpoint the problem. Syntax and runtime errors will both generate alert messages to help you find the problem, but with logic errors, you are left to your own devices. However, a debugger goes a long way toward helping you track down logic errors. You'll learn some techniques throughout the remainder of the lesson to rein in logic errors, as well as avoid errors in general.

Message Debugging

In a moment, you'll learn how to use a debugging tool to perform powerful bug hunting operations. Although debugging tools ultimately provide the best solution for tracking down bugs, there is a simpler approach that you might find useful in some situations. I'm referring to message debugging, which involves using a message box to display information about the state of a script at critical points in the code. Admittedly, this technique is somewhat archaic, but if you want a quick look into what's going on in a script, it's not a bad start.

8

Message debugging is carried by simply sprinkling calls to MsgBox() or WScript.Echo() at appropriate locations in your code, depending on whether you're using VBScript or JScript. If you're testing JScript code in a Web browser, you can use the alert() function instead of WScript.Echo(). You can use this technique for anything from looking at the value of variables to determining when or whether a function is being called. The results are extremely simple to interpret because you'll be presented with a message box window each time something important happens in your script.

The Script Debugger

To help make the detection of bugs easier, Microsoft has Script Debugger, which is freely available for debugging both JScript and VBScript code. The Script Debugger is a standalone application that is used to coordinate the debugging of a script that is executing in a Web browser, such as Internet Explorer. Wait a minute, what does Internet Explorer have to do with WSH? Well, as you probably know, JScript and VBScript both originated as scripting technologies for creating interactive Web pages. Not surprisingly, Web pages are still where the majority of scripting still takes place. Microsoft's Script Debugger focuses on the debugging of scripts executing within a Web page.

What does this mean for scripts that are designed to run solely in WSH? Well, it means that you won't be able to debug all WSH scripts using the Script Debugger. More specifically, you can't use WSH-specific objects, such as the WScript object, because the Internet Explorer object model doesn't support WScript. However, the core JScript and VBScript object models are supported under Internet Explorer, so you still have some flexibility when it comes to debugging scripts.

Preparing WSH Scripts for the Script Debugger

One significant issue related to the WScript object is that of displaying information in a script. If you recall, the Echo() method is called on the WScript object to display a text message in a window from WSH scripting code. Because the WScript object isn't supported in Internet Explorer, you can't display information using the Echo() method when debugging scripts. Instead, you can use the alert() function, which also accepts a string argument.

Because the Script Debugger operates in terms of a script executing within a Web page, it expects all scripts to be included as part of a Web page's code. This means that to debug a WSH script in the Script Debugger, you need to copy and paste the script's code into a Web page with a .html filename extension. The good news is that you only need a couple of lines of HTML code to house the script code. Following is an example:

```
<SCRIPT LANGUAGE="JScript">
  alert("Hello there!");
</SCRIPT>
```

In this example, the single line of script code is enclosed between the <SCRIPT> and </SCRIPT> HTML tags. Notice also that the scripting language is set using the LANGUAGE attribute of the <SCRIPT> tag. You should set this attribute appropriately based on whether you're using VBScript or JScript.

The Script Debugger's dependency on Web page scripts is certainly something that makes WSH script debugging a little trickier. However, it's worth the extra effort to be able to utilize debugging techniques afforded by using the Script Debugger.

Using the Script Debugger

Now that you understand how to prepare a WSH script for debugging using the Script Debugger, take the debugger for a test drive. Following is the code for a Web page named FreeSpace.html that includes a debugger-friendly version of the FreeSpace script you created back in Day 6, "Using Microsoft JScript with WSH":

LISTING 8.1   SCRIPT FOR FreeSpace.html

```
<SCRIPT LANGUAGE="JavaScript">
alert(GetFreeSpace("c:\\"));

function GetFreeSpace(drivePath) {
  var fso, drive, freeSpace;

  fso = new ActiveXObject("Scripting.FileSystemObject");
  drive = fso.GetDrive(fso.GetDriveName(drivePath));
  freeSpace = "Free Space on drive " + drivePath + " : " +
    Math.round(drive.FreeSpace / 1048576) + " MB";
  return freeSpace;
}
</SCRIPT>
```

The only change to the script code is the replacement of the WScript.Echo() method call with a call to alert() in the first line of script code. The <SCRIPT> and </SCRIPT> tags were also added to satisfy the Web browser.

With the script ready for the debugger, the next step is to open the FreeSpace.html Web page in a Web browser. The script immediately runs, in which case you should go along with it and allow it to execute once. After loading the script in a Web browser, you can launch the Script Debugger and get things started. If you have the Script Debugger properly installed, you can launch it by selecting Script Debugger, Open from the View menu in Internet Explorer.

> **Note**
>
> I've had trouble launching the Script Debugger using the menu command in Internet Explorer. If you have a similar problem, you can also launch the Script Debugger manually from Windows Explorer.

An alternative approach to running the Script Debugger is to launch it (MSSCRDBG.EXE) manually from Windows Explorer. When the debugger is up and running, select Running Documents from the View menu. A window similar to that in Figure 8.2 then appears.

FIGURE 8.2

The Running Documents window in the Script Debugger.

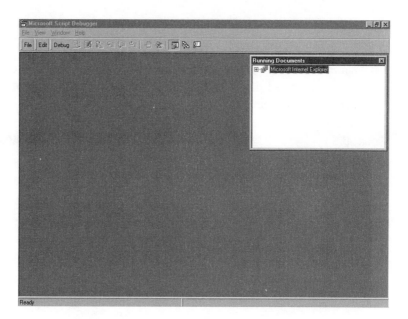

Click to open the Microsoft Internet Explorer tree, which will then display the different documents open in Internet Explorer (see Figure 8.3).

FIGURE 8.3

The Internet Explorer documents available for debugging in the Script Debugger.

Double-click the FreeSpace.html document to open it in the debugger (see Figure 8.4).

FIGURE 8.4

*The FreeSpace.html
document open for
debugging in the Script
Debugger.*

```
Read only: FreeSpace.html
<SCRIPT LANGUAGE="JavaScript">
alert(GetFreeSpace("c:\\"));

function GetFreeSpace(drivePath) {
  var fso, drive, freeSpace;

  fso = new ActiveXObject("Scripting.FileSystemObject");
  drive = fso.GetDrive(fso.GetDriveName(drivePath));
  freeSpace = "Free Space on drive " + drivePath + " : " +
    Math.round(drive.FreeSpace / 1048576) + " MB";
  return freeSpace;
}
</SCRIPT>
```

Select Break At Next Statement from the Debug menu to get the debugger ready. Now
return to Internet Explorer and refresh (reload) the FreeSpace.html page. The Script
Debugger immediately becomes active, and the first line of code in the script is highlighted as in Figure 8.5.

FIGURE 8.5

*The FreeSpace.html
halted in the Script
Debugger.*

```
Read only: file://C:\Books\TYWSH\Source\Chap08\FreeSpace.html [break]
<SCRIPT LANGUAGE="JavaScript">
alert(GetFreeSpace("c:\\"));

function GetFreeSpace(drivePath) {
  var fso, drive, freeSpace;

  fso = new ActiveXObject("Scripting.FileSystemObject");
  drive = fso.GetDrive(fso.GetDriveName(drivePath));
  freeSpace = "Free Space on drive " + drivePath + " : " +
    Math.round(drive.FreeSpace / 1048576) + " MB";
  return freeSpace;
}
```

At this point, the script is halted in the debugger, and you are ready to employ one of a
number of debugging techniques, described in the following sections:

- Breakpoints
- Single-stepping
- Variable access
- The call stack

Halting Scripts with Breakpoints

A *breakpoint* acts somewhat like a roadblock for program execution. It works like this:
You place breakpoint on a line of code, and when the script runs and gets to that line of
code, it stops. It's called a breakpoint because the script effectively takes a break at that

particular point in the code. Breakpoints are extremely useful in isolating certain parts of a script and analyzing them. You've actually already set a breakpoint in the `FreeSpace` script by halting the script at the first line of code. However, the Script Debugger gives you the freedom to place breakpoints anywhere within a script.

To understand the significance of breakpoints, imagine that you are interested in seeing what happens in a script at a particular point in the code. One option would be to single-step through the code a line at a time until you arrive at the code in question; you learn how to do this in a moment. However, some scripts have long loops that perform lots of iterations, which would take a long time to single-step through. Setting a breakpoint on the line of code solves this problem quite nicely. You set the breakpoint and then run the program in the debugger; when the debugger runs across the breakpoint, the program halts. You are then free to watch variables and even single-step through the code if you want.

To set a breakpoint to a specific line of script code, position the caret on the line of code in question and select Toggle Breakpoint from the Debug menu. This command actually toggles breakpoints, so you can use it to turn breakpoints on and off. You can also just press the F9 key as a shortcut to toggle breakpoints. There is also a Clear All Breakpoints command under the Debug menu to get rid of any breakpoints that you've set. Figure 8.6 shows a breakpoint set to the fourth line of code in the `GetFreeSpace()` function.

FIGURE 8.6

A breakpoint set in the `GetFreeSpace()` *function of the* `FreeSpace` *script.*

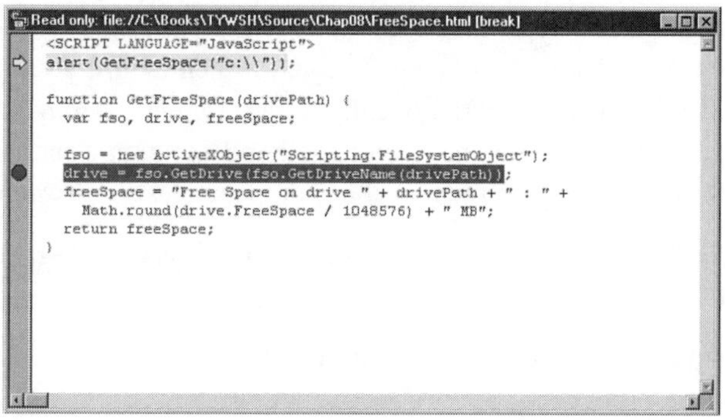

```
Read only: file://C:\Books\TYWSH\Source\Chap08\FreeSpace.html [break]

  <SCRIPT LANGUAGE="JavaScript">
  alert(GetFreeSpace("c:\\"));

  function GetFreeSpace(drivePath) {
    var fso, drive, freeSpace;

    fso = new ActiveXObject("Scripting.FileSystemObject");
    drive = fso.GetDrive(fso.GetDriveName(drivePath));
    freeSpace = "Free Space on drive " + drivePath + " : " +
      Math.round(drive.FreeSpace / 1048576) + " MB";
    return freeSpace;
  }
```

To run the script to this breakpoint, select Run from the Debug menu or press the F5 key. Control will return to Internet Explorer, where you must okay the use of the `FileSystemObject` ActiveX object (see Figure 8.7).

This is necessary because Web browsers have to be careful about allowing ActiveX objects to run. After confirming that it's okay to use the ActiveX object, control returns to the Script Debugger, where the highlight now rests on the line of code with the break-point, as in Figure 8.8.

Figure 8.7

An Internet Explorer window giving you an opportunity to confirm the use of an ActiveX object in script code.

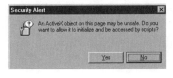

Figure 8.8

The FreeSpace *script halted at a breakpoint.*

```
Read only: file://C:\Books\TYWSH\Source\Chap08\FreeSpace.html [break]
    <SCRIPT LANGUAGE="JavaScript">
    alert(GetFreeSpace("c:\\"));

    function GetFreeSpace(drivePath) {
      var fso, drive, freeSpace;

      fso = new ActiveXObject("Scripting.FileSystemObject");
      drive = fso.GetDrive(fso.GetDriveName(drivePath));
      freeSpace = "Free Space on drive " + drivePath + " : " +
        Math.round(drive.FreeSpace / 1048576) + " MB";
      return freeSpace;
    }
```

Executing One Line at a Time

Single-stepping is the process of executing a script a line at a time, in single steps, and represents perhaps the most fundamental of all debugging strategies. The significance of single-stepping as a debugging technique is that it provides you with a way to see and control exactly what code is being executed, which in turn gives you insight into the flow of execution through a script. Typically, single-stepping through code isn't entirely useful by itself; you usually combine it with another debugging technique known as accessing variables to keep an eye on what happens to variables as you step through the code.

The Script Debugger gives you three different options for single-stepping through script code:

- Step into—executes the current line of code, stepping into any function that is called
- Step over—executes the current line of code without stepping into any called functions
- Step out—executes the current line of code, stepping out of a function if possible

The only real difference between these single-step approaches is how they handle function calls. You'll find menu commands for each of these approaches under the Debug menu in the Script Debugger. Try single-stepping once in the FreeSpace script to see how the highlight moves down a line of code in the Script Debugger.

Accessing Variables

Another Script Debugger debugging technique involves *accessing variables*. In general, setting breakpoints and single-stepping through code don't provide enough information alone to figure out problems in a script. It's helpful to be able to examine the contents of variables to see how they change in response to code being executed. By watching a variable in a debugger, you can quickly tell if the variable is somehow getting set to a value that doesn't jibe with the rest of the script code. If you keep an eye on a variable as you are single-stepping through code, you can learn a lot about what is happening to the variable.

To access a variable in the Script Debugger, you must use the Command Window; select Command Window from the View menu. The Command Window is a text window where you can issue commands to the Script Debugger and view the results. To check the value of a variable, type the variable name in the Command Window, as shown in Figure 8.9.

FIGURE 8.9

An uninitialized variable viewed in the Script Debugger's Command Window.

In this case, the script code has yet to initialize the `freeSpace` variable, so its value is returned as `undefined`. If you single-step through two more lines of code and try the command again, the value of the `freeSpace` variable appears (see Figure 8.10).

FIGURE 8.10

A variable viewed in the Script Debugger's Command Window.

You can directly modify a variable in the Command Window to see how it impacts the script. For example, try entering the following line in the Command Window:

```
freeSpace = "You're out of space!";
```

This overrides the calculated value of the `freeSpace` variable and results in the window in Figure 8.11 being displayed.

FIGURE 8.11

The modified output of the FreeSpace *script.*

One other interesting point about the Script Debugger's Command Window is that you can enter any script command directly in the Command Window and see the results. For example, entering the following line of code in the Command Window creates and initializes a variable named num:

```
num = 40;
```

You can then issue subsequent commands that utilize the variable:

```
alert(num / 5);
```

Figure 8.12 shows the results of this command.

FIGURE 8.12

Displaying the result of a calculation using the Command Window.

Keeping Track of Function Calls

The Script Debugger supports one other debugging feature that you will find useful in some situations. This is the *call stack* feature, which enables you to look at the list of functions that were called to arrive at a given point in a script. The call stack often sheds light on a problem that involves a nested function being called improperly or at an inopportune time.

To view the call stack in the Script Debugger, select Call Stack from the View menu. Figure 8.13 shows the call stack for the FreeSpace script when the debugger is halted within the GetFreeSpace() function.

FIGURE 8.13

The call stack displayed by the Script Debugger for the FreeSpace *script.*

As you can see, the call stack lists the two function levels associated with the current line of code: JScript global code and the GetFreeSpace() function. This list can prove extremely valuable in more complex scripts where you have function calls within function calls.

Dealing with Bugs

Although debugging certainly plays a vital role in eliminating bugs from your scripts, there is another line of defense that in many ways is more valuable. I'm referring to bug prevention, which involves you trying to conscientiously avoid bugs before they're ever created. As an analogy, it is commonly accepted that the most effective way to stay healthy is to practice preventive health care. This means that rather than just trying to take medicine for an illness after the fact, you try to avoid getting sick in the first place. Bug prevention in scripting works in a similar way by trying to initially avoid introducing bugs into a program.

As logical as bug prevention might sound, a surprising number of programmers don't employ enough bug prevention strategies in their code, and they pay for it later in the debugger. Just remember that bug detection is a much more difficult task than bug prevention, so try to focus on eliminating bugs as you develop code the first time around.

As astute as you might be with bug prevention, there will still be situations when you'll have to deal with bugs. Fortunately, both JScript and VBScript include some built-in language features that help handle bugs. In JScript, exception handling is the feature of choice, whereas in VBScript, the Err object comes in handy.

Exception Handling in JScript

Exception handling is something of a bug prevention mechanism in that it involves the detection and resolution of unexpected events that take place while a script is running, such as running out of memory. Exception handling is built into version 5.0 of JScript. An exception is defined as something (usually bad) that occurs in your program that you weren't expecting. In general, you can think of an exception as a type of runtime error.

To handle exceptions in JScript, you use the try-catch statement. The try part of the statement isolates a section of code as having the potential to cause trouble. The catch part of the statement contains special code that is executed if the try code indeed causes trouble. The code in the catch clause is referred to as an exception handler because it attempts to deal with, or handle, the exception.

The try-catch statement is named the way it is because when an exception occurs, it is referred to as being "thrown." Consequently, the code that handles an exception is effectively "catching" the exception and dealing with it. You can manually throw an exception by using the throw statement, like this:

```
if (num < 0)
  throw "num is less than zero"
```

The argument to the throw statement can be any legal JScript expression. The primary reason for throwing an exception is to pass it up to a higher context that you think might be able to better handle it. For example, you might throw an exception out of a function to allow the calling code to handle it. Listing 8.2 shows some code that demonstrates how to catch and throw exceptions in JScript:

LISTING 8.2 CATCHING AND THROWING EXCEPTIONS IN JSCRIPT

```
function NumTest(num) {
  try {
    if (num < 0)
      throw "num is less than zero";
    else if (num == 0)
      throw "num equals zero";
  }
  catch(e) {
    if (e == "num is less than zero")
      alert("LOCAL : " + e);
    else
      throw e;
  }
}

try {
  NumTest(-1);
}
catch(e) {
  alert("GLOBAL : " + e);
}
```

In this code, the NumTest() function throws an exception if the variable num is less than or equal to zero. The catch statement distinguishes between the two types of exceptions; it handles the less than zero exception locally but passes the equals zero exception out of the function. The code calling the function is itself placed in a try-catch statement to catch the exception thrown out of the function. You can test the code by changing the number passed into the NumTest() function.

VBScript and the `Err` Object

JScript isn't alone in providing special features for dealing with runtime errors. VBScript provides a very different approach to handling errors, but one that is useful all the same. The intrinsic `Err` object in VBScript is used to encapsulate information about a runtime error. When a runtime error occurs, the properties of the `Err` object are filled with information that uniquely identifies the error. This information can then be used to handle the error. Following are the different properties of the `Err` object, which reveal information about the current error:

- `Number`—A numeric value that identifies the type of error
- `Description`—A string that describes the error
- `Source`—The name of the object that generated the error
- `HelpFile`—A help file that is displayed when the user clicks Help in the error message window
- `HelpContext`—The context identifier for a topic in the help file

The most important properties of the `Err` object are `Number` and `Description` because they can be used to determine specifics about a given error. The `Err` object also supports the following two methods:

- `Clear()`—Clears all the properties in the object
- `Raise()`—Generates a runtime error and fills in the properties of the object

The `Clear()` method is used to clear the properties of the `Err` object, usually in response to handling an error. The `Raise()` method is roughly equivalent to throwing an exception in JScript because it generates an error using the `Err` object. More specifically, the `Raise()` method fills out the properties of the `Err` object, which can then be used as the basis for handling the error.

The `Err` object must be used with the `On Error Resume Next` VBScript statement to handle errors. The `On Error Resume Next` statement causes script execution to continue with the next statement when a runtime error occurs. By default, VBScript will stop executing a script when a runtime error occurs, which means runtime errors are fatal by default. The `On Error Resume Next` statement is the only way to handle runtime errors in a script.

The `On Error Resume Next` statement enables a script to continue executing even though a runtime error has occurred. The idea is that you will add error-handling code to try to resolve the error so that the script can continue executing safely. Following is a simple example of using the `On Error Resume Next` statement with the `Err` object to handle a runtime error:

```
On Error Resume Next

x = 6
y = 0
z = x / y

if Err.Number <> 0 Then
  MsgBox ("Error # " & CStr(Err.Number) & " " & Err.Description)
  Err.Clear
End If
```

In this example, the On Error Resume Next statement is first issued so that runtime errors won't cause a fatal script halt. Dividing by zero in the calculation of the z variable then intentionally creates a runtime error. The value of the Err.Number property is checked to see if an error has occurred; nonzero values indicate an error. If an error has indeed occurred, its number and description are displayed, and the Err object is cleared.

Avoiding Common Scripting Bugs

Now that you have a solid understanding of bugs, how to detect them, and how to handle with them, shift your attention to common bugs to avoid. Just as people have a tendency to misspell certain words in the English language more than others, script programmers have a tendency to make certain coding mistakes that result in bugs. By understanding these common mistakes, you'll be better equipped to avoid them in your own scripts. Following is my list of common scripting bugs that you should try hard to avoid:

- Assuming the wrong operator precedence
- Accidentally using the assignment (=) operator instead of the comparison operator (==)
- Using wrong data types
- Passing incorrect function and method arguments
- Mistaking the context of an object

The next few sections go into more detail about each of these common coding mistakes and give you some hints to help you to develop habits to avoid making them.

Parentheses and Precedence

A common programming area that is highly susceptible to bugs is operator precedence. I have to admit that I've personally fallen victim to operator precedence bugs in a few situations where I got confused and assumed the wrong operator precedence in an expression. The following VBScript code demonstrates how this can happen:

```
x = 37, y = 26
z = x + y / 7 ^ 8
```

8

All the operators in the second line of this code have different operator precedence. I consider this a risky piece of code because it's difficult to remember the exact precedence of each operator. It's all too easy to write code like this that you think is doing one thing when it is doing quite another. The solution is to explicitly group specific operations within parentheses to force their evaluation. Following is the same sample code with parentheses added to clarify the order of evaluation:

```
x = 37, y = 26
z = (x + (y / 7)) ^ 8
```

Notice how the use of parentheses clearly identifies the order of evaluation of this expression. Additionally, this code ignores operator precedence because the parentheses force the evaluation of each subexpression.

Speaking of parentheses, consider another problem that sometimes creeps into script code: unmatched parentheses. Parentheses always come in pairs, and the specific pairing of parentheses determines many things about the structure of script code, such as the order of operation. If you use an open parenthesis (() without a close parenthesis ()) or vice versa, you will experience some very interesting syntax errors. This same rule applies to curly braces ({}), which must also be paired appropriately.

Assignment and Comparison

The next bug you need to try hard to avoid is so prevalent that there is a programming practice specifically designed to sidestep it. I'm referring to the accidental use of the assignment operator (=) instead of the comparison (==) operator. Of course, this bug only applies to JScript, as VBScript uses the same operator (=) for both assignment and comparison. Take a look at the following code:

```
hungry = false;
if (hungry = true)
  alert("Let's eat!");
```

At a glance, this code looks perfectly fine, but it hides an extremely insidious bug. It is fairly rare that you would perform an assignment within an if conditional, which means that the conditional was intended to use the comparison (==) operator. Because the code looks a lot like it's supposed to and the interpreter doesn't generate a syntax or runtime error, this kind of bug is very hard to detect. Fortunately, there is a very simple programming practice to help keep it from occurring. Check out the modified if conditional:

```
if (true = hungry)
```

Unlike the first example, this code generates an error because it is illegal to assign something to a literal. Of course, this particular example could be further simplified by reducing the if conditional to this:

```
if (hungry)
```

Wrong Data Types

Variables in both VBScript and JScript don't have an explicit data type associated with them. This means that the scripting languages take care of converting data from one type to another depending on the context in which a variable is being used. For example, the following VBScript code shows how a number is automatically used as a string:

```
x = 12
MsgBox x
```

The MsgBox() function expects a string, but VBScript is smart enough to automatically convert the number stored in x to a string. This automatic data type conversion feature is what makes VBScript and JScript loosely-typed languages, which means that variables don't have explicit data types. Although this feature can make the development of scripts much easier, it can sometimes cause problems. For example, you might attempt to pass a number to a function that is expecting a string. The number you pass will automatically be converted to a string, which might or might not be meaningful to the function.

One solution to this problem, other than just being more careful about how you use variables, is to name variables according to their data type. For example, you might name string variables so that they begin with the prefix str. True/false Boolean values could begin with a b. There really is no set standard for this naming convention, so you're free to create your own standard to which you adhere. The main thing is to be consistent about how you name variables.

Following are suggested variable prefixes for VBScript code that are included in the VBScript documentation:

- Boolean—bln
- Byte—byt
- Date—dtm
- Double—dbl
- Error—err
- Integer—int
- Long—lng
- Object—obj
- Single—sng
- String—str

> **Note**
>
> Another issue related to variables is that of always explicitly declaring variables. In VBScript, this requires the use of the Dim statement, whereas in JScript, the var statement does the trick. Explicit variable declaration helps to avoid conflicts between local and global variables.

Function and Method Arguments

The next coding error might sound obvious, but you'd be surprised by how often it causes problems. I'm referring to incorrectly passing arguments to functions and methods. This problem touches on the previous bug I described because it's possible to pass the wrong type of data to a function or method without realizing it. However, this mistake goes further than just mistaking the data types of function and method arguments; it is quite possible to pass arguments to a function or method in the wrong order and not generate an error.

The simple solution to this problem is to double-check the syntax of functions and methods before writing code to call them. The VBScript and JScript documentation is very handy and provides a quick way to verify the arguments to functions and methods. I encourage you to use it whenever possible to avoid passing incorrect arguments.

Mistaken Object Context

The last of the common bugs I want you to steer clear of is attempting to use objects that aren't available in a given context or environment. For example, I mentioned earlier in the lesson that the WScript object is unique to WSH and isn't available when testing a script in a Web browser. It can be frustrating trying to use such an object in a Web browser script because Web browsers aren't always good about reporting unknown object references. In other words, it's possible that an unknown object reference would just do nothing.

Summary

This lesson introduced you to the exciting and frustrating world of script bugs, which are typically uncovered during the testing phase of script development. Okay, bugs aren't very exciting, but they sure can be frustrating! You learned in this lesson about the different types of errors that can rear their ugly heads in script code. Fortunately, you also learned some tips and techniques to help you track down and deal with bugs. One of these techniques involves the use of the Microsoft Script Debugger, which enables you to carefully determine the nature of script bugs. The lesson concluded by explaining some common script bugs and how to avoid them.

Q&A

Q Can I use a `.vbs` or `.js` script file directly in Microsoft's Script Debugger?

A No. Unfortunately, the Script Debugger is designed to debug scripts that reside in Web pages, which means that the Script Debugger operates on `.html` files with scripts embedded in them. You can circumvent this limitation to some extent by cutting and pasting script code into a "dummy" Web page for the purposes of debugging.

Q How can I avoid single-stepping through a loop with a lot of iterations in the Script Debugger?

A To avoid having to single-step through a lengthy loop, you can place a breakpoint just after the loop and then select Run from the Debug menu to run the script. The script will finish executing the loop and stop at the breakpoint following the loop.

Q Is it possible to filter and only handle certain types of VBScript errors using the `Err` object?

A Yes. The `Err.Number` property is a unique identifier that identifies the error type, which means that you can check this number to ignore certain types of errors. For example, the "Divide by zero" error code is 11, so you can check for the `Err.Number` property being set to 11 and do nothing to ignore "Divide by zero" errors.

DAY 9

Handling WSH Script Arguments and Reading/Writing Files

In this chapter you're going to cover some meat and potatoes topics. You're going to see how you can use arguments with your WSH scripts, and you'll see how you can use WSH scripts to read and write text files. For each, you'll see detailed examples that show you practical applications of the techniques discussed in the text. Before you dive into the detailed examples, you'll look at basic examples that will help you to understand the concepts.

On the ninth day of your introduction to WSH, you'll do the following:

- See how you can customize your WSH scripts with arguments and validate the arguments to ensure that they are correct
- Learn about reading and writing text files
- Dig into detailed examples that show complex arguments, a function that makes it easy to write log files, and a function for parsing INI files

Handling WSH Script Arguments and Reading and Writing Files

This chapter covers some standard techniques for handling arguments and manipulating files that you can use in many of your WSH scripts. For each task, you'll read about the purpose of the task, how it relates to the functions that you might use for your script, and finally, how you can implement code to perform the task.

First, you're going to take a look at how you can process the arguments for your script. You'll look at simple case arguments, arguments with different data types, and finally, complex arguments that require parsing. Next, you'll learn how you can read and write files, and you'll put the techniques into practice with functions that enable you to read and write .INI files and produce log files. When you finish this chapter, you'll have added some additional techniques to your scripting bag of tricks.

Processing Script Arguments

All scripts have the capability to take command-line arguments. When a script runs, the WSH scripting environment grabs any of the parameters that were specified on the command line and incorporates them into an object that is exposed as a property of the standard Wscript object. The property is called Arguments and it is implemented as a Collection object with one element for each of the command-line parameters. Each of the elements is a String that represents the argument.

For standard scripts, script arguments are the way that users interact with them. One of the reasons for this is the limitation of the WSH user interface. There's relatively little that you can do as the script is running to prompt the user for additional information. Consequently, command-line arguments are a popular way to enable users to control the behavior of WSH scripts. In the next few sections, you'll see how you can implement support for arguments for your scripts.

Accessing Arguments

You can retrieve the arguments for your script using the Wscript.Arguments property. When you access the command-line arguments through Wscript.Arguments, you can access them one by one, or you can access them using the VBScript For..Each statement. Here's a quick VBScript example that shows how you can access the arguments sequentially:

```
Dim iArg
Dim oArgs

Set oArgs = Wscript.Arguments
```

```
For iArg = 0 to oArgs.Count - 1
    Wscript.Echo "Arg #" & iArg & ": " & oArgs(iArg)
Next
```

If you run the preceding script using `cscript.exe`, it simply dumps the input arguments
to the console. The equivalent JScript follows, and the result of running the script is
shown in Figure 9.1:

```
var iArg;
var oArgs = WScript.Arguments;

for (iArg = 0; iArg < oArgs.length; iArg++) {
    WScript.echo("Arg #" + iArg + ": " + oArgs(iArg));
}
```

FIGURE 9.1

*Dumping arguments to
the screen.*

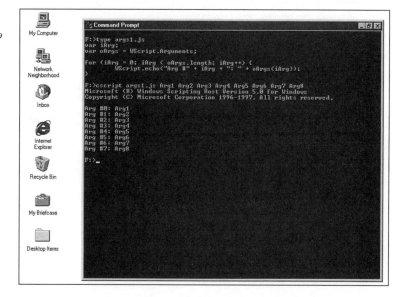

If you're using VBScript, it might be slightly more convenient to use the `For..Each`
statement. Here's an example that illustrates how you can dump the arguments using
`For..Each`:

```
Dim sArg
Dim oArgs

Set oArgs = Wscript.Arguments

For Each sArg In oArgs
    Wscript.Echo "Arg: " & sArg
Next
```

In JScript, the `for..in` statement provides basically the same functionality. However, in practice, the `for..in` statement appears to be much more limited than the VBScript `For..Each` statement. If you attempt to use `for..in` to iterate through the `Wscript.Arguments` collection, it will most likely fail.

Checking for Sufficient Arguments

As you can tell from the preceding code, accessing arguments from within a script is easy. However, the fact that you can access them doesn't mean that users specified valid parameters. In this section, you're going to look at how you can implement validation for your command-line script parameters.

The first and most basic check is a check to determine if sufficient parameters were specified. This is a very easy check to implement using either VBScript or JScript. Here's a common pattern to check for sufficient parameters for VBScript:

```
Dim oArgs

Set oArgs = Wscript.Arguments

'
' This script takes three parameters; check to ensure that the count
' of parameters is three. If it isn't, display the usage of the script
' and quit
'
If oArgs.Count <> 3 Then
    Wscript.Echo "USAGE:  myscript  [arg1] [arg2] [arg3]"
    Wscript.Echo ""
    Wscript.Echo "        This script ..."
    Wscript.Quit 1
End If

'
' The rest of the script follows...
'
```

The equivalent check using JScript is shown in the following code snippet:

```
var oArgs = WScript.arguments;

//
// This script takes three parameters; check to ensure that the count
// of parameters is three. If it isn't, display the usage of the script
// and quit
//
if (oArgs.length != 3) {
    WScript.echo("USAGE:  myscript  [arg1] [arg2] [arg3]");
    WScript.echo("");
    WScript.echo("        This script ...");
    WScript.quit(1);
}
```

```
//
// The rest of the script follows...
//
```

The previous check handles the most basic question: Did your script get all the arguments that it needs? In the next sections, you'll look at some more complex command-line argument validation. First, you'll look at how you can validate argument data types, and then you'll see how you can perform advanced command-line parsing.

Checking Argument Data Types

What if one of your arguments needs to be a number or a date? All the arguments are captured as strings. No validation is automatically done to ensure that arguments are particular data types. You have to implement your own validation. Suppose that you have a script that takes a number of iterations as an argument. You need to ensure that the number of iterations specified on the command line is actually a number. Here's an example, implemented using VBScript, that shows a check for the type of command-line argument:

LISTING 9.1 doecho.vbs—SCRIPT USING A NUMERIC COMMAND-LINE PARAMETER

```
Dim oArgs
Dim cIterations
Dim iIteration
Dim sMessage

Set oArgs = Wscript.Arguments

'
' Check the number of arguments that were specified on the command
line.
' If insufficient arguments were specified, display a usage message.
'
If oArgs.Count <> 2 Then
    Wscript.Echo "USAGE:  doecho [iterations] [message]"
    Wscript.Echo ""
    Wscript.Echo "        Displays the [message] for the"
    Wscript.Echo "        number of iterations specified in"
    Wscript.Echo "        the [iterations] parameter."
    Wscript.Quit 1
End If

'
' Now check the data type of the iterations parameter. It is the
' first argument (position 0) in the Arguments collection.
'
```

continues

LISTING 9.1 CONTINUED

```
If Not IsNumeric(oArgs(0)) Then
    Wscript.Echo "Error: The [iterations] parameter must be a "
    Wscript.Echo "           number. Instead it was '" & oArgs(0) &
"'."
    Wscript.Quit 1
End If

'
' The iterations parameter was a valid number, so iterate and
' display the message.
'
cIterations = CInt(oArgs(0))
sMessage = oArgs(1)
For iIteration = 1 to cIterations
    Wscript.Echo sMessage
Next
```

The previous script first checks to ensure that sufficient arguments are specified on the command line. If insufficient arguments are specified, it displays a usage message and terminates. Assuming that there are enough arguments, it checks to ensure that the iterations parameter is a number using the VBScript IsNumeric() function. If the iterations parameter is not a number, the script terminates and displays and error message. Otherwise, it's used in a loop to show a message; Figure 9.2 shows the results of running the script.

FIGURE 9.2

Output from the doecho.vbs script.

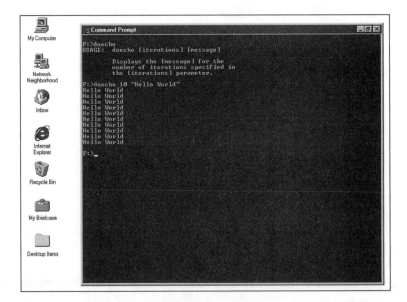

Take a look at the equivalent script using JScript. Here's the JScript code that implements the argument checking and message display loop:

LISTING 9.2   doecho.js—SCRIPT USING A NUMERIC COMMAND-LINE PARAMETER

```
var oArgs = WScript.Arguments;
var cIterations;
var iIteration;
var sMessage;

//
// Check the number of arguments that were specified on the command line.
// If insufficient arguments were specified, display a usage message.
//
if (oArgs.length != 2) {
    WScript.echo("USAGE:  doecho [iterations] [message]");
    WScript.echo("");
    WScript.echo("          Displays the [message] for the");
    WScript.echo("          number of iterations specified in");
    WScript.echo("          the [iterations] parameter.");
    WScript.quit(1);
}


//
// Now check the data type of the iterations parameter. It is the
// first argument (position 0) in the Arguments collection.
//
cIterations = parseInt(oArgs(0));
if (cIterations == NaN) {
    WScript.echo("Error: The [iterations] parameter must be a ");
    WScript.echo("          number. Instead it was '" + oArgs(0) + "'.");
    WScript.quit(1);
}


//
// The iterations parameter was a valid number, so iterate and
// display the message.
//
sMessage = oArgs(1)
for (iIteration = 1; iIteration <= cIterations; iIteration++) {
    WScript.echo(sMessage);
}
```

You can use a similar type of check to determine if a command-line parameter is a date. Dates can be very useful as parameters for your WSH scripts. You might want to have an archive script, for example, that archives all files older than a certain date. Another example is perhaps you have a script that performs a quick extract from a database. It can take a date parameter to provide a filter for the extract.

The next sample script takes a date parameter. Using the date, it filters and displays a list of the files in a folder that are older than that date:

LISTING 9.3   chkfiles.vbs—USING A COMMAND-LINE DATE PARAMETER

```
Dim oArgs
Dim dFile
Dim fso
Dim sFolder
Dim folder
Dim file

Set oArgs = Wscript.Arguments

'
' Check for sufficient arguments on the command line.
'
If oArgs.Count <> 2 Then
    Wscript.Echo "USAGE:  chkfiles [date] [folder]"
    Wscript.Echo ""
    Wscript.Echo "        Displays a list of the files in [folder]"
    Wscript.Echo "        that are older than the specified [date]."
    Wscript.Quit 1
End If

'
' Check the data type of the date parameter. It is the
' first argument (position 0) in the Arguments collection.
'
If Not IsDate(oArgs(0)) Then
    Wscript.Echo "Error: The [date] parameter must be a date value."
    Wscript.Echo "        Instead it was '" & oArgs(0) & "'."
    Wscript.Quit 1
End If
dFile = CDate(oArgs(0))

'
' Check to determine if the folder that was specified is a
' valid folder.
'
sFolder = oArgs(1)
Set fso = Wscript.CreateObject("Scripting.FileSystemObject")
If Not fso.FolderExists(sFolder) Then
    Wscript.Echo "Error: The [folder] parameter must be a " & _
"valid folder."
```

```
    Wscript.Echo "        Instead it was '" & sFolder & "'."
    Wscript.Quit 1
End If

'
' All parameters are valid, so open the folder and search for files are
' older than the specified date.
'
Wscript.Echo "chkfile.vbs: Displaying files older than '" & dFile &
➥"' in "
Wscript.Echo "                the '" & sFolder & "' folder."
Wscript.Echo "----------------------------------------------------------"
Set folder = fso.GetFolder(sFolder)
For Each file In folder.Files
    '
    ' Check the date of the file; if the date is older than the date
    ' specified on the command line, print the name of the file.
    '
    If file.DateLastModified < dFile Then
        Wscript.Echo file.Name & " (" & file.DateLastModified & ")"
    End If
Next
```

When the preceding script runs, it first checks to see if sufficient arguments were specified on the command line. This script requires two parameters; the user must specify a date to check files and the name of the folder to check within. After checking the number of arguments, it checks the type of the date parameter using the VBScript `IsDate()` function. If the parameter is not a date, the script terminates with an error message.

The next check performed by the script is an important one to note. It checks to determine if the folder is a valid folder using the `FileSystemObject.FolderExists()` method. The `FileSystemObject` has convenient methods that you can use to validate files and folders specified on the command line. For more information about the `FileSystemObject`, check Day 3, "The Scripting Object Model."

Assuming that both parameters are correct, the script grabs the specified folder and iterates through the files in the folder. The date for each file is checked using the file object's `DateLastModified` property. If the date is older than the date specified on the command line, the name of the file is printed with the date. You can easily extend this script to turn it into an archiving script. The output of the script is illustrated in Figure 9.3.

FIGURE 9.3

*Output from the
chkfiles.vbs script.*

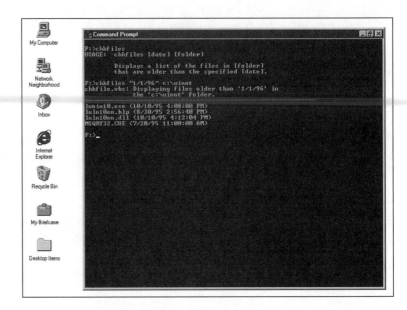

FIGURE 9.3

*Output from the
chkfiles.vbs script.*

Advanced Command-line Parsing

So far, you've covered basic use of command line arguments. The most sophisticated check that you've done is to check for the type of a parameter. Frequently, you might want to have much more complex arguments for your scripts. Take a look at an example of a command that takes complex arguments.

The standard DIR command, which has been used by literally anyone who has used Windows or DOS (well, everyone who's used DOS has used it), takes a substantial number of parameters. Figure 9.4 shows the parameters for DIR—which literally take up the entire screen!

DIR is typical of many of the command-line–driven utilities. Literally all the standard command-line utilities that come with Windows support some type of command-line arguments that enable the user to change the way that they work. You can implement the same type of sophisticated support for flexible command arguments in your scripts.

As an example, you're going to examine a script called mydir.vbs. The script doesn't do much; it's essentially a customized DIR command. It might not be too useful for you directly, but it's very likely that the techniques demonstrated within it will be useful for you as you implement your own scripts. The script takes one mandatory argument—the name of the folder for which you want to display the directory. It also takes the following three optional arguments: -a causes the script to display file attributes; -f logs the output of the script to a file; and -h displays a header before the directory listing. The listing of the script follows:

FIGURE 9.4

The parameters for the DIR command.

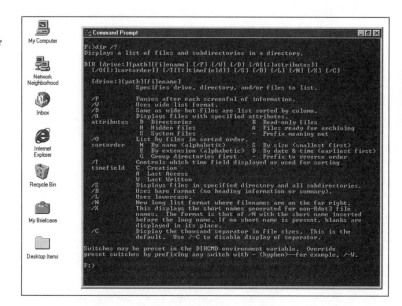

LISTING 9.4   mydir.vbs—ADVANCED COMMAND-LINE ARGUMENT PARSING

```
On Error Resume Next

'
' File Attribute Constants
'
Const Normal = 0
Const ReadOnly = 1
Const Hidden = 2
Const System = 4
Const Volume = 8
Const Directory = 16
Const Archive = 32
Const Alias = 64
Const Compressed = 128


'
' Execution flags
'
```

continues

LISTING 9.4   CONTINUED

```
Dim ShowAttribs
Dim ShowHeader
Dim LogFile


' Set default values for all of the execution flags
'
ShowAttribs = False
ShowHeader = False
LogFile = ""


' Miscellaneous variables
'
Dim oArgs
Dim sFolder
Dim folder
Dim fso
Dim iArg
Dim tsLog
Dim file
Dim sOutput


' Check the argument count and display a usage message if
' insufficient arguments are specified.
'
Set oArgs = Wscript.Arguments
If oArgs.Count < 1 Then
    Wscript.Echo "USAGE: mydir [folder] [options]"
    Wscript.Echo ""
    Wscript.Echo "        This displays a directory listing"
    Wscript.Echo "        of the [folder]. You may specify"
    Wscript.Echo "        the following optional parameters:"
    Wscript.Echo ""
    Wscript.Echo "        -a              Displays attributes"
    Wscript.Echo "        -fLogFile       Writes output to a log"
    Wscript.Echo "        -h              Output verbose header"
    Wscript.Quit 1
End If


' The first parameter should be a valid folder; check it using the
' FileSystemObject
'
sFolder = oArgs(0)
Set fso = Wscript.CreateObject("Scripting.FileSystemObject")
If Not fso.FolderExists(sFolder) Then
```

```
        Wscript.Echo "Error: The folder '" & sFolder & "' doesn't exist."
        Wscript.Quit 1
End If
Set folder = fso.GetFolder(sFolder)

'
' Now, for each of the remaining arguments, check the argument and set
' a flag if necessary. The flags will be used later as the script
' executes.
'
' Note that we start with the second argument, position one, instead
' of starting from the first argument at position 0 because we used it
' for the folder name.
'
For iArg = 1 to oArgs.Count - 1
    '
    ' Every argument must be at least two characters long so we
    ' check the length first
    '
    If Len(oArgs(iArg)) < 2 Then
        Wscript.Echo "Error: Invalid parameter format for '" & _
                oArgs(iArg) & "'."
        Wscript.Quit 1
    End If


    '
    ' Next we use "Select Case" to check each argument. Before we
' check each argument, we make sure that it is lowercase. That
    ' removes any case sensitivity. If an argument does not match
' one of the expected arguments, we output an error message
' with the invalid argument.
    '
    Select Case LCase(Left(oArgs(iArg), 2))
        Case "-a"
            '
            ' The -a argument indicates that the user wants the
            ' directory listing to include file attribute
            ' information. We set a global flag that will be used
            ' later.
            '
            ShowAttribs = True

        Case "-f"
            '
            ' The -f argument is used to specify a file that
' should be used for output from the script.
            '
            ' We strip off the filename by taking everything after
            ' the initial -f.
```

continues

LISTING 9.4   CONTINUED

```
            '
            LogFile = Right(oArgs(iArg), Len(oArgs(iArg)) - 2)
            If LogFile = "" Then
                Wscript.Echo "Error: If you specify the -F " & _
"flag, you must also specify a filename."
                Wscript.Quit 1
            End If

        Case "-h"
            '
            ' The -h argument indicates that the user wants
' the script to output a header for the directory
' listing.
            '
            ShowHeader = True

        Case Else
            Wscript.Echo "Error: Unrecognized parameter '" & _
                oArgs(iArg) & "'."
            Wscript.Quit 1
    End Select
Next

'
' All of the arguments have been parsed, so now we begin the meat
' of the script execution.
'


'
' First, open the logging file if one was specified.
'
If LogFile <> "" Then
    Set tsLog = fso.CreateTextFile(LogFile, True)
    If Err.Number <> 0 Then
        Wscript.Echo "Error: Unable to create logging file '" & _
LogFile & "'."
        Wscript.Echo "        (" & Err.Number & ") " & _
Err.Description
        Wscript.Quit Err.Number
    End If
Else
    Set tsLog = Nothing
End If

'
' Second, output the header to the log file and the screen if the user
' specified the show header flag (-h).
'
If ShowHeader Then
```

```vbs
    Dim sHeader
    sHeader = "---- mydir.vbs " & Now & " ----"
    WriteOutput sHeader
    WriteOutput "Arguments: "
    WriteOutput "      Show directory for " & sFolder & "."
    If ShowAttribs Then
        WriteOutput "      Show file attributes."
    End If
    If ShowHeader Then
        WriteOutput "      Show file header."
    End If
    If LogFile <> "" Then
        WriteOutput "      Log output to file '" & LogFile & "'."
    End If
    WriteOutput String(Len(sHeader), "-")
    WriteOutput ""
End If


' Show a header for the file listing
'
If Not ShowAttribs Then
    WriteOutput RPad("File", " ", 30) & " " & _
LPad("Created", " ", 20)
    WriteOutput String(30, "-") & " " & String(20, "-")
Else
    WriteOutput RPad("File", " ", 30) & " " & _
LPad("Created", " ", 20) & _
        " Attributes"
    WriteOutput String(30, "-") & " " & String(20, "-") & " " & _
        String(15, "-")
End If


' Finally, we iterate through the files in the directory and display
' information about them.
'
For Each file In folder.Files
    sOutput = RPad(file.Name, " ", 30) & " " & _
        LPad(file.DateCreated, " ", 20)

    '
    ' Add the attribute details to the output if the ShowAttribs
    ' flag is set.
    '
    If ShowAttribs Then
        Dim sAttrs
        sAttrs = ""
```

continues

LISTING **9.4**   CONTINUED

```
              If file.Attributes = Normal Then
                  sAttrs = sAttrs & "Normal, "
              End If
              If file.Attributes And ReadOnly Then
                  sAttrs = sAttrs & "ReadOnly, "
              End If
              If file.Attributes And Hidden Then
                  sAttrs = sAttrs & "Hidden, "
              End If
              If file.Attributes And System Then
                  sAttrs = sAttrs & "System, "
              End If
              If file.Attributes And Archive Then
                  sAttrs = sAttrs & "Archive, "
              End If
              If file.Attributes And Alias Then
                  sAttrs = sAttrs & "Alias, "
              End If
              If file.Attributes And Compressed Then
                  sAttrs = sAttrs & "Compressed, "
              End If


              '
              ' Strip off trailing ', '
              '
              sAttrs = Left(sAttrs, Len(sAttrs) - 2)
              sOutput = sOutput & " " & sAttrs
          End If
          WriteOutput sOutput
     Next

     Wscript.Quit 0

     '----------------------------------------------------------------
     ' SUB:  WriteOutput(sLine)
     ' DESC: Writes a single line of output to the display and/or log
     '       file if a log file was specified.
     '----------------------------------------------------------------
     Sub WriteOutput(sLine)
         Wscript.Echo sLine
         If Not tsLog Is Nothing Then
             tsLog.WriteLine sLine
         End If
     End Sub


     '----------------------------------------------------------------
     ' FUNC: Pad(sToPad, sPadding, nLength)
     ' DESC: Pads the 'sToPad' to the length specified by 'nLength'
```

```
'         using the 'sPadding' string.
'----------------------------------------------------------------
Function Pad(sToPad, sPadding, nLength)
    Pad = RPad(sToPad, sPadding, nLength)
End Function


'----------------------------------------------------------------
' FUNC: LPad(sToPad, sPadding, nLength)
' DESC: Pads the 'sToPad' to the length specified by 'nLength'
'         using the 'sPadding' string on the left of the string.
'----------------------------------------------------------------
Function LPad(sToPad, sPadding, nLength)
    If Len(sToPad) >= nLength Then
        LPad = sToPad
    Else
        LPad = String(nLength - Len(sToPad), sPadding) & sToPad
    End If
End Function


'----------------------------------------------------------------
' FUNC: RPad(sToPad, sPadding, nLength)
' DESC: Pads the 'sToPad' to the length specified by 'nLength'
'         using the 'sPadding' string on the right of the string.
'----------------------------------------------------------------
Function RPad(sToPad, sPadding, nLength)
    If Len(sToPad) >= nLength Then
        RPad = sToPad
    Else
        RPad = sToPad & String(nLength - Len(sToPad), sPadding)
    End If
End Function
```

The result of running the script is illustrated in Figure 9.5. You can see a list of files that shows the filename, date created, and file attributes.

The script begins with a check for the mandatory folder argument and then a check to ensure that the folder that was specified is really a valid folder. Next, there's a loop that iterates through the remaining arguments. The first two characters of each argument are checked using a Select Case statement. For each argument, a global flag is set or in the case of the file output, a filename is set.

After the arguments are checked, the script loops through the files in the specified folder and displays the information about each file. The script is peppered with descriptive comments, so if you want to learn more about how it works, just refer to the script code.

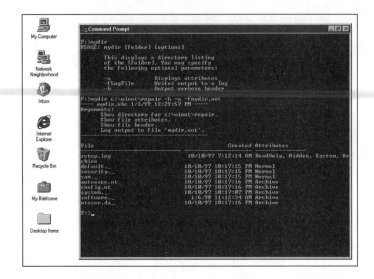

FIGURE 9.5

*File listing from the
mydir.vbs script.*

You can use this script as a starting point for scripts of your own. You can make the arguments for your scripts as complex or as simple as you want. Just remember not to make it so complex that a user has difficulty understanding how to use your script!

Reading and Writing Files

The capability to read and write files is essential if you want your script to be able to interact more with its environment. For example, you might want to have a script that creates a log file to document the functions that it performs. Alternatively, you might want to implement a script that uses an .INI file to store settings that change the script behavior. Those are two simple, common examples, both of which you'll explore in the following sections.

Introduction to Opening, Reading, and Writing Files

When you want to read or write files from your WSH scripts, you use the FileSystemObject. The FileSystemObject provides two methods that are essential for you: OpenTextFile() opens an existing text file, and CreateTextFile() creates a new text file. Each method returns a TextStream object. You use the TextStream methods to read or write the file.

Note

> It's important to be aware of file permission issues when you're trying to read and write files. If you're using the Windows NT operating system and the NTFS file system, any files may be protected with permission settings that may restrict the users that are allowed to read or write the files.

9

> You should make sure to incorporate error-handling for insufficient file per-
> missions within your code if you plan to use it under Windows NT.

The following short script shows how a file can be created and written to:

```
Dim fso
Dim ts
Dim i

If Wscript.Arguments.Count <> 1 Then
    Wscript.Echo "USAGE: makfile.vbs [file]"
    Wscript.Echo ""
    Wscript.Echo "        Creates a sample file."
    Wscript.Quit 1
End If

Set fso = Wscript.CreateObject("Scripting.FileSystemObject")
Set ts = fso.CreateTextFile(Wscript.Arguments(0))

ts.WriteLine "Example script!"

For i = 1 to 10
    ts.WriteLine "Hello World!"
Next
ts.Close

Wscript.Echo "File '" & Wscript.Arguments(0) & "' was created."
```

If you run the script and use the type command to display the results, you see something
like Figure 9.6.

FIGURE 9.6

*Results from the file
creation example.*

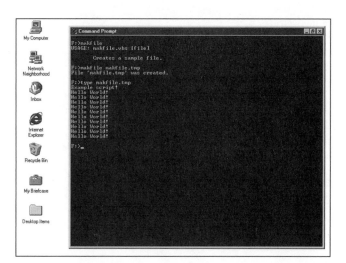

The script uses the `FileSystemObject.CreateTextFile()` method to create a text file. `CreateTextFile()` returns a `TextStream` object, which is then used to write some lines to the file.

That's file read and write access in a nutshell! To give you some additional help getting started, you're going to examine some additional techniques in the following two sections.

Writing Log Files

Writing log files is easy. You can implement your own text logs using techniques similar to those shown in the previous script. Alternatively, you can wrap log file access in a function so that it's even easier to use. You do so in the following script:

LISTING 9.5   WRITING LOG FILES USING A FUNCTION

```
Const ScriptName = "Logging Example"
Const LogFile = "logtest.log"

'
' Variable to hold the text stream for the log file
'
Dim Log
Set Log = Nothing

'
' Script code begins here
'
LogEvent "Script Startup..."

Wscript.Echo "This script does nothing but count from one to ten."
Dim i
For i = 1 to 10
    Wscript.Echo i
Next
LogEvent "Count from one to ten completed successfully."

'
' Now we output an end message and exit the script
'
LogEvent "Script finished."
Wscript.Quit 0

'-----------------------------------------------------------------
' SUB:  LogEvent(sEvent)
' DESC: Writes an event to the log file for the current script.
'-----------------------------------------------------------------
Sub LogEvent(sEvent)
```

```
    On Error Resume Next
    If Log Is Nothing Then
        Dim fso
        Set fso = Wscript.CreateObject("Scripting.FileSystemObject")
        Set Log = fso.CreateTextFile(LogFile, True)
        If Err.Number <> 0 Then
            Wscript.Echo "Error: Unable to create log file. Terminating."
            Wscript.Echo "         (" & Err.Number & ") " & Err.Description
            Wscript.Quit Err.Number
        End If
    End If
    Log.WriteLine ScriptName & ": " & sEvent
End Sub
```

The script wraps access to the log file within the LogEvent() function. LogEvent() takes care of all the details of opening and writing to the log file. First, it checks to determine whether a log file is currently open. If a log file is not open, it opens it. Next, it writes the event to the log file, preceded by a descriptive name for the script. The results of running the script are depicted in Figure 9.7.

FIGURE 9.7

Output from the logging demonstration.

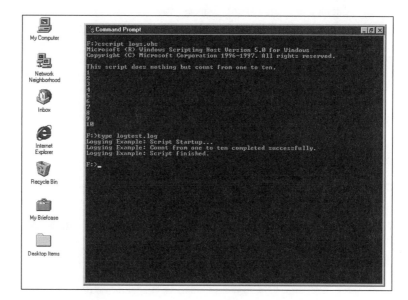

If you want, you can incorporate this logging function directly into your scripts. To incorporate the logging function into your script, you must include the ScriptName and LogFile constants, the Log variable, and the body of the LogEvent() subroutine.

Parsing .INI Files

For your next example, you're going to look at how you can access .INI files from WSH scripts. Initialization files, or text files that typically end with the extension .INI and have lines in the format *settingname=value*, are used by programs to store settings. These days, most programs store their settings in the Windows Registry, but many continue to use .INI files because they are convenient and make it very easy for users to change file settings.

You're going to take a look at a script example that shows how you can open and parse an .INI file. The following script contains a function called ParseINI(). The function opens and reads an .INI file and returns the values from the file in a Dictionary object. Take a look at the following code for it:

LISTING 9.6   ACCESSING .INI FILES

```
Dim dicIni, aItems, aKeys, i

'
' Check for sufficient arguments
'
If Wscript.Arguments.Count <> 1 Then
    Wscript.Echo "USAGE: parseini [file]"
    Wscript.Echo ""
    Wscript.Echo "        Parses the .ini file specified by"
    Wscript.Echo "        the [file] parameter."
    Wscript.Quit 1
End If

'
' Attempt to parse the .INI file
'
Set dicIni = ParseINI(Wscript.Arguments(0))

'
' Now display a count of the parameters found in the .INI file
'
Wscript.Echo "Finished reading '" & Wscript.Arguments(0) & "', " & _
    dicIni.Count & " parameters were found."
Wscript.Echo ""
Wscript.Echo "The parameters are listed below:"

'
' Dump the parameters listing from the dictionary object returned
' by ParseINI()
'
aItems = dicIni.Items
aKeys = dicIni.Keys
```

```
For i = LBound(aItems) To UBound(aItems)
    Wscript.Echo "'" & aKeys(i) & "' has value '" & aItems(i) "'."
Next

Wscript.Quit 0


'----------------------------------------------------------------
' FUNC: ParseINI(sIniFilename)
' DESC: This function returns a dictionary object containing the
'       settings from an INI file.
'----------------------------------------------------------------
Function ParseINI(sIniFilename)
    On Error Resume Next

    Dim fso
    Dim tsIni
    Dim iEquals
    Dim sKey
    Dim sVal

    Set ParseINI = Wscript.CreateObject("Scripting.Dictionary")
    Set fso = Wscript.CreateObject("Scripting.FileSystemObject")

    '
    ' Attempt to open the INI file and return if it fails
    '
    Set tsIni = fso.OpenTextFile(sIniFilename)
    If Err.Number <> 0 Then
        Wscript.Echo "Error: Unable to open .INI file '" & _
            sIniFilename & "'."
        Wscript.Echo "       (" & Err.Number & ") " & _
Err.Description
        Exit Function
    End If

    '
    ' Iterate through the contents of the INI file, reading one line
    ' at a time.
    '
    ' Each line in the INI file is expected to either be a comment,
' and begin with 'a', or is expected to be a setting definition
' in the format "name=value".
    '
    Do While Not tsIni.AtEndOfStream
        sLine = Trim(tsIni.ReadLine)
        If sLine <> "" Then
            If Left(sLine, 1) = "'" Then
                '
                ' This line is a comment, so ignore it.
                '
```

continues

LISTING 9.6 CONTINUED

```
        Else
            '
            ' Find the equals sign in the current line
            '
            iEquals = InStr(1, sLine, "=")
            If (iEquals <= 1) Then
                Wscript.Echo "Error: The following INI " & _
                    "line is invalid - '" & sLine & "'."
            Else
                '
                ' We've found a name and value pair
                '
                sKey = Left(sLine, iEquals - 1)
                sVal = Right(sLine, Len(sLine) - iEquals)


                '
                ' Add the key and value to the dictionary
                '
                ParseINI.Add sKey, sVal
                If Err.Number <> 0 Then
                    Wscript.Echo "Error: Unable to add " & _
                        "value '" & sVal & "' to " & _
                        "dictionary using key '" & sKey & "'"
                    Wscript.Echo "          (" & Err.Number & _
                        ") " & Err.Description
                End If
            End If
        End If
    End If
    Loop
End Function
```

The heart of the script example is in the ParseINI() function. The function first opens the .INI file specified on the command line. After the file is open, the function executes a loop that reads each line from the file. As each line is read, the line is checked to determine if it is a comment line, which begins with the ' character, or is a line in the format *Name=Value*. If it is in the format *Name=Value*, the name and value are parsed from the line, and the value is inserted into the Dictionary using the name as its key.

Figure 9.8 shows the output from the script after it has parsed a test.ini file. If you want, you can use the ParseINI() function verbatim in your scripts. It's particularly convenient because it hides all the logic of .INI file access from you and because it returns the .INI files in a Dictionary object, which makes it very easy for you to check specific .INI settings.

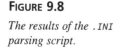

FIGURE 9.8

The results of the .INI parsing script.

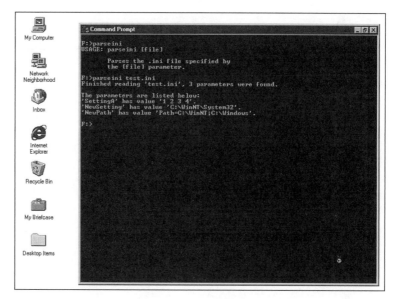

9

Summary

In this chapter, you've looked at some typical tasks that you need to accomplish with your WSH scripts. First, you looked at script argument handling. Script argument handling is basically pretty simple; it doesn't really get complex until your script requires complex parameters. If you extend your scripts by enabling them to take command-line parameters or arguments, you should include script argument validation as you did in the examples.

Next, you looked at file input and output. For file output, you took a look at how you can implement a logging function for your script. You can use the same techniques in the logging function to write any text file. For file input, you looked at an example that showed how you could open, read, and parse an .INI file. Again, the same techniques and function calls apply to any text file that you would read through a WSH script.

Hopefully, this chapter gives you some good ideas to help you implement functionality in your scripts and make your scripts robust! Subsequent chapters will provide additional techniques and details that will help you to write even more powerful WSH scripts.

Q&A

Q How can you tell how many parameters were specified on the command line for a script?

A You can use the Count property of the arguments collection that is accessed using the Wscript.Arguments property.

Q Can you read or write binary files using the standard WSH capabilities?

A No, you cannot. WSH only supports text files directly.

Q Which object is used to read or write a text file?

A The TextStream object is used to read or write a text file.

Workshop

The following section will help you test your comprehension of the material presented in this chapter and put what you've learned into practice. You'll find the answers to the quiz and exercises in Appendix A.

Quiz

1. What functions can you use to check the data type of script arguments?

2. Why is the Dictionary object particularly convenient to store .INI settings when they are read into memory?

3. What object can be used to verify files or folders that are specified as arguments for your script?

Exercises

1. Extend the script example that took a date parameter to take a range of dates instead.

2. Use the script from Exercise 1 to implement an archiving utility.

3. Create a script that can change settings in .INI files.

DAY 10

Replacing Batch Files with WSH Scripts

In this chapter, you're going to juxtapose the Windows Scripting Host with the original automation solution for the Windows platform—batch files. You'll learn the history of batch files, take a look at typical uses of them, examine some of their limitations, and then see how you can replace their functionality with more robust WSH scripts.

On the 10th day of your introduction to WSH, you'll

- Look at the history of Windows batch files and evaluate some of their limitations
- Compare batch file syntax with WSH script syntax
- See examples that illustrate how you can replace batch file techniques with corresponding WSH functionality

Batch File Background

Literally anyone who has used DOS or some flavor of Windows has run into batch files. If you've been using Microsoft operating systems for a while, you've probably had to run a SETUP.BAT file at one time or another. Certainly, if you're an administrator, you've no doubt run batch files, but you've also probably written them. If you've written batch files, you've no doubt been frustrated at one time or another by their very minimal capabilities.

In this chapter, you'll first read about the history of batch files, the limitations of batch files, the enhanced capabilities of WSH, and finally how you can replace your batch files with WSH scripts.

The History Of Batch Files

Batch files are the original automated "scripting" solution for the DOS platform. The DOS shell included a command interpreter that was able to run a sequence of DOS commands embedded in a plain text file, called a batch file, with the extension .BAT. The batch file can contain any standard DOS command; for example, it can contain the DIR command to display a directory listing. It can also call executable programs. You can use this capability to call your own programs, to call programs built into DOS (such as SORT), or to perform automated tasks using something like FTP. Batch files can also contain some rudimentary logic including branching using IF statements, iteration using GOTO, loops for multiple files using the FOR statement, and output to the user using ECHO. Figure 10.1 shows an example of a batch file that displays a partial directory listing and then pauses to wait for user input.

The batch file interpreter from DOS was incorporated into the original Windows 16-bit platform. When Windows NT was created, it also included the batch interpreter. Consequently, for years people have been limited to very basic command scripting capabilities on the Windows platform.

To be fair, over the years batch files have evolved slightly. The syntax for the aforementioned batch commands has changed a bit: Each of the commands has become a little more functional, and DOS/Windows has incorporated additional command programs, such as deltree, that can be leveraged within batch files. However, the basic capabilities for control over program flow remain unchanged. The limitations for program flow and automation have been eliminated with the introduction of WSH.

FIGURE 10.1

A simple example of a batch file.

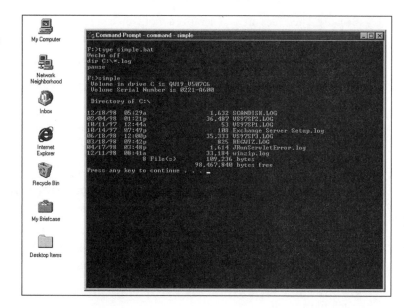

Typical Uses Of Batch Files

On the Windows platforms, batch files are basically used for any type of automated command scripting! Some of the standard uses for batch files include the following:

- **Shortcuts for commands**   The command lines for some console commands can get relatively long or be difficult to remember due to complex parameters. People frequently use batch files to provide an easier way to run commands on the command line. For example, you can create a batch file that contains `dir /o-d /p`, which displays a list of files sorted from newest to oldest with a pause when the screen is full.

- **Mapping directories**   If you need to map a directory or groups of directories, you can use batch files to automate the directory mapping.

- **General command batches**   This is certainly the most basic reason for using batch files. If you need to run a sequence of commands or programs on a repetitive basis, you can embed them within a batch file so that you don't need to type commands individually on the command line. If you're really ambitious, you can generalize and enhance your batch files by enabling them to use command line parameters.

Because batch files are a generalized tool, you can use them for any number of purposes. Batch files, however, have some basic limitations that render them ineffective or very difficult to use for certain tasks.

Problems with and Limitations of Batch Files

It's difficult to know where to begin when discussing the limitations of batch files because they have so many! If you've used batch files and a modern programming language such as C or Visual Basic, you know that in comparison, batch files are very weak. Some of the problems that batch files suffer from are listed in the following sections.

Batch Files Don't Provide Standard Programming Variables

Batch files provide no inherent support for variables. You can simulate standard variables by using environment variables. The problem with environment variables is that they are generally available to any programs running in the command shell. Consequently, environment variable names can collide, resulting in unintended effects.

Batch Files Provide Poor Error Handling

The only type of error handling supported by batch programs is the error level returned by programs or commands that run. The error level is just a number, so it does not include any descriptive information that might be similar to, for example, the VBScript Err.Description property.

Batch Files Have Weak Iteration Constructs

Batch files provide very weak iterative capabilities. There are two basic constructs for iteration: FOR and GOTO. FOR enables you to run a command for files that match one or more file specifications that might include wildcard characters. GOTO is the basic old go-to-label command that can be used to perform iteration; when used in conjunction with the IF statement, it can be used to perform a loop until a condition is satisfied.

Both the FOR and GOTO statements are very limited. For example, it is literally impossible to use either one to create a loop that goes from one to ten.

Note Some of these restrictions have been eliminated with command extensions provided by Microsoft. Later in this chapter, you'll look at some of the command extensions.

Batch Files Have Simplistic Command Branching

With batch files, you must implement your conditional logic and command branching using very basic IF statements. If you're used to standard programming languages that provide IF...THEN...ELSE... or SELECT CASE statements, the batch file IF statement is both tedious and error prone.

Batch Files Don't Have Subroutines

Most programming languages provide some type of subroutine that enables you to split up, modularize, and easily reuse code segments. Batch files are the exception. They have no inherent support for the definition of subroutines or functions. The closest that you can get to implementing subroutines is to call other batch files.

Batch Files Can't Access ActiveX Objects

Most modern Windows programs provide ActiveX objects that enable you to programmatically access programs to use their capabilities or to administer them. Later in this book, you'll see many examples that use WSH scripts to perform administrative tasks. Unfortunately, batch files do not have the capability to directly create or access ActiveX objects.

Batch Files Have No Debugging Utilities

If your batch file encounters an error, it might be difficult or next to impossible to debug the problem. That's because the batch file interpreter doesn't provide any debugging utilities. You can't stop code in the middle of execution, and you can't easily examine the contents of environment variables. You can include debugging statements that echo output to the user using the standard ECHO command. Those statements can indicate the current steps that the batch file is performing or can output the values of environment variables. That technique is effective, but it is nowhere near as convenient as a real debugger.

Benefits of WSH Over Batch Files

Unlike batch files, WSH provides a robust programming environment that enables you to automate tasks in the Windows environment. You've covered many of the advantages of WSH in preceding chapters, and you'll see more in subsequent chapters. What you'll do next is take a look at specific WSH features that are superior to capabilities in batch files. After that, you'll do a comparison that shows batch features or batch tasks relative to the equivalent WSH features.

Support For Complex Logic and Looping

WSH provides robust support for complex program logic and looping. It's important to note that the program logic and looping syntax depends on the scripting engine that is used. You saw detailed examples that show you how you can perform logic and looping using the VBScript and JScript languages on Day 5, "Using Microsoft VBScript with WSH," and Day 6, "Using Microsoft JScript with WSH."

Excellent Debugging Support

For WSH, excellent debugging features are available. In Day 8, "Testing and Debugging WSH Scripts," you looked at the Microsoft script debugger. The script debugger, depicted in Figure 10.2, provides lots of debugging functionality.

FIGURE 10.2

The Microsoft script debugger.

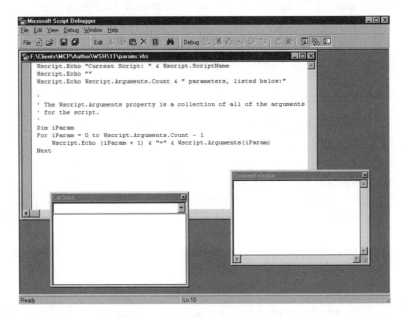

The script debugger enables you to trap errors that occur in your scripts, examine and modify the variables in your program during execution, and watch and control the flow of your script. There's also another alternative; if you have Microsoft Visual Studio 6.0, it provides an integrated script debugger. The script debugger is intelligent and launches itself if a runtime script error occurs. For example, say that I run the following script:

```
' FILE: badscrpt.vbs
' DESC: This will launch the Microsoft Visual Studio 6.0
'       script debugger.
```

```
' AUTH: Thomas L. Fredell
' DATE: 12/20/1998
'
' Copyright 1998 Macmillan Publishing
'

Dim object
Set object = Wscript.CreateObject("!!NOTANOBJECT!!")
object.NotAMethod

' Neither of the calls listed above will work
```

The script contains several errors. A runtime error is triggered by the
Wscript.CreateObject() call because it's called using an intentionally invalid object
ID. When the script runs, it fails and displays the dialog box shown in Figure 10.3.

FIGURE 10.3

A dialog box indicating that a script has encountered a runtime error.

If you select Yes from the dialog box, the Microsoft Visual Studio launches, and you
have the capability to step through and debug the script. Figure 10.4 shows Visual Studio
open for a script debugging session.

FIGURE 10.4

Using Visual Studio to debug a script.

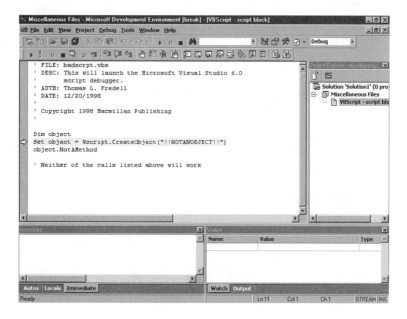

With batch files, there is no equivalent debugging capability. There's nothing built in to the operating system that enables you to debug them, and the Microsoft development tools don't help you to debug them either.

Support for Variables

WSH provides the capability for you to create and manipulate variables within your scripts. Unlike batch files, variables are constrained so they are only available within a single script during the execution of the script. This is a big advantage over batch files, which are restricted to using shared environment variables, because it eliminates potential conflicts that can occur between scripts. Furthermore, variables within WSH scripts can take any type of value including strings, numbers, and objects. In batch files, environment variables are always strings.

Comparing Batch File Usage With WSH

If you've used batch files before, you might wonder how you can translate your batch files into their WSH equivalent so that you can take advantage of the enhanced capabilities of WSH. In this section, you'll take a look at batch files in comparison to WSH features.

Note

As you go through this section, you'll notice that some of the WSH equivalents for batch file functions are much longer in terms of lines of code. That's one of the few advantages of batch files over WSH scripts. You might find that for certain tasks it's easier for you to implement batch files.

Batch Language and WSH Equivalents

First, you're going to take a look at some of the language constructs that are used in batch files and the equivalent language constructs in WSH. It's important to keep in mind that these language constructs are dependent on the WSH scripting language that you decide to use.

Using Variables

If you want to use variables in batch programs, you must use environment variables. Here's an example that shows how you might use environment variables in a batch program:

```
Rem Create an environment variable and set its value
Rem to the string 'Happy Holidays'
```

```
Set MY_VAR=Happy Holidays

Rem Here's where we would perform additional actions...

Rem At the end of the script, we need to set the variable
Rem to a blank string to cleanup the environment. If we
Rem don't do so, the command environment may contain
Rem lots of junk.
Set MY_VAR=
```

When you're using scripts with WSH, you don't need to use environment variables. That's much safer, and you don't need to clean up the variables at the end of your WSH script. Here's a short example that shows how you can use VBScript to create a variable:

```
' Allocate a variable, then set its value
Dim my_var
my_var = "Happy Holidays"

' NOTE: we don't need to cleanup the variable
```

Here's how you do the same type of thing using JScript:

```
' Allocate a variable, and set its value
var my_var = "Happy Holidays";
```

As you can see, the JScript code is actually somewhat shorter than the VBScript equivalent. In any case, like VBScript, you don't need to clean up the variable after you use it.

One thing that you can do with variables in WSH scripts is set them to values that are more than just strings. The following example shows how you can use VBScript to set variables that are numbers and objects:

```
' First allocate a variable to hold a number, then set its value
Dim num
num = 12

' Next, allocate a variable to hold an object, then create an
' object instance
Dim fileobject
Set fileobject = Wscript.CreateObject("Scripting.FileSystemObject")
```

When you use WSH variables, you have very few limitations. You also don't need to worry about collisions between variables that you use and variables that exist in other scripts.

10

Implementing Conditions and Logic

Batch programs use the IF statement in conjunction with GOTO statements to evaluate logical conditions and branch accordingly. Here's a batch file example that checks a condition:

```
Rem Create a variable to illustrate the use of the IF statement
Set MY_VAR=ValueA

Rem Now check the variable using IF - if the value of the variable is
Rem the string 'ValueA', the script will go to the label WasValueA
Rem and continue execution
IF .%MY_VAR%.==.ValueA. GOTO WasValueA

Rem This is the equivalent of the else clause
Echo MY_VAR was not ValueA
Goto BatchEnd

:WasValueA
Echo MY_VAR was ValueA

Rem We'll just fall through to the end of the batch sequence...

:BatchEnd
Rem This is the end of the batch sequence, so we'll cleanup
Rem the variable that we used.
Set MY_VAR=
```

That works okay when you have a simple condition. If you have a more complex condition, batch files quickly become messy. The following example is very similar to the first but includes a more complex condition:

```
Rem Create a variable to illustrate the use of the IF statement
Set MY_VAR=ValueB

Rem this time, we'll check for ValueA, ValueB, or other
IF .%MY_VAR%.==.ValueA. GOTO WasValueA
IF .%MY_VAR%.==.ValueB. GOTO WasValueB

Rem This is the equivalent of the last else clause
Echo MY_VAR was not ValueA or ValueB
Goto BatchEnd

:WasValueA
Echo MY_VAR was ValueA
Goto BatchEnd

:WasValueB
Echo MY_VAR was ValueB
```

```
Rem Fall through...

:BatchEnd
Rem This is the end of the batch sequence, so we'll cleanup
Rem the variable that we used.
Set MY_VAR=
```

Now, take a look at the WSH script equivalents. For the first simple case you can use the following VBScript:

```
' Create a variable to use to illustrate the use of
' the If...Then statement
Dim my_var
my_var = "ValueA"

' Now we use If...Then to evaluate our program's logic
If my_var = "ValueA" Then
    Wscript.Echo "my_var was ValueA"
Else
    Wscript.Echo "my_var was not ValueA"
End If
```

To do the same thing using JScript, you can use the following, which uses slightly different syntax but is conceptually identical:

```
// Create a variable to use to illustrate the use of the if statement
var my_var = "ValueA";

// Now we use if to evaluate our program's logic
if (my_var == "ValueA") {
    WScript.echo("my_var was ValueA");
} else {
    WScript.echo("my_var was not ValueA");
}
```

The advantage of the two examples is that the flow of the program is simple and easy to understand; the flow is certainly simpler and easier than the flow of the batch file. With the second batch file example, you can quickly see how code turns into spaghetti code that can be very difficult to debug and maintain. Now, take a look at the equivalent of the second batch file in VBScript:

```
' Create a variable to use to illustrate logical branching
Dim my_var
my_var = "ValueB"

' Now we use If...Then...ElseIf to evaluate our program's logic
If my_var = "ValueA" Then
    Wscript.Echo "my_var was ValueA"
ElseIf my_var = "ValueB" Then
    Wscript.Echo "my_var was ValueB"
```

10

```
Else
    Wscript.Echo "my_var was not ValueA"
End If

' And here's a cleaner alternative using the SELECT CASE statement
' this version is easier to expand if you need to handle multiple
' simple cases
Select Case my_var
    Case "ValueA"
        Wscript.Echo "my_var was ValueA"
    Case "ValueB"
        Wscript.Echo "my_var was ValueB"
    Case Else
        Wscript.Echo "my_var was not ValueA or ValueB"
End Select
```

That example demonstrates two different ways that you can perform branching logic in VBScript. Now take a look at similar functionality using JScript:

```
// Create a variable to use to illustrate logical branching
var my_var = "ValueB";

// Now we use if...else to evaluate our program's logic
if (my_var == "ValueA") {
    WScript.echo("my_var was ValueA");
} else if (my_var == "ValueB") {
    WScript.echo("my_var was ValueB");
} else {
    WScript.echo("my_var was not ValueA");
}

// And here's a cleaner alternative using the SELECT CASE statement
// this version is easier to expand if you need to handle multiple
// simple cases
switch (my_var) {
    case "ValueA":
        WScript.echo("my_var was ValueA");
        break;
    case "ValueB":
        WScript.echo("my_var was ValueB");
        break;
    default:
        WScript.echo("my_var was not ValueA or ValueB");
}
```

You can see that the JScript example is very similar to the VBScript example; the syntax varies a little. Both examples are much better structured than the batch file example. If you need to use complex logic, consider changing your batch files to WSH scripts so that you can make use of the more powerful, simpler language features.

Performing Iteration

In batch files there are two basic types of iteration; you can iterate over a group of files using the FOR command, or you can perform standard, plain-vanilla iteration using the GOTO statement. The second type of iteration is similar to the typical iteration that's used in a program for a while or for type of loop, but unfortunately it's much weaker.

Here's an example that illustrates the FOR command in a batch file:

```
@Echo Off
for %%f in (c:\winnt\system32\e*.dll) do echo %%f
```

If you run a batch file that contains the preceding commands, you see the results shown in Figure 10.5.

FIGURE 10.5

Results of running the for iteration example.

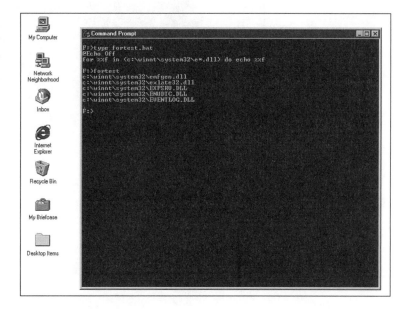

Typical batch files use GOTO in conjunction with IF statements to perform conditional iteration. Here's an example from gotoloop.bat that shows that type of iteration:

```
@Echo Off

:BeginLoop
Echo %1
Shift

If .%1.==.. Goto :ExitLoop
Goto BeginLoop

:ExitLoop
Echo Done!
```

The previous example shows a batch file loop that iterates through the parameters for the batch file. If the batch file is run with the command line gotoloop IterationA IterationB IterationC IterationD, you see the results in Figure 10.6.

FIGURE **10.6**

*Results of running
the goto iteration
example.*

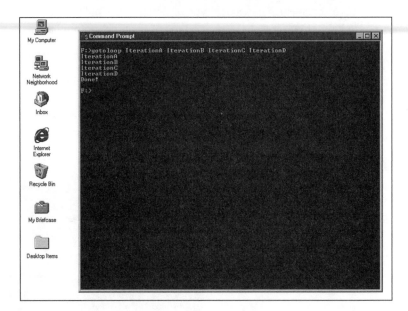

The batch file iteration techniques are effective but very clunky. They make it easy to iterate over multiple files but difficult to iterate for a specific number of times or until a complex condition is satisfied.

 Note

Some of these batch file restrictions have been eliminated with Windows NT command extensions. For example, the FOR command is extended to perform iteration for a specific sequence. The following code example illustrates the extended syntax:

```
for /L %%n in (1,1,10) do echo %%n
```

The output from a batch file containing that FOR example is shown in Figure 10.7. There are also some additional enhancements with the command extensions that make it possible to simulate subroutines using batch files. The extensions are very useful; however, they are still not as flexible or anywhere near as powerful as WSH scripts.

FIGURE 10.7

Example showing extended for syntax.

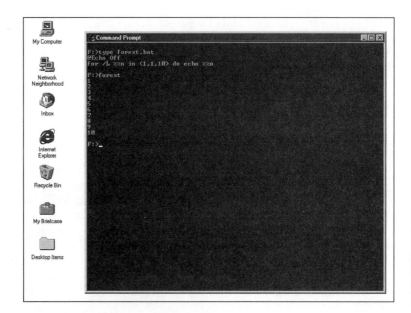

The Windows Scripting Host provides much better looping capabilities. You can easily create very flexible loops that use complex conditions and contain embedded loops. However, this is one situation where the WSH equivalent is not necessarily as simple or as short as the batch file version. Iterating over a group of files can be more complex but also more flexible using WSH. Here's an example that uses VBScript to iterate over all the files in the Windows NT system directory:

```
Dim fso, folder, file
Set fso = Wscript.CreateObject("Scripting.FileSystemObject")
Set folder = fso.GetFolder("C:\WINNT\SYSTEM32")

For Each file in folder.Files
    Wscript.Echo file.Name
Next
```

That's not too complex, but it gets worse. If you want to iterate over just a specific type of file, like all the DLLs that begin with the letter e, you need to implement additional file-checking logic. Here's an example that does the check:

```
Dim fso, folder, file, name
Set fso = Wscript.CreateObject("Scripting.FileSystemObject")
Set folder = fso.GetFolder("C:\WINNT\SYSTEM32")

For Each file in folder.Files
    name = LCase(file.Name)
```

10

```
' First check first letter of file name
If Left(name, 1) = "e" Then
    ' Check file extension
    If fso.GetExtensionName(name) = "dll" Then
        Wscript.Echo name
    End If
End If
Next
```

The output of the preceding example is depicted in Figure 10.8.

FIGURE 10.8

*Iterating over files
using VBScript.*

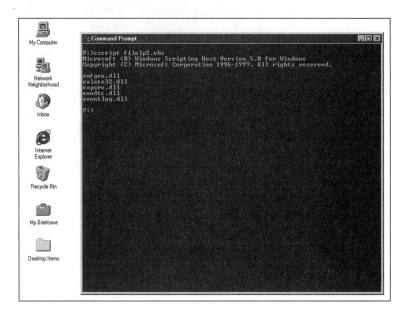

Both of those examples show some of the excellent looping capabilities provided by
WSH, but they also show that sometimes WSH scripts might not be as easy to implement
as batch files. Here's another simple example that illustrates the use of the while loop:

```
Dim count, name
count=1
Do While (count < 10) And (name <> "iteration5")
    name = "iteration" & count
    Wscript.Echo name
    count = count + 1
Loop
```

That's obviously a very trivial example, but it does demonstrate complex logic and com-
parisons that are much better than the capabilities provided by batch files.

Error Handling

With batch files, errors are captured using the IF ERRORLEVEL statement. When a batch file runs a command, the command might return a numeric DOS error level. Typically, an error level of zero represents success, whereas a nonzero error level is a failure number. Here's an example that shows the use of IF ERRORLEVEL:

```
@Echo Off
Type notafile.txt
If errorlevel 1 Goto :ErrOccurred
Echo No error occurred.
Goto :EndBatch

:ErrOccurred
Echo An error occurred with the type command!

:EndBatch
```

Assuming that the notafile.txt file doesn't exist, running the batch file produces the result shown in Figure 10.9. The Type command displays a text error and sets the DOS error level. That's more feedback than some other commands; many set the error level without displaying a descriptive message. The IF ERRORLEVEL logic is also very weak because you can't use it to check for a specific error level; it checks for an error equal to or greater than the error level that is specified.

FIGURE 10.9

A batch file that demonstrates error handling.

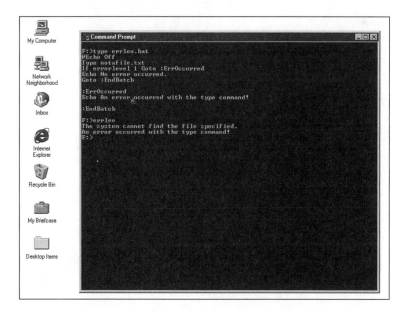

> **Note**
>
> This is another situation where the Windows NT command extensions improve the batch file capabilities. With the command extensions, the syntax for IF enables you to check for a specific error level using the %errorlevel% variable and the EQU operator. Here's a short example of the extended syntax:
>
> ```
> Type notafile.txt
> If %errorlevel% EQU 1 Echo The file wasn't found.
> ```

WSH scripts, assuming that you're using VBScript, provide much more robust error handling than batch files. (Unfortunately, the current version of JScript doesn't provide error handling capabilities.) VBScript provides an Err object that provides properties that include a numeric error code, a description of the error that occurred, and the source of the error. You can easily check for an error using logic that checks the Err.Number property. Here's an example that illustrates the check for an error:

```
' The following line must be included to set up VBScript error
' handling
On Error Resume Next

' We'll use a loop that will attempt to get a set of files; the
' last one is bogus and will cause an error to occur
Dim filelist, filename, fso, file
filelist = Array("user32.dll", "kernel32.dll", "not_a_dll.dll")
Set fso = Wscript.CreateObject("Scripting.FileSystemObject")
For Each filename In filelist
    Wscript.Echo "Getting the file object for " & filename & "..."
    Set file = fso.GetFile("c:\winnt\system32\" & filename)
    If Err.Number <> 0 Then
        Wscript.Echo "Unable to get file; an error occurred."
        Wscript.Echo "Err #" & Err.Number & ", " & Err.Description
    Else
        Wscript.Echo "Get file succeeded."
    End If
Next
```

The output of the script is shown in Figure 10.10. The script can easily be altered to check for a specific error number by changing the If Err.Number <> 0 Then line. Because of the capabilities of WSH, you can create scripts that notify users of problems and then enable them to retry operations. Here's a sample script that uses retry logic to prompt a user to enter a different filename if an error occurs:

FIGURE 10.10

A basic WSH error handling example.

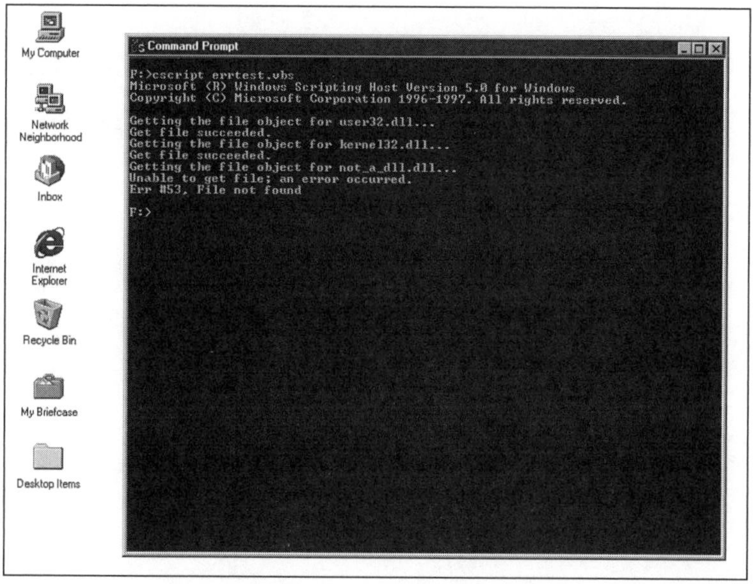

10

```
'
' The following line must be included to set up VBScript error
' handling
'
On Error Resume Next

'
' We'll use a loop that will attempt to get a set of files; the
' last one is bogus and will cause an error to occur
'
Dim filename, fso, shell, file, continue
filename = "not_a_dll.dll"
Set fso = Wscript.CreateObject("Scripting.FileSystemObject")
Set shell = Wscript.CreateObject("WScript.Shell")
Do
    Wscript.Echo "Getting the file object for " & filename & "..."
    Set file = fso.GetFile(filename)
    If Err.Number <> 0 Then
        '
        ' An error occurred when we tried to get the file,
        ' so ask the user if they'd like to retry with a
        ' different file
        '
        shell.Popup "Unable to get file; an error occurred." & _
            vbCrLf & "Err #" & Err.Number & ", " & Err.Description
        If shell.Popup("Would you like to try a different file?", _
```

```
        0, "Retry?", 4) = 6 Then
            '
            ' They selected yes, so ask for a new file name
            '
            filename = InputBox("Enter new file name:", _
                "Enter file name", filename)
            continue = True
            Err.Clear
        Else
            continue = False
        End If
    Else
        Wscript.Echo "Get file succeeded."
        continue = False
    End If
Loop Until Not continue
```

When the script runs, it fails because it tries the not_a_dll.dll file, which doesn't exist. When it fails, it displays a yes/no dialog box, shown in Figure 10.11, that enables the user to retry the operation.

FIGURE 10.11

The Retry? dialog box.

If the user selects yes, he is prompted to enter a new filename. The prompt dialog box is illustrated in Figure 10.12. When he reenters the filename, the loop in the script attempts to retry the file operation.

FIGURE 10.12

Prompt for new filename in retry operation.

This shows some of the power that is inherent in WSH error handling. These are just basic examples; you can easily extend them to perform additional error handling functions such as writing to a text log file.

Common Batch Usage and WSH Equivalents

In this section, you're going to examine some common techniques used in batch files, and you'll see how you can duplicate the functionality within your WSH scripts. For each section, you'll follow the pattern that you used in the previous section; first you'll see an example for a batch file, and then you'll see the corresponding WSH version.

Checking for File Existence

Checking for file existence within a batch file is easy. The IF statement provides a syntax that enables you to perform an action if a file exists. Here's an example of the syntax:

```
If Exist C:\WINNT\SYSTEM32\USER32.DLL Goto :FileExists
Echo The file doesn't exist.
Goto :EndOfBatch

:FileExists
Echo The file does exist.

:EndOfBatch
```

The syntax is effective but clunky due to the use of the batch file GOTO statement. Now, take a look at the equivalent functionality using WSH. To check for a file, you use the FileSystemObject like so:

```
Dim fso
Set fso = Wscript.CreateObject("Scripting.FileSystemObject")
If fso.FileExists("C:\WINNT\SYSTEM32\USER32.DLL") Then
    Wscript.Echo "The file exists."
Else
    Wscript.Echo "The file doesn't exist."
End If
```

Obviously, because you're using WSH, it is very easy for you to to incorporate additional complex logic for the file check. For example, you can check the size of file, or, if the file is a DLL or an executable, you can check internal file resources such as a version stamp. In Day 11, "Administering User Logins, Program Settings, Folders, and File Shortcuts Using WSH," you'll see additional examples that illustrate how you can use the FileSystemObject to check for files and perform other file operations.

Using Command-Line Parameters

Batch files can access nine command line parameters simultaneously. The syntax %N, where N represents the numeric index of the command line parameter, is used to access the parameter. The value %0 evaluates to the name of the batch file that was called, and %1 through %9 are the command parameters. You can specify more than nine parameters; to access them, the batch file uses the Shift command.

10

Here's an example of a batch file that simply dumps all its command line parameters:

```
@Echo Off
Echo Running: %0
Echo.
Echo Showing command line parameters...

:BegLoop
If .%1.==.. Goto ExitLoop
Echo %1
Shift
Goto BegLoop

:ExitLoop
Echo.
Echo Done.
```

Accessing command-line parameters is easier using WSH than it is using batch files. With WSH, you can easily access each command-line parameter, and you can tell from the beginning how many parameters are specified for the script. Here's a sample script that shows how you can access command-line parameters:

```
Wscript.Echo "Current Script: " & Wscript.ScriptName
Wscript.Echo ""
Wscript.Echo Wscript.Arguments.Count & " parameters, listed below:"

'
' The Wscript.Arguments property is a collection of all of
' the arguments for the script.
'
Dim iParam
For iParam = 0 to Wscript.Arguments.Count - 1
    Wscript.Echo (iParam + 1) & "=" & Wscript.Arguments(iParam)
Next
```

If you're converting a batch file to a WSH script, you can eliminate your shift statements and just make use of the Wscript.Arguments property to handle your parameters.

Displaying Messages to the User

With batch files, you have no choice for how you want to display a message to the user. All that you have is the Echo command, which writes a single line of text to the command console. Here's a basic example:

```
Echo Hello World!
```

You can certainly do the same type of thing with WSH scripts. You've used the Echo technique throughout this book. The difference is that you need to use the Wscript object, as so:

```
Wscript.Echo "Hello World!"
```

That's not all that you can do to display messages to the user using WSH. You can use internal functions or objects to display message boxes, or you can even make use of external custom objects to display your own UI. You'll see that technique demonstrated later in this book. For now, here's an example that displays dialog boxes using two different methods:

```
'
' The following technique is specific to VBScript because it makes use
' of the MsgBox function
'
MsgBox "Hello World!"


'
' This technique can be used for any script using any language because
' it uses a standard WSH object
'
Dim shell
Set shell = Wscript.CreateObject("WScript.Shell")
shell.Popup "Hello World!"
```

Pausing for User Input

There are only two standard options for getting user input with batch files. The most basic one, Pause, literally does nothing but display the message Press any key to continue . . . and wait for the user to press any of the keys on the keyboard. The more advanced one, Choice, was developed to provide more robust support for user input. Unfortunately, Choice was not designed for Windows NT 4.0. You can try to use it; beware that it is not officially supported. The following batch file uses the Choice command to display a list of choices and wait for user input:

```
@Echo Off

Rem
Rem First display menu
Rem
Echo MENU OPTIONS:
Echo.
Echo A  - Choice A
Echo B  - Choice B
Echo C  - Choice C
Echo.

Rem
Rem Display the choice prompt, then analyze the errorlevel.
Rem The errorlevel indicates which option was selected.
Rem
Choice /C:ABC Make your selection
If Errorlevel 3 Goto ChoiceC
If Errorlevel 2 Goto ChoiceB
```

```
If Errorlevel 1 Goto ChoiceA

Rem
Rem Fall-through here if errorlevel isn't set
Rem
Echo No selection was made.
Goto Done

:ChoiceA
Echo ChoiceA was selected!
Goto Done

:ChoiceB
Echo ChoiceB was selected!
Goto Done

:ChoiceC
Echo ChoiceC was selected!
Goto Done

:Done
```

Figure 10.13 shows the result of the batch file menu. The Choice technique is effective for batch files, but it is limited because it only enables the user to make selections from a canned menu. It also shows how weak the structure of batch files must be because of the lack of good programming constructs. With batch files, handling user input and logic is complex and error prone.

FIGURE 10.13

A batch file menu using the Choice *command.*

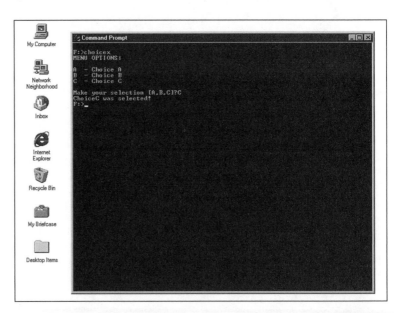

For WSH, the VBScript language provides the InputBox() function. Unfortunately, if you're using JScript, there is no standard mechanism for user input. Here's an example that uses InputBox() to prompt a user for a choice:

```
Dim menu, selection
menu = "MENU CHOICES:" & vbCrLf & vbCrLf & _
    "A - ChoiceA"  & vbCrLf & _
    "B - ChoiceB"  & vbCrLf & _
    "C - ChoiceC"  & vbCrLf & vbCrLf & _
    "Make your selection:"
selection = InputBox(menu, "Make a selection")

Select Case UCase(selection)
    Case "A"
        MsgBox "Selected ChoiceA"
    Case "B"
        MsgBox "Selected ChoiceB"
    Case "C"
        MsgBox "Selected ChoiceC"
    Case Else
        MsgBox "Your choice was not understood."
End Select
```

The result of this script is shown in Figure 10.14. The example shows both strengths and weaknesses of the WSH support for user input. The benefit of InputBox() is that it enables you to capture any type of user input. At the same time, the problem with InputBox() is that it doesn't enable you to constrain selections or to enable the user to select from a list. With VB, Java, C++, or any other language that enables you to create COM objects, you can define custom objects that can supplement your WSH scripts with custom interfaces.

FIGURE 10.14

A menu displayed using InputBox().

Mapping Network Drives

In the next chapter, you'll see how you can develop robust WSH scripts that perform drive mapping tasks. For now, you'll do a quick comparison that shows how you can map drives using batch files or scripts.

Your first example is a batch file that shows drive mapping. The batch file follows:

```
@Echo Off

Rem
Rem First ensure that drives don't have current mappings
Rem
Net Use X: /Delete
Net Use Y: /Delete
Net Use Z: /Delete

Rem
Rem Now map the drives
Rem
Net Use X: \\TLFSRV1\Clients
Net Use Y: \\TLFSRV1\Dev
Net Use Z: \\TLFSRV1\ROI
```

The batch file uses the standard Windows Net command. Net has options that enable you to create or remove drive mappings, among other things. The corresponding WSH script uses the WshNetwork object. WshNetwork provides all the networking functionality for WSH scripts. If you want to find out more about the WshNetwork object, refer back to Day 4, "The WSH Object Model." Here's the equivalent WSH script:

```
On Error Resume Next

'
' First we need to create an instance of the WshNetwork object
'
Dim network
Set network = Wscript.CreateObject("WScript.Network")

'
' Now we'll use the object to remove the current drive mappings
'
network.RemoveNetworkDrive "X:"
network.RemoveNetworkDrive "Y:"
network.RemoveNetworkDrive "Z:"

'
' And now we map the drives
'
network.MapNetworkDrive "X:", "\\TLFSRV1\Clients"
network.MapNetworkDrive "Y:", "\\TLFSRV1\Dev"
network.MapNetworkDrive "Z:", "\\TLFSRV1\ROI"
```

Scripts in the next chapter show you how you can map drives and perform checks to determine if drive mappings were created successfully.

Summary

This chapter began with a discussion of the history of batch files on the DOS/Windows platform. Batch files were developed as an effective and simple solution for command automation. They provide powerful but basic automation capabilities. Relative to robust programming languages, batch files are weak and cumbersome. However, there are tons of batch files out there, and you might have written a few of your own.

To help you to begin replacing your batch files or supplementing them with WSH scripts, you took a look at batch file syntax relative to WSH syntax. That gives you an idea of WSH equivalents for functionality that you might be using in batch files. Next, you examined several standard batch file usage scenarios. The batch file scenarios were juxtaposed with WSH script scenarios that illustrated corresponding WSH techniques.

Hopefully, this chapter has helped you to understand how you can use WSH scripts as a more robust substitute for batch files. With WSH, you have lots more flexibility and power than you ever do with standard batch files. In the upcoming chapters, you'll see practical examples that will help you to understand how you can make use of WSH scripts.

10

Q&A

Q **In batch files, environment variables are the only place that you can store temporary values. Typically, batch files need to clean up environment variables that they use before they terminate. Do WSH scripts also need to clean up variables that they use?**

A No, WSH scripts do not need to clean up variables that they use. The internal variables that are used by a script are only available while that script is executing; this prevents scripts from adversely affecting each other.

Q **Although batch files provide no debugging utilities, WSH scripts have excellent debugging tools. Name two tools that can be used to debug WSH scripts.**

A WSH scripts can be debugged using the Microsoft Script Debugger and the Microsoft Visual Studio.

Q **Error handling with batch files uses the IF ERRORLEVEL statement; what does WSH use for error handling?**

A For WSH, the Err object provides a number of properties that describe a runtime error. The Err object can be used in conjunction with standard VBScript If...Then statements to handle error conditions.

Workshop

The following section will help you test your comprehension of the material presented in this chapter and put what you've learned into practice. You'll find the answers to the quiz and exercises in Appendix A.

Quiz

1. What is the WSH equivalent of the batch file IF statement?

2. Why is error handling with WSH better than error handling with batch files?

3. What object do you need to use in WSH if you want to check for the existence of a file?

Exercises

1. Convert one of your most useful batch files into a WSH script.

2. Create a login script that takes a profile type as a parameter. Map different network directories according to the profile parameter.

3. Develop a WSH script that changes environment variables. Hint: In order to to do so, you need to use the WshShell object.

DAY 11

Administering User Logins, Program Settings, Folders, and File Shortcuts Using WSH

In this chapter, you're going to see how you can use the Windows Scripting Host to provide powerful user administration capabilities. On Day 10, you saw some standard techniques that you can use with WSH scripts. Day 10 showed you how to replace your existing batch files with more robust and complete scripts developed using WSH. Now you're going to put some of those techniques and ideas into action with scripts that will allow you to administer settings on user computers.

This chapter shows you how to create WSH login scripts, programmatically create directory mappings (and check to make sure that directory mappings succeed), check for the existence of files and check file timestamps, administer program Registry settings, and create shortcuts and directories. By the time you are finished with this chapter, you'll see how you can use WSH for administration tasks, and you'll have some code examples that you can put to work immediately in your own scripts.

On the 11th day of your introduction to WSH, you'll

- Discuss some scenarios where WSH can help for automating user administration
- View examples that show you how you can use WSH for standard administrative tasks
- Conclude with some ideas about how you can leverage WSH for administration

Overview of Administration Using WSH Scripts

The Windows Scripting Host is a generalized tool that allows you to perform a multitude of administrative tasks. You can use the objects that are built into WSH, such as the WshNetwork or WshShell objects, to administer drive mappings or program settings. You can also use standard scripting objects, such as the FileSystemObject, to check files and add folders. In this chapter, you'll see code examples that use those objects and others for user administration.

In this context, *user administration* means to administer the user's computer, including the Windows desktop, program settings, files, folders, and so on. It does not mean that you will actually be creating or modifying users with WSH scripts. That topic is discussed in Day 18, "Using WSH to Manipulate the Microsoft Active Directory." As Day 18 and several other chapters show you, WSH can really be used as a general administration tool because it can script any ActiveX objects. Because many of the Microsoft technologies expose ActiveX administration objects, they can be administered using WSH.

User Login Scripting

Today, user login scripting under Windows NT typically uses batch files. Batch files are useful, but they don't have anything close to the capabilities of WSH scripts. They have no real programming constructs and certainly no capability to leverage COM objects. Now you can replace them with more robust WSH scripts that perform more functions. With WSH scripts, you can perform many tasks and check the results much more easily than you ever could with standard batch files.

Directory Mappings

Directory mappings are typically done the old way using batch files. When you map drives, you use the net use command with the name of the server and share that you want to map to specified using the Universal Naming Convention (UNC) in the form \\server\share. For example, you may have a batch file that bitmaps to a directory using something like the following syntax:

```
net use V: \\tlfsrv1\clients
```

The problem is that it can be difficult to check whether the directory mapping succeeded. With WSH scripts, you can do the directory mapping using the WshNetwork object and check the result to ensure that the directory was mapped successfully.

Checking Files and File Versions

With batch files, it's literally impossible to check file versions. There's no good way, unless you extend batch files with external programs or utilities, to check file versions. Again, this is something you can do easily with WSH and the FileSystemObject. Later in this chapter, you'll see how you can perform this task using scripts.

Programs and Program Settings: .ini Files and the Registry

One major limitation of batch files is that they don't provide any capability to change program settings. With WSH, you can change program settings in both .ini files and in the Windows Registry. Later in this chapter, you use the WSH TextStream objects to change .ini settings, and the WshShell object to change Registry settings.

Shortcuts and Folders

With WSH objects, you can easily create new shortcuts and folders. You also can check for the existence of shortcuts or folders, and delete them or move them if appropriate. You can accomplish some of that using batch files, but again, some of the limitations of batch files are a lack of fine-granularity control and difficulty of verifying that commands were completed successfully.

Defining User Login Scripts

Defining user login scripts is easy; they are simply standard WSH scripts. Listing 11.1 provides a basic Hello World login script.

11

LISTING 11.1   Hello World LOGIN SCRIPT

```
// FILE: hellowld.js
// DESC: This is a very basic Hello World! script using JScript.
// AUTH: Thomas L. Fredell
// DATE: 12/8/1998
//
// Copyright 1998 Macmillan Publishing
//

var shell;

// Create WshShell object so we can use Popup()
shell = WScript.createObject("WScript.Shell");

// Now display Hello World!
shell.popup("Hello World!");
```

 Note

This is one of the few examples where we will use the Microsoft JScript lan-guage. Current versions of JScript provide no support for error handling, so it's difficult to use them to develop robust scripts. This will be fixed in upcoming versions of JScript, which will support robust error handling using a `try..catch` mechanism similar to the Java language.

Figure 11.1 shows the result of running this script. It's obviously a basic script, but note that you can easily change it to include functionality that you see throughout this chapter or any of the other chapters.

FIGURE 11.1

Hello World *login script.*

Next, you see how you can put this script into use as a login script.

Setting Up Login Scripts

To set up login scripts, go into the Windows NT User Manager for domains. Select a user, or multiple users, and press Enter, or select User, Properties from the menu. You'll see the dialog illustrated in Figure 11.2.

FIGURE **11.2**

User Properties dialog.

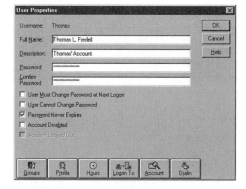

From the User Properties dialog, click the Profile button. You'll see a User Environment Profile dialog, as shown in Figure 11.3, which allows you to specify a logon script name.

FIGURE **11.3**

User Environment Profile dialog.

11

The default path to logon scripts is `C:\WINNT\system32\Repl\Import\Scripts`. Obviously, if Windows NT is installed on a different drive or in a different root directory, your path will be different. It's important to note that the aforementioned directory is also shared by default as `NETLOGON`. Put the `Hello World` script, `hellowld.js`, in the directory.

To make the `Hello World` script the user login script, you need to enter the following in the edit box next to logon script:

```
cscript \\Server\NETLOGON\hellowld.js
```

Caution

You may get inconsistent results using the aforementioned method. Sometimes it appears that the user manager has problems resolving the path to the script. Consequently, consider wrapping your scripts in the following batch file.

As an alternative, you can put the `cscript hellowld.js` command in a batch file. That can help you to eliminate any problems with directory dependencies. Here's a sample batch file that you could use:

```
@Echo Off
cscript hellowld.js
```

In either case, the result that the user sees when he logs in is illustrated in Figure 11.4.

FIGURE 11.4

Logging in with the `Hello World` *script.*

> **Caution**
>
> Users must have WSH installed locally to run WSH login scripts. In the last chapter of this book, we discuss how you can deploy WSH script solutions and the files that you need to distribute to end users for them to run WSH.

Retrieving User Information

When a user logs in, you can use a `WshNetwork` object to retrieve basic details about the user, such as the username. You can also use the name with other objects to perform useful functions. In Day 18, you see how to use WSH scripts with databases when users log in.

Mapping Directories

WSH makes it easy to map directories and perform other networking functions using the `WshNetwork` object. The `WshNetwork` object is described in detail in Day 2, "Writing a Simple Script Using WSH." This section shows you how you can use it to perform drive mapping. One of its biggest advantages is that it can be used to validate that mappings were completed successfully. Because you can perform validation, you can be more proactive in scripts to give the end user feedback about potential problems, or to alert the administrator about anomalous situations.

Next you'll see how you can create and validate network connections from WSH.

Creating Connections to Network Devices

Here is the basic VBScript code that is required to use the `WshNetwork` object to create drive mappings:

```
Dim network
Set network = Wscript.CreateObject("WScript.Network")
' Change the following line to match the server and drive
' that you want to connect to
network.MapNetworkDrive "Z:", \\TLFSRV1\Clients
```

Naturally, you would replace the arguments to the `MapNetworkDrive()` function with whatever is appropriate for your environment. Now, let's run a quick example that shows some of the usage of the object. Before running the script, drives in the Explorer look like Figure 11.5.

FIGURE 11.5

Before running drive mapping script.

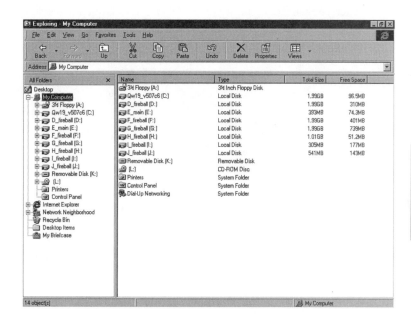

Now we'll run the following script shown in Listing 11.2.

LISTING 11.2   Mapdrive.vbs — DRIVE MAPPING SCRIPT

```
' FILE: mapdrive.vbs
' DESC: This script demonstrates how you can use the
'       WshNetwork object to map directories.
' AUTH: Thomas L. Fredell
' DATE: 12/8/1998
'
' Copyright 1998 Macmillan Publishing

Dim network
Set network = Wscript.CreateObject("WScript.Network")
```

continues

LISTING 11.2   CONTINUED

```
'
' Map some standard network drive letters
'
network.MapNetworkDrive "U:", "\\TLFSRV1\ROI"
network.MapNetworkDrive "V:", "\\TLFSRV1\NETLOGON"
network.MapNetworkDrive "Z:", "\\TLFSRV1\Clients"
```

After you run the script, if you go to the Explorer, you'll see something that looks like Figure 11.6. Next, you'll see how you can add checks to ensure that drive mappings were completed successfully.

FIGURE 11.6

After running drive mapping script.

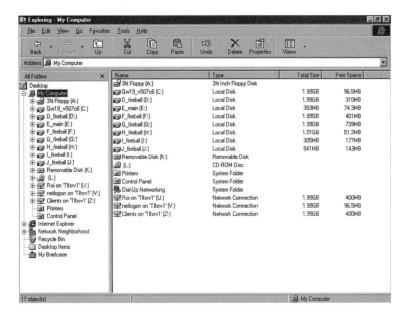

Checking for Successful Drive Mapping

There are a couple of ways that you can check to determine whether drive mappings were completed successfully. The most obvious way is to use the error handling that is built into the VBScript scripting language. The second way to do it is to check the drive mappings by enumerating them. You'll look at code to implement both ways.

First, let's look at using VBScript error handling. Using the previous example, Listing 11.3 adds a function that wraps the drive mapping with additional error checking.

LISTING 11.3   Mapdrv1.vbs—DRIVE MAPPING WITH ERROR CHECKING

```vbscript
' FILE: mapdrv1.vbs
' DESC: This script demonstrates how you can use VBScript
'       error checking to verify directory mappings.
' AUTH: Thomas L. Fredell
' DATE: 12/8/1998
'
' Copyright 1998 Macmillan Publishing


'
' Constants
'
Const ERR_DRIVE_IN_USE = -2147024811


'
' Create a network object that we'll use for drive mapping
'
Dim network
Set network = Wscript.CreateObject("WScript.Network")


'
' Map drives using our wrapper function with error
' handling
'
MapDrive network, "U:", "\\TLFSRV1\ROI"
MapDrive network, "V:", "\\TLFSRV1\NETLOGON"
MapDrive network, "Z:", "\\TLFSRV1\Clients"


'-----------------------------------------------------
' FUNC: MapDrive(NetObj, Local, Network)
' DESC: This wraps the MapNetworkDrive function with
'       a function that performs error checking.
'-----------------------------------------------------
Sub MapDrive(netObj, local, network)
    '
    ' Set up VBScript error handling
    '
    On Error Resume Next


    '
    ' Attempt to map a network connection, then check
    ' to see if an error occurred
    '
    netObj.MapNetworkDrive local, network
    If Err.Number <> 0 Then
        '
        ' The mapping failed; check the error code
        '
        Dim message, shell
```

continues

LISTING 11.3   CONTINUED

```
        If Err.Number = ERR_DRIVE_IN_USE Then
            message = "We were unable to map '" & Local & _
                "' to the network share '" & Network & "' " & _
                "because a there is already a local drive mapping."
        Else
            message = "We were unable to map '" & Local & _
                "' to the network share '" & Network & "'. " & _
                "The following error occurred: (" & Err.Number & _
                ") " & Err.Description
        End If
        Set shell = Wscript.CreateObject("WScript.Shell")
        shell.Popup message
    End If
End Sub
```

In the preceding script, you've added error checking to determine whether a drive mapping succeeded. This time, instead of directly calling the WshNetwork.MapNetworkDrive() method in the main body of our script, we call the new MapDrive() function that we've written. MapDrive() sets up error checking using VBScript On Error Resume Next and then calls WshNetwork.MapNetworkDrive(), immediately after which the Err error object is checked to determine whether an error occurred. If an error occurred, a descriptive message is displayed to the user, as illustrated in Figure 11.7.

FIGURE 11.7

Descriptive error message when drive mapping fails.

The preceding example is certainly better than no error checking, but it isn't as good as a script that actively validates the drive mappings. For example, what if a drive mapping is correct but an error occurred because the drive mapping already existed? The example shown in Listing 11.4 handles that case and shows a script that does the drive mapping validation using the EnumNetworkDrives property of the WshNetwork object:

LISTING 11.4   Mapdrv2.vbs—DRIVE MAPPING WITH VALIDATION USING EnumNetworkDrives

```
' FILE: mapdrv2.vbs
' DESC: This script demonstrates how you can use VBScript
'       error checking to verify directory mappings.
' AUTH: Thomas L. Fredell
' DATE: 12/8/1998
'
' Copyright 1998 Macmillan Publishing

'
' Constants
'
Const ERR_DRIVE_IN_USE = -2147024811

'
' Create a network object that we'll use for drive mapping
'
Dim network
Set network = Wscript.CreateObject("WScript.Network")

'
' Map drives using our wrapper function with error
' handling
'
MapDrive network, "U:", "\\TLFSRV1\ROI"
MapDrive network, "V:", "\\TLFSRV1\NETLOGON"
MapDrive network, "Z:", "\\TLFSRV1\Clients"

'
' Now set up to call a new function that will validate the
' drive mappings
'
Dim localDrives, netShares
localDrives = Array("U:", "V:", "Z:")
netShares = Array("\\TLFSRV1\ROI", _
    "\\TLFSRV1\NETLOGON", "\\TLFSRV1\Clients")
If Not ValidateConnections(network, localDrives, netShares) Then
    Dim shell
    Set shell = Wscript.CreateObject("WScript.Shell")
    shell.Popup "One or more network drive connections failed. " & _
        "You may encounter difficulties when running programs. " & _
        "Check with the system administrator to determine " & _
        "what needs to be done to fix your problem."
End If

'----------------------------------------------------
' FUNC: MapDrive(netObj, local, network)
' DESC: This wraps the MapNetworkDrive function with
'       a function that performs error checking.
'----------------------------------------------------
```

continues

LISTING **11.4** CONTINUED

```
Sub MapDrive(netObj, local, network)
    '
    ' Set up VBScript error handling
    '
    On Error Resume Next

    '
    ' Attempt to map the network drive, then
    ' check the error and perform an action accordingly
    '
    netObj.MapNetworkDrive local, network
    If Err.Number <> 0 Then
        '
        ' The mapping failed; check the error code
        '
        If Err.Number = ERR_DRIVE_IN_USE Then
            '
            ' We're not going to display the error here
            ' any more because we're going to check the
            ' mappings later
            '
        Else
            Dim message, shell
            message = "We were unable to map '" & Local & _
                "' to the network share '" & Network & "'. " & _
                "The following error occurred: (" & Err.Number & _
                ") " & Err.Description
            Set shell = Wscript.CreateObject("WScript.Shell")
            shell.Popup message
        End If
    End If
End Sub

'----------------------------------------------------
' FUNC: ValidateConnections(netObj, localDrives,
'        netShares)
' DESC: This attempts to validate drive mappings using
'        the EnumNetworkDrives property of the network
'        object.
'----------------------------------------------------
Function ValidateConnections(netObj, localDrives, netShares)
    Dim iLocal, localDrive, netShare
    Dim drives, iDrive
    Dim foundShare
    Dim shell

    '
    ' Assume success; this may be toggled to failure
```

```
' later
'
ValidateConnections = True

'
' Create a shell object that we may use later for
' popup messages
'
Set shell = Wscript.CreateObject("WScript.Shell")

'
' Get the list of network drives
'
Set drives = netObj.EnumNetworkDrives

'
' Now loop & scan for each expected local and network
' drive
'
For iLocal = LBound(localDrives) To UBound(localDrives)
    localDrive = localDrives(iLocal)
    netShare = netShares(iLocal)

    '
    ' Check if drive mapping exists
    '
    foundShare = ""
    For iDrive = 0 To drives.Count - 1
        If drives(iDrive) = localDrive Then
            foundShare = drives(iDrive + 1)
            Exit For
        End If
    Next

    '
    ' Now check the results
    '
    If foundShare = "" Then
        '
        ' No drive mapping was found; don't output a message
        ' because it was probably already noted by the
        '
        '
        ValidateConnections = False
    ElseIf StrComp(foundShare, netShare, _
        vbTextCompare) <> 0 Then
        '
        ' A drive mapping was found, but it's not
        ' what was expected; for this we'll output a
```

continues

LISTING **11.4**   CONTINUED

```
        ' message
        '
        shell.Popup "The local drive '" & localDrive & _
            "' is mapped to '" & foundShare & "', but " & _
            "it should be mapped to '" & netShare & "' " & _
            "instead."
            ValidateConnections = False
        End If
    Next
End Function
```

The preceding script includes a new function called ValidateConnections(). The function retrieves a list of drive mappings using the WshNetwork.EnumNetworkDrives and then checks two input parameters (localDrives and netShares) to determine whether the drive mappings are correct. If an expected drive mapping is not found, no error message is displayed because an error was probably displayed by the MapDrive() function. If a drive mapping is found but is not what was expected, an error message is displayed to the user. If either of those errors occurs, the ValidateConnections() function returns false to indicate that there was a problem with the drive mappings. The main body of the script checks the return value and, if an error occurred, displays an error message as depicted in Figure 11.8.

FIGURE **11.8**

Descriptive message to user indicating that there are some mapping problems.

Checking Files

One issue that administrators routinely face is ensuring that users have up-to-date files. For example, as new versions of ODBC drivers with various bug fixes or enhancements come out, it's important to be able to easily distribute and update files on user workstations.

There are certainly high-end solutions that provide this capability. Among others, Microsoft and Tivoli provide solutions for software distribution and updates. If you don't have one of these high-end solutions, you may have had to invent your own solution for checking files and file versions. If you've done this in the past, you've probably tried to do it using batch files. And, as anyone knows who has had experience with batch files, it can be difficult to do reliably.

In this section, you'll see how you can use WSH to check for the existence of files and to check file versions. You'll also see how you can use WSH to replace current files with updated files.

Checking for the Existence of a File

It is certainly possible to check for the existence of files using batch files. Listing 11.5 shows a quick way that you could do it using a batch file.

LISTING 11.5   BATCH PROGRAM—CHECK FOR FILE

```
@Echo Off
If .%1.==.. Goto NoFileSpecified
If Not Exist %1 Goto FileNotExist

Echo File '%1' was found successfully.
Goto Exit

:NoFileSpecified
Echo No file was specified on the command line.
Goto Exit

:FileNotExist
Echo The file '%1' does not exist.

:Exit
```

The key line in the batch file is the line If Not Exist %1 Goto FileNotExist. It is effective, but the type of feedback that you can give to users is limited. And it's difficult to implement complex logic because of the mess of Gotos.

Listing 11.6 presents a WSH script file that shows how you can use WSH to check for the existence of files.

11

LISTING 11.6   chkfile.vbs—CHECK FOR FILE

```
' FILE: chkfile.vbs
' DESC: This script demonstrates how you can use VBScript
'       to check for the existence of files.
' AUTH: Thomas L. Fredell
' DATE: 12/9/1998
'
' Copyright 1998 Macmillan Publishing

Dim file, filesys, shell

'
' First check arguments to script
'
If Wscript.Arguments.Count < 1 Then
    Wscript.Echo "USAGE: ChkFile [file]"
    Wscript.Echo ""
    Wscript.Echo "        Checks for the existence of a "
    Wscript.Echo "        specified file."
    Wscript.Quit 1
End If
file = Wscript.Arguments(0)

'
' Next create a FileSystemObject and use it to check
' if the file exists; also create WshShell object for
' Popup windows
'
Set filesys = CreateObject("Scripting.FileSystemObject")
Set shell = CreateObject("WScript.Shell")
If filesys.FileExists(file) Then
    '
    ' File does exist
    '
    shell.Popup "The file '" & file & "' does exist."
Else
    '
    ' File doesn't exist
    '
    shell.Popup "The file '" & file & "' does not exist."
    '
    ' ADD YOUR LOGIC HERE (to copy file, etc.)
    '
End If
```

Checking File Versions

A common requirement is to ensure that users have up-to-date files. For example, new ODBC DLLs are released fairly frequently, and it's typically a good idea to update to the latest version because it incorporates bug fixes.

With WSH, it's easy to check for file versions. The script given in Listing 11.7 implements a check that verifies file versions using the file last modified date and size. If it appears that a file is out of date, it will be replaced by the updated version.

LISTING 11.7   chkver.vbs—CHECK FILE VERSION

```
' FILE: chkver.vbs
' DESC: This script demonstrates how you can use VBScript
'       to check file versions.
' AUTH: Thomas L. Fredell
' DATE: 12/9/1998
'
' Copyright 1998 Macmillan Publishing


'
' CONSTANTS
'
' These constants are for the WshShell.Popup() function
'
Const ICON_STOP = 16
Const ICON_INFO = 64

Dim sFileToCheck, sMasterFile
Dim fileCheck, fileMaster
Dim tCopyFile
Dim filesys, shell


'
' By default, we assume that we will not have to copy the
' master file to the file that we are checking
'
tCopyFile = False


'
' First check arguments to script
'
If Wscript.Arguments.Count < 1 Then
    Wscript.Echo "USAGE: ChkVer [fileToCheck] [masterFile]"
    Wscript.Echo ""
    Wscript.Echo "        Checks the version of 'fileToCheck'"
    Wscript.Echo "        versus 'masterFile'. For our purposes,"
```

continues

11

LISTING **11.7**   CONTINUED

```
        Wscript.Echo "        same version means same timestamp"
        Wscript.Echo "        and same file length."
        Wscript.Quit 1
End If
sFileToCheck = Wscript.Arguments(0)
sMasterFile = Wscript.Arguments(1)


' Next create a FileSystemObject and use it to check
' if the file exists; also create WshShell object for
' Popup windows
'
Set filesys = CreateObject("Scripting.FileSystemObject")
Set shell = CreateObject("WScript.Shell")


' Check to make sure none of the file names contain
' wildcards
'
If (InStr(sFileToCheck, "*") > 0) Or _
   (InStr(sFileToCheck, "?") > 0) Or _
   (InStr(sMasterFile, "*") > 0) Or _
   (InStr(sMasterFile, "?") > 0) Then
    shell.Popup "Error: Either the master file, the file to" & _
        " check, or both contain wildcards.", 0, _
        "chkver.vbs", ICON_STOP
    Wscript.Quit 1
End If


' First, do a sanity check to ensure that the files have
' the same name
'
If StrComp(filesys.GetFileName(sFileToCheck), _
    filesys.GetFileName(sMasterFile), vbTextCompare) <> 0 Then
        '
        ' File names are different (ignoring path)!
        '
    shell.Popup "Error: The names of the files are different!" & _
        " The script will terminate execution.", 0, _
        "chkver.vbs", ICON_STOP
    Wscript.Quit 1
End If


' Check to see if the master file exists
'
```

```
If Not filesys.FileExists(sMasterFile) Then
    '
    ' File doesn't exist
    '
    shell.Popup "Error: The master file, " & sMasterFile & _
        ", doesn't exist. The script will terminate.", 0, _
        "chkver.vbs", ICON_STOP
    Wscript.Quit 1
Else
    Set fileMaster = filesys.GetFile(sMasterFile)
End If


'
' Check to see if the file that we need to check exists
'
If Not filesys.FileExists(sFileToCheck) Then
    '
    ' File doesn't exist
    '
    shell.Popup "The file '" & sFileToCheck & "' doesn't " & _
        "exist. The file will be copied from the master file.", _
        3, "chkver.vbs", ICON_INFO


    '
    ' Flag that we should copy the file
    '
    tCopyFile = True
Else
    '
    ' File does exist, so check version
    '
    Set fileCheck = filesys.GetFile(sFileToCheck)
    If fileCheck.DateLastModified < fileMaster.DateLastModified Then
        '
        ' File to check is older than the master file, so it
        ' should be copied
        '
        tCopyFile = True
    ElseIf fileCheck.Size <> fileMaster.Size Then
        '
        ' File to check is a different size; we take that
        ' as different, so we'll replace
        '
        tCopyFile = True
    End If
    '
    ' Release file object to ensure that we don't
    ' interfere with the file copy later
    '
```

11

continues

LISTING **11.7**   CONTINUED

```
        Set fileCheck = Nothing
    End If

    '
    ' Check if flag to copy file is set; if it is, do the copy
    '
    If tCopyFile Then
        On Error Resume Next
        filesys.CopyFile sMasterFile, sFileToCheck, True
        If Err.Number <> 0 Then
            '
            ' Error occurred during copy
            '
            shell.Popup "Error: The copy failed, additional error " & _
                "information is listed below." & vbCrLf & vbCrLf & _
                "(" & Err.Number & ") " & Err.Description, 0, _
                "chkver.vbs", ICON_STOP
            Wscript.Quit Err.Number
        Else
            '
            ' Show success; notice that the time-out is set
            ' so the message box will disappear after 5 seconds
            ' if user doesn't click on it first
            shell.Popup "The file " & sFileToCheck & " was " & _
                "successfully updated with " & sMasterFile, 5, _
                "chkver.vbs", ICON_INFO
        End If
    End If
```

The script takes two arguments; the first argument is the file that should be checked, and the second argument is the *master file*. If the file to check is older or a different size than the master file, it is replaced by the master file. Figure 11.9 shows the results after a file has been updated.

FIGURE 11.9

Message displayed to user after file is copied.

When the script runs, it first checks to ensure that neither of the file arguments contain a wildcard character. If either contains a wildcard, the results of running the script could be unpredictable. Next, the filenames are checked to ensure that they are the same. To do so, compare the names that are returned by the `FileSystemObject.GetFileName()` function. `GetFileName()` returns just the filename from a file path.

The script then checks to see whether the file that is being checked exists. If the file doesn't exist, you display a message to the user and set a flag indicating that you should copy the file. If it does exist, you check it against the master file using the `File.DateLastModified` and `File.Size` properties. If it is older or a different size than the master file, set the copy flag. Finally, if the copy flag is set, you attempt to copy the file and then display an error or success message depending on the result.

You'll notice that we have used some additional arguments to the `shell.Popup()` method. For the success message at the end of the script, we've added a timeout so that the message disappears automatically after five seconds. We've also added a title for the message dialog and an icon. The success message uses the information icon; the various error messages use the stop icon.

Program Registry Settings

On early versions of the Microsoft Windows platform, text files with the extension `.INI` were typically used to store program settings. That was a reasonable early solution but posed problems as programs began to share information and settings. As a solution, Microsoft developed the Windows Registry to provide a central repository for program, user, and system settings.

The Registry is a hierarchical data structure that is conceptually similar to a directory system. To examine the Registry, you can use the Windows standard `regedit` program. Figure 11.10 shows an example of the Windows Registry and program settings.

11

FIGURE 11.10

The Windows Registry and program settings.

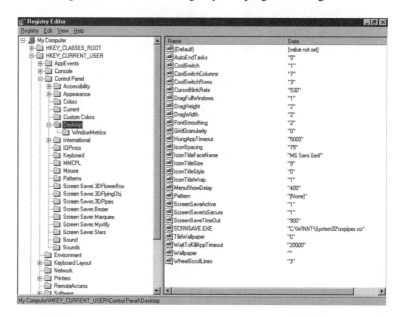

In the Registry, there are keys, subkeys, and values. Several standard root keys are used to navigate to program settings. Two of the most commonly used are the following:

- HKEY_CURRENT_USER   This is the root in the Registry for settings for the current user.
- HKEY_LOCAL_MACHINE   This is the root in the Registry for settings for the current machine.

Each Registry key can contain multiple values. A value consists of a name and the actual value, which may be a string, a DWORD, a binary value, or something else. Most modern Windows programs use the Registry to store their settings. Windows itself uses the Registry to store settings for Windows components. For example, the HKEY_CURRENT_USER\Software\Microsoft\Windows\CurrentVersion\Explorer\Advanced\Hidden Registry value is used to determine whether a user should see hidden files when she uses the Windows Explorer.

Many values are in the Registry. It's worthwhile to look through the Registry to see what types of information are stored. And, with WSH, you can alter Registry values and consequently change program settings. Next, you're going to look at some functions you can perform with WSH and the Registry.

Reading the Registry and Checking Program Settings

Reading the Registry from WSH is easy using the WshShell object. WshShell provides the RegRead() method, which allows you to read the value of a Registry key or Registry value. In Listing 11.8, you'll see how you can use the RegRead() method.

LISTING 11.8   chkreg.js—CHECK PROGRAM SETTINGS IN THE REGISTRY

```
// FILE: chkreg.js
// DESC: This script demonstrates how you can use VBScript
//       to check for program registry settings.
// AUTH: Thomas L. Fredell
// DATE: 12/9/1998
//
// Copyright 1998 Macmillan Publishing


//
// "Constants"
//
// These are paths to registry keys
//
var EXPLORER_SHOW_HIDDEN =
    "HKCU\\Software\\Microsoft\\Windows\\CurrentVersion\\" +
    "Explorer\\Advanced\\Hidden";
var CURRENT_WALLPAPER =
```

```
                "HKCU\\Control Panel\\Desktop\\Wallpaper";

//
// Instantiate a shell object; we'll use the
// RegRead() method
//
var shell = WScript.createObject("WScript.Shell");

//
// Retrieve and display some registry values
//
var nHidden = shell.RegRead(EXPLORER_SHOW_HIDDEN);
var sWallpaper = shell.RegRead(CURRENT_WALLPAPER);
WScript.Echo("chkreg.js: The setting for explorer to show " +
    "hidden files is " + nHidden + ".");
WScript.Echo("chkreg.js: The current wallpaper is '" +
    sWallpaper + "'.");
```

The chkreg.js is a simple example that reads and displays two Registry settings. There's not much to it. It sets some constants that are the paths to Registry values, it instantiates a WshShell object, and finally it calls the WshShell.RegRead() method. There are two important things to notice. First, instead of specifying HKEY_CURRENT_USER as the root for the Registry settings, we're using the abbreviation HKCU. The WshShell.RegRead() method recognizes abbreviations for commonly used Registry roots. Second, because this example uses JScript, the paths to the Registry keys must contain double-slashes because a single slash is an escape character (the same is not true for VBScript).

Changing Program Registry Settings

In Listing 11.9, you'll see how you can change settings in the Registry.

 Caution Before you make any changes to the Registry, make sure that you back up the Registry or create an emergency repair disk. By changing settings in the Registry, you could cause Windows or other programs to fail.

LISTING **11.9**   writereg.vbs—CHANGE PROGRAM SETTINGS IN THE REGISTRY

```
' FILE: writereg.vbs
' DESC: This script demonstrates how you can use VBScript
'       to modify program registry settings.
' AUTH: Thomas L. Fredell
' DATE: 12/9/1998
'
```

continues

LISTING 11.9   CONTINUED

```vbs
' Copyright 1998 Macmillan Publishing

'
' Constants
'
' These are paths to registry keys
'
Const NOTEPAD_KEY = "HKCU\Software\Microsoft\Notepad\"
Const EXPLORER_KEY = _
    "HKCU\Software\Microsoft\Windows\CurrentVersion\Explorer\Advanced\"

On Error Resume Next

'
' Instantiate a shell object; we'll use it for RegWrite()
'
Dim shell
Set shell = Wscript.CreateObject("WScript.Shell")

'
' First change value for Notepad's font
'
shell.RegWrite NOTEPAD_KEY & "lfFaceName", "Courier New"
If Err.Number <> 0 Then
    Wscript.Echo "An error occurred while changing notepad's font."
    Wscript.Echo "(" & Err.Number & ") " & Err.Description
    Wscript.Quit Err.Number
End If

'
' Next change Explorer to hide hidden files
'
shell.RegWrite EXPLORER_KEY & "Hidden", 0, "REG_DWORD"
If Err.Number <> 0 Then
    Wscript.Echo "An error occurred while changing 'show " & _
        "hidden' files in the explorer."
    Wscript.Echo "(" & Err.Number & ") " & Err.Description
Else
    Wscript.Echo "writereg.vbs: Changed registry settings."
    Wscript.Echo ""
End If
Wscript.Quit Err.Number
```

The preceding `writereg.vbs` script uses a structure similar to the `chkreg.js` script. Begin with embedded constants for Registry paths, instantiate a WSH shell object, and then change Registry settings using the `WshShell.RegWrite()` method. The two settings that you change are the font for the Windows Notepad program and the Show Hidden Files setting for the Windows Explorer.

Administering User Shortcuts and Folders

The Windows Scripting Host provides powerful capabilities to programmatically administer Windows shortcuts and folders. Using WSH, you can easily create or delete shortcuts and folders. In the next few sections, you'll look at WSH code that can be used to perform those functions.

Managing Shortcuts

Creating and deleting shortcuts is easy using WSH. To create shortcuts, we'll use the versatile `WshShell` object. `WshShell` provides a method called `CreateShortcut()` to create new shortcut objects. You can use that in conjunction with the `WshShell.SpecialFolders` property to create shortcuts on the Windows desktop and Start menu. To delete shortcuts, use `WshShell` in conjunction with the `FileSystemObject`.

The next few sections provide detailed code examples that illustrate some of the functions that you can perform with shortcuts using WSH.

Checking for a Shortcut

Listing 11.10 uses the `WshShell` object in conjunction with the `FileSystemObject` to check for the existence of a shortcut.

LISTING 11.10   `chkscut.vbs`—CHECK FOR SHORTCUTS

```
' FILE: chkscut.vbs
' DESC: This script demonstrates how you can use VBScript
'       to create Windows shortcuts.
' AUTH: Thomas L. Fredell
' DATE: 12/9/1998
'
' Copyright 1998 Macmillan Publishing

On Error Resume Next


' Check arguments & show usage if necessary
'
```

continues

LISTING **11.10**   CONTINUED

```
If Wscript.Arguments.Count <> 1 Then
    Wscript.Echo "USAGE:  chkscut.vbs  [shortcut file]"
    Wscript.Echo ""
    Wscript.Echo "        This checks to see if the 'shortcut file'"
    Wscript.Echo "        exists."
    Wscript.Echo ""
    Wscript.Quit 1
End If

Dim sLinkFile
Dim filesys

    '
    ' We'll accept file paths in the form <SpecialFolder>\file.lnk
    ' so first we need to expand the folder & resolve to
    ' an absolute path
    '
sLinkFile = ExpandFilePath(Wscript.Arguments(0))
Wscript.Echo "chkscut.vbs: Expanded path to link is '" & _
    sLinkFile & "'."

    '
    ' Check to see if file exists using FileSystemObject
    '
Set filesys = Wscript.CreateObject("Scripting.FileSystemObject")
If Not filesys.FileExists(sLinkFile) Then
    Wscript.Echo "chkscut.vbs: The shortcut link file doesn't exist."
Else
    Wscript.Echo "chkscut.vbs: The shortcut link file exists."
End If

    '-----------------------------------------------------------
    ' FUNC: ExpandFilePath(sPath)
    ' DESC: Returns a string that represents the expanded
    '       file path.
    '-----------------------------------------------------------
Function ExpandFilePath(sPath)
    On Error Resume Next

    Dim asPathSegments, iSeg, sSeg
    Dim sSpecialFolder
    Dim shell

        '
        ' We need a shell object to expand special folders
        '
    Set shell = Wscript.CreateObject("WScript.Shell")

        '
```

```
        ' First we'll split the input path into an array
        ' of strings using '\' as a delimiter; this will
        ' make the search easy, because we'll only have to
        ' iterate through an array, assuming the path is
        ' well-formed
        '
        asPathSegments = Split(sPath, "\")
        For iSeg = LBound(asPathSegments) To UBound(asPathSegments)
            sSeg = asPathSegments(iSeg)
            If Len(sSeg) > 2 Then
                '
                ' A special folder must be AT LEAST 3 characters,
                ' but in reality will be more ala <Desktop>
                '
                If (Left(sSeg, 1) = "<") And (Right(sSeg, 1) = ">") Then
                    '
                    ' Attempt to expand this path segment
                    '
                    sSpecialFolder = Mid(sSeg, 2, Len(sSeg) - 2)
                    asPathSegments(iSeg) = shell.SpecialFolders
➡(sSpecialFolder)
                End If
            End If
        Next

        '
        ' Now we can re-assemble the path and return it
        '
        ExpandFilePath = Join(asPathSegments, "\")
End Function
```

The script begins with a basic check to ensure that the command-line parameters are specified correctly. Next, we call an interesting function that we've developed called ExpandFilePath(), which takes the input argument and scans it for special embedded paths. For example, you can specify <Desktop>\file.lnk as the command-line argument. When that's passed to ExpandFilePath(), the function splits the path into an array using the VBScript Split() function. Next, each element of the array is checked to determine whether it is bracketed using < and >. If it is, the SpecialFolders property of a WshShell object is used to resolve it to a true path. Finally, the function reassembles the path using the Join() function.

The rest of the script is basic. A FileSystemObject is instantiated, and the FileExists() method is called to check for the link file. The output from the script is illustrated in Figure 11.11.

FIGURE **11.11**

Result of running the
chkscut.vbs *script.*

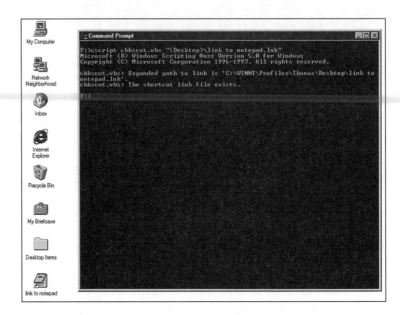

Creating a New Shortcut

The script example in Listing 11.11 shows how you can use the WSH objects to create
new shortcuts. The script creates two new shortcuts—one on the Windows desktop and
one on the Windows Start menu.

LISTING **11.11**   makescut.vbs—CODE SAMPLE TO CREATE SHORTCUTS

```
' FILE: makescut.vbs
' DESC: This script demonstrates how you can use VBScript
'       to create Windows shortcuts.
' AUTH: Thomas L. Fredell
' DATE: 12/9/1998
'
' Copyright 1998 Macmillan Publishing

On Error Resume Next

'
' Create shortcuts; we'll use our own function to wrap shortcut
' creation
'
Dim shortcut

Set shortcut = CreateShortcut("Desktop", _
    "link to notepad.lnk", "notepad.exe")
```

```
If Not shortcut Is Nothing Then
    shortcut.Description = "Link to Windows notepad"
    shortcut.Save
    Wscript.Echo "makescut.vbs: Created link to Windows notepad " & _
        "on Desktop."
End If

If GetOS() = "WINDOWS_NT" Then
    Set shortcut = CreateShortcut("StartMenu", _
        "Command Prompt.lnk", "cmd.exe")
    If Not shortcut Is Nothing Then
        shortcut.Hotkey = "CTRL+SHIFT+0"
        shortcut.Description = "Link to Command prompt"
        shortcut.Save
    End If
    Wscript.Echo "makescut.vbs: Created link to Windows NT " & _
        "command prompt on Start Menu."
End If

Wscript.Quit Err.Number

'-------------------------------------------------------------
' FUNC: CreateShortcut(sFolder, sFilename, sTarget)
' DESC: Creates a new shortcut object, saves it, then
'       returns it so additional attributes can be set.
'       sFolder must be the name of a predefined Windows
'       folder, like "Desktop".
'-------------------------------------------------------------
Function CreateShortcut(sFolder, sFilename, sTarget)
    Dim shell, sFolderPath, sFullPath
    Dim sErr
    On Error Resume Next
    Set shell = Wscript.CreateObject("WScript.Shell")
    If Err.Number <> 0 Then
        Wscript.Echo "Error: Unable to create shell object" & vbCrLf & _
            "        (" & Err.Number & ") " & Err.Description
        Exit Function
    End If

    '
    ' Determine full path to shortcut file using folder settings
    ' from shell object
    '
    sFolderPath = shell.SpecialFolders(sFolder)
    If Err.Number <> 0 Then
        sErr = "Error: Unable to retrieve path for folder '" & _
            sFolder & "'." & vbCrLf & vbCrLf & _
            "Details - (" & Err.Number & ") " & Err.Description
        shell.Popup sErr, 0, "CreateShortcut() Error", 16
```

continues

11

LISTING **11.11**   CONTINUED

```
            Exit Function
        End If
        If Right(sFolderPath, 1) <> "\" Then
            sFullPath = sFolderPath & "\" & sFilename
        Else
            sFullPath = sFolderPath & sFilename
        End If

        '
        ' Use shell object to create shortcut; check errors to
        ' ensure that it works
        '
        Set CreateShortcut = shell.CreateShortcut(sFullPath)
        If Err.Number <> 0 Then
            sErr = "Unable to create shortcut, path = '" & _
                sFullPath & "'." & vbCrLf & vbCrLf & _
                "Details - (" & Err.Number & ") " & Err.Description
            shell.Popup sErr, 0, "CreateShortcut() Error", 16
            Set CreateShortcut = Nothing
            Exit Function
        End If
        CreateShortcut.TargetPath = sTarget
        CreateShortcut.Save
    End Function

    '-------------------------------------------------------------
    ' FUNC: GetOS()
    ' DESC: Returns a string that represents the current
    '       operating system.
    '-------------------------------------------------------------
    Function GetOS()
        '
        ' We're going to get the OS using the current
        ' environment, so we need a shell object
        '
        Dim shell
        Set shell = Wscript.CreateObject("WScript.Shell")
        If Err.Number <> 0 Then
            Wscript.Echo "Error: Unable to create shell object" & vbCrLf & _
                "          (" & Err.Number & ") " & Err.Description
            Exit Function
        End If
        GetOS = UCase(shell.Environment("OS"))
    End Function
```

Most of the logic in the previous script is embedded in two functions: CreateShortcut() and GetOS(). The body of the script first calls CreateShortcut() to create a shortcut to the Windows Notepad on the desktop. Next, it calls the GetOS() function to check whether the current operating system is Windows NT. If it is Windows NT, the script creates a shortcut to the Windows NT command prompt on the Start menu.

The CreateShortcut() function contains all the logic for creating a Windows shortcut. It takes three arguments: the Windows folder in which the shortcut should be created, such as Desktop; the filename for the new shortcut file; and the target for the shortcut file. Within the function, it instantiates a WshShell object. The WshShell is used to find the absolute path to the Windows folder specified in the first argument and then it's used to create a new shortcut object, which is saved and returned to the caller of CreateShortcut().

The other primary function, GetOS(), returns a string that represents the current operating system. The guts of it are simple; it creates a WshShell object, which contains an Environment property that we access to get the value of the "OS" environment variable.

Note   Creating new shortcuts using WSH is easy as you can tell from the preceding example. Unfortunately, changing existing shortcuts isn't possible because the WshShell object doesn't provide a capability to get an object for an existing shortcut.

11

Deleting a Shortcut

The sample script in Listing 11.12 shows how you can delete a Windows shortcut. The structure of the example is similar to the Check Shortcut example.

LISTING 11.12   delscut.vbs—CODE SAMPLE TO DELETE A SHORTCUT

```
' FILE: delscut.vbs
' DESC: This script demonstrates how you can use VBScript
'       to delete Windows shortcuts.
' AUTH: Thomas L. Fredell
' DATE: 12/9/1998
'
' Copyright 1998 Macmillan Publishing

On Error Resume Next


'
' Check arguments & show usage if necessary
'
```

continues

LISTING **11.12**   CONTINUED

```
If Wscript.Arguments.Count <> 1 Then
    Wscript.Echo "USAGE:  delscut.vbs  [shortcut file]"
    Wscript.Echo ""
    Wscript.Echo "          This deletes the 'shortcut file'."
    Wscript.Echo ""
    Wscript.Quit 1
End If

Dim sLinkFile
Dim filesys

    '
    ' We'll use routine from chkscut.vbs to expand path
    '
sLinkFile = ExpandFilePath(Wscript.Arguments(0))
Wscript.Echo "delscut.vbs: Expanded path to link is '" & _
    sLinkFile & "'."

    '
    ' Check to see if file exists using FileSystemObject
    '
Set filesys = Wscript.CreateObject("Scripting.FileSystemObject")
If Not filesys.FileExists(sLinkFile) Then
    Wscript.Echo "delscut.vbs: The shortcut link file wasn't found."
Else
    filesys.DeleteFile sLinkFile, True
    If Err.Number = 0 Then
        Wscript.Echo "delscut.vbs: The shortcut link file " & _
            "was deleted successfully."
    Else
        Wscript.Echo "delscut.vbs: Unable to delete shortcut " & _
            "link file. (" & Err.Number & ") " & Err.Description
    End If
End If

    '-----------------------------------------------------------
    ' FUNC: ExpandFilePath(sPath)
    ' DESC: Returns a string that represents the expanded
    '       file path.
    '-----------------------------------------------------------
Function ExpandFilePath(sPath)
    On Error Resume Next

    Dim asPathSegments, iSeg, sSeg
    Dim sSpecialFolder
    Dim shell

    '
```

```
' We need a shell object to expand special folders
'
Set shell = Wscript.CreateObject("WScript.Shell")

'
' First we'll split the input path into an array
' of strings using '\' as a delimiter; this will
' make the search easy, because we'll only have to
' iterate through an array, assuming the path is
' well-formed
'
asPathSegments = Split(sPath, "\")
For iSeg = LBound(asPathSegments) To UBound(asPathSegments)
    sSeg = asPathSegments(iSeg)
    If Len(sSeg) > 2 Then
        '
        ' A special folder must be AT LEAST 3 characters,
        ' but in reality will be more ala <Desktop>
        '
        If (Left(sSeg, 1) = "<") And (Right(sSeg, 1) = ">") Then
            '
            ' Attempt to expand this path segment
            '
            sSpecialFolder = Mid(sSeg, 2, Len(sSeg) - 2)
            asPathSegments(iSeg) = shell.SpecialFolders
➥(sSpecialFolder)
        End If
    End If
Next

'
' Now we can re-assemble the path and return it
'
ExpandFilePath = Join(asPathSegments, "\")
End Function
```

This delete shortcut script is almost identical to the check shortcut script. The only differences are the messages and the use of the `FileSystemObject.DeleteFile()` method.

Managing Folders

You've seen how easy it is to check, create, and delete Windows shortcuts. Now you'll take a look at how you can perform similar functions with folders. When you understand how to manage shortcuts and folders with scripts, you will have the ability to write scripts that can reconfigure much of a user's Windows experience from the desktop and Start menu perspective.

Checking for a Folder

To check for a folder, Listing 11.13 uses the `FileSystemObject`. It provides a `FolderExists()` method that returns true if a folder exists, or false if it doesn't.

LISTING 11.13   `chkfldr.vbs`—CODE SAMPLE TO CHECK FOR A FOLDER

```
' FILE: chkfldr.vbs
' DESC: This script demonstrates how you can use VBScript
'        to check for a folder.
' AUTH: Thomas L. Fredell
' DATE: 12/9/1998
'
' Copyright 1998 Macmillan Publishing

On Error Resume Next

'
' Check arguments & show usage if necessary
'
If Wscript.Arguments.Count <> 1 Then
    Wscript.Echo "USAGE:  chkfldr.vbs  [folder path]"
    Wscript.Echo ""
    Wscript.Echo "          This checks for the existence"
    Wscript.Echo "          of 'folder path'."
    Wscript.Echo ""
    Wscript.Quit 1
End If


'
' Check to see if folder exists using FileSystemObject
'
Dim sFolderPath
Dim filesys
Dim tExists

sFolderPath = Wscript.Arguments(0)
Set filesys = Wscript.CreateObject("Scripting.FileSystemObject")

If filesys.FolderExists(sFolderPath) Then
    Wscript.Echo "chkfldr.vbs: The folder '" & _
        sFolderPath & "' was found."
Else
    Wscript.Echo "chkfldr.vbs: The folder '" & _
        sFolderPath & "' doesn't exist."
End If
```

The chkfldr.vbs script is simple. It begins with the standard argument check. Next it instantiates a FileSystemObject, which is used for the FolderExists() method to check for a folder.

Creating a New Folder

Creating a folder is as easy as checking for a folder. Examine the script in Listing 11.14, makfldr.vbs, and you'll see the similarities.

LISTING 11.14   makfldr.vbs—CODE SAMPLE TO CREATE A NEW FOLDER

```
' FILE: makfldr.vbs
' DESC: This script demonstrates how you can use VBScript
'       to create a new folder.
' AUTH: Thomas L. Fredell
' DATE: 12/9/1998
'
' Copyright 1998 Macmillan Publishing

On Error Resume Next

'
' Check arguments & show usage if necessary
'
If Wscript.Arguments.Count < 1 Then
    Wscript.Echo "USAGE:  makfldr.vbs  [folder1]..[folderN]"
    Wscript.Echo ""
    Wscript.Echo "        This allows you to create one or more"
    Wscript.Echo "        folders."
    Wscript.Echo ""
    Wscript.Quit 1
End If


'
' Create a FileSystemObject; we'll use it to create the
' new folder(s)
'
Dim sFolderPath
Dim filesys

Set filesys = Wscript.CreateObject("Scripting.FileSystemObject")

'
' Iterate through the arguments & create folders
'
For Each sFolderPath In Wscript.Arguments
    filesys.CreateFolder sFolderPath
```

continues

11

LISTING 11.14   CONTINUED

```
If Err.Number = 0 Then
    Wscript.Echo "makfldr.vbs: The folder '" & _
        sFolderPath & "' was created successfully."
Else
    Wscript.Echo ""
    Wscript.Echo "makfldr.vbs: An error occurred while " & _
        "creating the folder '" & sFolderPath & "'"
    Wscript.Echo "makfldr.vbs: (" & Err.Number & ") " &
Err.Description
    Wscript.Echo ""
    End If
Next
```

This script differs from the previous script because it takes multiple command-line arguments. A For..Each loop iterates through the arguments and creates directories accordingly.

Let's take a quick look at the effects of running the script. The before picture is illustrated in Figure 11.12.

FIGURE 11.12

Directories before running the makfldr.vbs *script.*

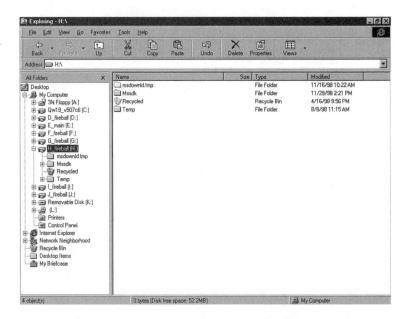

If you run the script using the command line makfldr H:\ROOT H:\ROOT\BIN
H:\ROOT\SRC H:\ROOT\HELP H:\ROOT\HELP\ADMIN, you'll see the output illustrated in
Figure 11.13, and if you go back to the Windows Explorer, you'll see something that
looks like Figure 11.14.

FIGURE 11.13

Output of the
makfldr.vbs *script.*

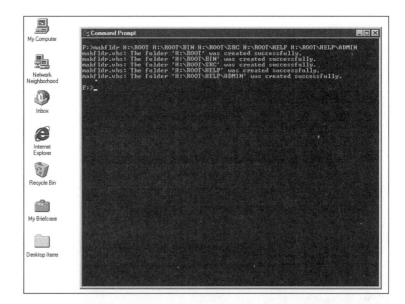

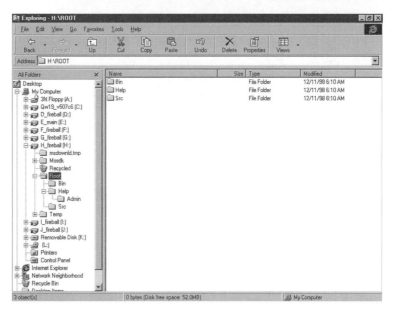

FIGURE 11.14

*Directories after run-
ning the* makfldr.vbs
script.

11

Deleting a Folder

Deleting a folder is just as simple as the preceding examples. Listing 11.15 uses the
`FileSystemObject.DeleteFolder()` method instead of `FolderExists()` or
`CreateFolder()`.

LISTING **11.15** `delfldr.vbs`—CODE TO DELETE FOLDER(S)

```
' FILE: delfldr.vbs
' DESC: This script demonstrates how you can use VBScript
'       to delete a folder.
' AUTH: Thomas L. Fredell
' DATE: 12/9/1998
'
' Copyright 1998 Macmillan Publishing

On Error Resume Next


'
' Check arguments & show usage if necessary
'
If Wscript.Arguments.Count < 1 Then
    Wscript.Echo "USAGE:  delfldr.vbs  [folder1]..[folderN]"
    Wscript.Echo ""
    Wscript.Echo "          This allows you to delete one or more"
    Wscript.Echo "          folders."
    Wscript.Echo ""
    Wscript.Quit 1
End If


'
' Create a FileSystemObject; we'll use it to delete the folder(s)
'
Dim sFolderPath
Dim filesys

Set filesys = Wscript.CreateObject("Scripting.FileSystemObject")


'
' Iterate through the arguments & delete folders
'
For Each sFolderPath In Wscript.Arguments
    filesys.DeleteFolder sFolderPath
    If Err.Number = 0 Then
        Wscript.Echo "delfldr.vbs: The folder '" & _
            sFolderPath & "' was deleted successfully."
    Else
        Wscript.Echo ""
        Wscript.Echo "delfldr.vbs: An error occurred while " & _
```

```
            "deleting the folder '" & sFolderPath & "'"
        Wscript.Echo "delfldr.vbs: (" & Err.Number & ") " &
➥Err.Description
        Wscript.Echo ""
    End If
Next
```

The flow of delfldr.vbs is identical to the makfldr.vbs script. The only differences are the messages and the call to DeleteFolder().

Summary

In this chapter, you've seen a number of examples that illustrate how you can use the WSH objects to perform standard administrative tasks. You've looked at examples that show how you can perform the following functions:

- Script user logins
- Check and change directory mappings
- Check files and file versions
- Examine and change program Registry settings
- Check for, create, and delete shortcuts and folders

You can take the script samples and the embedded functions and use them for your own scripts. You can even extend the standard capabilities with objects that plug into WSH. Later in this book, you'll see how to use the WSH objects with other objects to administer Windows NT server programs.

Q&A

Q What object should I use to access the Windows Registry?

A You can use the WshShell object to read and write the Windows Registry.

Q How can I determine the path to a user's desktop folder?

A The WshShell object provides a SpecialFolders property that allows you to determine the path to special Windows folders such as the desktop.

Q Which object should I use to change network directory mappings?

A You can use the WshNetwork object to change mappings.

DAY **12**

Automating Microsoft SQL Server Administration Using WSH Scripts

Day 12: Chapter Overview

In this chapter, you're going to see how you can use Microsoft SQL Server Management Objects to automate Microsoft SQL Server administration through WSH scripts. You'll learn how to automate SQL Server tasks, and you'll see scripts that give you examples you can use to create your own administrative scripts.

On the 12th day of your introduction to WSH, you'll do the following:

- Discover Microsoft SQL Server and SQL Server Administration
- Learn about the SQL Server Distributed Management Objects

- See examples that show WSH scripts that use the SQL Server Distributed Management Objects to administer Devices, Databases, and Tables

Introduction to SQL Server 6.5 Administration

Microsoft SQL Server is a very popular database server for the Windows NT platform. It provides a robust database engine, tight integration with the Windows NT operating system, and a powerful and easy-to-use management interface. With the management interface, you can create new databases or database devices, back up or restore databases, change SQL Server execution settings, and perform many other tasks.

Interestingly enough for you, the management interface uses ActiveX objects exposed by SQL Server to perform its functions. You can use the same ActiveX objects to perform your own administrative tasks programmatically. In this chapter, you'll see how you can use the ActiveX objects with WSH scripts to perform SQL Server administration.

 Note

> The concepts within this chapter are directly applicable to Microsoft SQL Server 7.0. The administration interface is different because with SQL Server 7.0, Microsoft incorporated SQL Server administration into the standard Microsoft Management Console (MMC) interface. However, the underlying objects are very similar.

First, you're going to take a look at some very typical administrative tasks for SQL Server. You'll run through the steps that you would perform using the standard management interface. You're going to focus on the tasks of creating and deleting devices, databases, and tables.

Next, you'll look at the administration objects that are available for SQL Server. For each object, you'll briefly examine the purpose of the object and its use.

Finally, you'll look at detailed script examples that will show you how you can use the administration objects in practice. In the examples, you'll find functions that you can cut and paste into your own scripts if you choose.

By the end of this chapter, you should have a clear idea of how administrative tasks can be performed with SQL Server and WSH scripts. You'll cover the basics in this chapter; using it as a foundation, you'll be able to create your own custom scripts.

Standard SQL Server Administration

If you're performing SQL Server administration, you'll most typically use the SQL Server Enterprise Manager. The Enterprise Manager, depicted in Figure 12.1, provides a Windows Explorer style view of an instance of SQL Server. You'll notice that different folders represent different "parts" of the SQL Server.

FIGURE 12.1

The SQL Server Enterprise Manager.

Table 12.1 summarizes the folders.

TABLE 12.1 SQL SERVER ENTERPRISE MANAGER FOLDERS

Folder Name	Description
Database Devices	Devices are the actual files in the file system that store information for SQL Server databases. A single database might be split among multiple devices. It's also very common for a database to use one device to store data and a separate device to store the database transaction log.
Backup Devices	Backup devices are used to store backups of databases.
Databases	Databases store all the information contained within SQL Server. Each database contains one or more tables, and each table consists of multiple rows and columns. If you expand the databases folder, you'll see a list of the databases on the server. If you expand a database, you'll see two folders: Group/Users contains all the valid groups and users for the database, and Objects contains all the components of the database, such as tables, views, and stored procedures.
Logins	This contains all the valid user logins for the SQL Server.

12

To perform an administrative task, you can right-click an object or folder and pick a selection from the context menu that appears. For example, if I right-click on the Databases folder, as depicted in Figure 12.2, a menu will appear that will give me the option to create a new database. If I right-click on a specific database in the databases folder, the context menu gives me the capability to delete the database or edit it. Each object in the Enterprise Manager provides an appropriate context menu that gives you quick access to management functions.

FIGURE 12.2

The context menu for the Databases folder.

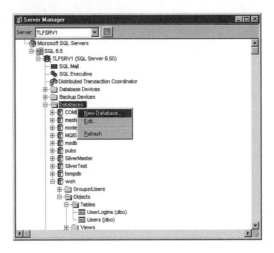

Alternatively, I could select one of the options on the Manage menu, such as Manage, Databases. If I do so, the Manage Databases dialog box will appear, as illustrated in Figure 12.3. Using the interface I can create, edit, or delete databases using convenient icons at the top-left of the interface.

There's yet another way to perform administrative tasks in SQL Server; you can use SQL commands in the SQL Query Tool. To display the SQL query window, you select Tools, SQL Query Tool from the menu. You can see the SQL query window illustrated in Figure 12.4; in the illustration, you can see a SQL query that will create a new database device.

FIGURE **12.3**

*The Manage
Databases dialog box.*

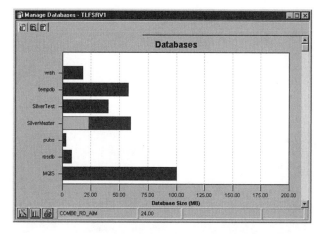

FIGURE **12.4**

The SQL Query Tool.

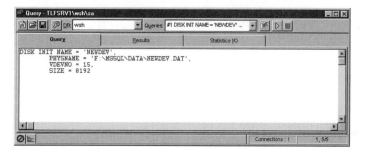

With the exception of the SQL query tool, all the other tools in the SQL Enterprise
Manager use the SQL Distributed Management Objects (DMO) provided by SQL Server.
The Distributed Management Objects provide a high-level, object-oriented interface for
SQL Server administration. Fortunately for you, you can access the SQL DMO objects
in your own programs to perform administrative tasks. In the next section, I'll discuss the
DMO objects and their capabilities.

Administration Objects

The SQL Server DMO administration objects can be used to administer literally any
SQL Server feature. Consequently, there are many objects in the DMO object hierarchy.
Figure 12.5 shows a diagram of the SQL DMO object hierarchy taken from the
Microsoft SQL Server online documentation.

FIGURE 12.5

*The Microsoft SQL
Server DMO object
hierarchy.*

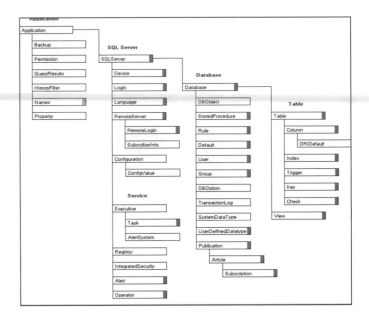

For all the details for the SQL DMO objects, please refer to the Microsoft SQL Server
documentation. You're going to use the objects in Table 12.2 in your WSH SQL Server
administration scripts.

TABLE 12.2 SQL SERVER DMO OBJECTS

Object Name	Description
SQLServer	The SQLServer object is the most important object in the SQL Server DMO object hierarchy. It's the object that you use to connect to an instance of SQL Server to perform administrative functions. It provides collections of databases and devices that can be used to add or remove databases or devices.
Device	The Device object represents preallocated storage that SQL Server uses to store databases, transaction logs, or database backups. To add a new device to an instance of SQL Server, you'll need to instantiate a Device object and add it to the SQLServer.Devices collection.
Database	The Database object contains information stored using a SQL Server. It provides the capability to change database attributes, execute database commands, and perform numerous other functions. For your purposes, you're going to use it to create a new database. You'll use it in conjunction with the Device and SQLServer objects.

Object Name	Description
Table	The Table object represents a table in a database. Table objects contain columns that represent the fields in a table.
Column	A Column object represents a single field within a database table.

Scripting the SQL Server Distributed Management Objects Using WSH

Now, you're going to see how you can use WSH to script the management objects provided by SQL Server. First, you'll see how you can connect to SQL Server to perform changes, and then you'll work with scripts that affect *database devices*. Database devices are the physical files that contain databases and their tables; you'll see how you can create and delete them.

Next, you'll look at creating and deleting databases. Databases contain one or more tables that store your information. Finally, you'll see how you can use WSH to create, modify, and delete database tables.

If you have SQL Server version 6.5 installed, you can follow along and execute the scripts as you go. If you have a different version, you might have problems because the management objects might be different.

Connecting to SQL Server

If you are working with the SQL Server Distributed Management Objects, you need to begin by connecting to a SQL Server. You do that by creating an instance of the SQLOLE.SQLServer object. Here's a code snippet that shows how it's done:

```
Dim sqlSrv

Set sqlSrv = Wscript.CreateObject("SQLOLE.SQLServer")
sqlSrv.Connect "My Server", "My Login", "My Password"
```

First, you create an instance of the SQLServer object using the standard Wscript.CreateObject() method. You use Wscript.CreateObject() when you create any new SQL Server objects, including devices, databases, tables, and columns. When you have the object instance, you connect to the SQL Server using the SQLServer.Connect() method, which takes the server name, user login ID, and user password as parameters. Most of your scripts that use the SQL Server objects will begin with similar code so that you can connect to SQL Server.

12

Creating and Deleting Devices

Devices contain databases on SQL Server. Before you can create a database, you must
have one or more devices to contain it. A typical configuration is to put the data portion
of a database on one device and the transaction log for the database on a separate device.
Doing so provides a significant performance enhancement. In either case, each device
corresponds to a single file in the NT file system.

To create devices, you use the Device object. To create the object, you use
Wscript.CreateObject("SQLOLE.Device"). After you've created the Device object, you
can change its settings by using its properties. When you've finished configuring it, you
tell SQL Server to create it by adding it to the SQLServer.Devices collection. The code
example in Listing 12.1 shows the details.

LISTING 12.1   CREATING DEVICES USING SQL SERVER MANAGEMENT OBJECTS

```
' FILE: Makedev.vbs
' DESC: This script demonstrates how you can create a new
'       device using the SQL Server management objects.
' AUTH: Thomas Fredell
' DATE: 1/16/99
'
' Copyright 1999 MacMillan Publishing
'


'
' Constants for the Server name, login ID, and password
' NOTE: YOU MUST CHANGE THESE TO MATCH YOUR ENVIRONMENT.
'
Const SERVER_NAME = "TLFSRV1"
Const LOGIN_ID = "sa"
Const LOGIN_PW = ""
Const DB_PATH = "F:\MSSQL\DATA\"


'
' The following are constants that were taken from the SQL
' server objects type library as viewed using the OLE view utility.
'
' This is the listing that was taken directly from the
' type information:
'
'     SQLOLEDevice_Unknown = 100,
'     SQLOLEDevice_Database = 0,
'     SQLOLEDevice_DiskDump = 2,
'     SQLOLEDevice_FloppyADump = 3,
'     SQLOLEDevice_FloppyBDump = 4,
'     SQLOLEDevice_TapeDump = 5,
'     SQLOLEDevice_PipeDump = 6,
```

```
'    SQLOLEDevice_CDROM = 7
'
' And here's the corresponding VBScript constant definitions:
'
Const SQLOLEDevice_Unknown = 100
Const SQLOLEDevice_Database = 0
Const SQLOLEDevice_DiskDump = 2
Const SQLOLEDevice_FloppyADump = 3
Const SQLOLEDevice_FloppyBDump = 4
Const SQLOLEDevice_TapeDump = 5
Const SQLOLEDevice_PipeDump = 6
Const SQLOLEDevice_CDROM = 7

Dim sqlsrv
Dim devNew

'
' First we create an instance of the SQL Server object.  We'll use the
' object to connect to an instance of SQL Server and make
' modifications.
'
Set sqlsrv = Wscript.CreateObject("SQLOLE.SQLServer")
sqlsrv.Connect SERVER_NAME, LOGIN_ID, LOGIN_PW

'
' Now we create a new device object.  The device object represents an
' SQL Server database device. We set all of the properties that we
' need to configure the device.
'
Set devNew = Wscript.CreateObject("SQLOLE.Device")
devNew.Name = "NEWDEV"
devNew.PhysicalLocation = DB_PATH & "NEWDEV.DAT"
devNew.Size = 10
devNew.Type = SQLOLEDevice_Database

'
' Finally, we add the new device to the SQL Server devices collection.
' Doing so causes SQL Server to actually create the new database
' device.
'
sqlsrv.Devices.Add devNew
sqlsrv.Devices.Refresh
```

Note   The code example begins with constants that are specific to my environment. Before you try to run the scripts in this chapter, you must change the
constants to suit your environment.

The example contains some constants that set up the name for SQL Server, the login ID and password that will be used to connect to the server, and the path for the physical file that will be used to store the new device that I create. This is followed by a bunch of constants for SQL Server devices. I pulled the constants from the type library that is associated with the SQL Server objects using the OLE View tool that comes with Visual Studio.

The OLE View tool is very useful for finding out information about the objects on your system. When you run it, it shows you a list of categories of information you can view organized as file folders like the Windows Explorer. If you scroll down and expand the category named Type Libraries, you'll see a list of the type libraries on your system, as shown in Figure 12.6.

FIGURE 12.6

The OLE View tool showing the list of type libraries.

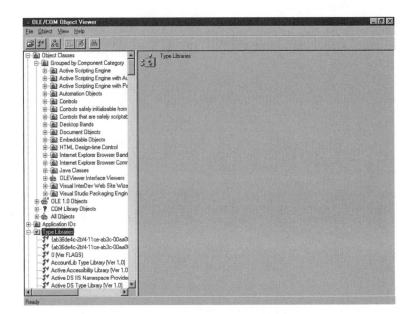

If you scroll down through the list of type libraries, you should find Microsoft SQLOLE Object Library, as illustrated in Figure 12.7. If you double-click on the library entry, the full Microsoft SQLOLE Object Library will come up in a type library viewer, which is shown in Figure 12.8. On the left side of the screen, you have categorized segments of the type information. On the right side of the screen, you see the full listing for the type library.

FIGURE 12.7

The OLE View tool with the Microsoft SQLOLE Object Library highlighted.

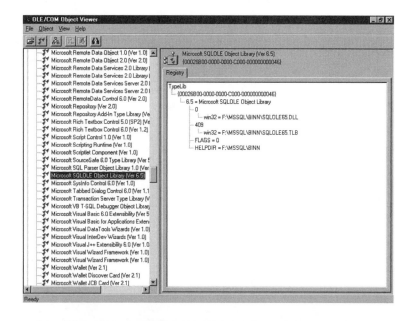

FIGURE 12.8

Viewing the Microsoft SQLOLE Object Library.

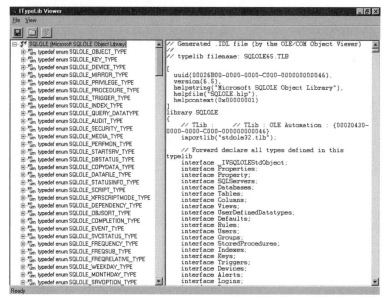

12

To get the constants for the SQL Server device types, I move down in the categorized type library on the left side of the screen until I find the entry labeled `typedef enum SQLOLE_DEVICE_TYPE`. If I click on the entry, I see the constants for the device types in the right side of the screen as shown in Figure 12.9.

FIGURE 12.9

Device constants from the Microsoft SQLOLE Library.

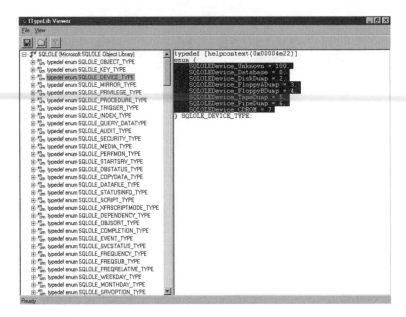

Unfortunately, I can't use the constants verbatim from the type library listing. First I have to reformat them into valid VBScript code. I do that manually using a standard text editor—in my case, Notepad. Figure 12.10 the shows the reformatted code in Notepad.

FIGURE 12.10

Reformatted constants in Notepad.

```
' WAS:
'       SQLOLEDevice_Unknown = 100,
'       SQLOLEDevice_Database = 0,
'       SQLOLEDevice_DiskDump = 2,
'       SQLOLEDevice_FloppyADump = 3,
'       SQLOLEDevice_FloppyBDump = 4,
'       SQLOLEDevice_TapeDump = 5,
'       SQLOLEDevice_PipeDump = 6,
'       SQLOLEDevice_CDROM = 7

' NOW:
Const SQLOLEDevice_Unknown = 100
Const SQLOLEDevice_Database = 0
Const SQLOLEDevice_DiskDump = 2
Const SQLOLEDevice_FloppyADump = 3
Const SQLOLEDevice_FloppyBDump = 4
Const SQLOLEDevice_TapeDump = 5
Const SQLOLEDevice_PipeDump = 6
Const SQLOLEDevice_CDROM = 7
```

That's a very handy technique that you can use to pull constants for your VBScript scripts. I used it throughout this chapter to get listings of constants that I use within the sample scripts.

Getting back to the script again, after the constants I create a SQLServer object that I use to connect to my database server. Next, I create a Device object. I configure the object by setting its Name, PhysicalLocation, Size, and Type properties. Finally, I add the Device object to the SQLServer.Devices collection using the SQLServer.Devices.Add() method. That's all there is to it! You'll notice the same coding pattern throughout the code examples.

If you run the script using cscript makedev.vbs from the command line and go back to the SQL Server Enterprise Manager, you'll see that a new device named NEWDEV has been created as illustrated in Figure 12.11.

FIGURE 12.11

The new device listed in the SQL Server Enterprise Manager.

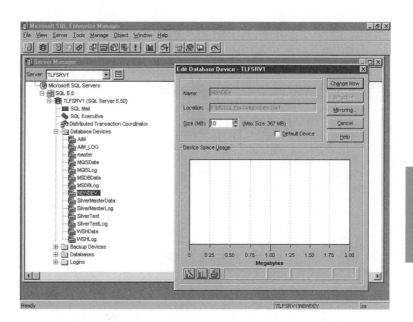

12

Creating and Deleting Databases

For your next example, you're going to see the VBScript code that is required to create a new database using the SQL Server objects. You'll notice that the flow of the code is very similar to the previous example. Take a look at the Listing 12.2, which shows the code required to create a database.

LISTING 12.2   CREATING A NEW DATABASE WITH VBSCRIPT

```
' FILE: Makedb.vbs
' DESC: This script demonstrates how you can create a new database
'       using the SQL Server management objects.
' AUTH: Thomas Fredell
' DATE: 1/16/99
'
' Copyright 1999 MacMillan Publishing
'


'
' Constants for the Server name, login ID, and password
' NOTE: YOU MUST CHANGE THESE TO MATCH YOUR ENVIRONMENT.
'
Const SERVER_NAME = "TLFSRV1"
Const LOGIN_ID = "sa"
Const LOGIN_PW = ""
Const DB_PATH = "F:\MSSQL\DATA\"

'
' The following are constants for SQL Server device types.
'
Const SQLOLEDevice_Unknown = 100
Const SQLOLEDevice_Database = 0
Const SQLOLEDevice_DiskDump = 2
Const SQLOLEDevice_FloppyADump = 3
Const SQLOLEDevice_FloppyBDump = 4
Const SQLOLEDevice_TapeDump = 5
Const SQLOLEDevice_PipeDump = 6
Const SQLOLEDevice_CDROM = 7

Dim sqlsrv
Dim dbNew
Dim tlog

'
' First we create an SQLServer object and connect to the server.
'
Set sqlsrv = Wscript.CreateObject("SQLOLE.SQLServer")
sqlsrv.Connect SERVER_NAME, LOGIN_ID, LOGIN_PW


'
' Next we called a new function that we've defined called
' "CreateDBDevice".  It hides the complexities involved in creating
' a new SQL Server database device.  We use it to create two new
' database devices.  The first is a device to hold data, and the
' second is a device to hold the database transaction log.
'
```

```
CreateDbDevice sqlsrv, "NEWDEV", DB_PATH & "NEWDEV.DAT", 10
CreateDbDevice sqlsrv, "NEWDEV_LOG", DB_PATH & "NEWDEV_LOG.DAT", 5
sqlsrv.Devices.Refresh True

'
' Here we create an instance of a database object, and set the
' properties for it using the devices that we created above.
'
Set dbNew = Wscript.CreateObject("SQLOLE.Database")
dbNew.Name = "NEWDB"
dbNew.ExtendOnDevices "NEWDEV=10"
Set tlog = dbNew.TransactionLog
tlog.DedicateLogDevices "NEWDEV_LOG=5"

'
' Finally, we add the new database object to the SQL Server databases
' collection.  Like the previous database device example, this causes
' SQL Server to create the database.
'
sqlsrv.Databases.Add dbNew
sqlsrv.Databases.Refresh True

Wscript.Quit 0
```

The first part of the code listing essentially calls a bunch of helper functions that you've created that make it easier to work with databases. You can reuse these functions within the code that you write. Those functions are listed as follows:

```
'----------------------------------------------------------------
' FUNC: CreateDbDevice()
' DESC: This is a wrapper function for the CreateDevice() function.
'       It makes it very easy for us to create a new database device;
'       using it, we don't need to know any special SQL Server
'       constants.
'----------------------------------------------------------------
Sub CreateDbDevice(sqlsrv, sName, sLocation, nSize)
    CreateDevice sqlsrv, sName, sLocation, nSize, _
SQLOLEDevice_Database
End Sub
```

The next function, CreateDevice(), is particularly long. However, you'll notice that much of the code consists of error handling logic, so it really isn't that complex.

```
'----------------------------------------------------------------
' FUNC: CreateDevice()
' DESC: This function creates a new SQL Server device.
'----------------------------------------------------------------
Sub CreateDevice(sqlsrv, sName, sLocation, nSize, nType)
    On Error Resume Next
```

12

```
Dim dev, devNew

'
' First, we check to see if the device already exists using
' the device name.
'
Set dev = sqlsrv.Devices(sName)

If Err.Number <> 0 Then
    '
    ' If an error was triggered, we assume that the database
    ' device doesn't exist, so we create a new device.
    '
    EchoErr
    Set devNew = Wscript.CreateObject("SQLOLE.Device")
    If Err.Number <> 0 Then EchoErr

    devNew.Name = sName
    devNew.PhysicalLocation = sLocation
    devNew.Size = nSize
    devNew.Type = nType

    sqlsrv.Devices.Add devNew
    If Err.Number <> 0 Then EchoErr
    sqlsrv.Devices.Refresh
    If Err.Number <> 0 Then EchoErr
Else
    '
    ' No error was triggered, so a device with the specified
    ' name already exists in the SQL Server devices collection.
    ' Consequently, we don't create a new device; we simply
    ' output a message to the user.
    '
    MsgBox "Device '" & sName & "' already exists."
End If
End Sub


'-------------------------------------------------------------------
' FUNC: EchoErr()
' DESC: This is a simple function that dumps the current error
'       to the screen.
'-------------------------------------------------------------------
Sub EchoErr()
    Wscript.Echo "ERROR: (" & Err.Number & ") " & Err.Description
End Sub
```

The example begins with the standard SQL Server constants, the creation of an instance of the SQLServer object, the creation of two devices using a CreateDevice() subroutine, and the creation of a Database object. After the Database object is created, it is configured by setting some of its properties and calling some of its methods. If you would like more information about the properties and methods of the object, please refer to the SQL Server books online. Finally, the Database object is added to the SQLServer.Databases collection using the SQLServer.Databases.Add() method. Again, you notice a pattern that is similar to what you saw when you created a new device.

The example is actually more complex than what is necessary to simply create a database because it also creates two new devices. One device will contain the data for the database; the other device will contain the database transaction log. You'll notice that the code to create the devices has been packaged in a convenient CreateDevice() subroutine. If you want, you can reuse that subroutine and other functions and subroutines for your own scripts.

Listing 12.3 demonstrates how you can delete a database and database devices.

LISTING 12.3   DELETING DATABASES AND DATABASE DEVICES

```
' FILE: Deldb.vbs
' DESC: This script demonstrates how you can delete a database
'       using the SQL Server distributed management objects.
' AUTH: Thomas Fredell
' DATE: 1/16/99
'
' Copyright 1999 MacMillan Publishing
'


'
' Constants for the Server name, login ID, and password
' NOTE: YOU MUST CHANGE THESE TO MATCH YOUR ENVIRONMENT.
'
Const SERVER_NAME = "TLFSRV1"
Const LOGIN_ID = "sa"
Const LOGIN_PW = ""

Dim sqlsrv
Dim fso
Dim devDb
Dim devLog
Dim sFileName

'
' First we connect to the SQL Server.
'
```

continues

LISTING 12.3 CONTINUED

```
Set sqlsrv = Wscript.CreateObject("SQLOLE.SQLServer")
sqlsrv.Connect SERVER_NAME, LOGIN_ID, LOGIN_PW

'
' Next, we remove the database from the SQL Server databases
' collection.
'
sqlsrv.Databases.Remove "NEWDB"
sqlsrv.Databases.Refresh True

'
' Finally, delete the devices that were associated with the database.
'
DeleteDevice sqlsrv, "NEWDEV"
DeleteDevice sqlsrv, "NEWDEV_LOG"
sqlsrv.Devices.Refresh True

Wscript.Quit 0


'-----------------------------------------------------------------
' FUNC: DeleteDevice()
' DESC: This deletes a device from the SQL Server.
'-----------------------------------------------------------------
Sub DeleteDevice(sqlSrv, sDevName)
    Dim fso
    Dim dev
    Dim sFilename

    On Error Resume Next

    '
    ' Instantiate a File systemObject. We'll need to use the object to
    ' delete the physical file that represents a device. When you
    ' delete a device using the SQL Server Enterprise Manager,
    ' the file that represents the device is deleted automatically.
    ' That's not the case when you delete a device using the
    ' SQL Server DMO objects.
    '
    Set fso = Wscript.CreateObject("Scripting.File systemObject")

    '
    ' Next, get the device from the SQL Server devices collection.
    ' Get the physical filename of the device using the
    ' PhysicalLocation property. we'll use it later to delete the
    ' file for the device.
    '
    Set dev = sqlSrv.Devices("NEWDEV")
    sFileName = dev.PhysicalLocation
```

```
'
' Remove the device using the Device.Remove method, then delete
' the device file using the File systemObject that we created
' earlier.
'
dev.Remove
fso.DeleteFile sFileName, True
End Sub
```

The aforementioned code example shows another pattern that is very common when using the SQL Server objects. To delete something, you typically remove it from a collection. For example, close to the beginning of the script, you see a call to `sqlsrv.Databases.Remove "NEWDB"`. That call removes the NEWDB database from the SQLServer.Databases collection, which causes it to be deleted.

Next, the script uses a `DeleteDevice()` subroutine to delete the devices that were associated with the NEWDB database. I've created `DeleteDevice()` because deleting a device is a little more complicated than deleting other types of objects in SQL Server. For most objects, removing them from a collection is sufficient to delete them. However, when you remove a device from the Devices collection, the actual physical file for the device is not deleted. Consequently, my `DeleteDevice()` subroutine is intelligent enough to find the physical file for the device and delete it using the standard WSH File systemObject.

Creating and Deleting Tables

The next step that you need to create a fully functional database is to create a database table. Listing 12.4 shows how you can create a database table.

Note If you want to run this example, it assumes that you have created a database named NEWDB using the aforementioned makedb.vbs sample script.

LISTING 12.4   CREATING DATABASE TABLES

```
' FILE: MakeTbl.vbs
' DESC: This script demonstrates how you can create a new
'       table using the SQL Server management objects.
' AUTH: Thomas Fredell
' DATE: 3/5/99
'
' Copyright 1999 MacMillan Publishing
'
```

continues

LISTING **12.4**   CONTINUED

```
'
' Constants for the Server name, login ID, and password
' NOTE: YOU MUST CHANGE THESE TO MATCH YOUR ENVIRONMENT.
'
Const SERVER_NAME = "TLFSRV1"
Const LOGIN_ID = "sa"
Const LOGIN_PW = ""

Dim sqlsrv
Dim db
Dim tblNew
Dim colNew
Dim keyNew

'
' First we create an SQLServer object and connect to the server.
'
Set sqlsrv = Wscript.CreateObject("SQLOLE.SQLServer")
sqlsrv.Connect SERVER_NAME, LOGIN_ID, LOGIN_PW

'
' Now we get the database in which we want to create
' a new table; we're using the NEWDB that we created
' in an earlier script.
'
Set db = sqlsrv.Databases("NEWDB")

'
' Now we'll create a table that holds product information.
'
Set tblNew = Wscript.CreateObject("SQLOLE.Table")
tblNew.Name = "Products"

'
' Create the columns for the product information. For each
' product, we will maintain a product name and price.
'
Set colNew = Wscript.CreateObject("SQLOLE.Column")
colNew.Name = "ProductName"
colNew.AllowNulls = False
colNew.Datatype = "varchar"
colNew.Length = 50
tblNew.InsertColumn colNew, ""

Set colNew = Wscript.CreateObject("SQLOLE.Column")
colNew.Name = "ProductPrice"
colNew.AllowNulls = False
colNew.Datatype = "money"
colNew.Identity = False
```

```
tblNew.InsertColumn colNew, ""

'
' Add the new products table to the database
'
db.Tables.Add tblNew
```

The example connects to SQL Server and then accesses a specific database using the `SQLServer.Databases` collection. Accessing a database is easy because you can index into the `SQLServer.Databases` collection using the name of the database. Next, I create a new `Table` object using `Wscript.CreateObject("SQLOLE.Table")`. The `Table` object contains `Column` objects that represent the fields in the table. To add the columns, I need to create individual `Column` objects, change the settings for each `Column`, and then add the `Column` to the `Table` object using the `Table.InsertColumn()` method. After I've finished adding columns to the table, I create the table in the database by adding it to the `Database.Tables` collection.

If you run the sample script, you will see a new `Products` table created in the `NEWDB` database, as illustrated in Figure 12.12.

FIGURE 12.12

The new Products table shown in the SQL Server Enterprise Manager.

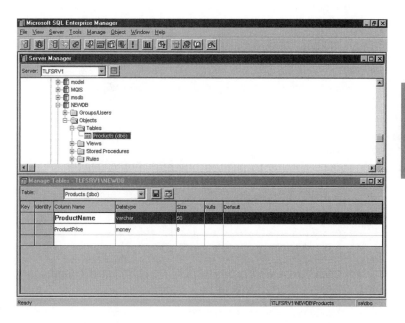

What if you want to add a new column to the `Products` table? Doing so is very easy. All that you need to do is retrieve the `Table` object for the `Products` table and then use its methods to make changes. In Listing 12.5, you add a `ProductURL` column to the `Products` table.

LISTING 12.5 CREATING NEW COLUMNS

```vbs
' FILE: ChngTbl.vbs
' DESC: This script demonstrates how you can change a
'       database table using the SQL Server management
'       objects.
' AUTH: Thomas Fredell
' DATE: 3/5/99
'
' Copyright 1999 MacMillan Publishing
'


'
' Constants for the Server name, login ID, and password
' NOTE: YOU MUST CHANGE THESE TO MATCH YOUR ENVIRONMENT.
'
Const SERVER_NAME = "TLFSRV1"
Const LOGIN_ID = "sa"
Const LOGIN_PW = ""

Dim sqlsrv
Dim db
Dim tbl
Dim colNew


'
' First we create an SQLServer object and connect to the server.
'
Set sqlsrv = Wscript.CreateObject("SQLOLE.SQLServer")
sqlsrv.Connect SERVER_NAME, LOGIN_ID, LOGIN_PW


'
' Now we get the database that contains the table we want
' to change, then we get the table from the database's
' Tables collection.
'
Set db = sqlsrv.Databases("NEWDB")
Set tbl = db.Tables("Products")


'
' Create a new column to add to the table; we'll add
' a ProductURL column.
'
Set colNew = Wscript.CreateObject("SQLOLE.Column")
colNew.Name = "ProductURL"
colNew.AllowNulls = True
colNew.Datatype = "varchar"
colNew.Length = 200


'
' Insert the column into the table; we have to prepare
```

```
' it for changes first.
'
tbl.BeginAlter
tbl.InsertColumn colNew, ""
tbl.DoAlter
tbl.Refresh
```

To change the table, you connect to SQL Server, retrieve the database from the
`SQLServer.Databases` collection, and then retrieve the `Table` object from the
`Database.Tables` collection. Next, you create a new Column object, set the name of the
column to `ProductURL`, and set the characteristics of the column—including the fact that
it should allow nulls, should be a variable-length character field, and should have a maximum length of 200 characters.

Before you can add the column to the table, you call the `Table.BeginAlter()` method.
`Table.BeginAlter()` prepares the table for a batch of changes. Then, you insert the new
column into the table using the `Table.InsertColumn()` method, and finally, you tell the
table to go ahead and make the changes using the `Table.DoAlter()` method.

Deleting a table is very easy. You might guess—correctly—that deleting a table probably
involves the `Database.Tables` collection and the `Remove()` method. Listing 12.6 shows
how you can delete the `Products` table that you created using a previous script.

LISTING 12.6   DELETING TABLES

```
' FILE: DelTbl.vbs
' DESC: This script demonstrates how you can delete a
'       database table using the SQL Server management
'       objects.
' AUTH: Thomas Fredell
' DATE: 3/5/99
'
' Copyright 1999 MacMillan Publishing
'


'
' Constants for the Server name, login ID, and password
' NOTE: YOU MUST CHANGE THESE TO MATCH YOUR ENVIRONMENT.
'
Const SERVER_NAME = "TLFSRV1"
Const LOGIN_ID = "sa"
Const LOGIN_PW = ""

Dim sqlsrv
Dim db
```

continues

12

LISTING **12.6**   CONTINUED

```
Dim tbl

'
' First we create a SQLServer object and connect to the server.
'
Set sqlsrv = Wscript.CreateObject("SQLOLE.SQLServer")
sqlsrv.Connect SERVER_NAME, LOGIN_ID, LOGIN_PW

'
' Now we get the database in which we want to delete
' the Products table.
'
Set db = sqlsrv.Databases("NEWDB")

'
' And delete the table by removing it from the
' database tables collection.
'
db.Tables.Remove "Products"
db.Tables.Refresh
```

The table delete script is very straightforward. First, you connect to SQL Server. Next, you retrieve the database that you need from the SQLServer.Databases collection. Finally, you call the Database.Tables.Remove() method with the name of the table that you want to delete.

Putting It All Together

So far, you've seen how you can create devices, databases, and database tables. Now, you're going to put those techniques together in a sample script that creates a new database from scratch. Listing 12.7 will create a data device, a transaction log device, a database, and Customers and Orders tables.

LISTING **12.7**   CREATING A NEW DATABASE FROM SCRATCH

```
' FILE: CreateDb.vbs
' DESC: This script demonstrates how you can create new
'       devices, database and tables using the SQL Server
'       management objects.
' AUTH: Thomas Fredell
' DATE: 3/5/99
'
' Copyright 1999 MacMillan Publishing
'
```

```
' Constants for the Server name, login ID, and password
' NOTE: YOU MUST CHANGE THESE TO MATCH YOUR ENVIRONMENT.
'
Const SERVER_NAME = "TLFSRV1"
Const LOGIN_ID = "sa"
Const LOGIN_PW = ""
Const DB_PATH = "F:\MSSQL\DATA\"


' The following are constants for SQL Server device types.
'
Const SQLOLEDevice_Unknown = 100
Const SQLOLEDevice_Database = 0
Const SQLOLEDevice_DiskDump = 2
Const SQLOLEDevice_FloppyADump = 3
Const SQLOLEDevice_FloppyBDump = 4
Const SQLOLEDevice_TapeDump = 5
Const SQLOLEDevice_PipeDump = 6
Const SQLOLEDevice_CDROM = 7


' SQL Server Key Types
'
Const SQLOLEKey_Unknown = 0
Const SQLOLEKey_Primary = 1
Const SQLOLEKey_Unique = 2
Const SQLOLEKey_Foreign = 3

Dim sqlsrv
Dim devDb
Dim devLog
Dim dbNew
Dim tblCustomers
Dim tblOrders
Dim colNew
Dim keyNew
Dim tlog


' First we create an SQLServer object and connect to the server.
'
Set sqlsrv = Wscript.CreateObject("SQLOLE.SQLServer")
sqlsrv.Connect SERVER_NAME, LOGIN_ID, LOGIN_PW


' For our example, we're going to create new devices and a new
' database.
'
Set devDb = CreateDbDevice(sqlsrv, "NEWDEV", _
    DB_PATH & "NEWDEV.DAT", 10)
```

12

continues

LISTING 12.7   CONTINUED

```
Set devLog = CreateDbDevice(sqlsrv, "NEWDEV_LOG", _
    DB_PATH & "NEWDEV_LOG.DAT", 5)
Set dbNew = CreateDatabase(sqlsrv, "NEWDB", devDb, 10, devLog, 5)
```

All of the preceding code is used to set up the devices and the database that will hold your new table. The following body of code is used to actually create the new table and add columns to the table. The code is long, but it's primarily because there are a lot of properties that you need to set on the column objects that are contained within the table:

```
'
' Now we'll create a table that holds customer information in the
' database
'
Set tblCustomers = Wscript.CreateObject("SQLOLE.Table")
tblCustomers.Name = "Customers"


'
' Create the columns for the customer information and add them
' to the table. Our customers table will contain customer id,
' customer name, email address, and phone number columns. The customer
' id will be an automatically incremented unique id that will serve
' as the primary key.
'
Set colNew = Wscript.CreateObject("SQLOLE.Column")
colNew.Name = "CustomerID"
colNew.AllowNulls = False
colNew.Datatype = "int"
colNew.Identity = True
colNew.IdentityIncrement = 1
colNew.IdentitySeed = 0
colNew.Length = 4
tblCustomers.InsertColumn colNew, ""

Set colNew = Wscript.CreateObject("SQLOLE.Column")
colNew.Name = "CustomerName"
colNew.AllowNulls = False
colNew.Datatype = "varchar"
colNew.Identity = False
colNew.Length = 50
tblCustomers.InsertColumn colNew, ""

Set colNew = Wscript.CreateObject("SQLOLE.Column")
colNew.Name = "CustomerEmail"
colNew.AllowNulls = True
colNew.Datatype = "varchar"
colNew.Identity = False
colNew.Length = 70
tblCustomers.InsertColumn colNew, ""
```

```
Set colNew = Wscript.CreateObject("SQLOLE.Column")
colNew.Name = "CustomerPhone"
colNew.AllowNulls = True
colNew.Datatype = "varchar"
colNew.Identity = False
colNew.Length = 20
tblCustomers.InsertColumn colNew, ""

'
' Now set up primary key for Customers
'
Set keyNew = Wscript.CreateObject("SQLOLE.Key")
keyNew.Name = "CustomerID"
keyNew.Type = SQLOLEKey_Primary
keyNew.KeyColumns.Add "CustomerID"
tblCustomers.Keys.Add keyNew

'
' Add the new customers table to the database
'
dbNew.Tables.Add tblCustomers
```

Now that you've finished setting up the customers table, you can create the customer order table. The code is similar to the customers table code in that lots of properties need to be set:

```
'
' Create a table to contain customer order information
'
Set tblOrders = Wscript.CreateObject("SQLOLE.Table")
tblOrders.Name = "Orders"

'
' Create the columns for the order details information and add them
' to the table. Our orders table is very simple; it contains a
' customer id that refers to the Customers table, a date for the
' order, and an order amount.
'
Set colNew = Wscript.CreateObject("SQLOLE.Column")
colNew.Name = "CustomerID"
colNew.AllowNulls = False
colNew.Datatype = "int"
colNew.Identity = False
colNew.Length = 4
tblOrders.InsertColumn colNew, ""

Set colNew = Wscript.CreateObject("SQLOLE.Column")
colNew.Name = "OrderDate"
colNew.AllowNulls = False
colNew.Datatype = "datetime"
```

12

```
colNew.Identity = False
colNew.Length =
tblOrders.InsertColumn colNew, ""

Set colNew = Wscript.CreateObject("SQLOLE.Column")
colNew.Name = "OrderAmount"
colNew.AllowNulls = False
colNew.Datatype = "money"
colNew.Identity = False
colNew.Length = 70
tblOrders.InsertColumn colNew, ""

'
' Set up foreign key relationship with Customers table
'
Set keyNew = Wscript.CreateObject("SQLOLE.Key")
keyNew.Name = "FK_CustomerID"
keyNew.Type = SQLOLEKey_Foreign
keyNew.KeyColumns.Add "CustomerID"
keyNew.ReferencedTable = "Customers"
keyNew.ReferencedColumns.Add "CustomerID"
tblOrders.Keys.Add keyNew

'
' Add the new orders table to the database
'
dbNew.Tables.Add tblOrders

Wscript.Quit 0
```

The following functions are very useful "wrapper" functions that you can reuse for your own scripts. They'll enable you to easily create databases and database devices. Before you use them, you might want to alter the error handling logic as appropriate for your script:

```
'------------------------------------------------------------------
' FUNC: CreateDatabase()
' DESC: This is a wrapper function for the CreateDevice() function.
'       It makes it very easy for us to create a new database device;
'       using it, we don't need to know any special SQL Server
'       constants.
'------------------------------------------------------------------
Function CreateDatabase(sqlsrv, sName, devDb, nDbSize, devLog,_
    nLogSize)
    On Error Resume Next

    Dim tlog

    '
```

```
    ' First, we check to see if the database already exists using
    ' the database name.
    '
    Set CreateDatabase = sqlsrv.Databases(sName)

    If Err.Number <> 0 Then
        '
        ' If an error was triggered, we assume that the database
        ' doesn't exist, so we create a new database.
        '
        EchoErr
        Set CreateDatabase = Wscript.CreateObject("SQLOLE.Database")
        If Err.Number <> 0 Then EchoErr

        CreateDatabase.Name = sName
        CreateDatabase.ExtendOnDevices devDb.Name & "=" & nDbSize
        Set tlog = CreateDatabase.TransactionLog
        tlog.DedicateLogDevices devLog.Name & "=" & nLogSize

        sqlsrv.Databases.Add CreateDatabase
        If Err.Number <> 0 Then EchoErr
    Else
        '
        ' No error was triggered, so a device with the specified
        ' name already exists in the SQL Server databases
        ' collection.
        '
        MsgBox "Database '" & sName & "' already exists."
    End If
End Function


'-------------------------------------------------------------------
' FUNC: CreateDbDevice()
' DESC: This is a wrapper function for the CreateDevice() function.
'       It makes it very easy for us to create a new database device;
'       using it, we don't need to know any special SQL Server
'       constants.
'-------------------------------------------------------------------
Function CreateDbDevice(sqlsrv, sName, sLocation, nSize)
    Set CreateDbDevice = CreateDevice(sqlsrv, sName, sLocation, _
        nSize, SQLOLEDevice_Database)
End Function


'-------------------------------------------------------------------
' FUNC: CreateDevice()
' DESC: This function creates a new SQL Server device.
'-------------------------------------------------------------------
Function CreateDevice(sqlsrv, sName, sLocation, nSize, nType)
    On Error Resume Next
```

12

```
'
' First, we check to see if the device already exists using
' the device name.
'
Set CreateDevice = sqlsrv.Devices(sName)

If Err.Number <> 0 Then
    '
    ' If an error was triggered, we assume that the database
    ' device doesn't exist, so we create a new device.
    '
    EchoErr
    Set CreateDevice = Wscript.CreateObject("SQLOLE.Device")
    If Err.Number <> 0 Then EchoErr

    CreateDevice.Name = sName
    CreateDevice.PhysicalLocation = sLocation
    CreateDevice.Size = nSize
    CreateDevice.Type = nType

    sqlsrv.Devices.Add CreateDevice
    If Err.Number <> 0 Then EchoErr
Else
    '
    ' No error was triggered, so a device with the specified
    ' name already exists in the SQL Server devices collection.
    ' Consequently, we don't create a new device; we simply
    ' output a message to the user.
    '
    MsgBox "Device '" & sName & "' already exists."
End If
End Function

'-----------------------------------------------------------------
' FUNC: EchoErr()
' DESC: This is a simple function that dumps the current error
'       to the screen.
'-----------------------------------------------------------------
Sub EchoErr()
    Wscript.Echo "ERROR: (" & Err.Number & ") " & Err.Description
End Sub
```

After you run the script using cscript createdb.vbs, you'll see two new tables in the NEWDB database in the SQL Server Enterprise Manager, as illustrated in Figures 13.13 and 13.14.

FIGURE 12.13

The new Customers *table shown in the SQL Server Enterprise Manager.*

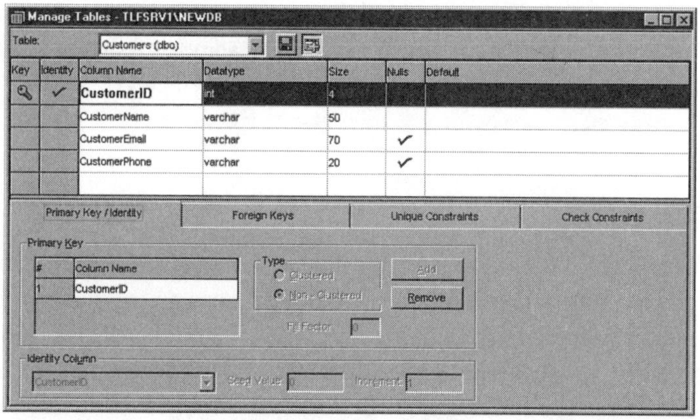

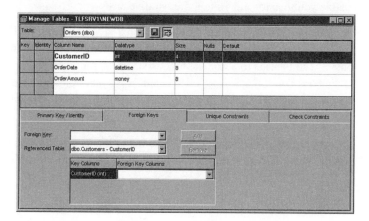

FIGURE 12.14

The new Orders *table shown in the SQL Server Enterprise Manager.*

12

The script begins with the standard connection to SQL Server. It creates two devices using my CreateDBDevice() function, and then it creates a new database using my CreateDatabase() function. After it's created the database, it creates two tables in the database using code that is similar to the previous example that illustrated the creation of a Products table.

It's a bit more complicated than the previous example because the tables include some more advanced features. The Customers table that the script creates includes an auto increment ID field, CustomerID, that is the primary key and unique identifier for a customer record. It designates the CustomerID as the primary key for the table by creating a Key object that is added to the Table.Keys collection. The Products table is related to the Customers table through the CustomerID field. To enforce the relationship between the tables, you've created a foreign key relationship, again using the Table.Keys collection. The table schema is very simple, but is more similar to the type of schema that you would encounter in practical use.

Take note of the functions within the script that you can make use of in your own VBScript code. You can use the CreateDatabase() function to simplify the task of creating a new database, and you can use the CreateDBDevice() and CreateDevice() functions to make it easy for you to create new devices.

Summary

You began this chapter with a review of Microsoft SQL Server and SQL Server administration. SQL Server is an excellent database engine that has become increasingly popular due to its ease of use and tight integration with Windows NT. Administering SQL Server is fairly easy; however, some administrative tasks might be repetitive, tedious, or error-prone. You can simplify SQL Server administration by implementing WSH scripts that enable you to automate your administrative tasks.

After discussing SQL Server administration and the SQL Server Distributed Management Objects, you dug into code examples that illustrate how the management objects can be used to automate tasks such as creating and deleting devices, databases, and tables. You can use those code examples as a baseline to create your own automation scripts, or you can just reuse some of the useful functions embedded within them.

In this chapter, you've only begun to scratch the surface of automation possibilities that are available with the SQL Server Distributed Management Objects used through WSH scripts. There is much more that you can do! I suggest that you experiment with WSH scripts, get to know the SQL Server objects, and refer to the SQL Server books online when you need a little extra help.

Q&A

Q What is the root object that you'll typically use to begin altering SQL Server databases?

A Most of your scripts (perhaps all) will begin with the instantiation of a SQLServer object that you'll use to connect to a database server.

Q When you are creating new objects in SQL Server, such as databases, devices, or tables, there is a certain pattern that your code will typically follow. What is the pattern?

A Generally speaking, when you create a new SQL Server object, your code will begin with the instantiation of a new object, such as a device object, using Wscript.CreateObject() (like Wscript.CreateObject("SQLOLE.Device")). Next, you'll set the properties of the object and potentially call various methods to complete the configuration of it. Finally, you'll add the object to the appropriate SQL Server collection (like `sqlsrv.Devices.Add devNew`).

Q If you delete a device using the SQL Server 6.5 Distributed Management Objects (DMO), what do you need to do in order to reclaim the disk space used by the device?

A If you delete a device using the DMO objects, you need to delete the physical file that represents the device. You can do so in your script using the standard `File systemObject`.

12

DAY 13

Automating Microsoft IIS Administration Using WSH Scripts

Microsoft provides an excellent Web server, Microsoft Internet Information Server (IIS), as a free add-on for the Windows NT operating system. IIS comes with a good, fairly easy-to-use administration interface, but it doesn't provide any macro capability to automate typical functions that you might perform. If you are an ISP who takes care of many clients on a single server, or even if you are an MIS person who is charged with setting up new intranet sites using IIS, you know that the lack of automation can be frustrating and inefficient.

Thankfully, Microsoft provides capabilities to administer IIS through IIS Administration Objects. Using WSH, you can easily develop scripts that perform many IIS administration functions using the administration objects. In this chapter, you'll learn you how IIS administration works and how you can use the IIS objects through WSH.

On the 13th day of your introduction to WSH, you'll

- Get an introduction to Microsoft IIS and administrative scripting capabilities
- Learn about the administration components for IIS
- See script examples that illustrate the use of the IIS objects from WSH scripts

Introduction to Using WSH to Administer IIS

This chapter gives you some examples of how you can use Microsoft's Windows Scripting Host to automate the administration of the Internet Information Server. First you'll get a quick overview of IIS, and then the chapter discusses IIS components and administration functions. Finally the chapter shows some concrete examples that illustrate how you can automate IIS administration with WSH scripts.

IIS Overview

Microsoft Internet Information Server is Microsoft's standard Web server for the Windows NT operating system. IIS provides robust Web server functionality and includes components that provide mail, NNTP, gopher, and FTP functionality.

When you install NT 4.0, you can select to install IIS 3.0. If you want a more updated version of IIS, you can install the Windows NT option pack. The option pack provides several useful server components including Microsoft IIS 4.0, Microsoft Message Queues (MSMQ), Microsoft Transaction Server (MTS), Microsoft Index Server, and Microsoft Certificate Server. For your purposes, you're going to focus on IIS 4.0.

When you're running the IIS, there's relatively little to see. Like most NT server functions, there's really no user interface for the server task itself. The most basic indication that a server task is running is its listing in the services applet within the Control Panel. If you're running IIS, you'll see something like Figure 13.1.

FIGURE 13.1

The IIS Web service listing.

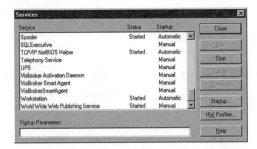

There is more to IIS than just the entry in the services listing. An administration interface provides many functions that enable you to affect the way that IIS runs.

The administration interface uses the standard Microsoft Management Console (MMC). Using the Management Console, you can start and stop the IIS server processes, you can create new Web sites, you can change folder options and site configuration details, and more. The Management Console is depicted in Figure 13.2.

FIGURE 13.2

IIS administration using the Microsoft Management Console.

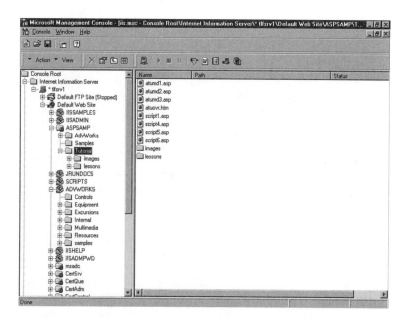

The Management Console is an excellent tool, but it does have some problems. As your site begins to grow, or as you host multiple sites using an IIS server, it can become difficult to keep track of all the settings for different folders and Web sites. Unfortunately, the management console doesn't have any concept of macros that enable you to automate tasks. Luckily for you, there's more than one way to administer IIS. IIS exposes administration objects that you can use from any software that can use COM objects. Consequently, you can create administration scripts using a tool such as WSH to automate your administration functions.

13

Note

If you're running NT and you're not familiar with the Microsoft management console, it's probably worthwhile for you to get acquainted with it. All the latest versions of the Microsoft BackOffice server programs integrate with the Microsoft Management Console, so you can go to one place for your administration needs. And, when you need to automate your administrative tasks, it's highly likely, at least with Microsoft server tasks, that you'll be able to write WSH scripts that access appropriate administration objects.

The next few sections discuss the configuration and automation capabilities of IIS. First you'll look at the IIS metabase, which contains configuration settings for IIS. Next, you'll examine the IIS administration objects. You'll use those objects later in this chapter to create automated administration scripts.

BACKING UP YOUR IIS CONFIGURATION

It's important to back up your current IIS configuration before you make changes to it. Let's take a quick look at how you can back up your configuration.

Backing up your configuration is easy using the IIS Management Console. First, select the base IIS service by left-clicking on it. Next, right-click to display the context menu. Select Backup/Restore Configuration from the menu, illustrated in Figure 13.3.

Next, you'll see the Configuration Backup and Restore dialog, illustrated in Figure 13.4. You can use this dialog to back up and restore IIS configurations. It's easy to use; just click on the button that represents the action you want to perform. *Make sure that you back up your IIS configuration before you run any of the scripts in this chapter.*

FIGURE 13.3

The IIS context menu.

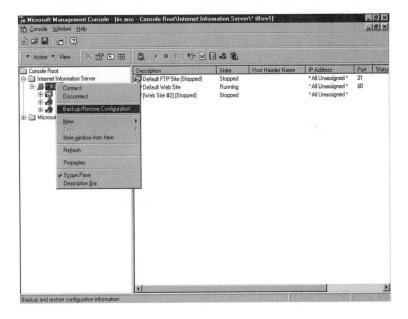

FIGURE 13.4

IIS Configuration Backup and Restore dialog.

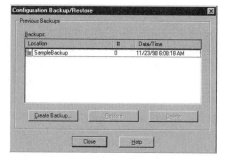

IIS Metabase

IIS stores its configuration settings in a hierarchical database called the *metabase*. The metabase contains configuration settings for the overall IIS service, Web sites, virtual directories, directories, and files. If you refer back to Figure 13.2, you'll notice these different components listed in the IIS Management Console. Figure 13.5 illustrates the structure of the IIS metabase.

FIGURE 13.5

The IIS metabase structure.

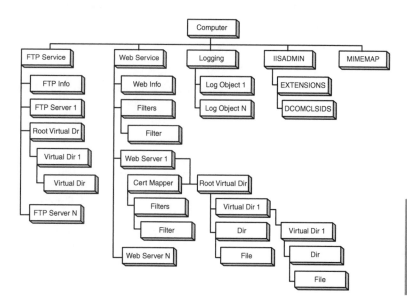

13

The use of the metabase with IIS is somewhat nonstandard relative to other Windows NT programs. Typically, most NT programs store their settings in the Windows Registry. If the settings are very large, the program can also use disk-based storage for the configuration details. The IIS metabase is memory resident while IIS is running, but persists on disk when IIS is shut down. For administration purposes, you can access and configure the metabase using the management console. However, the IIS metabase can be accessed by other programs using the Microsoft Active Directory Service Interfaces (ADSI) standard.

Microsoft's ADSI is a standard that enables client applications to communicate with various directory services including the Windows NT directory service, LDAP directories, NetWare NDS, and any other services that implement the ADSI standard for directory service providers. The IIS metabase leverages ADSI to provide access to the IIS configuration details. When you use ADSI, you specify a path, similar to an URL, which enables you to access an object through a directory. The first part of the URL, which typically specifies the protocol, designates the type of directory service that you want to access. For IIS, ADSI paths begin with the prefix IIS://. After the prefix, you specify the hierarchical path to the IIS metabase object that you want to access. The hierarchical path, which is referred to as the *namespace*, takes the following form:

```
IIS://[MachineName]/[Service]/[Website]/Root/[Virtual
➥Directory]/[Directory]/[File]
```

Each of the components of the path or namespace is described in the following minitable:

IIS METABASE NAMESPACE COMPONENTS

Component	Description
[Service]	This is the Internet service that you want to access using the ADSI path. It might be one of the following: W3SVC—the Web service; MSFTPSVC—the FTP service; MimeMap—current MIME encoding mappings; Logging—current logging settings.
[Website]	This is the number that corresponds with the Web site that you want to access. The default Web site can be accessed using the number 1.
Root	This indicates the virtual Root directory, which is the parent of any virtual directories or directories located underneath the Web site.
[Virtual Directory]	This designates a virtual directory.
[Directory]	This designates a standard directory.
[File]	This designates a specific file within a directory or a virtual directory.

You can use any of these components to access administration settings for part of an IIS site. For example, you can use the following path to access the overall settings for the IIS Web service on the local machine:

```
IIS://Localhost/W3SVC
```

The following example shows a more detailed path that accesses a specific file within a directory for one of the IIS samples:

```
IIS://Localhost/W3SVC/1/IISSAMPLES/ExAir/Catalog/MoreInfo.asp
```

If you were to describe this path, you would say that it begins with the prefix that designates IIS; next, it specifies the Web service; after that it specifies the default Web site using the number 1; then it specifies the IIS samples virtual directory, two subdirectories, and finally the MoreInfo.asp page.

It's important that you understand the IIS metabase and ADSI path conventions when you write scripts that administer IIS programmatically. Your scripts will use the GetObject() function with an IIS metabase path to retrieve IIS administration objects. The following section discusses the various IIS administration objects.

IIS Administration Objects

IIS administration objects enable you to change settings stored in the IIS metabase. Because the metabase has a hierarchical structure, you can easily make changes that affect large portions of your IIS configuration. You can also make small, specific changes because you can access the IIS metabase through ADSI down to file-level granularity. Figure 13.6 shows a diagram of the IIS administration objects hierarchy.

If you compare Figure 13.6 to Figure 13.5, the IIS metabase structure, you'll notice that there are many similarities between the administrative objects and the structure of the metabase. That makes it easy to relate the administration objects back to the corresponding configuration settings in the metabase.

This discussion of the IIS administration objects first looks at the standard properties and methods associated with any ADSI objects. Next, you'll look at some specific characteristics unique to IIS. Finally, this section describes special IIS properties.

This discussion does not provide a full reference for all the IIS administration objects. As you can see from Figure 13.6, there are many objects, and each of the objects has several properties and methods. If you want to find more information about the IIS administration objects, refer to the Microsoft product documentation that accompanies the IIS distribution.

13

FIGURE **13.6**

The IIS administration objects.

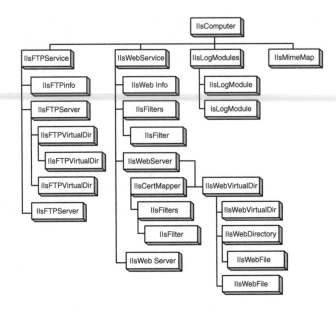

> **Caution**
>
> Be careful when you use the IIS administration objects to create Web sites. It is easy to create "partial" site instances that are not fully functional. Always back up your metabase before you make any changes.

ADSI Object Properties for IIS Administration Objects

The following minitable lists the standard properties for all the ADSI objects. All these properties are read-only String values.

Property	Description
Name	This is the name of the object that is used within the underlying IIS namespace.
ADsPath	This is the path that is used with the GetObject() function to retrieve IIS administration objects. The AdsPath uniquely identifies a specific object.
Class	This is the name of the ADSI schema class of the IIS administration object.
GUID	This is a unique identifier for objects of this ADSI schema.

Property	Description
Parent	This is the ADsPath of the parent IIS container object.
Schema	This is the ADsPath of the object that represents the object schema class in the schema.

ADSI Object Methods for IIS Administration Objects

The following minitable lists the standard methods for ADSI objects.

ADSI OBJECT METHODS

Method	Description
Get(Property)	This retrieves the value of a specific named property from an object. The name is passed as a string using the Property argument. An alternative syntax is to use object.Property.
GetEx(Property)	This retrieves the value or values for a specific property of an object.
GetInfo	This reinitializes the IIS administration objects' values by rereading them from the metabase.
GetInfoEx	For IIS administration objects, this performs the same function as the GetInfo() method.
Put(Property, Value)	This sets the value of a specific property of the IIS administration object. Alternatively, you can use the syntax object.Property = "newvalue".
PutEx(ControlCode,Property,Value)	This method enables you to either set the value of a specific property of an IISadministration object, or to remove aproperty from an administration object.To set a property, pass the value 2 for the ControlCode argument. To remove a property, pass the value 1 for ControlCode. You might want to remove a property so that inherited properties can pass down successfully. If a value for a specific property on subobject is set, it will not be overridden by an inherited property until the property is removed from the subobject.
SetInfo	This writes the current values of an IIS administration object back to the IIS metabase.

13

ADSI Container Properties for IIS Administration Objects

Some of the IIS administration objects can contain other administration objects. The following minitable describes the standard container properties for ADSI or, in your example, IIS administration objects.

ASDI Container Property	Description
_NewEnum	This returns an Enumerator object that can be used to retrieve the objects contained within the ADSI container object. This property is used by the VBScript For..Each loop.
Count	This returns the number of objects in the container.

ADSI Container Methods for IIS Administration Objects

The following methods listed in the following minitable apply to any of the IIS administration objects that act as ADSI containers. For example, you can use these with any of the directory or virtual directory objects.

ADSI Container Method	Description
CopyHere(SourceName, NewName)	This returns a new copy of the source object using the name specified with the NewName parameter. The copied object remains in the original container.
Create(KeyType, Name)	This creates a new object in the IIS administration object container. The KeyType parameter specifies the type for the IIS object, and the Name specifies the new name for the object.
Delete(KeyType, Name)	This deletes an object from the IIS administration object container. The KeyType parameter specifies the type of object to delete, and Name specifies the name of the object.
GetObject(Class, ChildName)	This retrieves a specific child object from an IIS administration object. The Class parameter represents the type of administration object to retrieve, such as IIsWebServer, and ChildName represents the name of the subobject.
MoveHere(SourceName, NewName)	This copies an object from SourceName to NewName and deletes the original object.

Standard IIS Administration Object Methods

The methods listed in the following minitable are available from all the IIS administration objects. It is not a standard ADSI object method; it is provided specifically for IIS administration objects.

IIS Administration Object Method	Description
GetDataPaths (Property, Flag)	This returns a String list of all the paths where a specific property is located. You can use this to find properties in sub objects that are overriding inherited properties from their containing objects. The Property parameter specifies the property to find. The Flag parameter can be either IIS_ANY_PROPERTY, which retrieves paths whether or not the property is inheritable, or IIS_INHERITABLE_ONLY, which only retrieves inheritable properties.

Administering IIS Using WSH Scripts

The IIS administration objects provide many capabilities for programmatically administering IIS Web servers. So far you've looked at the IIS administration objects and the various properties and methods that they expose. This section shows how you can use the objects to automate typical administration tasks. You'll see a couple of different examples, and hopefully when you're finished you'll have some ideas for your own scripts. To help you get started, at the end of the chapter are some exercises that enable you to try your hand at modifying the sample scripts.

The first example is a basic example that shows you how to retrieve an IIS administration object and examine the properties associated with it. The next example shows how you can programmatically create a new Web site. After that, you'll see how WSH scripts can be used to scan Web sites for configuration settings. Finally, you'll look at an example that illustrates how you can perform changes to groups of Web sites programmatically.

Hopefully, the following script examples will be useful for you. The intention is not to fulfill all your needs with the examples but to provide you with a foundation of knowledge that will help you to create your own scripts.

13

Introductory Script: Dump Web Settings

The following script given in Listing 13.1 is a simple example that illustrates how you can use the IIS administration objects from your WSH scripts. After the script, you'll see the output of the script and a detailed description of the script's inner workings.

LISTING **13.1**   iisinfo.vbs DUMP WEB SETTINGS

```
' FILE: iisinfo.vbs
' DESC: This displays information about the current IIS installation
'       and metabase.
' AUTH: Thomas L. Fredell
' DATE: 11/16/98
'


Option Explicit

On Error Resume Next

Dim oArgs, sServer, nInstance, sIISPath
Dim oIISSrv, sTmp

' First check args to ensure that a computer is specified
Set oArgs = Wscript.Arguments
If oArgs.Count <> 2 Then
    Wscript.Echo "USAGE:  iisinfo  [computer] [instance]"
    Wscript.Echo ""
    Wscript.Echo "         Displays information about the IIS server"
    Wscript.Echo "         instance located on the specified computer"
    Wscript.Echo "         using IIS administration objects."
    Wscript.Echo ""
End If
sServer = oArgs(0)
nInstance = oArgs(1)

' Next connect to the IIS server and dump details
' Note: IIS uses ADSI conventions, so we need to create the path to
'       the IIS server in the ADSI directory.
sIISPath = "IIS://" & sServer & "/w3svc/" & CInt(nInstance)
Set oIISSrv = GetObject(sIISPath)
If Err.Number <> 0 Then
    ShowErr "Unable to connect to IIS server instance using '" & _
        sIISPath & "'."
    Wscript.Exit Err
End If
sTmp = "iisinfo.vbs: Dumping configuration details for server " & _
    "at '" & sIISPath & "'"
Wscript.Echo sTmp
Wscript.Echo String(Len(sTmp), "-")
```

```
    Wscript.Echo ""
    DumpObject oIISSrv

    ' End of script
    Wscript.Exit 0


Sub ShowErr(sDescription)
    Wscript.Echo "iisinfo.vbs: " & sDescription
    Wscript.Echo "iisinfo.vbs: An error occurred - code: " & _
        Hex(Err.Number) & " - " & Err.Description
End Sub


Sub DumpObject(o)
    DumpADSIProperties o
    Wscript.Echo "AccessExecute: " & o.AccessExecute
    Wscript.Echo "AccessFlags: " & o.AccessFlags
    Wscript.Echo "AccessNoRemoteExecute: " & o.AccessNoRemoteExecute
    Wscript.Echo "AccessNoRemoteRead: " & o.AccessNoRemoteRead
    Wscript.Echo "AccessNoRemoteScript: " & o.AccessNoRemoteScript
    Wscript.Echo "AccessNoRemoteWrite: " & o.AccessNoRemoteWrite
    Wscript.Echo "AccessRead: " & o.AccessRead
    Wscript.Echo "AccessScript: " & o.AccessScript
    Wscript.Echo "AccessSSL: " & o.AccessSSL
    Wscript.Echo "AccessSSL128: " & o.AccessSSL128
    Wscript.Echo "AccessSSLFlags: " & o.AccessSSLFlags
    Wscript.Echo "AccessSSLMapCert: " & o.AccessSSLMapCert
    Wscript.Echo "AccessSSLNegotiateCert: " & _
        o.AccessSSLNegotiateCert
    Wscript.Echo "AccessSSLRequireCert: " & o.AccessSSLRequireCert
    Wscript.Echo "AccessWrite: " & o.AccessWrite
'
'   Wscript.Echo "AdminACL: " & CInt(o.AdminACL)
'   This won't work because AdminACL is a binary reference
'
    Wscript.Echo "AllowKeepAlive: " & o.AllowKeepAlive
    Wscript.Echo "AllowPathInfoForScriptMappings: " & _
        o.AllowPathInfoForScriptMappings
    Wscript.Echo "AnonymousPasswordSync: " & o.AnonymousPasswordSync
    Wscript.Echo "AnonymousUserName: " & o.AnonymousUserName
    Wscript.Echo "AnonymousUserPass: " & o.AnonymousUserPass
    Wscript.Echo "AppAllowClientDebug: " & o.AppAllowClientDebug
    Wscript.Echo "AppAllowDebugging: " & o.AppAllowDebugging
    Wscript.Echo "AppFriendlyName: " & o.AppFriendlyName
    Wscript.Echo "AppIsolated: " & o.AppIsolated
    Wscript.Echo "AppOopRecoverLimit: " & o.AppOopRecoverLimit
    Wscript.Echo "AppPackageID: " & o.AppPackageID
    Wscript.Echo "AppPackageName: " & o.AppPackageName
```

13

continues

LISTING **13.1**   CONTINUED

```
Wscript.Echo "AppRoot: " & o.AppRoot
Wscript.Echo "AppWamClsid: " & o.AppWamClsid
Wscript.Echo "AspAllowOutOfProcComponents: " & _
        o.AspAllowOutOfProcComponents
Wscript.Echo "AspAllowSessionState: " & o.AspAllowSessionState
Wscript.Echo "AspBufferingOn: " & o.AspBufferingOn
Wscript.Echo "AspCodepage: " & o.AspCodepage
Wscript.Echo "AspEnableParentPaths: " & o.AspEnableParentPaths
Wscript.Echo "AspExceptionCatchEnable: " & _
        o.AspExceptionCatchEnable
Wscript.Echo "AspLogErrorRequests: " & o.AspLogErrorRequests
Wscript.Echo "AspMemFreeFactor: " & o.AspMemFreeFactor
Wscript.Echo "AspQueueTimeout: " & o.AspQueueTimeout
Wscript.Echo "AspScriptEngineCacheMax: " & _
        o.AspScriptEngineCacheMax
Wscript.Echo "AspScriptErrorMessage: " & o.AspScriptErrorMessage
Wscript.Echo "AspScriptErrorSentToBrowser: " & _
        o.AspScriptErrorSentToBrowser
Wscript.Echo "AspScriptFileCacheSize: " & _
        o.AspScriptFileCacheSize
Wscript.Echo "AspScriptLanguage: " & o.AspScriptLanguage
Wscript.Echo "AspScriptTimeout: " & o.AspScriptTimeout
Wscript.Echo "AspSessionTimeout: " & o.AspSessionTimeout
Wscript.Echo "AuthAnonymous: " & o.AuthAnonymous
Wscript.Echo "AuthBasic: " & o.AuthBasic
Wscript.Echo "AuthFlags: " & o.AuthFlags
Wscript.Echo "AuthNTLM: " & o.AuthNTLM
Wscript.Echo "AuthPersistence: " & o.AuthPersistence
Wscript.Echo "CacheControlCustom: " & o.CacheControlCustom
Wscript.Echo "CacheControlMaxAge: " & o.CacheControlMaxAge
Wscript.Echo "CacheControlNoCache: " & o.CacheControlNoCache
Wscript.Echo "CacheISAPI: " & o.CacheISAPI
Wscript.Echo "CGITimeout: " & o.CGITimeout
Wscript.Echo "ConnectionTimeout: " & o.ConnectionTimeout
Wscript.Echo "CreateCGIWithNewConsole: " & _
        o.CreateCGIWithNewConsole
Wscript.Echo "CreateProcessAsUser: " & o.CreateProcessAsUser
Wscript.Echo "DefaultDoc: " & o.DefaultDoc
Wscript.Echo "DefaultDocFooter: " & o.DefaultDocFooter
Wscript.Echo "DefaultLogonDomain: " & o.DefaultLogonDomain
Wscript.Echo "DirBrowseFlags: " & o.DirBrowseFlags
Wscript.Echo "DirBrowseShowDate: " & o.DirBrowseShowDate
Wscript.Echo "DirBrowseShowExtension: " & _
        o.DirBrowseShowExtension
Wscript.Echo "DirBrowseShowLongDate: " & o.DirBrowseShowLongDate
Wscript.Echo "DirBrowseShowSize: " & o.DirBrowseShowSize
Wscript.Echo "DirBrowseShowTime: " & o.DirBrowseShowTime
Wscript.Echo "DontLog: " & o.DontLog
Wscript.Echo "EnableDefaultDoc: " & o.EnableDefaultDoc
```

```
Wscript.Echo "EnableDirBrowsing: " & o.EnableDirBrowsing
Wscript.Echo "EnableDocFooter: " & o.EnableDocFooter
Wscript.Echo "EnableReverseDns: " & o.EnableReverseDns
Wscript.Echo "FrontPageWeb: " & CStr(o.FrontPageWeb)
Wscript.Echo "HttpCustomHeaders: " & _
    Join(o.HttpCustomHeaders, ", ")
Wscript.Echo "HttpErrors: " & Join(o.HttpErrors, ", ")
Wscript.Echo "HttpExpires: " & o.HttpExpires
Wscript.Echo "HttpPics: " & Join(o.HttpPics, ", ")
Wscript.Echo "HttpRedirect: " & o.HttpRedirect

'  Wscript.Echo "IPSecurity: " & o.IPSecurity
'  We can't display this because it's a binary reference.
'
Wscript.Echo "LogExtFileBytesRecv: " & o.LogExtFileBytesRecv
Wscript.Echo "LogExtFileBytesSent: " & o.LogExtFileBytesSent
Wscript.Echo "LogExtFileClientIp: " & o.LogExtFileClientIp
Wscript.Echo "LogExtFileComputerName: " & _
    o.LogExtFileComputerName
Wscript.Echo "LogExtFileCookie: " & o.LogExtFileCookie
Wscript.Echo "LogExtFileDate: " & o.LogExtFileDate
Wscript.Echo "LogExtFileFlags: " & o.LogExtFileFlags
Wscript.Echo "LogExtFileHttpStatus: " & o.LogExtFileHttpStatus
Wscript.Echo "LogExtFileMethod: " & o.LogExtFileMethod
Wscript.Echo "LogExtFileProtocolVersion: " & _
    o.LogExtFileProtocolVersion
Wscript.Echo "LogExtFileReferer: " & o.LogExtFileReferer
Wscript.Echo "LogExtFileServerIp: " & o.LogExtFileServerIp
Wscript.Echo "LogExtFileServerPort: " & o.LogExtFileServerPort
Wscript.Echo "LogExtFileSiteName: " & o.LogExtFileSiteName
Wscript.Echo "LogExtFileTime: " & o.LogExtFileTime
Wscript.Echo "LogExtFileTimeTaken: " & o.LogExtFileTimeTaken
Wscript.Echo "LogExtFileUriQuery: " & o.LogExtFileUriQuery
Wscript.Echo "LogExtFileUriStem: " & o.LogExtFileUriStem
Wscript.Echo "LogExtFileUserAgent: " & o.LogExtFileUserAgent
Wscript.Echo "LogExtFileUserName: " & o.LogExtFileUserName
Wscript.Echo "LogExtFileWin32Status: " & o.LogExtFileWin32Status
Wscript.Echo "LogFileDirectory: " & o.LogFileDirectory
Wscript.Echo "LogFilePeriod: " & o.LogFilePeriod
Wscript.Echo "LogFileTruncateSize: " & o.LogFileTruncateSize
Wscript.Echo "LogOdbcDataSource: " & o.LogOdbcDataSource
Wscript.Echo "LogOdbcPassword: " & o.LogOdbcPassword
Wscript.Echo "LogOdbcTableName: " & o.LogOdbcTableName
Wscript.Echo "LogOdbcUserName: " & o.LogOdbcUserName
Wscript.Echo "LogonMethod: " & o.LogonMethod
Wscript.Echo "LogPluginClsId: " & o.LogPluginClsId
Wscript.Echo "LogType: " & o.LogType
Wscript.Echo "MaxBandwidth: " & o.MaxBandwidth
Wscript.Echo "MaxBandwidthBlocked: " & o.MaxBandwidthBlocked
Wscript.Echo "MaxConnections: " & o.MaxConnections
```

13

continues

LISTING **13.1**   CONTINUED

```
        Wscript.Echo "MaxEndpointConnections: " & _
            o.MaxEndpointConnections
'
'    Wscript.Echo "MimeMap: " & o.MimeMap
'    This is a sub-object of IISMimeMap type, so we aren't going
'    to dump the contents.
'
        Wscript.Echo "NetLogonWorkstation: " & o.NetLogonWorkstation
        Wscript.Echo "NTAuthenticationProviders: " & _
            o.NTAuthenticationProviders
        Wscript.Echo "PasswordCacheTTL: " & o.PasswordCacheTTL
        Wscript.Echo "PasswordChangeFlags: " & o.PasswordChangeFlags
        Wscript.Echo "PasswordExpirePrenotifyDays: " & _
            o.PasswordExpirePrenotifyDays
        Wscript.Echo "PoolIDCTimeout: " & o.PoolIDCTimeout
        Wscript.Echo "ProcessNTCRIfLoggedOn: " & o.ProcessNTCRIfLoggedOn
        Wscript.Echo "PutReadSize: " & o.PutReadSize
        Wscript.Echo "Realm: " & o.Realm
        Wscript.Echo "RedirectHeaders: " & o.RedirectHeaders
        Wscript.Echo "ScriptMaps: " & Join(o.ScriptMaps, ", ")
        Wscript.Echo "SecureBindings: " & Join(o.SecureBindings, ", ")
        Wscript.Echo "ServerAutoStart: " & o.ServerAutoStart
        Wscript.Echo "ServerBindings: " & Join(o.ServerBindings, ", ")
        Wscript.Echo "ServerComment: " & o.ServerComment
        Wscript.Echo "ServerListenBacklog: " & o.ServerListenBacklog
        Wscript.Echo "ServerListenTimeout: " & o.ServerListenTimeout
        Wscript.Echo "ServerSize: " & o.ServerSize
        Wscript.Echo "ServerState: " & o.ServerState
        Wscript.Echo "SSIExecDisable: " & o.SSIExecDisable
        Wscript.Echo "UNCAuthenticationPassthrough: " & _
            o.UNCAuthenticationPassthrough
        Wscript.Echo "UploadReadAheadSize: " & o.UploadReadAheadSize
        Wscript.Echo "UseHostName: " & o.UseHostName
End Sub

Sub DumpADSIProperties(o)
        Wscript.Echo "Name: " & o.Name
        Wscript.Echo "ADsPath: " & o.ADsPath
        Wscript.Echo "Class: " & o.Class
        Wscript.Echo "GUID: " & o.GUID
        Wscript.Echo "Parent: " & o.Parent
        Wscript.Echo "Schema: " & o.Schema
End Sub
```

The output of the script is basic; it essentially shows you a dump of the various properties of a given Web site on a specific machine. You can see the output in Figure 13.7.

FIGURE 13.7

The output of the
iisinfo.vbs *script.*

The structure and functioning of the script are also simple. First, the script begins with a check to ensure that all the necessary script command-line parameters have been passed. Next, it uses the parameters to dynamically create a string that represents an ADSI path to an IIS administration object. It calls the GetObject() function using the path to retrieve the associated administration object. Next, it calls the DumpObject() function to dump all the properties associated with the administration object. The first line in DumpObject() calls the DumpADSIProperties() function, which dumps the standard ADSI object properties, and then it dumps IIS properties. You'll notice that there are many properties for the IIS objects. The properties are not discussed in this chapter, but if you'd want to find out more about them, refer to the documentation provided by Microsoft for IIS.

You'll notice this pattern of using the GetObject() function throughout the code examples in this chapter. It's the first way that you get an IIS administration object. After you have the first object, you can navigate to additional administration objects using the standard ADSI container object properties and methods.

Create a New Web Site

Listing 13.2 shows how you can use a WSH script, createweb.vbs, to create a new Web site. Creating a new Web site might be a fairly intricate process, depending on how many settings you define from the beginning. The site created in this example will be simple; the only special setting that you're going to define is a cgi-bin directory. You can extend the script to include whatever steps you want.

13

The script takes the following arguments, in order: computer—this is the name of the computer on which you want to create the new Web site; hostname—this is the name of the host that you want the Web site to be associated with, for example "www.test.com"; instance—this is the instance number of the Web server that you want to create; and rootdir—this is the physical directory on disk that should become the root for the Web site.

LISTING 13.2   USING createweb.vbs TO CREATE A WEB SITE

```
' FILE: createweb.vbs
' DESC: This script illustrates how you can programmatically
'       create a web site using IIS administration objects.
' AUTH: Thomas L. Fredell
' DATE: 11/23/98
'
' Copyright 1998 Macmillan Publishing

Option Explicit

On Error Resume Next

Dim oArgs, sComputer, sHostName, sRootDir
Dim oService, nNewServer, oServer, oVDir, oDir
Dim oFS, sBasePath, sCGIDir
Dim sTmp

' Step 1: Check script arguments
Set oArgs = Wscript.Arguments
If oArgs.Count <> 4 Then
    Wscript.Echo "USAGE:  createweb  [computer] [hostname]" & _
                 " [instance] [rootdir]"
    Wscript.Echo ""
    Wscript.Echo "        Creates a new IIS web site on "
    Wscript.Echo "        [computer] using the [hostname]."
    Wscript.Echo "        [instance] specifies the web server"
    Wscript.Echo "        and [rootdir] specifies the root"
    Wscript.Echo "        directory on the file system."
    Wscript.Echo ""
    Wscript.Quit 1
End If
sComputer = oArgs(0)
sHostName = oArgs(1)
nNewServer = oArgs(2)
sRootDir = oArgs(3)

' Step 2: Get the object that represents the web service
Set oService = GetObject("IIS://" & sComputer & "/W3SVC")

' Step 3: Create a new virtual server
```

```
' Determine the new virtual server number by
' iterating through the current servers
oService.GetInfo
Set oServer = oService.Create("IIsWebServer", nNewServer)
If Err.Number <> 0 Then
    ShowErr "Unable to create server."
    Wscript.Quit Err.Number
End If

' Step 4: Configure the new server
oServer.DefaultDoc = "default.htm, index.htm"
oServer.ServerComment = "New server created by createweb.vbs"
oServer.ConnectionTimeout = 600
oServer.ServerBindings = ":80:" & sHostName
oServer.SetInfo
If Err.Number <> 0 Then
    ShowErr "An error occurred while setting configuration params."
    Wscript.Quit Err.Number
End If

' Step 5: Create virtual root directory for the new site
Set oVDir = oServer.Create("IIsWebVirtualDir", "ROOT")
If Err.Number <> 0 Then
    ShowErr "Unable to create virtual root directory."
    Wscript.Quit Err.Number
End If

' Step 6: Configure the virtual root directory
Set oFS = CreateObject("Scripting.FileSystemObject")
sBasePath = oFS.GetAbsolutePathName(sRootDir)
oVdir.Path = sBasePath
oVdir.AccessRead = True
oVdir.AccessWrite = True
oVdir.AccessScript = True
oVdir.SetInfo
If Err.Number <> 0 Then
    ShowErr "Unable to save settings for virtual root."
    Wscript.Quit Err.Number
End If
oVdir.AppCreate False
If Err.Number <> 0 Then
    ShowErr "Unable to define virtual root as application."
    Wscript.Quit Err.Number
End If
oVdir.SetInfo

' Step 7: Create and configure a cgi-bin directory
' First ensure that the physical directory exists
sCGIDir = sBasePath & "\cgi-bin"
```

13

continues

LISTING **13.2**   CONTINUED

```
If Not oFS.FolderExists(sCGIDir) Then
    ' Create the physical cgi-bin directory
    oFS.CreateFolder sCGIDir
End If

' Then create the IIsWebDirectory object & configure it
Set oDir = oVDir.Create("IIsWebDirectory", "cgi-bin")
If Err.Number <> 0 Then
    ShowErr "Unable to create cgi-bin directory."
    Wscript.Quit Err.Number
End If
oDir.AccessRead = False
oDir.AccessWrite = False
oDir.AccessScript = True
oDir.AccessExecute = True
oDir.SetInfo
If Err.Number <> 0 Then
    ShowErr "Error setting cgi-bin configuration."
    Wscript.Quit Err.Number
End If

' Step 8: Start the web server
oServer.Start
If Err.Number <> 0 Then
    ShowErr "Unable to start new web server."
    Wscript.Quit Err.Number
End If

' Step 9: Done! Quit execution
Wscript.Echo "createweb.vbs: Successfully created new web site."
Wscript.Echo "createweb.vbs: Instance #=" & nNewServer
Wscript.Echo "createweb.vbs: Host Name=" & sHostName
Wscript.Echo "createweb.vbs: Root Dir=" & sRootDir
Wscript.Quit 0

'-----------------------------------------------------
' SUB:  ShowErr(Description)
' DESC: Displays information about a runtime error.
'-----------------------------------------------------
Sub ShowErr(sDescription)
    Wscript.Echo "createweb.vbs: " & sDescription
    Wscript.Echo "createweb.vbs: An error occurred - code: " & _
        Hex(Err.Number) & " - " & Err.Description
End Sub
```

You can see the output of the script from the command line in Figure 13.8. If you go to the Microsoft Management Console, illustrated in Figure 13.9, you'll notice that a new Web site has been created.

FIGURE 13.8

The command-line output of createweb.vbs.

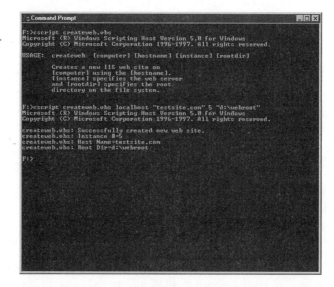

FIGURE 13.9

The resulting Web site in the Microsoft Management Console.

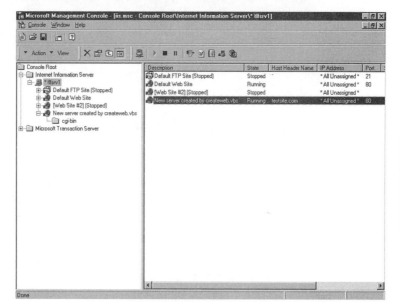

13

Comments in the script divide the script into different steps. Step one ensures that the proper arguments have been specified for the script. That's a standard step that will be included in any of the sample scripts that take arguments. Step two retrieves the Web service object using an ADSI path; it uses the GetObject() function that's standard for accessing the IIS administrative objects. Step three creates a new Web server object using the instance number specified on the command line.

Step four sets some of the properties for the Web server. There are many properties to choose from; if you examine the code for the first example, you'll see a list of them. Step five creates a new virtual root directory for the Web site, and in step six, it is configured. For the configuration, you set the path for the root directory, then you set access rights, and finally you set it up as an out-of-process application.

Step 7 creates and configures the cgi-bin directory. First the code checks to ensure that the physical cgi-bin directory actually exists. If the physical directory doesn't exist, it is created using the FileSystemObject that was described in Day 2. Next a Web directory object for cgi-bin is created, and the access rights are set. The only access that you'll enable is script and execute access. That's plenty of access for the cgi-bin directory and this will ensure that no one downloads any CGI executables that you put in the directory.

Finally, step 8 starts the Web server; you check to ensure that it actually starts by validating that no error occurs. Step 9 stops execution and displays information about the site that was created.

The script is relatively simple. For the most part, you use the standard ADSI methods to create new objects. You also use some of the IIS specific properties to set configuration parameters. You can modify it for your purposes by creating different objects, such as different directories, or by setting different properties.

Scanning Sites for Configuration Settings

One of the benefits of using WSH scripts to administer IIS Web servers is that you can perform automated tasks that would be infeasible or impractical using the standard Management Console. The script example shown in Listing 13.3 illustrates a task that would be difficult if not automated. The following script, scanweb.vbs, scans a Web site and determines whether any .EXE files are located within directories with either access read or access write permissions set.

The scanweb.vbs script takes the following arguments, in order: computer—this is the name of the computer that contains the Web site to scan, and hostname—this is the host-name of the Web site that you want to scan.

LISTING 13.3   USING scanweb.vbs TO FIND CONFIGURATION SETTINGS

```vbs
' FILE: scanweb.vbs
' DESC: This script illustrates how you can programmatically
'       scan a web site using IIS administration objects.
' AUTH: Thomas L. Fredell
' DATE: 11/23/98
'
' Copyright 1998 Macmillan Publishing

Option Explicit

On Error Resume Next

Dim oArgs, sComputer, sHostName
Dim oService, oServer, oVDir, oFS
Dim sBindings, sToFind, tFound
Dim sTmp

' Step 1: Check script arguments
Set oArgs = Wscript.Arguments
If oArgs.Count <> 2 Then
    Wscript.Echo "USAGE:  scanweb [computer] [hostname]"
    Wscript.Echo ""
    Wscript.Echo "        [computer] = this is the computer to scan"
    Wscript.Echo "        [hostname] = this is the hostname to scan"
    Wscript.Echo ""
    Wscript.Echo "        This scans an IIS web site to determine if"
    Wscript.Echo "        executable programs are in directories"
    Wscript.Echo "        that have read or write access."
    Wscript.Echo ""
    Wscript.Quit 1
End If
sComputer = oArgs(0)
sHostName = oArgs(1)

' Step 2: Get the object that represents the web service
Set oService = GetObject("IIS://" & sComputer & "/W3SVC")

' Step 3: Find the specific web server
oService.GetInfo
sToFind = ":" & sHostName & ":"
tFound = False
For Each oServer In oService
    sBindings = Join(oServer.ServerBindings, ":") & ":"
    ' sBindings should now be a string in the form:
    '    IP1:Port1:Hostname1:IPn:Portn:Hostnamen:
    If Err.Number <> 0 Then
        Err.Clear
```

13

continues

LISTING 13.3 CONTINUED

```
        Else
            tFound = (InStr(sBindings, sToFind) > 0)
            If tFound Then Exit For
        End If
Next
If Not tFound Then
    Wscript.Echo "scanweb.vbs: Unable to find hostname."
    Wscript.Quit 1
End If

' Step 4: Get the ROOT directory for the site
Set oFS = Wscript.CreateObject("Scripting.FileSystemObject")
Wscript.Echo "scanweb.vbs: Beginning scan on " & sHostName
Wscript.Echo ""
Set oVDir = oServer.GetObject("IIsWebVirtualDir", "ROOT")
If Err.Number <> 0 Then
    ShowErr "Unable to get root directory."
    Wscript.Quit Err.Number
End If

' Step 5: Recursively iterate through the directory & all
' sub-directories, checking for .EXE files
ScanDir oVDir, ""

' Step 6: Done! Quit execution
Wscript.Echo ""
Wscript.Echo "scanweb.vbs: Site scan complete."
Wscript.Quit 0

'--------------------------------------------------------
' SUB:  ScanDir(oDir)
' DESC: Scans a directory for executable files, then
'       checks directory access permissions.
'--------------------------------------------------------
Sub ScanDir(oDir, sParentPath)
    Dim obj
    Dim tReadOrWrite
    Dim sThisParentPath

    If oDir.Class = "IIsWebVirtualDir" Then
        sThisParentPath = oDir.Path
    Else
        sThisParentPath = sParentPath & "\" & oDir.Name
    End If
    Wscript.Echo "Scanning " & oDir.ADsPath & "..."
    Wscript.Echo "          " & "(" & sThisParentPath & ")"

    ' Check if we need to examine this directory for .exe files
    If oDir.AccessRead Or oDir.AccessWrite Then
```

```
            ' This is a read or write directory, so check for .exe
            Dim oFolder
            Dim oFiles
            Dim oFile
            Dim iFile

            ' We scan files using a FileSystemObject, because
            ' we may not get IIsFile objects for every file
            Set oFolder = oFS.GetFolder(sThisParentPath)
            If Err.Number <> 0 Then
                ShowErr "Unable to get folder '" & _
                    sThisParentPath & "'."
                Err.Clear
            Else
                ' Scan files within the directory
                Set oFiles = oFolder.Files
                For Each oFile In oFiles
                    If InStr(UCase(oFile.ShortName), ".EXE") > 0 Then
                        Wscript.Echo "          WARNING: This " & _
                            "read or write directory contains a .exe"
                        Exit For
                    End If
                Next
                If Err.Number <> 0 Then
                    ShowErr "An error occurred while checking files."
                    Err.Clear
                End If
            End If
        End If

    Wscript.Echo ""

    ' Finally we recurse and check sub-directories
    For Each obj In oDir
        Select Case obj.Class
            Case "IIsWebVirtualDir"
                ScanDir obj, sThisParentPath
            Case "IIsWebDirectory"
                ScanDir obj, sThisParentPath
        End Select
    Next
End Sub

'----------------------------------------------------------
' SUB:  ShowErr(Description)
' DESC: Displays information about a runtime error.
'----------------------------------------------------------
Sub ShowErr(sDescription)
    Wscript.Echo "scanweb.vbs: " & sDescription
```

continues

LISTING **13.3** CONTINUED

```
    Wscript.Echo "scanweb.vbs: An error occurred - code: " & _
        Hex(Err.Number) & " - " & Err.Description
End Sub
```

The scanweb.vbs script enables you to specify a computer and a hostname to begin a site scan. You'll run it on the sample Web site that you created with the previous script, after you've added some .EXE files. Figure 13.10 shows a directory listing of the Web site that you're going to scan. The results of the scan are illustrated in Figure 13.11.

FIGURE **13.10**

The directory listing of the Web site that will be scanned.

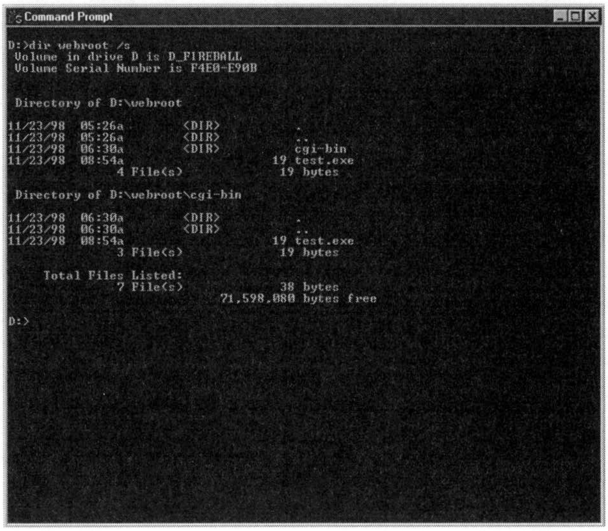

If you examine how the script functions, you'll notice that it begins with the typical check for correct command-line parameters in step 1. In step 2, you get an object for the IIsWebService on the specified computer. In step 3, you iterate through all the IIsWebServer objects associated with the IIsWebService until a Web server is found that matches the hostname specified on the command line. The hostname check is done using the ServerBindings property; ServerBindings is a list of strings in the form "*IP address:Port number:hostname*".

Next, in step 4, assuming that you found the correct Web server, you access the root directory of the Web server. Just before you access the root directory, you instantiate a WSH FileSystemObject. The FileSystemObject will be used when you scan directories for the files that they contain. You begin the directory scanning by calling the ScanDir() function in step 5.

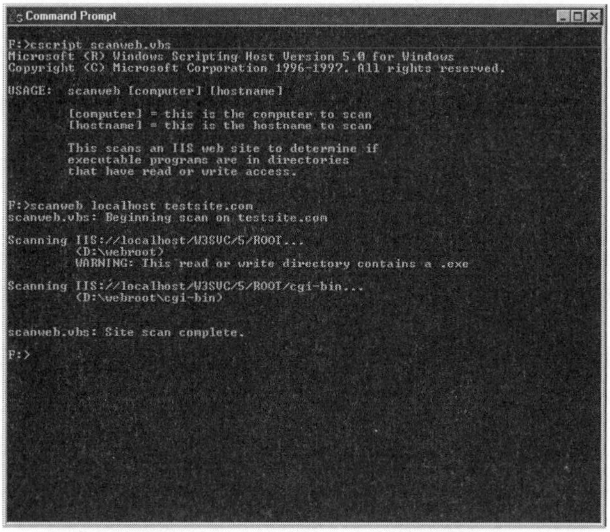

Figure 13.11

The output from the scanweb.vbs *script.*

ScanDir() is where most of the work occurs in this script. It first determines the path for the current directory that is being scanned. If the current directory is a virtual directory, the Path property returns the correct physical file directory. However, if it is a standard directory, in other words an IIsWebDirectory object, it does not have a Path property. Consequently, you must append the value of the Name property to the parent path to calculate the physical directory. Next, a message is displayed that indicates the directory and physical file folder that is being scanned. The AccessRead and AccessWrite properties of the directory are checked to determine whether either is enabled. If either is enabled, the physical file directory is scanned for files with the extension .EXE. If a file is found with the .EXE extension, a warning message is printed. The example illustrated in Figure 13.11 shows the warning message.

The last part of the ScanDir() function causes the recursion. If the directory contains any IIsWebDirectory or IIsWebVirtualDir objects, the ScanDir() function is called with the subdirectory.

The script finishes execution when there are no more directories upon which to call ScanDir(). Step 6 simply outputs a "finished" message and then calls the standard Wscript.Quit() function.

13

Performing Mass Changes to Groups of IIS Web Sites

Listing 13.4 shows how you can perform mass changes to groups of IIS Web sites. You'll provide a put function that enables you to put a specific file within a directory that matches a regular expression search criterion. This time you've implemented the script using the JScript language because the language contains inherent support for regular expression searches.

The name of the script is putfile.js, and you can refer to the source code in Listing 13.4. The script takes the following arguments, in order: computer—this is the name of the computer that contains the Web site; instance—this is the instance number of the Web site; file—this is the file that you want to put on the Web site; and direxp—this is a regular expression that will be used to match directories.

LISTING **13.4** USING putfile.js TO CHANGE WEB SITE GROUPS

```
// FILE: putfile.js
// DESC: This script illustrates how you can programmatically
//       replace a file within a web site using IIS
//       administration objects.
// AUTH: Thomas L. Fredell
// DATE: 11/24/98
//
// NOTE: This script uses JScript for regular expression
//       functionality, so consequently, with this version
//       of JScript, there is no capability for robust
//       error checking and handling.
//
// Copyright 1998 Macmillan Publishing

var oArgs, sComputer, nInstance, sFile, sDirExp;
var oRootDir, oFS, oRegEx;

// Step 1: Check script arguments
oArgs = WScript.arguments;
if (oArgs.length != 4) {
    WScript.echo("USAGE:  putfile [computer] [instance] " +
        "[file] [direxp]");
    WScript.echo("");
    WScript.echo("         [computer] = this is the computer");
     WScript.echo("                        to scan");
    WScript.echo("         [instance] = this is the web server");
    WScript.echo("                        to scan");
    WScript.echo("         [file]     = this is the file to");
    WScript.echo("                        add to the directory");
    WScript.echo("         [direxp]   = this is a regular");
    WScript.echo("                        expression filter that");
```

```
        WScript.echo("                    will be used to match");
         WScript.echo("                      directories");
        WScript.echo("");
        WScript.echo("        This puts a specific file in every");
        WScript.echo("        directory that matches a regular");
        WScript.echo("        expression search pattern.");
        WScript.echo("");
        WScript.quit(1);
    }
    sComputer = oArgs(0);
    nInstance = oArgs(1);
    sFile = oArgs(2);
    sDirExp = oArgs(3);
    oRegEx = new RegExp(sDirExp);

    // Step 2: Get the root of the specified web server
    oRootDir = GetObject("IIS://" + sComputer + "/W3SVC/" +
        nInstance + "/ROOT");

    // Step 3: Iterate through the directories on the web server
    WScript.echo("putfile.js: Beginning scan for matching directories...");
    WScript.echo("");
    oFS = new ActiveXObject("Scripting.FileSystemObject");
    PutFile(oRootDir, "", sFile, oRegEx);

    // Step 4: Done! Quit execution
    WScript.echo("");
    WScript.echo("putfile.js: Finished adding file to sites.");
    WScript.quit(0);


//////////////////////////////////////////////////////
// FUNC: PutFile(oDir, sParentPath, sFile, oRegEx)
// DESC: Puts a file recursively into matching
//       IIsWebDirectory or IIsWebVirtualDir.
//////////////////////////////////////////////////////
function PutFile(oDir, sParentPath, sFile, oRegEx) {
    var obj;
    var sThisParentPath;
    var oFolder;
    var enumDirs;

    // Determine what the next "parent path" will be
    if (oDir.Class == "IIsWebVirtualDir")
        sThisParentPath = oDir.Path;
    else
        sThisParentPath = sParentPath + "\\" + oDir.Name;

    // Check if the current directory name matches the
    // directory expression
```

continues

13

LISTING **13.4**   CONTINUED

```
if (oRegEx.test(oDir.Name)) {
    var sFilename, sDestination;

    // It matches, so put the file in its directory
    WScript.echo("putfile.js: Found matching " +
        "directory - " + oDir.Name);

    // Get just the file name
    sFilename = oFS.getFileName(sFile);

    // Calculate the new name & path
    sDestination = oFS.buildPath(sThisParentPath,
        sFilename);

    // Now copy the file
    WScript.echo("                Copy " + sFile +
        " to " + sDestination);
    oFS.copyFile(sFile, sDestination, true);
}

// Now recurse and check sub-directories
enumDirs = new Enumerator(oDir);
obj = enumDirs.item();
while (obj != null) {
    switch (obj.Class) {
        case "IIsWebVirtualDir":
        case "IIsWebDirectory":
            PutFile(obj, sThisParentPath, sFile, oRegEx);
    }
    enumDirs.moveNext();
    obj = enumDirs.item();
}
}
```

In Figure 13.12, you've run the putfile.js script to place a test.htm file in all the directories on a Web site. That functionality would enable you to, for example, automatically replace all the index.htm or default.htm files throughout a site. Figure 13.13 shows the result when a regular expression is used as a filter. In that example, you've used a filter expression that only selects directories that begin with the letters cgi You could use that with your site to replace every instance of a cgi script that you use with an updated version.

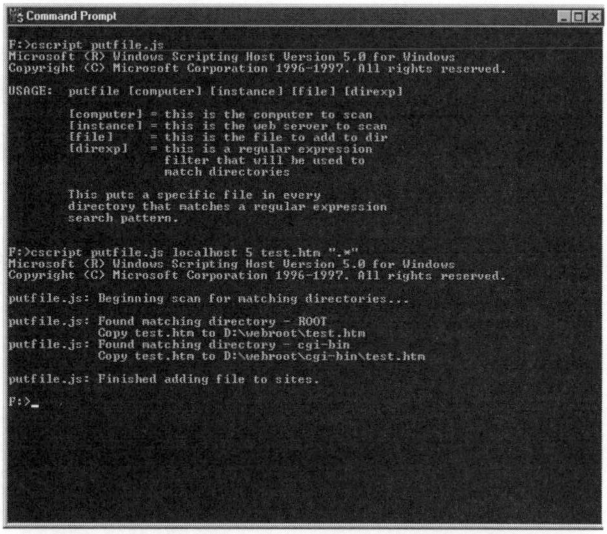

FIGURE **13.12**

Using putfile.js *to put the* test.htm *file in all the directories of a Web site.*

FIGURE **13.12**

Using putfile.js *to put the* test.htm *file in all the directories of a Web site.*

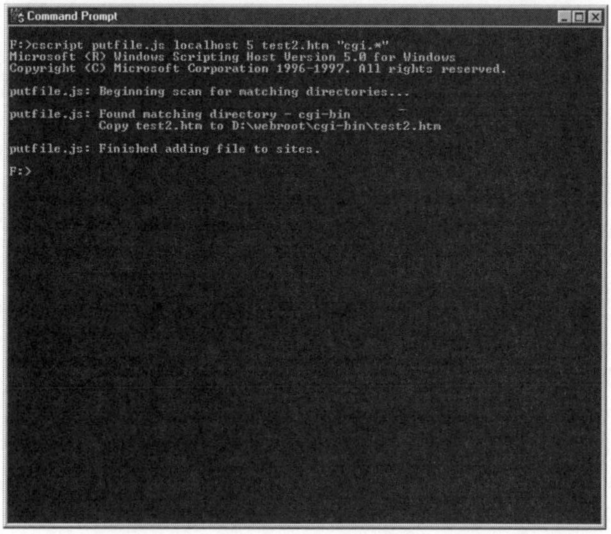

FIGURE **13.13**

Using putfile.js *with the directory filter* cgi* *to put the* test2.htm *file in all directories that begin with the letters* cgi.

13

Like the other scripts, the example begins with a check for command-line parameters in step 1. In step 2, the root directory of the Web site is associated with the instance command-line parameter. Step 3 creates an instance of a FileSystemObject that is used in the PutFile() function. Then PutFile() is called with the Web site root directory, the name of the file to put on the site, the parent directory (which at the root is blank), and the regular expression object that contains the search expression that used to match directories.

Most of the work in this script occurs in the PutFile() function. It begins by calculating the current "parent directory." This is necessary because you need to concatenate the path if the function is called with a standard IIsWebDirectory object. Next, the function checks the current directory to determine whether it matches the regular expression filter for the directory name. If the current directory matches, it determines the new path for the file, copies the file to the directory, and displays a message indicating that it copied the file. Finally, PutFile() calls itself recursively with the subdirectories that it finds. When PutFile() returns, step 4 is executed, which displays a "Done" message and quits the script.

This script can be useful if you need to perform mass changes to a Web site. You can reuse the techniques for directory matching that are implemented in the PutFile() function, and you can replace the functionality that occurs. For example, instead of putting a file in directories on a site, you could easily alter this script to delete files. Alternatively, if you only want to change directory settings on a site, you could replace the logic in PutFile() that copies files with logic that changes directory settings instead.

Summary

IIS is an excellent Web server with a good administration interface provided by the Microsoft Management Console. The Management Console works well; however, as your sites grow, it can become difficult to keep track of and maintain everything. Consequently, you might want to automate some of your administrative tasks using scripts. Those scripts can use the IIS administration objects, which provide access to the IIS metabase that contains IIS administration settings.

This chapter shows you a few examples of various scripts that use the IIS administration objects. Those scripts are just the beginning. You can modify them, if they are similar enough to what you want to accomplish, or you can take ideas from them to create your own scripts. In any event, if you're an IIS administrator who is frustrated with the capabilities of the standard Management Console, now you have the capability to create your own scripts to automate your IIS administration.

Q&A

Q **What objects can I access using the GetObject() function?**

A Assuming that you can specify the full ADSI path, you can access any IIS administration objects, anywhere in the hierarchy, directly using GetObject().

Q Will a property in a subobject override an inherited property from a parent object?

A Yes, if a property is explicitly set in a subobject, it will override an inherited property.

Q How can I remove properties from subobjects so that they use inherited properties instead?

A You can use the `PutEx()` function to remove properties from subobjects. After you've removed a property from it, the subobject will use the value from an inherited property.

13

DAY **14**

Overview of WSH and Application Scripting Capabilities

By Ian D. Morrish

Day 14: Chapter Overview

WSH includes some useful built-in functions, but the real power comes from the capability to automate other applications and make use of the Component Object Model (COM).

Scripting has become the glue that can tie all the pieces together. Whether it is WSH, Active Server Pages, Commerce Server Pipe Lines, or Transaction Server, you will see that scripting is everywhere. This chapter will explain the programmer's terminology that you need to understand in order to make use of all the cool stuff programmers have provided in their applications and components.

In this chapter, you will learn about the following:

- Definitions of terms
- Object models
- Tools to help identify component capabilities

Introduction to Scripting Applications

In the old DOS days, you often used a batch file to run a program that could take command-line parameters. The program would start using these parameters, and the required action was completed. Windows applications have become so feature-rich that the number of command-line options required to support all the possible combinations of actions that you might want to perform would be unmanageable.

Running Applications the Standard Way

Applications can be run in many ways on the Windows platform:

- From a shortcut to the application
- From the Explorer window
- As batch files
- By file association

For an application such as Microsoft Word, you have limited control over what happens when you start the application. Using the command line to execute the application, you can specify a filename to automatically open the application and some switches to control its behavior, as in the following example:

```
Winword.exe /tautomate /mstart
```

This command causes Word to start, load a template file called `automate`, and then run a macro in that template called `start`.

Other applications might make more extensive use of command-line options. For example, PKZip from PKWARE, Inc. (`http://www.pkware.com/`), has the following command-line options:

```
Usage:  PKZIP [options] zipfile [@list] [files...]

-a               Add files
-b[drive]        create temp zipfile on alternative drive
-d               Delete files
-e[xx,x,n,f,s,0] Use [Extreme¦eXtra¦Normal (default)¦Fast¦Super
➥fast¦Store]
-f               Freshen files
```

```
-l                  display software License agreement
-m[f,u]             Move files [with Freshen ¦ with Update]
-u                  Update files
-p¦P                store Pathnames¦p=recursed into¦P=specified & recursed
↪into
-r                  Recurse subdirectories
-s[pwd]             Scramble with password [If no pwd is given, prompt for
↪pwd]
-v[b][r][m][t][c] View .ZIP [Brief][Reverse][More][Technical][Comment]
sort by [d,e,n,o,p,s] [Date¦Extension¦Name¦natural
↪Order(default)¦Percentage¦Size]
-&[f¦u¦l            Span disks [Format¦Unconditional format¦Low density
  h¦w¦v]            High density¦Wipe disk¦enable dos Verify¦
  [s[drive]]        Back up entire disk w/ subdirs (-rp) [drive to back up]]
```

Most people would use a GUI-based compression program such as WINZip, but I have yet to find one that can be automated. The problem with using the DOS program is that there is a limit to the number of files you can specify on the command line. Long filenames also have a big impact on this.

Running Applications with Macros

Many Windows applications can be automated by using built-in macro capabilities. These work well for power users who want to automate common tasks. Macro languages enable a user to record repetitive tasks so that they can be repeated when required. They generally require the user to start the application and then to select the required macro to run. The user then watches the macro perform the actions that would otherwise be achieved through keyboard or menu actions. Microsoft developed Visual Basic for Applications to provide powerful automation within applications.

VBA can be used from within an application to automate other applications, but compared with WSH, it has a much greater overhead.

Running Applications Using OLE Automation

When Microsoft combined a number of applications into an office suite, they found that people wanted to combine features from one application with the documents created in another application. For example, a user might want to embed a range of cells from an Excel spreadsheet in a Word document.

Dynamic data exchange (DDE) was the first attempt at enabling data and commands to be sent to other applications. This developed into object linking and embedding (OLE), which supported drag-and-drop and in-place editing. OLE Automation was developed as a way of enabling other applications to access the functions of an application.

14

For example, the menu item in Word to open a document can be automated with the following script:

```
Set objWord = Wscript.CreateObject("Word.Application")
appWord.Documents.Open("C:\test.doc")
```

Note This is not a complete script, and the next chapter, "Scripting the Microsoft Office Suite," covers automating Word in more detail.

OLE Automation is exposed through the Component Object Model (COM). COM is also the basis for many small components (utilities) that have been developed that don't have any user interface and can only be accessed through automation. These are often called ActiveX controls.

Compare the previous PKZip command-line example with this component from Inner Media Inc.:

```
Set oZip = Wscript.CreateObject("dzactxctrl.dzactxctrl.1")
oZip.ItemList = "C:\test.doc"
oZip.ZIPFile = "C:\test.zip"
oZip.ActionDZ = 4 'Add to zip
Wscript.Echo "Done " & oZip.ErrorCode
```

You can download a 30-day evaluation copy of this control from http://www.innermedia.com/html/free_demos.htm.

Not all controls are suitable for use with WSH. Some controls require a user interface that is provided by the hosting application. WSH does not manage windows and cannot use these types of controls. An example of such a control is the Microsoft `ProgressBar` control that is often used in VB applications or in Internet Explorer Web pages.

Definition of Terms

A good understanding of the terms used when describing the use of components and OLE Automation will help most when you have to talk to a programmer or post questions to the newsgroups. It will also help you understand what I'm talking about in the rest of the chapter.

COM (Component Object Model)

This is a standard that defines the interface through which your script or other components can communicate with a COM component or OLE Automation application. The term "object" can get very confusing, and most COM objects should just be called "components."

COM is more significant than the language used to create the component or application because it is a language-independent standard. It fits in well with the object-oriented programming methods.

Interface

An interface is a collection of functions that can be accessed through the name of the interface. All COM components support at least the Iunknown interface. This provides the information required by high-level languages to query the component for additional information. Windows also uses this interface to track the use of the component and remove it from memory when it is no longer required.

Idispatch is an interface that makes a COM component an Automation object. It is used by applications that can explore all the interfaces available in a component. Such an application is the Microsoft OLE Viewer, which you will be looking at later in this chapter. Most functions of a small component are accessed by WSH through this interface.

Method

A method is a function that performs an action. Just like a function in VBScript, a method can also accept parameters. A method usually initiates an action, such as opening, saving, getting, and putting.

Property

A property is a variable used by a function or attribute of an object. It can be read or written; however, it can sometimes be read-only. Things such as color, size, height, and width are properties. This is where you must remember that VBScript only supports variants, which might not be compatible with some components.

Events

When you call an object's method, your script will wait for the function to complete if the object is synchronous. This means that next line of your script will not be executed until the method you called is complete.

Some objects are asynchronous, which means that program execution will not wait for the method to complete. In this case, the object will use events to let the calling application know that a state has changed or a task has been completed. These types of objects are a bit more difficult to use with WSH because you must make the script wait for the event to happen.

14

Object

Within an application, there can be a number of objects that have their own specific methods and properties. For example, Microsoft Outlook has many objects, including the following:

- Application object
- NameSpace object
- Explorer object
- Folders Collection object
- Items Collection object

To access these objects, you reference them by assigning them a variable name—the same as creating the application variable. For example, to determine the current folder a user is viewing in Outlook, you can use the following code:

```
Set objOL = Wscript.CreateObject("Outlook.Application")
Set olFolder = objOL.ActiveExplorer.CurrentFolder
CurFolder = olFolder
Wscript.Echo "Current folder name = " & CurFolder
```

The second Set statement (olFolder) has given you a reference to the current folder. See the description of object models later in this chapter.

Collections

An object is often a container holding a number of items that in turn have properties. For example, your Inbox is an object within the folders object. Each mail item within the Inbox has several properties, such as sender's name, date/time sent, subject, and message text.

You can programmatically iterate through the collection of items with the For Each statement or the object might support a count property that you can use for the upper bound of a For...Next loop. For example, this code will tell you how many items are in your currently selected Outlook folder:

```
Set objOL = Wscript.CreateObject("Outlook.Application")
Set olFolder = objOL.ActiveExplorer.CurrentFolder
CurFolder = olFolder
Set oFolderItems = olFolder.Items ' get collection of items in folder
NumItems = oFolderItems.Count
Wscript.Echo "Current folder name = " & CurFolder & vbLF &_
        "Number of items = " & NumItems
```

Note   Outlook collections start at 1, as opposed to arrays, which start at 0.

By adding this code to the previous example, you can access the properties of each item:

```
For I = 1 to NumItems
    Set oMyItem = oFolderItems(I)
    Wscript.Echo oMyItem.Subject
Next
```

Instantiate

Instantiate is the term used when you create an instance of an object. WSH does this for you when you use the `Wscript.CreateObject` command. This involves loading it into memory if it is not already there and using the `Iunknown` interface to register the fact that WSH is using the object.

Program ID

The program ID is the key piece of information you need to instantiate the object you want to automate. It is the string you use in the `Wscript.CreateObject` command. How to find the program ID is covered later in this chapter.

There are two Program IDs. A version-independent ID is normally the one you use unless you want to use methods that are only in a particular version, in which case you would use the version-specific ID. For example, if you want to use a specific method available in Outlook 2000, you could use the following command to ensure that an older version of Outlook is not used:

```
Set appOutl = Wscript.CreateObject("Outlook.Application.9")
If Err.Number <>0 Then
    Wscript.Echo "Outlook 2000 required"
    Wscript.Quit()
End If
```

CLSID

Everything that has a COM interface is defined in the Registry. The CLSID is a unique 128-bit identifier. You will find these in the Registry under `HKEY_CLASSES_ROOT\CLSID`. For example, Word 2000 has a CLSID of:

```
000209FF-0000-0000-C000-000000000046
```

14

When you use the `Wscript.CreateObject` command, the program ID is found in the Registry, and the relevant CLSID key contains the information Windows needs to make the object available.

These Registry keys are created when you install an application or register a component with the `regsvr32.exe` program.

Type Library

This is an interface (`ItypeLib` or `ItypeInfo`) that is not required but is very useful if you have it. It is a way of documenting the parameters that are supported by each function. This is how an object viewer application such as the Microsoft OLE Viewer can display property names and data types supported by an object.

Understanding Object Models

The Object Model is a visual representation of what is available in the COM interface of a component or OLE–Automation-enabled application (you can also call this an OLE Automation Server).

A well-documented object model is invaluable when trying to automate a complicated application such as Microsoft Outlook. You will usually find an object model in the application's documentation or online help. See Figure 14.1 for an example of the Outlook 2000 object model.

FIGURE 14.1

The Outlook 2000 object model.

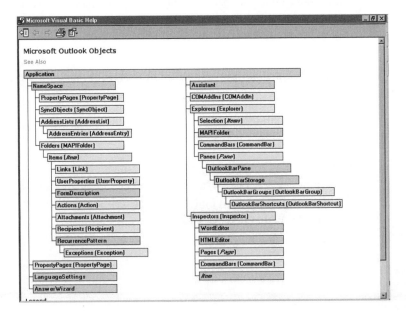

You can drill down into each object to get more information by clicking it.

For example, look at the `Explorers` object. This is a collection of all Outlook windows (not all of them might be visible). For each window, you can access the `CommandBars` object. This is a collection of all menus and toolbars. Having access to this object lets you execute any menu or toolbar command.

Here is a sample script that will bring up the Out of Office dialog box:

```
Set objOutlook = Wscript.CreateObject("Outlook.Application")
Set objOlEx = objOutlook.ActiveExplorer
Set objOlCB = objOlEx.CommandBars
Set menu = objOlCB("Menu Bar")
Set Tools = menu.Controls("Tools")
Set myTool = Tools.Controls("Out of Office Assistant...")
myTool.Execute
```

Active Explorer is a quick way of referencing the currently active Outlook Explorer window. After you have a reference to the `CommandBars` object, you can specify the menu bar and then each menu and submenu just as seen when using the application interactively.

You can find the name of each toolbar with the following code:

```
Set objOutlook = Wscript.CreateObject("Outlook.Application")
Set objOlEx = objOutlook.ActiveExplorer
Set objOlCB = objOlEx.CommandBars
For each cbar in objOlCB
  Wscript.Echo cbar.Name '& " " & _
cbar.NameLocal & " " & cbar.Visible
Next
```

As you can see, the Outlook object model is very powerful, and if it weren't for COM and OLE Automation, you would not have access to these features from WSH.

Here are some links to other object model diagrams available on the Web:

- IE4: `http://www.microsoft.com/mind/1098/working/workingfig01.htm`
- Office Applications:
  `http://www.microsoft.com/officedev/articles/OMG/default.htm`
- Advanced Data Objects:
  `http://msdn.microsoft.com/library/techart/adosql_2.htm`

14

Tools

You would be surprised how many OLE–Automation-capable applications and COM components are available on your Windows PC. There are two powerful applications that can help you understand how to use these objects.

The first is Microsoft's free OLE Viewer. You can download this from `http://www.microsoft.com/com`. The other is the VBA editor that ships with Microsoft Office.

OLE Viewer

This application searches the Registry to display a list of all registered objects. You can view all the objects or list them by category, as seen in Figure 14.2.

FIGURE 14.2

The OLE/COM object viewer.

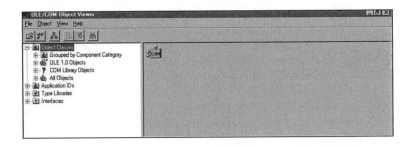

The group Grouped by Component Category relates to Internet Explorer, not WSH. Although you might be able to use some of these controls with WSH, IE will display a warning if an HTML document contains a component that is not in this category.

Expand the All Objects folder and wait a while (see Figure 14.3). Scroll down to Internet Explorer (Ver1.0) and expand it.

Because this object has an `Idispatch` interface (third item in the left window), you can probably automate it. You can see the program ID in the right window.

You can now create an instance of Internet Explorer using the following code:

```
Set objIE = Wscript.CreateObject("InternetExplorer.Application")
```

To find what methods and properties are available, double-click the `Idispatch` interface and select the View TypeInfo button. Depending on the version of IE, you might see different results. A typical view is shown in Figure 14.4.

FIGURE 14.3

The All Objects folder in expanded view.

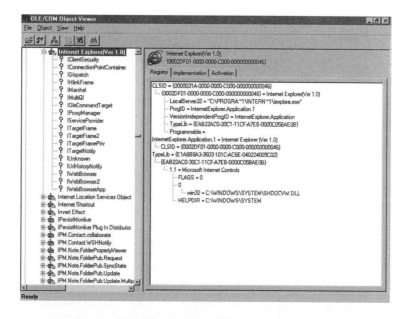

FIGURE 14.4

Idispatch interface with the View TypeInfo button selected.

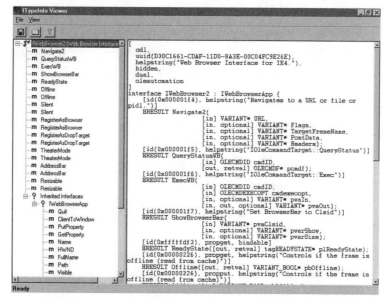

If you expand the Inherited Interfaces, you will see even more available methods. This is where the experimentation starts.

14

Find the Visible method and highlight it. You will see the following information displayed:

```
[id(0x00000192), propput, helpstring("Determines whether the application
➡is visible or hidden.")]HRESULT Visible([in] VARIANT_BOOL pBool);
```

This tells you how to use the method. VARIANT_BOOL means that the value can be 0 or 1, so you can add another line to your script:

```
objIE.Visible=1
```

Now, look at the Navigate2 method:

```
[id(0x000001f4), helpstring("Navigates to a URL or file or pidl.")]

HRESULT Navigate2(
                [in] VARIANT* URL,
                [in, optional] VARIANT* Flags,
                [in, optional] VARIANT* TargetFrameName,
                [in, optional] VARIANT* PostData,
                [in, optional] VARIANT* Headers);
```

This tells you that you must supply the URL as a VARIANT (other parameters are optional). This is the last line of the script:

```
objIE.navigate2 "http://msdn.microsoft.com/scripting"
```

Two items are shown for most methods. This means that you read and write parameters. If there is only one item, it will be for [in] (write) or [out] (read-only) use.

VBA Editor

The VBA editor is a little more user-friendly for VBScript developers because VBA has a lot in common with VBScript.

After starting an Office application, you can access the VBA development environment by pressing the Alt and F11 keys.

In the Tools menu, select References. Then select Microsoft Internet Controls, as shown in Figure 14.5.

If you want to work with a DLL or OXC not in this list, you can use the Browse icon to locate the control.

Now, you can use the Object Browser by selecting in the View menu. Select SHDocVw from the top drop down list (Figure 14.6).

The right window gives a good representation of the properties (hand icon), methods (green icon), and events (lightning). Read-only properties are indicated by a dot to the left of the hand.

FIGURE 14.5

Tools menu in the VBA development environment.

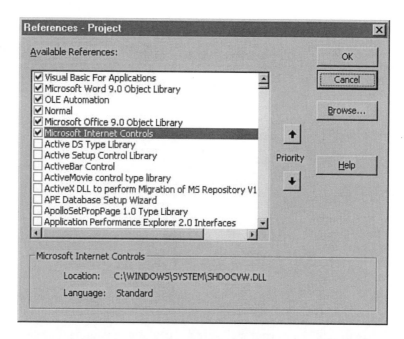

FIGURE 14.6

SHDocVw in the Object Browser.

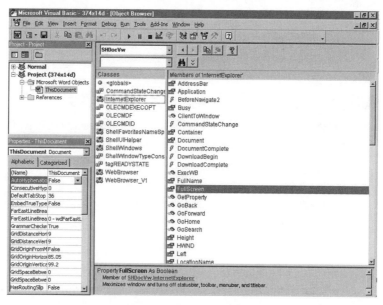

You can even use the Code editor to write some of your code. Create a new module by using the Insert, Module menu. The first line of code, although not valid in WSH, enables Intellisense for the object (see Figure 14.7).

Day 14

FIGURE **14.7**

Intellisense enabled.

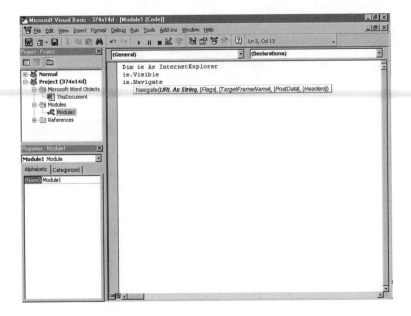

You could now copy and paste this code with minor modification into your normal script editor (Visual Notepad).

The Macro editor can also be used to generate automation code that with some modification can be copied into your VBScript.

Microsoft COM Components

COM is a key technology in Microsoft's development strategy. The fact that a Windows Script Host file can perform such a powerful and wide range of tasks is a testament to the success of this technology. Other chapters in this book will cover the following components:

- ADSI (Active Directory Services Interface)
- IIS Admin Object
- ADO (Advanced Data Objects)

There is a large number of third-party COM components available that have been developed for Active Server Pages that are ideal for use with WSH. These components are all synchronous and don't rely on events. There is a good list of components at http://www.activeserverpages.com/components/toc.asp, where you can find DNS lookup, POP3, and NT permission components that are free or shareware.

Applications That Can Be Automated

On a lighter side, Microsoft Agent is a user interface that uses an animated character to communicate with a user through text-to-speech and dialog boxes. The software is freely available from `http://msdn.microsoft.com/agent`.

This script will use the Agent COM component to display the Merlin character, move it to a new location, and if you have the text-to-speech software installed, will speak a message. You might have to change the path to `merlin.acs` depending on your installation.

Sample code:

```
Dim AgentControl
On Error Resume Next
Set AgentControl = CreateObject("Agent.Control.1")
If IsObject(AgentControl) Then
  AgentControl.Connected = True
  Dim merlin
  On Error Resume Next
  AgentControl.Characters.Load "merlin", "C:\Program Files\Microsoft
➥Agent\characters\merlin.acs"
  set merlin= AgentControl.Characters ("merlin")
merlin.Get "state", "Showing"
merlin.Get "state", "Speaking"
merlin.MoveTo 10, 10
merlin.Show
merlin.Get "state", "Moving"
merlin.MoveTo 257, 177
merlin.Speak ("Isn't it about time you started doing some real work?")
merlin.Hide
End If
wscript.echo "What do you think?"
```

Summary

I hope you now appreciate two things: COM is here to stay, and it is important for you to understand how to take advantage of this technology through scripting. This is probably the hardest thing for NT Administrators and Systems engineers to grasp, but if you want to be a smart and valuable (better paid) member of your team, you can't avoid it.

The next time you have to add or update 20 NT accounts, I'm sure you will be thinking about COM and not User Manager for Domains.

14

Q&A

Q I'm using a component in a script on my development machine, but it fails to run on other PCs. I have registered the component using `Regserv32`, but it still doesn't work. Why not?

A Some components require a license to be used in "design-time mode." If you have Visual Basic installed on your PC, this license is installed. Each time the component is instantiated, it checks for the existence of the required license. When the component is shipped with an application, it operates in runtime mode, which doesn't require a license. Unfortunately, WSH appears to the component as a design-time environment and requires the license.

Q I have successfully installed a COM object using `regserv32.exe`, but I get a runtime error when trying to use the object in a script. What can I do?

A The COM object might have other dependencies, such as the VB runtime or the ATL library (C++ components often require this). There can also be other operating system dependencies relating to OLE and COM infrastructure. You should check with the component's vendor for the requirements.

Q The component I'm automating disappears as soon as my script disappears. Applications such as MS Office don't behave like this. What is the difference?

A When you start an Office application, it runs in its own memory space, so when the script exits Office, the application continues running. Other components might run in the same memory as WSH, which means that the component will be destroyed as soon as the script exits.

DAY 15

Scripting the Microsoft Office Suite

By Michael Morrison

One of the most powerful uses of Windows Script Host (WSH) is the control of applications with scripts. For example, you can use WSH to create scripts that automate data-entry or document processing tasks. Microsoft's Office Suite is perhaps the most popular suite of applications in use on the Windows platform, so it's important to understand how WSH integrates with Office. This lesson explores how to create scripts in both VBScript and JScript that can be used to interact with and control Office applications such as Excel and Word.

Today you will learn

- How to write scripts that interact with and control Microsoft Office applications
- How to create and manipulate Excel spreadsheets using WSH scripts
- How to create and manipulate Word documents using WSH scripts

- How to make sure that Office objects are valid
- How to create scripts that share information between two Office applications

Microsoft Office Scripting with WSH

As you learned in the preceding lesson, applications make themselves open to scripting environments via their object models. The Microsoft Office Suite is no different in this regard; in fact, Office provides an incredibly powerful application object model for scripting. Virtually anything that you can do in an Office application using the application's user interface can also be done programmatically using a script. For example, you might consider creating a script that generates random love notes in Word—or maybe I should just stay out of your love life!

Scripting Microsoft Office applications is typically a two-step process:

1. Obtain an object reference.
2. Manipulate the object via properties and methods.

Because VBScript and JScript are both object-based languages, you must always interact with Office applications via objects defined in an application's object model. The first step involves obtaining a reference to a specific object. This reference is then used as the basis for accessing properties and calling methods, which is where it gets interesting. Now you will take a close look at these two steps.

Referencing Objects

Just as you can't write anything without picking up a pen or pencil, you can't do anything with an object without obtaining a reference to it. Fortunately, obtaining an object reference in Office applications is very straightforward; it requires only a knowledge of the application's object model. Details on each application's object model are available in the Visual Basic Reference section of the application's online help.

 Note All Office applications share a similar object model. After you've learned to script one of them, you will be ready to use them all.

Office application object models are organized as a *hierarchy* of objects, which means that you typically must start high up in the hierarchy and "drill down" to get a reference to the object you need. The Application object is the top-level object in all Office applications. To initially obtain a reference to the Application object for an Office application, you must use the `CreateObject()` method, which is provided by the `WScript` object:

```
Dim appWord
Set appWord = WScript.CreateObject("Word.Application")
appWord.Visible = True
```

Note

> In some situations, you might want to move up the object hierarchy from a lower object. In this case, you use the `Parent` property to obtain a reference to an object's parent. You then use the `TypeName()` function to determine the type of object returned by any expression, not just expressions containing the `Parent` property.

In this example, a variable named `appWord` is created to hold a reference to the `Application` object for an instance of the Word application. Word is specified as the application by passing `"Word.Application"` as the object type to `CreateObject()`. The last line of code makes the application window appear; otherwise, the application would be hidden.

Admittedly, this code doesn't do much. You might try something a little more interesting:

```
appWord.Documents.Add()
appWord.Documents.Add()
appWord.Documents.Add()
MsgBox(appWord.ActiveDocument.Name)
```

This sample code calls the `Add()` method on the `Documents` collection to add three new documents to Word. It then displays the filename of the active document using the `ActiveDocument` object, which is a special object under the `Application` object that references the currently active document in an Office application.

I just mentioned the fact that the `Documents` object is a *collection*, which means that it serves as a container for holding multiple objects. Collections appear in the object models for all Office applications and serve as a great way to manage multiple entities of the same type. The `Documents` object in Word is a good example of a collection; it holds a list of the `Document` objects open in a given Word session. Similarly, Excel has a `Workbooks` collection that contains a list of the workbooks open in a given Excel session. You can obtain a reference to a single member of a collection using the `Item` property or method, like this:

```
appWord.Documents.Item(1).CheckSpelling()
```

This code checks the spelling of the first document in the application's document list. The `Item` method is the default method for most collections, so you could reduce the preceding code to the following:

```
appWord.Documents(1).CheckSpelling()
```

Of course, all the code thus far has been VBScript code. The following is a JScript equivalent of the simple script you've been studying:

```
var appWord
appWord = WScript.CreateObject("Word.Application");
appWord.Visible = true;

appWord.Documents.Add();
appWord.Documents.Add();
appWord.Documents.Add();
appWord.Documents.Item(1).CheckSpelling();
```

As you can see, the JScript code closely parallels the VBScript code. That is the power of having both scripting languages reliant on common object models.

Manipulating Objects

You've learned how to obtain a reference to an `Application` object, and you've even had a peek at manipulating the object using properties and methods. Now you will dig a little deeper into how properties and methods are used on Office objects to control Office applications.

Manipulating objects primarily involves an understanding of the properties and methods available for use in a given object. You dig into the object models for Word and Excel a little later in the lesson. For now, you will focus on a few examples of popular properties and methods used to control Office applications.

The `Close()` method is common across all Office applications and is used to close a document or window. Here is an example of JScript code that closes the active document in Word:

```
appWord.ActiveDocument.Close();
```

Of course, you usually have to open a document before closing it. This is an example of VBScript code that opens a document in Word:

```
appWord.Documents.Open("C:\My Documents\HiMom.doc")
```

As you can see, the `Open()` method takes a single argument, which is the filename of the document to open. Some methods take more interesting arguments. For example, the `ComputeStatistics()` method takes an argument that specifies a statistic in which to

15

calculate on a Word document. The following statistic constants are valid for use with the ComputeStatistics() method:

- wdStatisticCharacters—The number of nonspace characters in the document
- wdStatisticCharactersWithSpaces—The number of characters in the document, including spaces
- wdStatisticWords—The number of words in the document
- wdStatisticLines—The number of lines in the document
- wdStatisticParagraphs—The number of paragraphs in the document
- wdStatisticPages—The number of pages in the document

The next example uses the ComputeStatistics() method to calculate and display the number of words in a document:

```
MsgBox(appWord.ActiveDocument.ComputeStatistics(wdStatisticWords))
```

This type of script code is very useful for writers such as me. For example, I can use it to determine whether my word count or page count is getting too large in a particular lesson. If I'm short on content, I can create a script that will randomly add phrases such as "How are you doing?" just to fill out a lesson. By the way, how are you doing? Just kidding.

Thus far, I've focused on manipulating objects by calling methods. You can also do some neat things by simply querying and setting properties. For example, this code displays a message in the status bar of Word by setting the StatusBar property of the Application object:

```
appWord.StatusBar = "Howdy partner!"
```

You could personalize this by using the UserName property:

```
appWord.StatusBar = "Howdy, " & appWord.UserName & "!"
```

This code builds a message string by inserting the username set in Word. The result of running this code on my computer is Howdy, Michael Morrison!

Scripting Microsoft Excel

As you probably already know, Microsoft Excel is a major part of the Office Suite and is geared toward creating powerful spreadsheets for managing and manipulating numerical data. Excel is particularly well suited to scripting because of the ease with which its data can be accessed. Consider how easy it is to reference a cell in an Excel spreadsheet versus navigating through paragraphs of text in a Word document. Don't worry, you will learn how to write scripts that interact with Word documents a little later in the day, but for now you will start off with Excel spreadsheets.

Excel's object model provides a variety of objects that you can use to build scripts. However, most of the time you will use four primary objects when creating Excel scripts:

- Application
- Workbook
- Worksheet
- Range

The familiar Application object represents an instance of an Excel application session. The Application object also serves as the basis for navigating through the object hierarchy and obtaining references to other objects. The Workbook object represents a single Excel workbook, which can contain multiple worksheets. An individual worksheet in a workbook is represented by the Worksheet object. Finally, the Range object represents a selection of one or more contiguous cells in a worksheet.

The Excel Application Object

Like Application objects for all Office applications, Excel's Application object takes on the task of controlling the application window and providing access to general application features. The Application object contains a collection of workbooks in the Workbooks property, which is the property you will typically use as the basis for digging into data that is stored in cells of a worksheet. The Application object also includes a Windows property that is a collection of child windows open in the application.

You obtain a reference to an Excel Application object by calling the CreateObject() method on the WScript object and passing "Excel.Application" as the only argument:

```
Dim appXL
Set appXL = WScript.CreateObject("Excel.Application")
appXL.Visible = True
```

Notice that the Visible property of the Application object is set to True; this is necessary for the application window to become visible.

The Application object contains lots of properties and methods that can be used to automate Excel and perform interesting tasks. These are some of the more commonly used properties of the Application object:

- Windows
- Workbooks
- Cells

- ActiveWindow
- ActiveWorkbook
- ActiveSheet

The Windows object is a collection of Window objects representing open windows in the current Excel application session. You obtain references to individual Window objects by indexing the Windows collection or by using the ActiveWindow property. The following code displays the caption of the first window in the Windows collection:

```
MsgBox(appXL.Windows(1).Caption)
```

You can also close a window by calling the Close() method on a Window object. Here is an example of closing the active window by calling Close() on the ActiveWindow property:

```
appXL.ActiveWindow.Close()
```

The Workbooks object is a collection of Workbook objects representing open workbooks. You obtain references to individual Workbook objects by indexing the Workbooks collection or by using the ActiveWorkbook property. This code checks whether changes have been made to necessitate saving the current workbook:

```
If appXL.ActiveWorkbook.Saved = False Then
  MsgBox("Somebody save me!")
End If
```

As you can see, the Saved property of the active Workbook object is used to see whether the workbook has to be saved. If so, a message is displayed to the user. Of course, Excel automatically prompts users to save a workbook if they attempt to close the workbook with unsaved changes. However, you still might find a need for automatically saving a workbook using a script.

Getting back to the Excel Application object, Cells is a two-dimensional collection of cells that represent all the cells in the active worksheet. You can use the Cells object to get or set the contents of a specific cell. To do so, you must specify the row and column coordinates of the cell within the worksheet, like this:

```
appXL.ActiveSheet.Cells(2, 3).Value = 3.14
```

This sample code sets the cell in the second row and third column to 3.14.

The last object of interest with respect to the Application object is the ActiveSheet object, which represents the currently active worksheet. You can use the ActiveSheet object to manipulate the active worksheet. Here is an example of printing the active worksheet by calling the PrintOut() method on the ActiveSheet object:

```
appXL.ActiveSheet.PrintOut()
```

The Excel Workbook Object

Workbooks form the basis of information storage and retrieval in Excel. All content that you manipulate in Excel is saved as a workbook, which can later be opened. To open a workbook programmatically, you simply call the Open() method on the Workbooks object, like this:

```
appXL.Workbooks.Open("C:\My Documents\Taxes.xls")
```

If the workbook file doesn't exist or the path was entered wrong, the script will fail, and Excel will automatically be closed. After you open a workbook, you're free to manipulate it at will using script code. For example, you can get the value of a specific cell by using the Cells property, like this:

```
MsgBox(appXL.ActiveSheet.Cells(4, 2).Value)
```

Note If you don't specify a full path when using the Open() method, Excel will assume that the file is in the current folder.

Unless you have a specific file in mind to open in Excel, you might want to allow the user to browse and select the file to open. You can do this by calling the GetOpenFilename() method, which displays the standard File Open dialog box. This method returns a string path for the file selected by the user, which you can then pass to the Open() method to actually open the file. This example demonstrates how it is accomplished:

```
fileName = appXL.GetOpenFilename()
If fileName <> False Then
  MsgBox("Getting ready to open " & fileName & "!")
  appXL.Workbooks.Open(fileName)
End If
```

The return value of GetOpenFilename() is checked with an If statement because it is possible for the user to cancel out of the File Open dialog box, in which case GetOpenFilename() will return False. If the fileName variable isn't set to False, the workbook is opened with a simple call to Open().

If you would like to start out with a new workbook instead of opening an existing one, you can use the Add() method on the Workbooks object. The Add() method creates an empty workbook, which you can populate with data and manipulate to your heart's desire:

```
book = appXL.Workbooks.Add()
```

15

After you've made changes to a workbook, either directly in Excel or programmatically from a script, you can save it using either the Save() or SaveAs() methods in the Workbook object. You should always use SaveAs() when saving a workbook for the first time, because the workbook doesn't yet have a filename. Fortunately, you can use the GetSaveAsFilename() method to display the standard File Save As dialog box, which allows the user to browse and enter a filename for the workbook. The following saves a workbook using this approach:

```
fileName = appXL.GetSaveAsFilename()
If fileName <> False Then
  MsgBox("Getting ready to save " & fileName & "!")
  book.SaveAs(fileName)
End If
```

 Note   If you call the Save() or Close()method on the Workbooks collection, all the workbooks in the collection will be saved or closed.

You might notice that the SaveAs() method is called on a variable named book, which must have been previously set to a Workbook object. The best place to set such a variable is when you first add or open a workbook.

Closing a workbook is as simple as calling the Close() method on a Workbook object:

```
book.Close()
```

The Excel Worksheet Object

A workbook represents a collection of worksheets, which are the primary objects that you manipulate within Excel. The Worksheet object represents an individual worksheet in a workbook. It also provides a host of properties and methods that can be used to manipulate data stored in a worksheet. One such property that you've already learned about is the Cells property, which provides access to cells in a worksheet. You saw earlier in the lesson how to use the Cells property in conjunction with the ActiveSheet property of a workbook in order to manipulate cells in the active worksheet.

Another useful property defined in the Worksheet object is Range, which allows you to work with a range of cells in a worksheet. You will learn how to use the Range object in the next section. If you're only interested in working with a single row or column of worksheet data, you can use the Rows and Columns properties. The Rows property is an object that acts as a collection of all of the rows in a worksheet. Likewise, the Columns property acts as a collection of all of the columns in a worksheet.

There are also some useful methods defined in the Worksheet object. One of these methods is Calculate(), which is used to calculate a worksheet, or a range of cells within a worksheet. The following code shows how to calculate a worksheet by calling the Calculate() method:

```
appXL.ActiveSheet.Calculate()
```

If you happen to have a worksheet with some text in it, you might consider spell-checking the worksheet. The CheckSpelling() method does just the trick:

```
appXL.ActiveSheet.CheckSpelling()
```

The Excel Range Object

Although you can use the Cells property of a worksheet to access individual cells, the real power of accessing worksheets comes in the form of the Range object. The Range object represents a range of cells and is used throughout the Excel object hierarchy to represent a selection of cells. The Range object is not exactly a collection, but it can certainly represent multiple cells. This makes the Range object somewhat unique because it can represent either a single cell or range of cells.

Perhaps the simplest way to use the Range object is to access an individual cell using the name of the cell in Excel's A1-style naming convention. This naming convention uses letters for the column names and numbers for the row names, as displayed in Excel. The following sets the value of an individual cell using the Range object:

```
appXL.ActiveSheet.Range("B3").Value = 23
```

This code sets the cell at location B3 to 23. You can also set a cell to a formula by providing the formula as a string for the Formula property, like this:

```
appXL.ActiveSheet.Range("B4").Formula = "=(B3 - 8) / 5"
```

The real power of ranges doesn't enter the picture until you start dealing with ranges of cells. Here's how to initialize a two-dimensional range of cells to zero:

```
appXL.ActiveSheet.Range("A1:E5").Value = 0
```

Alternatively, you might want to clear a range of cells instead of setting them to zero:

```
appXL.ActiveSheet.Range("A1:E5").ClearContents()
```

Scripting Microsoft Word

Because all Office applications adhere to a similar object model, you will find that scripting Word is very similar to scripting Excel. The primary difference between scripting each of these applications has to do with their each operating on very different types of data. Even so, the manner in which objects are handled is very similar when scripting all Office applications. For example, the Application object is used as the application for both Word and Excel. These are some of the most important objects you will encounter when scripting Word:

- Application
- Document
- Range
- Selection
- Find and Replacement

Similar to its role in the Excel object model, here the Application object represents an instance of a Word application session. The Application object also serves as the basis for navigating through the object hierarchy and obtaining references to other objects such as Document objects. The Document object is somewhat akin to the Workbook object in Excel and represents a Word document. The Range object represents a selection of one or more contiguous text elements in a document. Although these elements could be words, sentences, or paragraphs, it's more accurate to think of a Range object as representing a series of characters. The Selection object is similar to the Range object except that it applies to the currently selected text in a document; the text selected in a Range object doesn't affect the document selection.

The Find and Replacement objects encapsulate the criteria required to perform a find and replace operation. The information stored in these objects reflects the options in the standard Find and Replace dialog box.

The Word Application Object

The Application object in Word functions very much like the Application object for Excel. In the context of Word, the Application object contains a collection of documents in the Documents property. The Application object also includes a Windows property that is a collection of child windows open in the application.

You obtain a reference to a Word Application object by calling the CreateObject() method on the WScript object and passing "Word.Application" as the only argument:

```
Dim appWord
Set appWord = WScript.CreateObject("Word.Application")
appWord.Visible = True
```

You must set the Visible property of the Application object to True to make sure that the application window is visible.

Not surprisingly, the `Application` object contains a wide range of properties and methods that can be used to automate Word and perform interesting tasks. These are some of the more commonly used properties of the `Application` object:

- `Windows`
- `Documents`
- `ActiveWindow`
- `ActiveDocuments`
- `Options`

The `Windows` object is a collection of `Window` objects representing open windows in the current Word application session. You obtain references to individual `Window` objects by indexing the `Windows` collection or by using the `ActiveWindow` property. This code displays the caption of the first window in the `Windows` collection:

```
MsgBox(appWord.Windows(1).Caption)
```

You can also close a window by calling the `Close()` method on a `Window` object. The following closes the active window by calling `Close()` on the `ActiveWindow` property:

```
appXL.ActiveWindow.Close()
```

At this point, you probably realize how similar the script code is for various Office applications. The reality is that after you've learned how to script one Office application, it requires very little additional knowledge to script other Office applications. Let's continue learning the basics of scripting Word!

The `Documents` object is a collection of `Document` objects representing open documents. You obtain references to individual `Document` objects by indexing the `Documents` collection or by using the `ActiveDocument` property. Here is an example that checks whether changes have been made to necessitate saving the current document:

```
If appWord.ActiveDocument.Saved = False Then
  MsgBox("Somebody please save me!")
End If
```

This code should look familiar because it is very similar to the code you saw earlier that performs a similar function in Excel.

There are a few capabilities of the `Application` object that you didn't learn about in the discussion of Excel. For one, you can switch the view to Print Preview by setting the `PrintPreview` property to `True`, like this:

```
appWord.PrintPreview = True
```

Simple! You can also control the application's graphical user interface by getting and setting property values such as `DisplayStatusBar`, which determines whether the status bar is visible. The following code toggles the status bar's visibility:

```
appWord.DisplayStatusBar = Not appWord.DisplayStatusBar
```

In addition to controlling the Word application's appearance, you can also alter the application's options using the `Options` property. The `Options` object includes a variety of properties that can be accessed to alter the functionality of Word—for example:

```
With appWord.Options
  .AllowDragAndDrop = False
  .AllowFastSave = True
  .BackgroundSave = True
  .SaveInterval = 15
End With
```

The options encapsulated in the `Options` object correspond to the options that can be viewed and set using the Options command from Word's Tools menu. You might want to check out these options in Word to get an idea of the options you can alter programmatically.

The Word `Documents` Object

Like workbooks in Excel, Word documents form the basis of information storage and retrieval in Word. All content that you manipulate in Word is saved within the context of a document, which can later be opened. To open a document programmatically, you simply call the `Open()` method on the `Documents` object, like this:

```
appWord.Documents.Open("C:\My Documents\Bio.doc")
```

After you've opened a document, you're ready to get to work entering and formatting document data.

 Note
> If you don't specify a full path when using the `Open()` method, Word will assume that the file is in the current folder.

To give the user a say in what document is opened, you can call the `GetOpenFilename()` method, which displays the standard File Open dialog box. This method returns a string path for the file selected by the user, which you can then pass to the `Open()` method to actually open the file. The following example demonstrates how this is accomplished:

```
fileName = appWord.GetOpenFilename()
If fileName <> False Then
  appWord.Documents.Open(fileName)
End If
```

To start out with a new document rather than open an existing one, you can use the Add() method on the Documents object. Similar to its counterpart in Excel's Workbooks object, the Add() method in Documents creates an empty document.

```
doc = appWord.Documents.Add()
```

After making changes to a document, either directly in Word or programmatically from a script, you can save it using either the Save() or SaveAs() methods in the Documents object. You should always use SaveAs() when saving a document for the first time, because the document doesn't yet have a filename. The GetSaveAsFilename() method displays the standard File Save As dialog box, which allows the user to browse and enter a filename for the document. You can call this method before calling SaveAs() to allow the user to enter the filename. The following code saves a document using this approach:

```
fileName = appWord.GetSaveAsFilename()
If fileName <> False Then
  doc.SaveAs(fileName)
End If
```

The SaveAs() method is called on a variable named doc, which must have been previously set to a Documents object. The best place to set such a variable is when you first add or open a workbook. You could also use the ActiveDocument property to save the current document, like this:

```
fileName = appWord.GetSaveAsFilename()
If fileName <> False Then
  appWord.ActiveDocument.SaveAs(fileName)
End If
```

Closing a document is as simple as calling the Close() method on a Documents object:

```
book.Close()
```

You can determine how many documents are open in a given Word session by looking at the Count property of the Documents object, like this:

```
MsgBox("There are " & appWord.Documents.Count & " documents open.")
```

Note   If you call the Save() or Close() method on the Documents collection, all the documents in the collection will be saved or closed.

To print a document, you simply call the PrintOut() method on a Documents object:

```
wordApp.ActiveDocument.PrintOut()
```

A topic closely related to printing is the setup of the page, which can be altered using the PageSetup property of the Documents object. The PageSetup object provides a host of properties that represent the various options available in Word's Page Setup dialog box. This code sets the margins for the active document using the PageSetup property:

```
With appWord.ActiveDocument.PageSetup
  .LeftMargin = InchesToPoints(0.5)
  .RightMargin = InchesToPoints(0.5)
  .TopMargin = InchesToPoints(1.0)
  .BottomMargin = InchesToPoints(1.0)
End With
```

As you've already learned, the Documents object is powerful and gives you lots of flexibility when it comes to manipulating Word documents. Take a look at one more use of the Documents object before moving on. I'm referring to *revision marks*, which are used in Word as a means of keeping track of document changes. You can turn revision tracking on and off by setting the TrackRevisions property, like this:

```
wordApp.ActiveDocument.TrackRevisions = True
```

The Word Range and Selection Objects

Because a Word document essentially consists of a group of sequentially arranged formatted characters, you typically manipulate a document by adding or selecting characters. The Word object model provides a suite of objects that make the selection and manipulation of text very straightforward. Two of the most important classes in this model are Range and Selection. Both these objects represent a range of contiguous characters; the difference between them has to do with their relationship to Word's current user selection.

The Selection object mirrors the currently selected text that the user sees with a highlight. If no text is selected, the Selection object represents the insertion point in the document, which is the location of the user input caret. Like the Selection object, the Range object also represents a selection of text, but it has no association with the highlighted text selection visible in Word. In other words, the Range object is an all-purpose selection object that enables you to select and manipulate text without the selection being visibly highlighted in Word. Another difference between ranges and selections is that you can create multiple Range objects, whereas only one Selection object can be active at any given time. This makes sense because there can be only one physical selection active in Word.

You can use the Range and Selection objects to perform all kinds of interesting tasks in Word, such as creating paragraphs, inserting text, and applying formatting and font styles. You can also use these objects to select a portion of a document to search for a word or phrase. Ranges and selections are defined by starting and ending character positions, which are calculated relative to the first character in a document. The first character in a document has the character position of zero. If a range or selection identifies the insertion point, the starting and ending character positions are equal.

Note The remainder of this section focuses on ranges because they are generally more flexible than selections. However, keep in mind that using the Selection object is very similar to using the Range object.

A range is identified by three primary properties:

- Start—The starting character position for the range
- End—The ending character position for the range
- StoryType—The type of story selected by the range

Not surprisingly, the Start and End properties represent the starting and ending character positions of the range. The StoryType property is a little more interesting. A *story* is an area of a document that contains text that is distinct from other parts of a document. For example, the body, header, and footer are all considered stories. The StoryType property can have one of 11 values that identify the story type of the range:

- wdMainTextStory
- wdPrimaryFooterStory
- wdPrimaryHeaderStory
- wdFirstPageFooterStory
- wdFirstPageHeaderStory
- wdEvenPagesFooterStory
- wdEvenPagesHeaderStory
- wdFootnotesStory
- wdCommentsStory
- wdEndnotesStory
- wdTextFrameStory

You typically don't have to worry about the story type of a range, so you can move on to working with ranges. The following example shows how to apply bold formatting to the first 20 characters in the active document:

```
appWord.ActiveDocument.Range(0, 20).Bold = True
```

15

As you can see, the range of characters is specified to the Range() method, which returns a Range object. The Bold property of this object is then set to apply bold formatting to all the characters in the range. Although this example is functional, you typically think of a Word document as a series of words, sentences, and paragraphs, as opposed to individual characters. The following example uses a range to italicize the first four words in the active document:

```
appWord.ActiveDocument.Range(0, appWord.ActiveDocument.Words(4).End)
➥.Italic = True
```

This example makes use of the Words collection, which references all the words in a document. Also, Sentences, Paragraphs, and Sections properties of the Document object allow you to work with sentences, paragraphs, and sections as opposed to words or characters. The following code alters the font size of the third sentence in the active document and then inserts a new paragraph before and after the paragraphs:

```
Set range = appWord.ActiveDocument.Sentences(3)
range.Font.Size = 40
range.InsertParagraphBefore()
range.InsertParagraphAfter()
```

In this example, the Sentences collection is indexed to return a range containing the third sentence in the document.

Keep in mind that all the range examples you've seen thus far have no effect on Word's text selection. I alluded to the fact earlier in the lesson that the Range object is more flexible than the Selection object. These are the specific reasons why:

- You can use multiple Range objects, whereas only one Selection object is allowed per document window.

- Using Range objects doesn't affect the text selected in Word.

- Range objects are a little faster to use than the Selection object.

Note

Although the main benefit to using ranges is that they don't affect the text selection, you can use the Range object as the basis for selecting text. For example, you might want to reflect a range visually, in which case you would use the range to alter the selection. The Select() method in the Range object enables you to accomplish this task by applying a range to the selection.

Before moving on, you must tackle one last topic related to ranges: looping. This example shows how to loop through a range of characters and apply the underline formatting style to each:

```
Set range = appWord.ActiveDocument.Words(1)
For i = 1 To 30
  range.Underline = True
  Set range = range.Next(1)
Next
```

Here, the Next() method is called to alter the range and select one character after another.

The Word Find and Replacement Objects

You've learned how to use the Range object to select specific ranges of text. Although this approach certainly has its benefits, you might want to select ranges of text by searching for a particular word or phrase. Additionally, you might want to search and replace text in a document. The Find and Replacement objects make both these tasks possible. If you've used the Find or Replace commands in Word, you've already seen these objects at work. Issuing the Find command in Word is equivalent to calling the Find() method on the Selection object in script code.

The following example shows how to use the Find() method to locate the next occurrence of the word *sneaky*:

```
With appWord.Selection.Find
  .Forward = True
  .Text = "sneaky"
  .Execute()
End With
```

The Forward property of the Find object is first set to True to indicate that the search should be performed forward through the document. The search text is set via the Text property. Finally, the Execute() method is called to start the search. If the end of the document is reached before the search text is found, the search is stopped.

The Replacement object is a property of the Find object, which means that you use the Find object to perform both the find and replace operations. The properties in the Find and Replace objects correspond to the options available in Word's Find and Replace dialog box. Keep in mind that you can use the Find object with a range, as well as the selection, which doesn't affect the visible selection in Word.

Making Sure That Objects Are Valid

15

Now that you understand how to develop scripts for Excel and Word using their respective scripting object models, it's important to point out a couple issues regarding runtime errors. Because script code regularly uses object references to access objects through properties and methods, it's possible to generate runtime errors by inadvertently using the wrong object in a given context. You can avoid such errors by checking the type of an object before attempting to access it.

The TypeName() function returns the type of an object. The following is an example of checking the type of the object returned by the Add() method in Excel:

```
Set book = appXL.Workbooks.Add()
if TypeName(book) <> "Workbook" Then
  MsgBox("Error adding workbook.")
End If
```

In this example, you know that the correct return type of the Add() method is Workbook, so you can check to make sure that the type name of the book variable is Workbook before accessing the variable.

Another trick to help avoid runtime errors is to use the global IsObjectValid property. This property applies to all objects and can be used to determine whether an object reference is valid. The IsObjectValid property is set to True if an object is valid or otherwise to False. An *invalid object* is one for which no memory has been allocated or for which the memory has already been freed. Either way, attempting to use the object will result in a runtime error. This code checks the book variable to see whether it is valid:

```
if IsObjectValid(book) = False
  MsgBox("The workbook isn't valid.")
End If
```

Scripting Multiple Office Applications

The final topic today pulls together much of what you've learned about Microsoft Office scripting in a simple example. The topic to which I'm referring is that of controlling multiple Office applications with a single script. This is a powerful use of scripting because it enables you to share information between applications. Here is a sample script that performs the following steps:

1. Opens an Excel workbook
2. Retrieves a value from a cell in an Excel worksheet
3. Builds a sentence string containing the value
4. Creates a Word document and adds the sentence to it

```
Dim appWord
Dim appXL

Set appWord = WScript.CreateObject("Word.Application")
appWord.Visible = True
Set appXL = WScript.CreateObject("Excel.Application")
appXL.Visible = True

appXL.Workbooks.Open("C:\My Documents\Finance\Plan99.xls")
appWord.Documents.Add()

sentence = "The value is " & appXL.Cells(4, 3).Value & "."
appWord.ActiveDocument.Words(1).InsertAfter(sentence)
```

This script uses scripting elements that you learned today. The only new skill you're exercising is the ability to merge the scripting of multiple applications within a single script.

Summary

This lesson explores the possibilities for using Windows Script Host to control and interact with Microsoft Office applications. You learned the basics of Office scripting, including how to obtain object references and how to access properties and methods of objects. You then learned the specifics of how to write scripts to interact with Excel and Word, the two most popular Office applications. From there, you learned a few tips regarding error prevention. Finally, you combined what you learned today to create a script that shares data between Excel and Word.

Keep in mind that today you only scratched the surface of what can be accomplished with WSH and Office. Office applications have very extensive object models that offer all kinds of interesting opportunities for scripting. My objective today was to lay the groundwork for you to explore these opportunities on your own.

Q&A

Q I've read through the Visual Basic reference that ships with Word and Excel, and some of the examples differ from the code in this lesson. Why is this?

A The reason for a disparity between the sample code in the Visual Basic documentation for Office applications has to do with the applications themselves supporting the Visual Basic for Applications (VBA) programming language. Although VBScript is similar to VBA, VBScript isn't quite as full featured. Therefore, VBScript code is more simplified than VBA code.

Q Can I also use JScript to script Office applications?

A Of course! VBScript and JScript are both fully supported in Office applications. I focused primarily on VBScript today just to make things more consistent. Besides, this will make it easier for you to understand the code if you should poke around in the VBA documentation that ships with Office.

Q Is there a relationship between scripting code in Word and the code associated with a Word macro?

A Yes. Word macros are actually just VBA programs, which means that they adhere to the same object model used by VBScript and JScript. One neat trick to learning how to carry out certain tasks is to first record a macro and then study the resulting code. In many cases, you will be able to convert this code to VBScript without too much work, which will enable the code to run under WSH.

15

Day 16

Using WSH to Access Databases Through Microsoft Active Data Objects (ADO)

As you've seen throughout this book, the Windows Scripting Host is a powerful, open technology for scripting and automation. One of the ways that you may want to extend your scripts is by integrating them with a database. Doing so really opens up the possibilities for your scripts. Imagine, for example, a user login script that retrieves information about a user from a centralized database. Conceivably, the user's entire desktop could be reconfigured using the settings from the database! Or you could develop reporting scripts that extract information to the user's local machine. Those are some basic examples. After you've read this chapter, you'll no doubt be able to think of situations where you may be able to apply database access.

To access databases, you'll use the Microsoft Active Data Objects (ADO). ADO is Microsoft's new standard for a database object model, and it's typically used for data access through Active Server Pages. In this chapter, you'll get a full introduction to ADO.

On the 16th day of your introduction to WSH, you'll

- Get an introduction to databases and data access via ADO
- See a reference for the ADO objects
- View examples that illustrate the use of the ADO objects from WSH scripts

Introduction to Database Access

In this chapter, you'll learn how you can access RDBMS systems from your WSH scripts using the Microsoft ADO technology. First the chapter discusses the history of data access; that will put ADO in context and help you to understand how it relates to earlier data access technologies such as ODBC, DAO, and RDO. After that the chapter delves into the details of ADO with plenty of examples that will show you how you can use it with your WSH scripts.

Persistent data storage is one of the most important requirements for literally any system. Systems that require users to log in must somehow store information about a user's login ID and password. Transaction systems must record and store information about, for example, customer orders. Financial analysis systems may store information about historical and current stock prices. Those are some basic examples—there are many others.

In the past, numerous approaches have been taken to support persistent data storage. In the old days, data for an application may have been stored in a simple flat file—sometimes just a basic text file. That's essentially the approach taken by legacy systems that use ISAM files. The limitations of flat text files are manifold; they have no abstraction to support complex analysis and aggregation of information stored in records. Soon people began to create database systems that supported more robust record creation, deletion, and modification, as well as searching and other advanced functions. Today, Relational Database Management Systems, or RDBMSs, have become popular. Some examples of common RDBMSs include Oracle, Microsoft SQL Server, IBM DB2, and Sybase Adaptive Server.

RDBMSs store information in tables. Each table is structured as a set of rows and columns. The columns represent individual fields, whereas the rows represent individual data records, which are comprised of multiple columns. RDBMSs allow you to create relationships between information stored in different tables. This allows you, for example, to store information about a customer once and relate that information to any number of orders. Because the customer information is stored once, it only needs to be updated once.

With RDBMS systems, it can be complex to store objects developed using object-oriented languages such as C++ or Java in relational tables. That's because the concepts underlying object design are pretty different from the concepts for relational tables. Consequently, object-oriented database management systems, or OODBMSes, have been gaining popularity. Rather than using table concepts, OODBMSes support the storage of information as objects, so the mapping from objects implemented in object-oriented languages such as C++ or Java to data storage is greatly simplified. There also hybrids such as object-relational systems that make it easier to store objects within RDBMSs by providing the logic to take object representations and break them down into relational table representations.

For this chapter's purposes, you're going to look at ways that you can access RDBMS systems. You'll start with a look at SQL and ODBC, and then you'll look at some of Microsoft's early object models for data access, and finally you'll examine the latest technology for database access, Microsoft Active Data Objects (ADO), and see how you can use it in your WSH scripts.

ODBC and SQL

In the early days, every database vendor had its own unique interface to its database system. To use a particular vendor's database, you needed to write code that used its function libraries and its specific syntax. The situation was improved by the advent of a standard language for database access—the Structured Query Language, or SQL.

SQL uses text statements to perform database functions. Using SQL, you can add information to tables in a database, retrieve data from tables, combine and aggregate information from several tables, delete or change information, and change the structure of database tables. For example, if you had a database of books, you might retrieve a list of authors by selecting information from a table of authors using syntax such as SELECT * FROM Authors. The syntax of SQL is standardized by ANSI, and it's become the most common language to interface with RDBMSs.

A further improvement was developed by Microsoft—Open Database Connectivity, or ODBC. ODBC specifies an interface between applications and database engines. Applications can use ODBC to pass SQL strings to databases and to retrieve information without requiring code specific to an individual database vendor's API. ODBC serves as an abstraction layer between the application and the database. For a database to be used through ODBC, you must have an ODBC driver for the database. The ODBC driver translates between the standard ODBC API used by applications and the specific API provided by a database vendor. The ODBC architecture is illustrated in Figure 16.1.

FIGURE 16.1

The ODBC Architecture; a unified interface to RDBMS systems.

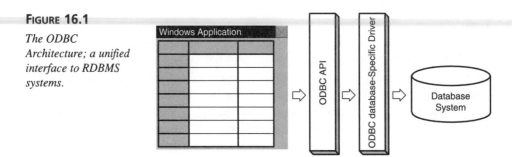

From an application perspective, using ODBC has the advantage of insulating you from vendor-specific details. It's become the standard for database access for the Windows platform. There are some problems with ODBC, however. ODBC is based on C-language coding conventions. Consequently, it can be difficult to use from object-oriented languages such as C++ or Visual Basic. Microsoft's solution to this issue has been to provide object models that sit on top of ODBC and/or other database technologies. The first object model was Data Access Objects (DAO), next came Remote Date Objects (RDO), and finally we have ADO. In the next few sections, we'll discuss each, then we'll dive into ADO details.

Microsoft DAO and RDO

Microsoft's first object model for database access was Data Access Objects, or DAO. DAO was based on the Microsoft Jet database engine, which is the same database engine used by the Microsoft Access database, at least up to Access 97. Later versions of Access use an engine that's similar to the engine in Microsoft SQL Sever. DAO provides easy access to Microsoft Access databases and also to RDBMS databases through ODBC support that's built into the Jet engine. The object model for DAO is illustrated in Figure 16.2.

DAO became popular with Visual Basic as the standard data access mechanism for version 3.0 of that language. However, certain problems with DAO began to materialize. First, the DAO object model is complex and relatively "heavy." To retrieve information from a database, you need to instantiate multiple DAO objects, a process that is both memory intensive and tedious. Second, DAO provides slow access to ODBC databases. For organizations that were using VB to access RDBMS systems through DAO's ODBC support, the speed, or lack thereof, was a common problem.

FIGURE **16.2**

The DAO object model.

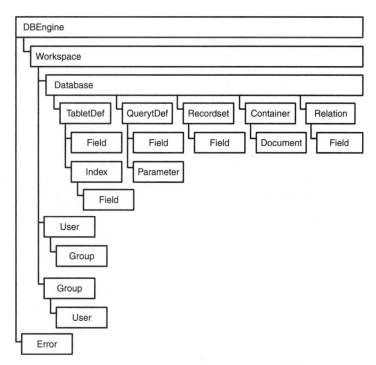

Microsoft's solution to the speed problem was the Remote Data Objects, or RDO. RDO was no longer based on the Microsoft Jet Database engine. It was intended to be a more efficient, less memory-intensive object interface to ODBC databases. It is much faster than using DAO to access ODBC databases but, as you can see from the illustration of the RDO object model in Figure 16.3, it's still chock-full of objects.

FIGURE **16.3**

The RDO object model.

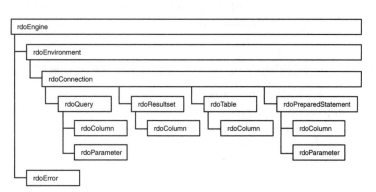

Because of the complexity of their object models, neither DAO nor RDO was particularly great for use in lightweight environments such as Active Server Pages (ASP). So Microsoft created a new object model, the Active Data Objects, or ADO.

Microsoft ADO

Microsoft ADO is the latest data access object model from Microsoft. It's a high-speed, efficient, and easy-to-use object-oriented framework for database access. ADO allows you to manipulate data in databases that are exposed through the OLE DB standard. OLE DB is an object standard for database access that supersedes the ODBC standard. To access a database through OLE DB, it must have an OLE DB provider. Conceptually, the OLE DB provider performs a similar function to an ODBC database driver.

Because many databases already provide ODBC drivers, Microsoft includes the Microsoft ODBC Provider for OLE DB. The Microsoft ODBC Provider allows ADO objects to access ODBC databases through OLE DB, so you can use any database with ODBC support through ADO immediately. Because it has an open model with standard interfaces implemented through providers, one of the major benefits of OLE DB is that it can be used both with relational and non-relational data sources. For our discussion, we're going to focus on the practical issue of using the ADO objects for data access in WSH scripts, but if you want more information about OLE DB, refer to the Microsoft Web site at www.microsoft.com.

Microsoft ADO also includes a capability called the Remote Data Service (RDS). RDS enables you to do *data remoting*. With data remoting, you move data from the server to the client in one step. Any data manipulation is done on the client, and updates are returned to the server in a single round trip. RDS can be used for Web applications to transfer data dynamically to and from a Web page for remote data access applications. We won't cover the RDS capabilities in this chapter, so if you want more details, refer to Microsoft ADO documentation.

The Microsoft Active Data Objects (ADO)

The Microsoft Active Data Objects can allow you to easily integrate your WSH scripts with database systems. Take a quick look at the ADO object model depicted in Figure 16.4. That's the object model that you'll be working with to access databases.

FIGURE 16.4

The ADO object model.

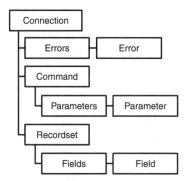

16

Note

> The diagram doesn't show the Properties collection associated with the Connection, Command, Recordset, and Field objects. The Properties collection can be used to attach dynamic attributes to the aforementioned ADO objects using Property objects. You can use all the other ADO objects without ever using the Property or Properties objects. Specific database providers may use the Properties to expose special capabilities.

ADO has a simple object model, and there are few dependecies between objects. If you want to quickly retrieve data or change data, you may only need to use the Recordset object! The Recordset is the object that you'll use most frequently because it represents a database result set. A *result set* is a sequence of records retrieved from a database. It may be the result of the execution of a SQL command, it may be the contents of a database table, or it may be the results of the execution of a database stored procedure. You can use Recordset objects to retrieve, add, or modify database information.

Note

> For those of you who are unfamiliar with stored procedures, a *stored procedure* is essentially a compiled set of SQL commands stored on a database server. You can access a stored procedure using a syntax similar to a function call that you might make using VBScript.

All Recordsets use a database connection. To establish a connection, you use a connection string. Recordsets may either use a connection string directly or an instance of a Connection object that you pre-prepare using a connection string; in either case, ADO ensures that the Recordset is associated with a Connection object. The connection string specifies all the details that are necessary to connect to a database. It typically includes the provider, or driver, that should be used, the name of the database server and database, and the username and password to use when connecting. We'll cover connection strings in more detail in the documentation for the `Connection.ConnectionString` property later in the chapter.

In addition to using it to connect to databases, you can use the `Connection` object to change data in databases using transactions. A *transaction* allows you to treat several database changes as a unit of work. This may be useful, for example, in a situation where you are maintaining bank accounts. Say you want to transfer money from one account to another. You need to decrement the value of the first account and then increment the value of the second account. You must ensure that both accounts are updated; if one is updated but the other isn't, the accounts will no longer be correct. Transactions allow you to treat both the increment and the decrement as atomic operations, so that either both succeed or both fail. You can find out more about the capabilities of the `Connection` object, including support for transactions, in the documentation for the `Connection` object later in this chapter.

The last major ADO object that you need to understand is the `Command` object. The `Command` object represents a SQL statement, a table name, or a stored procedure. You can use it as a convenient way to call a stored procedure that you might use multiple times; it has methods and properties that allow you to describe the characteristics of the stored procedure. Later in the chapter, you can find more details about the `Command` object, and you can see examples of its usage.

The ADO objects are easy to use from WSH, and you can exploit them for numerous purposes. Any time you need to retrieve, store, or modify data, you can use the ADO objects to go directly to a database system. In this chapter you'll see reference information for each object; make sure that you review the examples for the objects because they'll show you basic usage of the objects from ADO. After the reference material for each object, we'll take a step back and review some of the ways that you can use ADO from WSH to perform useful tasks.

Connection Object

The `Connection` object is the root of the ADO object hierarchy. It represents a connection to an OLE DB data source. The connection may be the equivalent of an actual network connection to a database server in a client/server system.

Connection Properties

Property Name	Description
Attributes	This returns or sets the characteristics of a connection. The valid attributes for a connection include the following constants: adXactCommitRetaining—ensures that calling CommitTrans will automatically start a new transaction; adXactAbortRetaining—ensures that calling RollbackTrans will automatically start a new transaction.
CommandTimeout	This specifies how many seconds to wait while executing a command before returning an error and terminating the command request. The default value is 30 seconds. If a command doesn't complete execution within the number of seconds specified by CommandTimeout, ADO will cancel the command and raise an error. If you set CommandTimeout to zero, ADO will wait indefinitely for the command to complete.
ConnectionString	This string specifies the connection to a database. It may either be a datasource name (DSN) or a connection string with embedded parameters. The DSN may be any registered datasource. The connection string may contain the following parameters: Provider—this specifies the name of the OLE DB provider; Data Source—this specifies the name of a registered data source; User ID—this is the user ID to use for the connection; Password—this specifies the password to use when opening the connection; File Name—this is the name of a provider-specific file that contains connection information; Remote Provider—this is the name of the provider to use when opening a client-side connection if the Remote Data Service is being used; Remote Server—this specifies the path name of the server to use when opening a connection using the Remote Data Service.

continues

16

Property Name	*Description*
ConnectionTimeout	This indicates how many seconds to wait when creating a connection to a data source before the connection attempt fails with an error. The default value is 15 seconds. You can only set this property when a connection is closed; it is read-only when a connection is open.
CursorLocation	This allows you to choose between various cursor libraries for a provider. Typically, you can either choose a client-side cursor library or a server-side library. This setting only affects database connections that are established after the property is set. If the connection is open, this property is read-only; if it is closed, the property is read/write. The valid constants for this property are: adUseClient—this uses the client-side cursor engine, the Microsoft Client Cursor Provider, which provides special features such as dis-associated recordsets; adUseClientBatch—this has the same effect as adUseClient; adUseServer—this is the default, which indicates that data provider or driver-supplied cursors should be used.
DefaultDatabase	This string specifies the default database for a connection. If a default database is set, SQL strings may access objects in that database using an unqualified syntax.
IsolationLevel	This long value sets the isolation level for transactions that are performed using the Connection object. This is a read/write property, but any changes to it don't take effect until the next time that you call the BeginTrans method. The following constants may be used to set the isolation level: adXactUnspecified—this indicates that the IsolationLevel cannot be determined from the provider; adXactChaos—this indicates that you cannot overwrite pending changes from more highly isolated transactions; adXactBrowse—this indicates that you can view uncommitted changes in other transactions; adXactReadUncommitted—this has

Property Name	Description
	the same function as `adXactBrowse`; `adXactCursorStability`—this is the default isolation level, which means that from one transaction you can only view committed changes from other transactions; `adXactReadCommitted`—this has the same function as `adXactCursorStability`; `adXactRepeatableRead`—this indicates that from one transaction you cannot see changes made in other transactions, but that requerying can bring new recordsets; `adXactIsolated`—this indicates that transactions are isolated from other transactions; `adXactSerializable`—this has the same function as `adXactIsolated`.
`Mode`	The `Mode` property is used to set or get the access permissions used by the provider for a database connection. The property can only be set when the `Connection` is closed. The valid values for the `Mode` property are: `adModeUnknown`—this is the default mode and indicates that the permissions haven't been set or can't be determined. `adModeRead`—this indicates read-only; `adModeWrite`—this indicates write-only; `adModeReadWrite`—this indicates read/write is allowed; `adModeShareDenyRead`—this prevents others from opening a connection with read capabilities; `adModeShareDenyWrite`—this prevents others from opening a connection with write capabilities; `adModeShareExclusive`—this prevents others from opening a connection; `adModeShareDenyNone`—this prevents others from opening new connections with any permissions.
`Provider`	This string can be used to set or get the name of the provider for the database connection. It is read-only when a connection is open and read/write when it is closed. It can also be set using the `ConnectString` property or the `ConnectString` parameter for the

continues

Property Name	Description
	Connection.Open() method. The default provider is the Microsoft OLE DB Provider for ODBC (MSDASQL).
State	This returns the state of the Connection object. It will be one of the following constants: adStateClosed—this is the default setting, which indicates that the object is closed; adStateOpen—this indicates that the object is open.
Version	This returns the version number of the ADO objects that are in use.

Connection Methods

Method Name	Description
BeginTrans()	This begins a new transaction for the database connection. Within a transaction, no changes to the database are committed until CommitTrans() is called. Any changes within the transaction established by BeginTrans() can be rolled back using RollbackTrans(). When BeginTrans() is called as a function, it returns a Long indicating the level of nesting of the transaction. With some providers, you can nest transactions. No nested transactions are actually committed until the "outermost" transaction is committed.
Close()	This closes the current database connection and any active Recordsets associated with the connection.
CommitTrans()	This saves any database changes and ends the current transaction. It may also begin a new transaction depending on the Connection.Attributes property settings.

Method Name	Description
Execute(Command, RecsAffected, Options)	This executes a database command. `Execute()` may either be used as a statement, such as `connection.Execute "DELETE * FROM Authors WHERE LastName LIKE 'A'"`, or as a function returning a `RecordSet`, such as `Set recordset = connection.Execute("SELECT * FROM Authors")`. The first parameter, `Command`, is the database command that you want to execute. The second, `RecsAffected`, is a `Long` value that will contain the number of rows affected by the command, if supported by the provider. The `Options` parameter indicates how the provider should evaluate the command; it may be one of the following constants: `adCmdText`—this indicates that the provider should evaluate `CommandText` as a text command; `adCmdTable`—this indicates that the `CommandText` specifies a table name; `adCmdStoredProc`—this indicates that `CommandText` specifies a stored procedure; `adCmdUnknown`—this indicates that the type of command is unknown.
Open(ConnectString, User, PW)	This method opens a connection to a datasource. The `ConnectString` parameter must specify a valid datasource connection string. The `User` parameter is the username for the datasource connection, and `PW` is the password.

Caution

You can specify the username and password using either the `Open()` parameters or within the connection string, but don't specify it in both places or the results will be unpredictable.

continues

Method Name	Description
OpenSchema(QueryType, Criteria, SchemaID)	This returns a RecordSet containing database schema information from the datasource provider. QueryType specifies the type of schema query to run, and Criteria is an array of values that may be used to limit the results for the query type. There are three QueryTypes that are required by the OLE DB specification: adSchemaTables, adSchemaColumns, and adSchemaProvider. These QueryType and the corresponding Criteria constants are listed in the following table. There are many other QueryTypes; check the Microsoft ADO documentation for additional listings. The final parameter, SchemaID, may be used to specify a GUID for a provider-specific schema query.

QueryType	Criteria Constants
adSchemaColumns	TABLE_CATALOG
	TABLE_SCHEMA
	TABLE_NAME
	COLUMN_NAME
adSchemaProviderTypes	DATA_TYPE
	BEST_MATCH
adSchemaTables	TABLE_CATALOG
	TABLE_SCHEMA
	TABLE_NAME
	TABLE_TYPE
RollbackTrans()	This ends the current transaction and cancels any changes. Depending on the Connection.Attributes property, it may also begin a new transaction.

Connection Collections

Collection Name	Description
Errors	This contains a collection of Error objects generated by a provider when a failure occurs.
Properties	This contains a collection of Property objects associated with an ADO object. This may be used by a provider to supplement the standard ADO properties with dynamic properties.

16

Connection Code Sample

First we'll begin with a simple example that shows you how you can use the Connection object to connect to a database. The following example instantiates a connection and then connects to a hard-coded database. The example in Listing 16.1 uses the standard pubs database that comes with Microsoft SQL Server 6.5.

 Note

All the examples for the ADO objects use the Microsoft SQL Server pubs database example. If you do not have access to the pubs database or SQL Server, just substitute a different relational database—or even a simple database such as Access—that you have handy. The only thing that you need to change is the SQL query and the datasource connection strings. If you run the samples, you'll need to change the connection strings anyway to reference your database server.

LISTING 16.1   Connect1.vbs

```
' FILE: Connect1.vbs
' DESC: This shows basic usage of the Connection object.
' AUTH: Thomas L. Fredell
' DATE: 10/31/1998
'
' Copyright 1998 Macmillan Publishing
'

Dim connection
Dim sConnectionString

' My connection string is hardcoded to a Microsoft SQL Server database
sConnectionString = "driver={SQL Server};server=TLFSRV1;uid=sa;" & _
    "pwd=;database=pubs"

Set connection = WScript.CreateObject("ADODB.Connection")
```

continues

LISTING **16.1**   CONTINUED

```
connection.ConnectionString = sConnectionString
connection.Open
If Err.Number <> 0 Then
    Wscript.Echo "Err# " + Err.Number + " - " + Err.Description
Else
    Wscript.Echo "Connected to pubs database using <" +
➥connection.Provider + ">."
End If
```

Figure 16.5 illustrates the results of running the connect1.vbs script.

FIGURE 16.5

The results of running the connect1.vbs *script.*

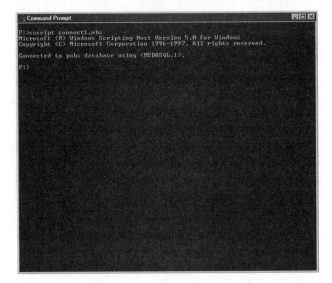

The preceding example is simple and shows only the most basic code involved in connecting to a database using WSH and ADO. Listing 16.2 shows a more sophisticated example that uses a Connection object to open a database and display all the tables in the database using the OpenSchema() method:

Note

You'll notice that there are some inline constants at the beginning of my code. Those constants were pulled from the adovbs.inc file that comes with ADO. The file contains all the ADO constants. Unfortunately, WSH doesn't have a file inclusion mechanism—so I can't just include the contents of adovbs.inc at runtime. There's also a corresponding file for JavaScript called adojavas.inc. You'll need those files if you plan to use any of the ADO constants in your WSH scripts.

LISTING **16.2**   Connect2.vbs

```
' FILE: Connect2.vbs
' AUTH: Thomas L. Fredell
' DESC: This illustrates how you can use an ADO Connection through
'    WSH and VBScript to access a database and display information
'    about the tables in the database.
' DATE: 10/31/1998
'
' Copyright 1998 Macmillan Publishing
'

' ADO Constants
'
' NOTE: Have to copy these in because WSH can't dynamically
'       include files at runtime.
'
Const adSchemaTables = 20

'
' Check parameters
'
If Wscript.Arguments.Count <> 5 Then
    ' Show the usage
    Wscript.Echo "USAGE: connect2.vbs [driver] [server] [user]" & _
"[password] [database]"
    Wscript.Echo ""
    Wscript.Echo "        Connects to a database and displays" & _
"information about"
    Wscript.Echo "        the tables within the database."

    ' And quit
    Wscript.Quit 0
End If

Dim sDriver, sServer, sUser, sPassword, sDatabase
Dim sConnect
Dim connDb
Dim rsetTables
Dim sTablesListing
Dim oShell

'
' Get parameters for connection
'
sDriver = Wscript.Arguments(0)
sServer = Wscript.Arguments(1)
sUser = Wscript.Arguments(2)
sPassword = Wscript.Arguments(3)
sDatabase = Wscript.Arguments(4)
```

continues

LISTING 16.2   CONTINUED

```
'
' Create connection string
'
sConnect = "driver=" + sDriver + ";server=" + sServer + ";uid=" + _
    sUser + ";pwd=" + sPassword + ";database=" + sDatabase


'
' Now attempt to open the connection
'
On Error Resume Next
Set connDb = WScript.CreateObject("ADODB.Connection")
connDb.ConnectionString = sConnect
connDb.Open
If Err.Number <> 0 Then
    ShowErr "Unable to connect to database."
End If
WScript.Echo "Connected to '" + sDatabase + "' on '" + sServer + "'"


'
' Use the connection to get the table schema
'
Set rsetTables = connDb.OpenSchema(adSchemaTables)
If Err.Number <> 0 Then
    ShowErr "Unable to open the schema."
End If


'
' Now retrieve and dump the table listing
'
sTablesListing = ""
Do While Not rsetTables.EOF
    sTablesListing = sTablesListing & rsetTables.Fields(2) & _
Chr(10) & Chr(13)
    If Err.Number <> 0 Then ShowErr "An error occurred."
    rsetTables.MoveNext
Loop
Set oShell = Wscript.CreateObject("Wscript.Shell")
oShell.Popup sTablesListing, 0, "Table listing from '" & sDatabase & "'"


'
' Quit with no error
'
Wscript.Quit 0


'-------------------------------------------------------------------
' SUBR: ShowErr(sDesc)
' DESC:   Displays information about the current error then quits.
```

```
' ----------------------------------------------------------------
Sub ShowErr(sDesc)
    Wscript.Echo "Error: " & sDesc
    Wscript.Echo "Err# " & Err.Number & " - " & Err.Description
    Wscript.Quit Err.Number
End Sub
```

When I run the script using cscript connect2.vbs "{SQL Server}" TLFSRV1 sa ""
pubs for the command line, the script runs, connects to the database, retrieves the table
names, and then displays a dialog box containing the list of names. Figure 16.6 shows
the output from the script.

16

FIGURE 16.6

*The results of running
the* connect2.vbs
script.

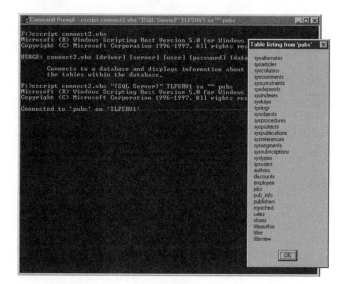

Command Object

The Command object represents a specific command that you want to execute against a datasource. It may be a straight SQL statement, a parameterized query, or a stored procedure.
You can use it to do a query and retrieve a recordset, to change the database structure, to
execute a bulk change—anything that you can do with a standard database command.

Command Properties

Property Name	Description
ActiveConnection	This is the connection for the Command object. It is a read-write property and may be set using either a Connection object or a valid connection string. If a connection string is used, the provider will create a new Connection object using the definition.
CommandText	This is a read-write string that contains a provider command. The command may be a SQL statement, a table name, or a stored procedure call.
CommandTimeout	This specifies how many seconds to wait while executing a command before returning an error and terminating the command request. The default value is 30 seconds. If a command doesn't complete execution within the number of seconds specified by CommandTimeout, ADO will cancel the command and raise an error. If you set CommandTimeout to zero, ADO will wait indefinitely for the command to complete.
CommandType	This indicates the type of the command that will be executed. It may be one of the following constants: adCmdText—this evaluates the command as text (such as a SQL statement); adCmdTable—this evaluates the command as a table name; adCmdStoredProc—this evaluates the command as a stored procedure; adCmdUnknown—this indicates that the type of command is unknown. If you know what type of command you will use, setting the CommandType will increase the speed of ADO's execution because it doesn't have to determine the type of the command at runtime.
Name	This string value allows you to assign or retrieve an object's name.

Property Name	Description
Prepared	This is a boolean value that indicates whether the provider should save a prepared (compiled) version of the command specified by CommandText. Some providers may not support this property and will either return an error or ignore the value if you change the Prepared property.
State	This returns the state of the Command object. It will be one of the following constants: adStateClosed—this is the default setting, which indicates that the object is closed; adStateOpen—this indicates that the object is open.

Command Methods

Method Name	Description
CreateParameter(Name, Type, Direction, Size, Value)	This creates a new Parameter object. The parameters for CreateParameter() are passed in to the corresponding properties on the new object. See the information about the Parameter object for more details.

Note

When you call CreateParameter(), the new Parameter object is not automatically added to the Command.Parameters collection. If you want to, you must add it manually to the Parameters collection using the Parameters.Add() method.

Execute(RecsAffected, Parameters, Options)	This executes a database command. Execute() may either be used as a statement, such as command.Execute RecCount, or as a function returning a recordset, such as Set recordset = command.Execute(). The first parameter, RecsAffected, is a Long value that will contain the number of rows affected by the command, if supported by the provider. The Parameters parameter is a Variant array of parameter values that should be used with the Command;

continues

Method Name	Description
	they may override parameters that are in the Command.Parameters collection. The Options parameter indicates how the provider should evaluate the command; it may be one of the following constants: adCmdText—this indicates that the provider should evaluate CommandText as a text command, like a SQL statement; adCmdTable—this indicates that the command specifies a table name; adCmdStoredProc—this indicates that command specifies a stored procedure; adCmdUnknown—this indicates that the type of command is unknown.

Note

> If your command uses output parameters, you must specify the parameters using Parameter objects in the Command.Parameters collection. You can't pass output parameters in the Parameters argument to the Execute() method.

Command Collections

Collection Name	Description
Parameters	This is a collection containing all the Parameter objects associated with the Command.
Properties	This contains a collection of Property objects associated with an ADO object. This may be used by a provider to supplement the standard ADO properties with dynamic properties.

Command Code Sample

The script given in Listing 16.3, Command1.vbs, provides a simple example illustrating how you can use the Command object to run a query against a database; Figure 16.7 illustrates the results of running the script.

LISTING **16.3** Command1.vbs

```
' FILE: Command1.vbs
' AUTH: Thomas L. Fredell
' DESC: This illustrates how you can use an ADO Command through
```

```
'     WSH and VBScript to run a command against a database.
' DATE: 10/31/1998
'
' Copyright 1998 Macmillan Publishing
'

Dim command, recordset

' My connection string is hardcoded to a Microsoft SQL Server database
sConnectionString = "driver={SQL Server};server=TLFSRV1;uid=sa;" & _
    "pwd=;database=pubs"

' Create a command object, then set the connection and command
Set command = WScript.CreateObject("ADODB.Command")
command.ActiveConnection = sConnectionString
command.CommandText = "SELECT * FROM authors"

' Execute a query to retrieve the names of book authors
Set recordset = command.Execute()
Do While Not recordset.EOF
    Wscript.Echo recordset.Fields("au_lname") + ", " + _
        recordset.Fields("au_lname")
    recordset.MoveNext
Loop
```

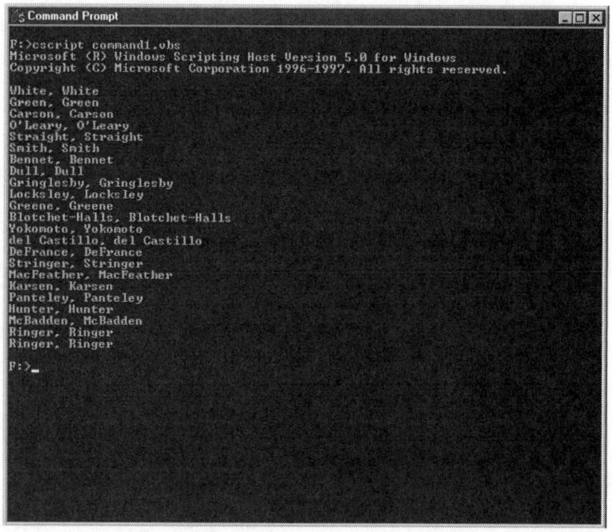

FIGURE 16.7

The results of running the command1.vbs *script.*

Recordset Object

The Recordset object represents the results of executing a database command. You can use a Recordset to retrieve and page through information returned by a command, you can use it to add new rows to a table, and you can use it to change data within a table. When you create a Recordset, you can walk through the Recordset using navigation methods such as MoveNext() and MovePrevious(). See the following sections for more details regarding the use of recordsets.

Recordset Properties

Property Name	Description
AbsolutePage	This can be used to identify the page number on which the current record is located. AbsolutePage is 1-based like AbsolutePosition. It may either return a page number or one of the following constants: adPosUnknown—this indicates that the current position is unknown; adPosBOF—this indicates that the record pointer is at BOF (Beginning Of File); adPosEOF—this indicates that the record pointer is at EOF (End Of File).
AbsolutePosition	This returns the ordinal position of the current record in the Recordset. It may also return one of the constants listed for AbsolutePage.
ActiveConnection	This is the connection for the Recordset object. It is a read-write property and may be set using either a Connection object or a valid connection string. If a connection string is used, the provider will create a new Connection object using the definition.
BOF	This returns true if the current record is before the first record or false if it is not.
Bookmark	This returns a Variant that represents a bookmark that can be used to save the position of the current record. To return to a record, you can set the Bookmark property using a previous bookmark value. Not all recordsets support bookmark functionality; see the CursorType property for more details.

Property Name	Description
CacheSize	This controls how many records the provider keeps in its buffer and how many should be retrieved into local memory. This must be greater than zero.
CursorLocation	This allows you to choose between various cursor libraries for a provider. Typically, you can either choose a client-side cursor library or a server-side library. This setting only affects database connections that are established after the property is set. If the connection is open, this property is read-only; if it is closed, the property is read/write. The valid constants for this property are: adUseClient—this uses the client-side cursor engine, the Microsoft Client Cursor Provider, which provides special features such as dis-associated recordsets; adUseClientBatch—this has the same effect as adUseClient; adUseServer—this is the default, which indicates that data provider or driver-supplied cursors should be used.
CursorType	This property can be used to set or get the type of cursor that is used for the Recordset. If the Recordset is open, the property is read-only, but it is read/write when the Recordset is closed. The valid constants for this property are: adOpenForwardOnly—this is the default, which specifies a forward-only cursor; adOpenDynamic—with this, cursor additions, changes, and deletions by other users are visible, and all types of movement through the recordset are allowed, except for bookmarks if they aren't supported by the provider; adOpenKeyset—this is like a dynamic cursor, except that you can't see records that other users add; adOpenStatic—this is a static copy of a set of records that you can use to find data or generate reports—any changes made by other users are not visible.
EditMode	This indicates the edit status for the current record. It will be one of the following constants: adEditNone—this indicates that no edits are in progress;

continues

Property Name	Description
	adEditInProgress—this indicates that data in the current record has been modified; adEditAdd—this indicates that AddNew() has been invoked.
EOF	This returns true if the current record is after the last record or false if it is not.
Filter	This can be set using a Variant to selectively screen out records in a Recordset object. The Filter may be either a string using clauses concatenated with AND or OR operators, an array of bookmark values, or a Filter constant. It may be one of the following constants: adFilterNone—this removes the current filter; adFilterPendingRecords—this allows you to view only records that have changed but have not yet been committed (this only applies to batch update mode); adFilterAffectedRecords—this allows you to view only records affected by the last Delete, Resync, UpdateBatch, or CancelBatch call; adFilterFetchedRecords—this allows you to view records from the results of the last call to retrieve records from the database.
LockType	This indicates the type of lock that should be placed on records when editing. It may be one of the following constants: adLockReadOnly—this is the default, indicating read-only; adLockPessimistic—this specifies pessimistic locking, which the provider typically implements by locking the record at the datasource immediately upon editing; adLockOptimistic—this specifies optimistic locking, which the provider typically implements by locking records only when Update() is called; adLockBatchOptimistic—this specifies optimistic batch updates and is required for batch update mode.
MarshalOptions	This indicates which records are to be marshaled back to the server when using the ADO Remote Data Service. It may be one of the following constants:

Property Name	Description
	adMarshalAll—this is the default, indicating that all rows are returned to the server; adMarshalModifiedOnly—this indicates that only modified rows are returned.
MaxRecords	This may be used to specify the maximum number of rows returned by the provider. If this property is zero, all requested rows will be returned.
PageCount	This indicates how many pages, or groups of records, are contained in the Recordset. If the provider doesn't support this property, PageCount will return -1.
PageSize	This may be used to get or set the number of records that make up a logical page of data. This defaults to 10.
RecordCount	This indicates how many records are in the Recordset. If ADO cannot determine the number of records, this will return -1.

Caution

Be careful when you use the RecordCount property. Depending on the capabilities of the provider and datasource, all records may have to be retrieved and counted to return an accurate count value.

Source	This may be used to set the source for the Recordset using a Command object or a string containing a SQL statement, stored procedure call, or table name. It may be used to get a string representing the current datasource. This is read-only for open Recordsets and read-write for closed Recordsets.
State	This returns the state of the Recordset object. It will be one of the following constants: adStateClosed—this is the default setting, which indicates that the object is closed; adStateOpen—this indicates that the object is open.

continues

Property Name	Description
Status	This indicates the status of the current record. It may be one of the following values: adRecOK—indicates that the record was successfully updated; adRecNew—indicates that the record is new; adRecModified—indicates that the record was modified; adRecDeleted—indicates that the record was deleted; adRecUnmodified—indicates that the record was not modified; adRecInvalid—indicates that the record was not saved because its bookmark is invalid; adRecMultipleChanges—indicates that the record was not saved because it would affect multiple records; adRecPendingChanges—indicates that the record was not saved because it refers to a pending insert; adRecCanceled—indicates that the record was not saved because the operation was canceled; adRecCantRelease—indicates that the new record was not saved because of record locks; adRecConcurrencyViolation—indicates that the record was not saved because optimistic concurrency was in force; adRecIntegrityViolation—indicates that the record was not saved because integrity constraints were violated; adRecMaxChangesExceeded—indicates that the record was not saved because of too many pending changes; adRecObjectOpen—indicates that the record was not saved because of a conflict with an open storage object; adRecOutOfMemory—indicates that the record was not saved because the computer has run out of memory; adRecPermissionDenied—indicates that the record was not saved because the user has insufficient permissions; adRecSchemaViolation—indicates that the record was not saved because it violates the database structure; adRecDBDeleted—indicates that the record has already been deleted.

Recordset Methods

Method Name	Description
AddNew(Fields, Values)	For updatable Recordsets, this method can be used to create a new record. The Fields argument can contain a field name, an array of field names, or an array of integers indicating positions in the record. The Values argument can either be a single Variant value or an array of Variants. The number of Fields specified must match the number of Values, but both parameters are optional.
CancelBatch(AffectRecords)	This cancels any pending changes in the current Recordset if it is in batch update mode. The AffectRecords parameter determines how many records will be affected by CancelBatch(). The constant values for AffectRecords are: adAffectCurrent—this cancels pending updates for the current record; adAffectGroup—this cancels pending updates for records that match the current Filter, if the Filter property is set to one of the valid predefined constants; adAffectAll—this is the default, which cancels pending updates for all the records in the Recordset, even if they are hidden by the Filter.
CancelUpdate	This cancels any changes made to the current record or, if a record is being added, discards the new record.
Clone	This returns a duplicate Recordset from the current Recordset. Creating a clone of a Recordset is more efficient than instantiating a new Recordset using the same command parameters. Only Recordsets that support bookmarks can be cloned.
Close	This closes the Recordset, releasing any associated resources and locks.

continues

Method Name	*Description*
Delete(AffectRecords)	This deletes the current record or a group of records in the Recordset. The AffectRecords parameter may be used to determine which records will be affected. It may be one of the following constants: adAffectCurrent—this is the default, which deletes just the current record; adAffectGroup—this deletes all the records that satisfy the current Filter property setting, if the Filter is set to one of the predefined constants.
GetRows(Rows, Start, Fields)	This method returns a two-dimensional array containing field values from a Recordset. The Rows parameter is a Long indicating the number of rows to retrieve; it defaults to the constant adGetRowsRest, which returns the rest of the rows from the Recordset. Start is an optional parameter that specifies the bookmark for the record from which GetRows() should begin retrieving records. It may be a bookmark or one of the following constants: adBookmarkCurrent—this starts at the current record; adBookmarkFirst—this starts at the first record; adBookmarkLast—this starts at the last record. Fields is an optional parameter that specifies the fields whose values should be retrieved by GetRows(). It may be a single field name, an array of field names, a positional field index, or an array of indices.
Move(NumRecords, Start)	This moves the position of the current record. NumRecords specifies how many record positions to move; if it is positive, it moves forward through the recordset, and if it is negative, it moves backward. The Start parameter may specify a starting position either as a bookmark or as one of the following constants: adBookmarkCurrent—this starts at the current record; adBookmarkFirst—this starts at the first record; adBookmarkLast—this starts at the last record.
MoveFirst	This moves to the first record in the Recordset.

Method Name	*Description*
MoveLast	This moves to the last record in the Recordset.
MoveNext	This moves to the next record in the Recordset from the current record.
MovePrevious	This moves to the previous record in the Recordset.
NextRecordset (RecordsAffected)	This returns a Recordset that represents the results of the next command in a compound command statement or of a stored procedure that returns several result sets. RecordsAffected is an optional parameter into which the provider will return the number of records affected by the command or stored procedure.
Open(Source, ActiveConnection, CursorType, LockType, Options)	This opens a new cursor into a result set. Source is an optional Variant that evaluates to a Command object, SQL statement, table name, or stored procedure call. ActiveConnection is an optional Variant that evaluates to either a Connection object or a valid connection string. CursorType is an optional value that specifies the type of cursor that should be used for the Recordset. The valid constants for CursorType are: adOpenForwardOnly; adOpenDynamic; adOpenKeyset; and adOpenStatic. For more details, review the Recordset.CursorType documentation. LockType is an optional value that specifies the type of lock that should be used; it may be one of the following constants: adLockReadOnly; adLockPessimistic; adLockOptimistic; and adLockBatchOptimistic. For more details, review Recordset.LockType. Options is an optional value that indicates how the provider should evaluate the Source argument if it isn't a Command object; it may be one of the following constants: adCmdText—this evaluates the Source as text (such as a SQL statement); adCmdTable—this evaluates the Source as a table name; adCmdStoredProc—this evaluates the Source as a stored procedure; adCmdUnknown—this indicates that the type of Source is unknown.

continues

16

Method Name	*Description*
Requery	This causes the Recordset to re-execute the source query.
Resync(AffectRecords)	This refreshes the data in the current Recordset. AffectRecords may be one of the following constants: adAffectCurrent—this refreshes just the current record; adAffectGroup—this refreshes the records that satisfy the current Filter, if it is set to one of the pre-defined constants; and adAffectAll—this is the default, which refreshes all the records in the Recordset. Calling Resync() does not cause the underlying Recordset command to be re-executed.
Supports(CursorOptions)	This returns a boolean value that indicates whether the provider supports all the options specified in the CursorOptions parameter. CursorOptions is a Long value that may consist of one or more of the following constant values (combined using the VBScript Or operator or the JavaScript ¦): adAddNew indicates that AddNew() may be used to add new records; adApproxPosition indicates that AbsolutePosition and AbsolutePage can be set; adBookmark indicates that you can use the Bookmark property; adDelete indicates that you can delete records using Delete(); adHoldRecords indicates that you can retrieve more records or change the next position without committing all pending changes; adMovePrevious indicates that you can use MoveFirst(), MovePrevious(), Move(), and GetRows(); adResync indicates that you can use Resync(); adUpdate indicates that you can use Update(); adUpdateBatch indicates that you can use batch updating via UpdateBatch() and CancelBatch().
Update(Fields, Values)	This saves any changes that have been made to the current record of the Recordset. You can use the Fields and Values arguments to specify values that should be set during the Update() call. The Fields argument can contain a field name, an array of field names, or an array of integers indicating positions in

Method Name	Description
	the record. The `Values` argument can either be a single `Variant` value or an array of `Variants`. The number of `Fields` specified must match the number of `Values`, but both parameters are optional.
UpdateBatch(AffectRecords)	This writes all pending batch changes to the underlying database. `AffectRecords` is an optional parameter that specifies which records should be affected. It may be one of the following constants: `adAffectCurrent`—this writes changes only for the current record; `adAffectGroup`—this writes changes for the records that match the current `Filter` setting, if it is one of the predefined `Filter` constants; and `adAffectAll`—this is the default, which writes changes for all the records in the Recordset object.

Recordset Collections

Collection Name	Description
Fields	This is a collection containing all the `Field` objects associated with the `Recordset`. There is one `Field` object for each column in the result set represented by the `Recordset`.
Properties	This contains a collection of `Property` objects associated with an ADO object. This may be used by a provider to supplement the standard ADO properties with dynamic properties.

Recordset Code Sample

The script shown in Listing 16.4, `recset1.js`, provides a simple example illustrating how you can use the `Recordset` object to run a query and view the query results.

Note   This script example is implemented using the JScript language. As emphasized earlier in this book, you can use either JScript or VBScript for your WSH scripting tasks. The language is obviously different, but you still use the objects—in this case ADO—the same way.

LISTING 16.4   recset1.js

```
// FILE: Recset1.js
// AUTH: Thomas L. Fredell
// DESC: This demonstrates basic usage of the Recordset object.
// DATE: 11/1/1998
//
// Copyright 1998 Macmillan Publishing
//

var recordset;
var sSource, sConnection;
var sAuthors;
var shell;

// The source will be a SQL statement that retrieves a list of authors
sSource = "SELECT au_lname, au_fname FROM authors " +
    "ORDER BY au_lname, au_fname";

// The connection string is hardcoded to a Microsoft
// SQL Server database
sConnection = "driver={SQL Server};server=TLFSRV1;uid=sa;" +
    "pwd=;database=pubs";

// Create a recordset object, then open a result set
recordset = WScript.CreateObject("ADODB.Recordset");
recordset.open(sSource, sConnection);

// Now dump the list of authors to the screen
sAuthors = "";
while (!recordset.EOF)
{
    sAuthors = sAuthors + recordset.fields("au_lname") + "\n";
    recordset.moveNext();
}
shell = WScript.createObject("Wscript.Shell");
shell.popup(sAuthors, 0, "List of authors in pubs database");
```

Listing 16.4 shows how easy it is to use the Recordset object to retrieve and navigate a result set. Figure 16.8 shows the result of running the script.

FIGURE 16.8

The result of running the recset1.js *script.*

Field Object

The Field object represents a column of data retrieved in a result set. Field objects are stored in the Recordset.Fields collection. You can use them to retrieve field values, get information about field values such as the numeric precision, or change existing field values.

Field Properties

Property Name	Description
ActualSize	This is a read-only property that returns a Long indicating the actual length of a Field object's value.
Attributes	The read-only Attributes property indicates the characteristics of the Field object. Its value may be the sum of one or more of the following constant values: adFldMayDefer—this indicates that the field values are not retrieved from the datasource with the whole record, but only explicitly accessed; adFldUpdatable—this indicates that you can update the field; adFldUnknownUpdatable—this indicates that the provider can't determine whether you can update the field; adFldFixed—this indicates that the field is

continues

Property Name	*Description*
	fixed-length; adFldIsNullable—this indicates that the field accepts the Null value; adFldMayBeNull—this indicates that the field value may return Null; adFldLong—the field is a long binary field, so you can use AppendChunk() and GetChunk(); adFldRowID—the field contains a record ID (such as a record number or unique identifier; adFldRowVersion—the field contains some kind of time or date stamp used for update tracking; adFldCacheDeferred—this indicates that the provider caches field values, so subsequent reads come from the cache.
DefinedSize	This is a Long value that returns the data capacity of the Field.
Name	This can be used to retrieve the name of a Field.
NumericScale	This returns a Byte value that indicates how many decimal places will be used to resolve numeric values.
OriginalValue	This returns the original field value, which may be different from the current Value if the field has been changed.
Precision	This returns a Byte value that indicates the maximum total number of digits that will be used to represent values in a numeric Field.
Type	This returns the type of the Field value. It may be one of the following constants: adArray—this indicates that the data is a safe-array and will be Or'd together with one of the other data type constants; adBigInt—the field value is an 8-byte signed integer; adBinary—the field value is binary; adBoolean—the field value is a boolean; adByRef—this is Or'd together with another one of the data type constants and indicates that the field value is a pointer to data; adBSTR—the field value is a null-terminated character string; adChar—the field value is a String; adCurrency—the field value is currency; adDate—the field value is a

Property Name	Description
	date, stored as a `Double`; `adDBDate`—the field value is a date in the format `yyyymmdd`; `adDBTime`—the field value is time in the format `hhmmss`; `adDBTimeStamp`—the field value is a date-time stamp in the format `yyyymmddhhmmss`, plus a fraction; `adDecimal`—the field value is a fixed precision and scale numeric value; `adDouble`—the field value is a double-precision floating point; `adEmpty`—no value is specified for the field; `adError`—the field value is a 32-bit error code; `adGUID`—the field value is a GUID (Globally Unique Identifier); `adIDispatch`—the field value is a pointer to an ActiveX `IDispatch` interface; `adInteger`—the field value is a 4-byte signed integer; `adIUnknown`—the field value is a pointer to an ActiveX `IUnknown` interface; `adNumeric`—the field value is a fixed precision and scale numeric value; `adSingle`—the field value is a single-precision floating point; `adSmallInt`—the field value is a 2-byte signed integer; `adTinyInt`—the field value is 1-byte; `adUnsignedBigInt`—the field value is an 8-byte unsigned integer; `adUnsignedInt`—the field value is a 4-byte unsigned integer; `adUnsignedSmallInt`—the field value is a 2-byte unsigned integer; `adUnsignedTinyInt`—the field value is a 1-byte unsigned integer; `adVariant`—the field value is a `Variant`; `adVector`—this indicates that the field value is an OLE DB `DBVECTOR` structure and will be `Or`'d together with another data type; and `adWChar`—the field value is a null-terminated Unicode string.
`UnderlyingValue`	This returns the current field value from the database. This may be different from the `OriginalValue` property if the value of the field in the database has changed.
`Value`	This is a `Variant` that may be used to retrieve or set the value of the current `Field`.

16

Field Methods

Method Name	Description
AppendChunk(Data)	This method is used to append data to a large text or binary field. The Data parameter is a Variant that you want to append to the field value.
GetChunk(Size)	This returns a Variant containing a chunk of data retrieved from a large text or binary field. Size is a Long value that indicates how many characters or bytes should be retrieved.

Field Collections

Collection Name	Description
Properties	This contains a collection of Property objects associated with an ADO object. This may be used by a provider to supplement the standard ADO properties with dynamic properties.

Field Code Sample

The script in Listing 16.5, field1.js, provides a simple example that shows how you can use the Field object to retrieve information about the fields in a Recordset.

LISTING **16.5**   field1.js

```
// FILE: Field1.js
// AUTH: Thomas L. Fredell
// DESC: This demonstrates basic usage of the Field object.
// DATE: 11/1/1998
//
// Copyright 1998 Macmillan Publishing
//

var recordset;
var sSource, sConnection;
var iField;
var field;

// Setup source and connection strings
sSource = "SELECT * FROM authors";
sConnection = "driver={SQL Server};server=TLFSRV1;uid=sa;" +
    "pwd=;database=pubs";

// Create a recordset object, and open a result set
```

```
recordset = WScript.CreateObject("ADODB.Recordset");
recordset.open(sSource, sConnection);

// Iterate through the fields and display information about each
WScript.echo("Dumping fields from '" + sSource + "' resultset...\n");
for (iField = 0; iField < recordset.fields.count; iField++) {
    WScript.echo("Field #" + iField + ": " +
        recordset.fields(iField).name);
    WScript.echo("Defd Size: " + recordset.fields(iField).definedSize);
    WScript.echo("Fld Value: " + recordset.fields(iField).value);
    WScript.echo();
}
```

16

Figure 16.9 shows the results of running field1.js.

FIGURE 16.9

The results of running the field1.js script.

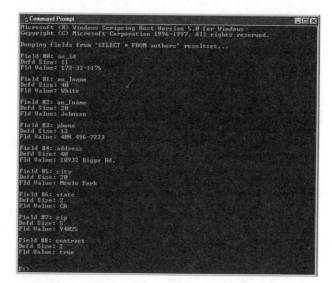

Fields Collection

Multiple Field objects may be stored in a Fields collection. The Fields collection is one of the properties of the Recordset object and contains all the fields associated with the current recordset.

Fields Properties

Property Name	Description
Count	This indicates the number of Field objects in the Fields collection.

Fields Methods

Method Name	Description
Item	This returns a specific Field object using either the field name or ordinal position in the Fields collection.
Refresh	This is available for the Fields collection, but it has no effect.

Parameter Object

The Parameter object represents a parameter associated with a parameterized query or stored procedure. You can use Parameter objects with the Command object to define the specific parameters with datatypes for the underlying database command. To create a parameter, you call the Command.CreateParameter() method. That's not enough to associate the parameter with the command, however. You must also call the Command.Parameters.Append() method to actually add the parameter to the list of parameters associated with the Command.

Parameter Properties

Property Name	Description
Attributes	This is a read-only property that indicates that the attributes of the Parameter. It can be a sum of any of the following constants: adPropNotSupported—this indicates that parameter is not supported; adPropRequired—this indicates that the user must specify a parameter value before the data source is initialized; adPropOptional—this indicates that the user does not need to specify a parameter value before the data-source is initialized; adPropRead—this indicates that the user can read the parameter value; adPropWrite—this indicates that the user can change the parameter value.
Direction	This determines whether the parameter is an in parameter, an out parameter, an in-out parameter, or a return value. You can use the Direction to specify the parameter type. It must be one of the following constants: adParamInput—this is the default, which indicates that the parameter is an input parameter; adParamOutput—the parameter is an output parameter; adParamInputOutput—the parameter is both an input and output parameter; and adParamReturnValue—the parameter is a return value.

Property Name	Description
Name	This is the name of the parameter.
NumericScale	This can be used to set or get a Byte value that indicates how many decimal places will be used to resolve numeric values.
Precision	This can be used to set or get a Byte value that indicates the maximum total number of digits that will be used to represent values in a numeric Field.
Size	This can be used to set or get the maximum size in bytes or characters of a Parameter value.
Type	This can be used to set or get the type of the Parameter. It can be one of the following constants: adArray—this indicates that the data is a safe-array, and will be Or'd together with one of the other data type constants; adBigInt—the field value is an 8-byte signed integer; adBinary—the field value is binary; adBoolean—the field value is a boolean; adByRef—this is Or'd together with another one of the data type constants and indicates that the field value is a pointer to data; adBSTR—the field value is a null-terminated character string; adChar—the field value is a String; adCurrency—the field value is currency; adDate—the field value is a date, stored as a Double; adDBDate—the field value is a date in the format yyyymmdd; adDBTime—the field value is a time in the format hhmmss; adDBTimeStamp—the field value is a date-time stamp in the format yyyymmddhhmmss, plus a fraction; adDecimal—the field value is a fixed precision and scale numeric value; adDouble—the field value is a double-precision floating point; adEmpty—no value is specified for the field; adError—the field value is a 32-bit error code; adGUID—the field value is a GUID (Globally Unique Identifier); adIDispatch—the field value is a pointer to an ActiveX IDispatch interface; adInteger—the field value is a 4-byte signed integer; adIUnknown—the field value is a pointer to an ActiveX IUnknown interface; adLongVarBinary—the field is a long binary; adLongVarChar—the field value is a long String value; adLongVarWChar—the field value is a long null-terminated string value; adNumeric—the field

16

Property Name	Description
	value is a fixed precision and scale numeric value; adSingle—the field value is a single-precision floating point; adSmallInt—the field value is a 2-byte signed integer; adTinyInt—the field value is 1-byte; adUnsignedBigInt—the field value is an 8-byte unsigned integer; adUnsignedInt—the field value is a 4-byte unsigned integer; adUnsignedSmallInt—the field value is a 2-byte unsigned integer; adUnsignedTinyInt—the field value is a 1-byte unsigned integer; adUserDefined—the field value is user-defined; adVarBinary—the field value is binary; adVarChar—the field value is a String; adVariant—the field value is a Variant; adVector—this indicates that the field value is an OLE DB DBVECTOR structure and will be Or'd together with another data type; adVarWChar—the field value is a null-terminated Unicode string; and adWChar—the field value is a null-terminated Unicode string.
Value	This can be used to set or get the Variant value of the parameter.

Parameter Methods

Method Name	Description
AppendChunk(Data)	This method is used to append data to a large text or binary Parameter. The Data parameter is a Variant that you want to append to the parameter value.

Parameter Collections

Collection Name	Description
Properties	This contains a collection of Property objects associated with an ADO object. This may be used by a provider to supplement the standard ADO properties with dynamic properties.

Parameter Code Sample

The example in Listing 16.6, param1.js, shows how you can use the Parameter object to set the parameter(s) for a stored procedure that you call. In the example, you'll see how you can use the standard Microsoft SQL Server sp_helpdb stored procedure to retrieve details about the pubs database.

LISTING **16.6**   param1.js

```
// FILE: Param1.js
// AUTH: Thomas L. Fredell
// DESC: This demonstrates basic usage of the Parameter object.
// DATE: 11/1/1998
//
// Copyright 1998 Macmillan Publishing
//

// Constants from adojavas.inc
var adBSTR = 8;
var adParamInput = 0x0001;
var adCmdStoredProc = 0x0004;

// Local variables
var command;
var parameter;
var recordset;
var sSource, sConnection;
var iField;
var field;

// Setup source and connection strings
sConnection = "driver={SQL Server};server=TLFSRV1;uid=sa;" +
    "pwd=;database=pubs";

// Create a command; we'll use the standard 'sp_helpdb'
// stored procedure to retrieve information about the
// pubs database
command = WScript.CreateObject("ADODB.Command");
command.activeConnection = sConnection;
command.commandText = "sp_helpdb";
command.commandType = adCmdStoredProc;

// 'sp_helpdb' takes only one parameter - the name of the
// database
parameter = command.createParameter("dbname", adBSTR,
    adParamInput);
command.parameters.append(parameter);
parameter.value = 'pubs';

// Execute the stored procedure and dump the information
// about the database
//
// NOTE: sp_helpdb returns multiple result-sets
//
recordset = command.execute();
while (recordset != null) {
    while (!recordset.eof) {
```

continues

LISTING 16.6   CONTINUED

```
        for (iField = 0; iField < recordset.fields.count;
            iField++) {
            WScript.echo(recordset.fields(iField).name + ": " +
                recordset.fields(iField).value);
        }
        recordset.moveNext();
    }
    WScript.echo();
    recordset = recordset.nextRecordset();
}
```

The first step in the script is to instantiate a new Command object and connect it to a data-base, which you do by setting the ActiveConnection property. Next you create a new Parameter object by calling the Command.CreateParameter() method. You append the Parameter to the Command.Parameters collection using the Append method and then call Command.Execute() to run the stored procedure, which returns multiple result sets. Finally, iterate through the result sets and dump the information about the pubs table to the screen. Figure 16.10 shows the results of running the param1.js script. The benefit of using parameters and commands is that you could check a different table easily by just changing the Parameter.Value property and rerunning the query by calling Command.Execute().

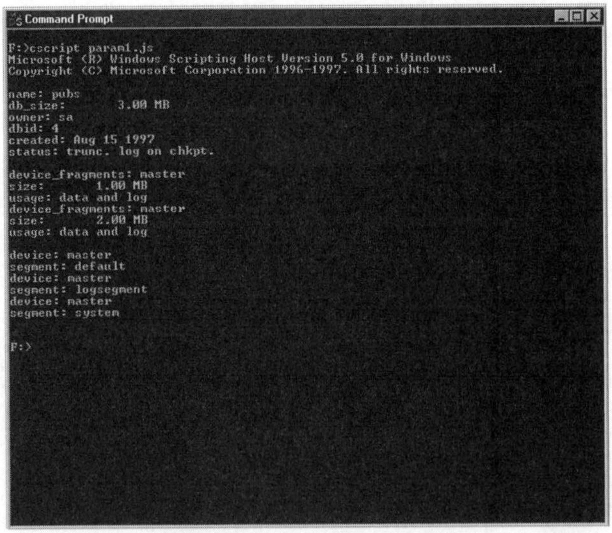

FIGURE 16.10

The results of running the param1.js *script.*

Parameters Collection

The Parameters collection contains all the Parameter objects that are associated with a Command object. If you create a Parameter using Command.CreateParameter(), you must explicitly add it to the Parameters collection using the Parameters.Append() method.

Parameters Properties

Property Name	Description
Count	This is the number of Parameter objects in the collection.

Parameters Methods

Method Name	Description
Append(Parameter)	This method is used to append a Parameter to the collection. The Type property of the Parameter object must be set before you append it.
Delete(Index)	This deletes a Parameter from the collection using either the ordinal position in the collection or the parameter name.
Item(Index)	This retrieves a Parameter from the collection using either the ordinal position in the collection or the name.
Refresh	This retrieves provider-side parameter information for the query specified in the Command object associated with the Parameters collection.

Property Object

Property objects can be used by a datasource provider to associate dynamic properties with ADO objects.

Property Properties

Property Name	Description
Attributes	This is a read-only property that can be a sum of any of the following constants: adPropNotSupported—this property is not supported by the provider; adPropRequired—the user must specify a value before the datasource is initialized; adPropOptional—this indicates that the user doesn't need to set a value before the datasource is initialized; adPropRead—the user can read the property value; and adPropWrite—the user can set the property value.

continues

16

Property Name	Description
Name	This is a read-only string that contains the name of the Property.
Type	This is a read-only property that returns the type of the Property. See the listing for Field.Type for more information about type constants.
Value	This is a read-write Variant that contains the value for the Property.

Properties Collection

The Connection, Command, Recordset, and Field objects all have an associated Properties collection. The datasource provider may use the Properties collection to associate dynamic properties with the ADO objects.

Properties Properties

Property Name	Description
Count	This is the number of Property objects in the collection.

Properties Methods

Method Name	Description
Item(Index)	This retrieves a Property from the collection using either the ordinal position in the collection or the name.
Refresh	If the provider uses the Properties collection, this will cause the provider to populate the Properties collection with Property objects.

Error Object

The Error object contains information about a single error that occurred when executing an operation on an ADO object.

Error Properties

Property Name	Description
Description	This is a string that describes the error.
HelpContext	This returns the context ID for the topic in the Windows help file indicated in the HelpFile property.

Property Name	Description
HelpFile	This returns a string that contains the fully resolved path for a Windows help file.
NativeError	This returns a provider-specific error code.
Number	This indicates which error occurred.
Source	This is a string that indicates the ADO object that generated the error.
SQLState	This is the five-character ANSI SQL standard error code.

Errors Collection

The Errors collection may contain multiple Error objects. Any time an operation is performed with any ADO object, multiple Error objects may be generated. You can use this collection to retrieve information about errors that occur.

Errors Properties

Property Name	Description
Count	This is the number of Error objects in the collection.

Errors Methods

Method Name	Description
Clear	This removes all existing Error objects from the collection.
Item(Index)	This retrieves an Error from the collection using the ordinal position in the Error collection.

Summary

We began this chapter with the context of a discussion of databases and data access methods. The tools that Microsoft provides for data access have matured over the years; the first was Open Database Connectivity (ODBC). ODBC was a good start because it provided an abstraction layer that allowed an application to access multiple different types of databases through a single API. Next came DAO and RDO, which were object-oriented data access tools. Both were relatively inefficient and suffered from complex, memory-intensive object models.

Next we discussed ADO, which is Microsoft's latest approach to object-oriented data access. ADO has a lightweight object model which is both efficient and easy to use. We reviewed the properties, methods, and collections associated with each ADO object, and we looked at examples that illustrated the use of each object from WSH scripts.

The next step is to take a look at specific tasks that you can use ADO to perform from your WSH script. You'll see some examples with full source code in the next chapter, Day 17, "Using ADO for WSH Scripting Tasks."

Q&A

Q **I can create a `Recordset` and access a database without ever creating a separate `Connection` object. Why would I want to create a separate `Connection`?**

A A standalone `Connection` object can be useful if you want to reuse a database connection for multiple `Recordset` objects. One of the benefits of reusing a `Connection` is that you only have to set the `Connection` properties once.

Q **Why should I use a `Command` object instead of just passing a command string to a `Recordset`?**

A `Command` objects are most useful when you want to retrieve recordsets by running a stored procedure. If you use a `Command` object, you can set parameters for a stored procedure easily rather than having to dynamically generate a string with embedded parameters for the stored procedure.

Q **How would you perform a transaction using ADO objects?**

A We'll cover transactions in more detail in the next chapter, but here's a quick example. You would begin by establishing a `Connection` to the database that you want to access. Next you would call `Connection.BeginTrans()` to begin the transaction. At that point, you could call `Connection.Execute()` or `Command.Execute()` to execute a SQL statement, or you could modify the records in a `Recordset`. When you are finished making your changes, call `Connection.CommitTrans()` to finalize the changes. If an error occurs, you can call `Connection.RollbackTrans()` to cancel the changes.

DAY 17

Using ADO for WSH Scripting Tasks

In the last chapter, you got a taste for the possibilities that arise when you integrate a database with your WSH scripts. You received an introduction to each of the ADO objects; you can refer back to that reference information as you go through this chapter and as you implement your own scripts.

Now you're going to see how you can leverage ADO in your WSH scripts to perform really useful tasks. First the chapter recaps ADO, the ADO objects, and how you can put them to use. Then the chapter digs into specific examples with detailed code that shows you how to use ADO and WSH. Hopefully, you'll even be able to reuse the code for your own scripts.

On the 17th day of your introduction to WSH, you'll

- Review ADO and examine typical ADO usage patterns
- See detailed examples with code walk-throughs that show you how to use ADO and WSH
- Learn ways that you can leverage ADO for your own tasks

Using ADO for WSH Scripting Tasks

The preceding chapter discussed the basics for the Microsoft ADO objects. In this chapter, you'll delve into the details of how you can use the ADO objects to perform useful scripting tasks. Before that, however, we'll review the ADO objects and examine some typical ADO usage patterns.

The ADO Objects

If you've been reading this book sequentially, the ADO object model depicted in Figure 17.1 will be familiar to you. The diagram illustrates the various ADO objects that you can use to interact with databases.

FIGURE 17.1

The ADO object model.

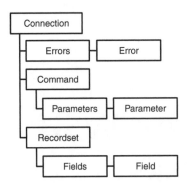

For our purposes, we're going to focus on the use of the Connection, Command, and Recordset objects. The Connection object will be used connect to a database. The Command and Recordset objects will be used to execute database commands; we'll use Command when we need to run something that doesn't return information and Recordset when we need to retrieve data.

Note

> We're making an arbitrary distinction between the use of the Command and Recordset objects for this example. Bear in mind that there's a lot of overlap between the two, but the Command object is more convenient for robustly calling parameterized database stored procedures.

The next few sections quickly cover basic WSH techniques for using the aforementioned objects.

Connecting to a Database

For the examples in this chapter, you'll connect to a database using a `Connection` object that you create. Creating the instance of the `Connection` object is easy; you create it the same way you would create any other COM object in a WSH script. Here's a basic example:

```
Dim connection
Set connection = Wscript.CreateObject("ADODB.Connection")
```

After you've created the `Connection` object, you need to tell it what datasource to connect to. You do that using the `ConnectionString` property. The `ConnectionString` property uses a database connection syntax that specifies the database provider, database, and server details. For more information about connection strings, refer to the preceding chapter. Here's an example that shows how you can set the connection string:

```
connection.ConnectionString = "driver=SQL Server;server=" & _
    "TLFSRV1;uid=sa;pwd=password;database=wsh"
```

After the connection string is set, you can tell the `Connection` object to attempt to connect to the database by calling the `Connection.Open()` method; here's a basic example:

```
connection.Open
```

Alternatively, you can pass a connection string or other arguments directly to the `Open()` method. That saves you the step of setting the `ConnectionString` property and then calling `Open()`.

The sample scripts in this chapter use the aforementioned technique to create database connections. After you've created the database connection, it will be used as `Command` and `Recordset` objects.

Changing Database Records

The example will use a stored procedure to create a new record in a database. That's one way that you can change or add new records; you can also use straight SQL statements to insert or update records. To call the stored procedure, you'll use a `Command` object. You can use a `Command` object to execute any type of database command, including a straight SQL statement or a stored procedure. In the example, you're going to use a stored procedure.

To create a `Command` object, you can use the standard `CreateObject()` method as illustrated in the following code snippet:

```
Dim command
Set command = Wscript.CreateObject("ADODB.Command")
```

As a refresher, here's the similar syntax that you would use for Microsoft JScript:

```
var command;
command = WScript.CreateObject("ADODB.Command");
```

After you've created the command object, you need to connect it to a database. To do so, use the ActiveConnection property. Set ActiveConnection to an instance of a Connection object that you create before you create the Command object. The basic flow is like the following:

```
Dim connection, command
Set connection = Wscript.CreateObject("ADODB.Connection")
connection.ConnectionString = "...";
Set command = Wscript.CreateObject("ADODB.Command")
Set command.ActiveConnection = connection
' Now set the rest of the command properties
```

After you've set up the basic properties of the Command object, as we've just demonstrated, you can set the command string that the object will use. The command string is stored in the CommandText property. Set it to the value of a stored procedure like so:

```
command.CommandText = "my_stored_proc"
command.CommandType = adCmdStoredProc
```

Notice that we also set the CommandType property to the stored procedure constant (adCmdStoredProc). ADO can generally determine the command type by examining the text and checking the database, but it's faster if we just go ahead and set the CommandType directly.

The last step before running the command is to add parameters for the stored procedure. To add parameters, we instantiate Parameter objects using the Command.CreateParameter() method, set their properties, and then add them to the parameters collection for the Command object. Here's a basic example:

```
Set parameter = command.CreateParameter("Param1")
parm.Type = adVarChar
parm.Size = 10
parm.Direction = adParamInput
parm.Value = "TestParam1"
command.Parameters.Append parameter
```

The example creates a basic input-only Parameter object that contains a variable-length text string and then adds it to the Command parameters list. After you've added all the necessary parameters, you can execute the command using the Execute() method:

```
command.Execute
```

You'll see this pattern again in the addlog.vbs script.

Retrieving Database Records

Retrieving database records is easy using the `Recordset` object. There are basically three ways that you can get a `Recordset`. You can use either the `Connection.Execute()` or `Command.Execute()` methods to run a query that returns a `Recordset`, or alternatively you can instantiate a `Recordset` separately and use the `Recordset.Open()` method.

Use the latter technique to retrieve the `Recordset` for our `viewlogs.vbs` script. Basically, perform the following steps:

1. Create the `Recordset` object.

```
Dim recordset
Set recordset = WScript.CreateObject("ADODB.Recordset")
```

2. Retrieve the `Recordset` by running a query using the `Recordset.Open()` method.

```
recordset.Open "SELECT * FROM MyTable", _
    connection, adOpenForwardOnly, _
    adLockReadOnly, adCmdText
```

17

Naturally, you can use whatever options you need to use for the `Open()` method. For example, you may retrieve a `Recordset` using a table name instead of a SQL command. To do so, you would replace the `adCmdText` value with `adCmdTable`.

Recording User Logins in a Database

The code example for this chapter involves a series of scripts that allow you to record login information in a database and retrieve basic tabular reports about user logins. The main script is `addlog.vbs`. The following sections discuss the script and how it functions. You can easily extend the script to leverage databases to perform your custom functions when users log in.

First we'll discuss the database that we'll use to record user logins, then we'll examine the `addlog.vbs` script that records their logins, and finally we'll look at the `viewlogs.vbs` script that lists user logins.

Creating the Login Database and Tables

Our example requires a Microsoft SQL Server database named `wsh`. The database contains two tables: `Users` and `UserLogins`. `Users` contains a list of usernames with unique numeric IDs. `UserLogins` contains a list of user logins that includes the user ID, the name of the computer on which the user logged in, and the time at which the user logged in.

If you want to create the SQL Server database so that you can execute the examples, first you need to create a device that can be used to host the database. In Figure 17.2, you'll see the SQL Server dialog in the Enterprise Manager that's used to create a new device. In the illustration, it's being used to create a WSHData device.

FIGURE 17.2

Creating the WSHData *device.*

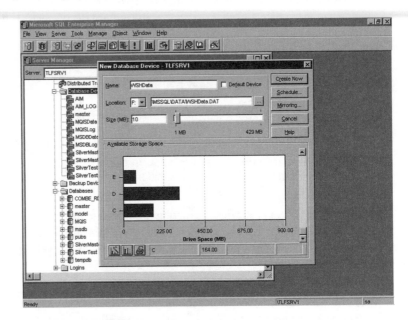

For this example, we've also created a separate device, WSHLog, to hold transaction logs. Figure 17.3 shows the WSHLog device as it is being created.

FIGURE 17.3

Creating the WSHLOG *device.*

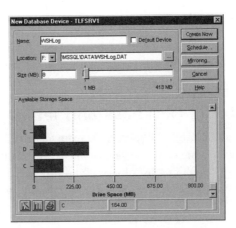

Note If you want more details about creating SQL Server database devices, refer to the Microsoft SQL Server documentation. Also, note that you can use whatever database devices you want to create the wsh database.

After the devices have been created, create a new database named wsh. The wsh database will contain the Users and UserLogins tables, as well as a stored procedure that you'll use later in your scripts. Figure 17.4 shows the New Database dialog that was used to create the wsh database.

FIGURE 17.4

Creating the wsh database.

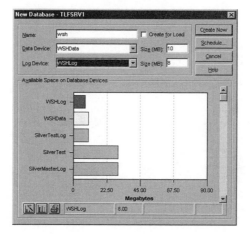

17

The last step to complete the setup of the wsh database is to run a SQL script that creates the database tables and stored procedure. Our SQL script for the database, which is in the file logtbls.sql, is as follows:

```
USE wsh
GO

/*
** Create the Users table
*/
CREATE TABLE dbo.Users (
    UserID int IDENTITY (1, 1) NOT NULL ,
    Username char (20) NULL
)
GO

/*
** Create the User logins table
*/
```

```
CREATE TABLE dbo.UserLogins (
    UserID int NOT NULL ,
    Time datetime NOT NULL ,
    Computer varchar (40) NOT NULL
)
GO

/*
** Create the record login stored procedure
*/
CREATE PROCEDURE sp_recordlogin(
    @Username VARCHAR(20),
    @Computer VARCHAR(40)
    )
AS

DECLARE @UserId INT

BEGIN TRANSACTION

-- Check to ensure that user exists; if user does not,
-- then create new user
IF NOT EXISTS (SELECT UserID FROM Users WHERE Username = @Username)
BEGIN
    -- Create new user record
    INSERT Users (Username) VALUES (@Username)
END

-- Now SELECT & store the user ID
SELECT @UserID = (SELECT UserID FROM Users WHERE Username = @Username)

-- Add a new login record
INSERT UserLogins (UserID, Time, Computer)
    VALUES (@UserID, GETDATE(), @Computer)

-- Finally, commit the transaction
COMMIT
GO
```

To run the SQL script to create the tables, you can use the isql command-line utility. Here's the command line that I used to create my database:

```
isql -S tlfsrv1 -U sa -P "" -i logtbls.sql
```

The database is a simple database; all the logic stored within the database is in the sp_recordlogin() stored procedure. sp_recordlogin() takes two parameters. The first is the name of the user who's logging in, and the second is the computer the user is logging in to. The stored procedure handles checks to see whether the user is already in the Users table and then records the login details in the UserLogins table. The addlog.vbs script is really primarily an interface to the sp_recordlogin() procedure.

Recording Information About User Logins: `addlog.vbs`

The script shown in Listing 17.1, `addlog.vbs`, connects to the aforementioned wsh database and records the information about a single user login. After the script, we'll discuss some of the implementation details.

LISTING 17.1 `addlog.vbs`—USER LOGIN INFORMATION

```
' FILE: addlog.vbs
' DESC: This illustrates how you can use ADO to record
'       details about a user login in a database.
' AUTH: Thomas L. Fredell
' DATE: 11/30/1998
'
' Copyright 1998 Macmillan Publishing
'


' ADO Constants (these are from adovbs.inc, which is
'                included with the ADO installation)
'
Const adVarChar = 200
Const adParamInput = &H0001
Const adCmdStoredProc = &H0004

On Error Resume Next

Dim oNet
Dim sDriver, sServer, sUser, sPassword, sDatabase
Dim sConnect
Dim connDb
Dim cmdAddLog
Dim parm
Dim cRecs

'
' 1. Create a WshNetwork object that we can use
' to get the user name & current computer
'
Set oNet = Wscript.CreateObject("Wscript.Network")
If Err.Number <> 0 Then
    ShowErr "Unable to create Wscript.WshNetwork object"
    Wscript.Quit Err.Number
End If
Wscript.Echo "addlog.vbs: Recording login for " & _
    oNet.UserName & " on " & oNet.ComputerName

'
```

continues

17

LISTING 17.1   CONTINUED

```
' 2. Get parameters for connection
'
sDriver = "SQL Server"
sServer = "TLFSRV1"
sUser = "sa"
sPassword = ""
sDatabase = "wsh"

'
' 3. Create connection string
'
sConnect = "driver=" + sDriver + ";server=" + sServer + ";uid=" + _
    sUser + ";pwd=" + sPassword + ";database=" + sDatabase

'
' 4. Now attempt to connect to the database
'
Set connDb = WScript.CreateObject("ADODB.Connection")
connDb.ConnectionString = sConnect
connDb.Open
If Err.Number <> 0 Then
    ShowErr "Unable to connect to database."
End If
WScript.Echo "addlog.vbs: Connected to " & sDatabase & _
    " database on " & sServer

'
' 5. Log the user by calling the sp_recordlogin
' stored procedure.
'
' NOTE: We'll use an ADO command to do this, but you
' could do it with just a single Recordset object
'
Set cmdAddLog = WScript.CreateObject("ADODB.Command")
Set cmdAddLog.ActiveConnection = connDb

'
' 6. Set characteristics of the Command object
'
cmdAddLog.CommandText = "sp_recordlogin"
cmdAddLog.CommandType = adCmdStoredProc

'
' 7. Create parameter for the user name
'
Set parm = cmdAddLog.CreateParameter("Username")
parm.Type = adVarChar
parm.Size = 20
```

```
parm.Direction = adParamInput
parm.Value = oNet.UserName
cmdAddLog.Parameters.Append parm
If Err.Number <> 0 Then
     ShowErr "Error creating username parameter"
End If


' 8. Create parameter for the computer name
'
Set parm = cmdAddLog.CreateParameter("Computer")
parm.Type = adVarChar
parm.Size = 40
parm.Direction = adParamInput
parm.Value = oNet.ComputerName
cmdAddLog.Parameters.Append parm
If Err.Number <> 0 Then
     ShowErr "Error creating computer parameter"
End If


' 9. Now attempt to execute the stored procedure
'
cmdAddLog.Execute cRecs
If (Err.Number <> 0) Or (cRecs <> 1) Then
     ShowErr "Error recording user login"
Else
     Wscript.Echo "addlog.vbs: Finished recording user login"
End If


' 10. Quit with no error
'
Wscript.Quit 0


'----------------------------------------------------------------
' SUBR: ShowErr(sDesc)
' DESC:    Displays information about the current error then quits.
'----------------------------------------------------------------
Sub ShowErr(sDesc)
     Wscript.Echo "Error: " & sDesc
     Wscript.Echo "Err# " & Err.Number & " - " & Err.Description
     Wscript.Quit Err.Number
End Sub
```

17

When you run the script, you'll see something like the output depicted in Figure 17.5.

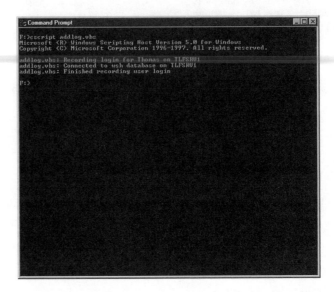

The script performs the following steps:

1. It creates a WshNetwork object. The WshNetwork object allows you to determine the current user and computer.

2. It sets the parameters for the connection to the database. You'll need to change these parameters to reflect your SQL Server environment.

3. The script creates a connection string using the parameters from step 2.

4. The script instantiates a new Connection object, sets the ConnectionString for the object using the string from step 3, and attempts to open a connection to the specified database.

5. The script creates a new Command object that uses the database connection from step 4.

6. The script sets the basic properties of the Command object; it calls a stored procedure named sp_recordlogin.

7. The script creates an input parameter for the username. Note that the value of the username is set using the value retrieved from the WshNetwork object that was instantiated in step 1.

8. The script creates an input parameter for the username and sets its value using the Computer property of the WshNetwork object.

9. The script finally executes the Command object. If all goes correctly, the sp_recordlogin procedure executes, and the user's login details are recorded.

10. The script quits with no error code.

The script builds on the steps discussed earlier in this chapter. You can replace the command with whatever command you want to run. It's completely flexible; you can do anything that's possible with any of the ADO objects or other COM objects.

Setting Up the addlog.vbs Script

To use the addlog.vbs script, you need to set up Windows NT user profiles to call the script when users log in. You can do so using the standard NT User Manager application. Figure 17.6 shows an example of user properties as viewed in the User Manager.

FIGURE 17.6

The properties for a user in the NT User Manager.

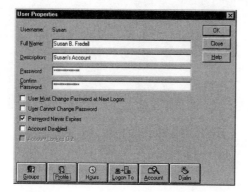

To set the login script, you need to click the Profile button. After doing so, you'll see the dialog illustrated in Figure 17.7.

FIGURE 17.7

A user profile in the NT User Manager.

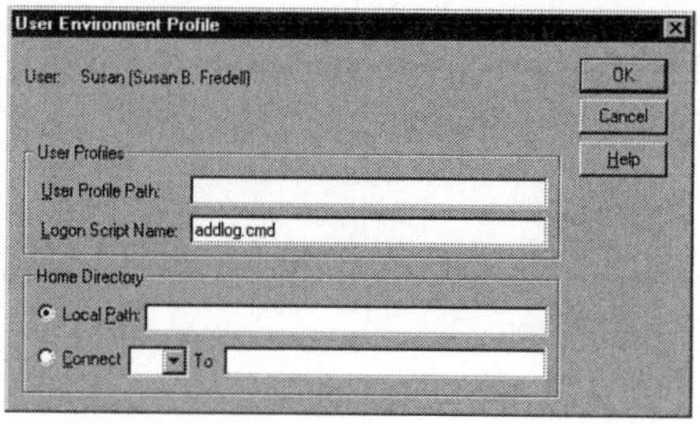

17

You'll notice that the Login Script Name field has the value `addlog.cmd`. We've created the `addlog.cmd` batch file to run the login recorder script. The batch file has the following steps:

```
@Echo Off
cscript \\TLFSrv1\NetLogon\addlog.vbs
Pause
```

When a user logs in, the `addlog.vbs` script executes, and the user sees the output illustrated in Figure 17.8.

FIGURE 17.8

Logging in with the addlog.vbs *script.*

Retrieving User Login Details: `viewlogs.vbs`

The `addlog.vbs` script takes care of the details of recording a user login, but it doesn't provide any capability to view the details of who logged in, when, and to which computers. The script presented in Listing 17.2, `viewlogs.vbs`, provides that functionality.

LISTING 17.2 viewlogs.vbs—USER LOGIN DETAILS

```
' FILE: viewlogs.vbs
' DESC: This illustrates how you can use ADO to retrieve
'       details about user logins from a database.
' AUTH: Thomas L. Fredell
' DATE: 11/30/1998
'
' Copyright 1998 Macmillan Publishing
'


'
' ADO Constants (these are from adovbs.inc, which is
'                included with the ADO installation)
'
Const adOpenForwardOnly = 0
Const adLockReadOnly = 1
Const adCmdText = &H0001
```

```
On Error Resume Next

Dim oArgs, iArg, sArg
Dim sComputerName, sUserName
Dim sDriver, sServer, sUser, sPassword, sDatabase
Dim sConnect
Dim sSQL
Dim connDb
Dim rsetLogs


'
' 1. Check for sufficient parameters
'
Set oArgs = Wscript.Arguments
If (oArgs.Count < 1) or (oArgs.Count > 2) Then
    ShowUsage
    Wscript.Quit 1
End If


'
' Check parameter validity
'
sComputerName = ""
sUserName = ""
For iArg = 0 To oArgs.Count - 1
    sArg = Trim(oArgs(iArg))
    If Len(sArg) < 3 Then
        Wscript.Echo ""
        Wscript.Echo "viewlogs.vbs: Parameter '" & _
            sArg & "' is too short."
        Wscript.Echo ""
        ShowUsage
        Wscript.Quit 1
    Else
        ' Check parameter prefix
        Select Case Left(sArg, 2)
            Case "-c"
                sComputerName = Right(sArg, Len(sArg) - 2)
            Case "-u"
                sUserName = Right(sArg, Len(sArg) - 2)
            Case Else
                Wscript.Echo ""
                Wscript.Echo "viewlogs.vbs: Invalid " & _
                    "parameter prefix '" & Left(sArg, 2) & "'"
                Wscript.Echo ""
                ShowUsage
                Wscript.Quit 1
        End Select
    End If
Next
```

continues

LISTING 17.2 CONTINUED

```
'
' 2. Display a message indicating the type of query that
' will occur
'
Wscript.Echo ""
If sComputerName = "" Then
    Wscript.Echo "viewlogs.vbs: Displaying information for " & _
        "user " & sUserName
ElseIf sUserName = "" Then
    Wscript.Echo "viewlogs.vbs: Displaying information for " & _
        "computer " & sComputerName
Else
    Wscript.Echo "viewlogs.vbs: Displaying information for " & _
        "user " & sUserName & " on computer " & sComputerName
End If
Wscript.Echo ""


'
' 3. Generate SQL statement that will be used to retrieve
' user login details
'
sSQL = "SELECT UserName, Computer, Time " & _
    "FROM wsh.dbo.Users Users, wsh.dbo.UserLogins UserLogins " & _
    "WHERE (Users.UserID = UserLogins.UserID) "

If sComputerName <> "" Then
    sSQL = sSQL & _
        "AND (UserLogins.Computer = '" & sComputerName & "') "
End If

If sUserName <> "" Then
    sSQL = sSQL & _
        "AND (Users.UserName = '" & sUserName & "') "
End If

'
' 4. Set parameters for database connection
'
sDriver = "SQL Server"
sServer = "TLFSRV1"
sUser = "sa"
sPassword = ""
sDatabase = "wsh"

'
' Create connection string
'
sConnect = "driver=" + sDriver + ";server=" + sServer + ";uid=" + _
```

```
            sUser + ";pwd=" + sPassword + ";database=" + sDatabase

    '
    ' Now attempt to connect to the database
    '
    Set connDb = WScript.CreateObject("ADODB.Connection")
    connDb.ConnectionString = sConnect
    connDb.Open
    If Err.Number <> 0 Then
        ShowErr "Unable to connect to database."
    End If


    '
    ' 5. Create a recordset using the SQL command that
    ' we defined above
    '
    Set rsetLogs = WScript.CreateObject("ADODB.Recordset")
    rsetLogs.Open sSQL, connDb, adOpenForwardOnly, _
        adLockReadOnly, adCmdText
    If Err.Number <> 0 Then
        ShowErr "Error running logs query"
    End If


    '
    ' 6. Now we iterate through the results and dump them to
    ' the screen
    '
    Do While Not rsetLogs.EOF
        Wscript.Echo rsetLogs("UserName") & _
            rsetLogs("Computer") & "    " & _
            rsetLogs("Time")
        rsetLogs.MoveNext
    Loop


    '
    ' 7. cQuit with no error
    '
    Wscript.Quit 0


    '------------------------------------------------------------
    ' SUBR: ShowErr(sDesc)
    ' DESC:    Displays information about the current error then quits.
    '------------------------------------------------------------
    Sub ShowErr(sDesc)
        Wscript.Echo "Error: " & sDesc
        Wscript.Echo "Err# " & Err.Number & " - " & Err.Description
        Wscript.Quit Err.Number
    End Sub
```

continues

LISTING 17.2 CONTINUED

```
'-----------------------------------------------------------------
' SUBR: ShowUsage()
' DESC:     Displays usage details for this script.
'-----------------------------------------------------------------
Sub ShowUsage()
    Wscript.Echo "USAGE:  viewlogs  -c[computer] -u[username]"
    Wscript.Echo ""
    Wscript.Echo "        Displays details of user logins. You may"
    Wscript.Echo "        specify either a computer or a username,"
    Wscript.Echo "        or both."
    Wscript.Echo ""
    Wscript.Echo "        Example:"
    Wscript.Echo "        "
    Wscript.Echo "        viewlogs -cTlfsrv1 -uThomas"
    Wscript.Echo "        "
End Sub
```

When you run the script, you'll see something like the output depicted in Figure 17.9.

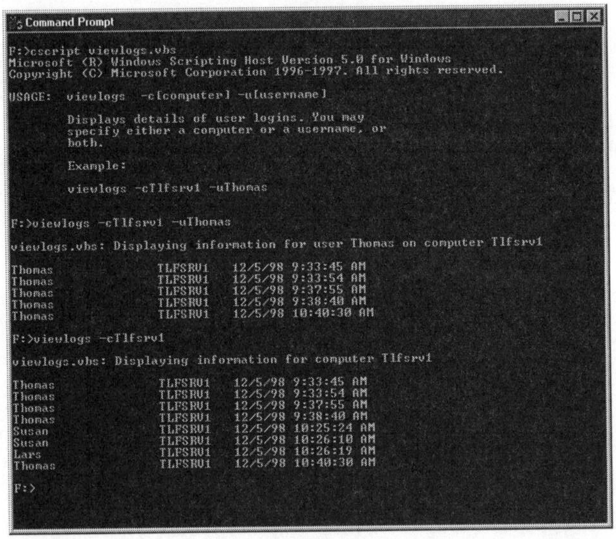

FIGURE 17.9

The results of running the viewlogs.vbs *script.*

The script performs the following steps:

1. The script checks the parameters that were specified on the command line. There must be at least one parameter, and the parameter must be in the form specified in the ShowUsage() function.

2. A message is displayed indicating the type of query that will occur.

3. The script dynamically generates a SQL statement that will be used to retrieve the user login details. If you examine the code, you'll notice that the WHERE clause is modified dynamically depending on the command-line parameters used to execute the script.

4. The script sets connection parameters, creates a connection string, and attempts to connect to the database that contains the user login information.

5. The database query is performed. First create a Recordset object, and then call the Open() method using the SQL statement that was dynamically generated in step 3.

6. Assuming that the query in step 5 was successful, iterate through the returned Recordset and display the query results.

7. This is the end of the script; it quits with no error code.

Like the addlog.vbs script, this script builds on the steps discussed earlier in this chapter. You can easily modify it to incorporate your own database connection parameters, and you can change it to incorporate whatever SQL statement you need to use.

Summary

This chapter demonstrates how you can use the ADO objects to access databases to create useful WSH scripts. Our example provides the capability to record user login details in a database and to retrieve the details dynamically using a command-line interface.

You can use the code from the examples as a building block for your own code that leverages ADO objects. The objects are easy to use, and you'll find that they integrate naturally with the scripts that you create.

Q&A

Q **Is it necessary to create a separate Connection object before you create a Command object?**

A No. You can pass a valid connection string directly to a Command object using the ActiveConnection property.

Q Is it necessary to create a separate `Connection` object before you create a `Recordset` object?

A No. If you want, you can pass a connection string directly to the `Recordset.Open()` method.

Q What object can you use to retrieve the current username and computer?

A You can get the current username and computer using the `WshNetwork` object, which provides `Username` and `Computer` properties.

DAY **18**

Using WSH to Manipulate the Microsoft Active Directory

By Stephen Campbell

Day 18: Chapter Overview

Today, you will use Windows Scripting Host and the Microsoft Active Directory to manage users and computers in a Windows NT domain. But the Active Directory enables you to do much more. It provides a standard set of tools to access any directory object, whether it is part of a Windows NT or Windows 2000 domain, a Novell Netware user list, or any other directory that supports the Lightweight Directory Access Protocol (LDAP).

Today you will do the following:

- Get a basic understanding of the Microsoft Active Directory and its underlying technologies.
- See the Active Directory Object Model for Windows NT 4 and Windows 2000 systems.

- See examples of managing the computer's resources such as printer queues and share names.
- See examples of adding and removing users and groups.
- See how what you have learned applies to the Windows 2000 environment.

Before You Get Started

Before you can run the Windows NT 4 examples in this chapter, you need to install ADSI version 2.0 or higher, the Active Directory components, onto your Windows NT 4 or Windows 95 system. This is available for no charge from the Microsoft Web site at `http://www.microsoft.com/ntserver/nts/downloads/other/ADSI2/default.asp`. At the time of this writing, a beta of ADSI Version 2.5 is available at `http://www.microsoft.com/ntserver/nts/downloads/previews/ADSI25/default.asp`.

The full Active Directory is the central component of Windows 2000 Server, formerly called Windows NT 5 Server. The examples at the end of this chapter require Windows NT 5 Beta 2, Windows 2000 Server Beta 3, or later. (As an aside, Windows NT 5 Workstation has been renamed to Windows 2000 Professional.)

Overview of the Microsoft Active Directory

What is a directory? In an abstract sense, it is a list of objects, such as people, companies, computers, or buildings, with some information about those objects, such as street address, phone number, SSN, name, or digital signature certificate.

Most of the time, you use a directory to find information about an object when you know some other information about that object. For example, you find a phone number when you know the name of the person. You find the name of the laser printer when you know its location. The directory you use most often, of course, is the telephone book, but there are lots of others that you use, such as the zip code directory, your NT domain accounts database, and your email address book.

Directories look a lot like databases, and in many cases they are implemented using database technology. Some of the important things that make directories unique are the following:

- The information is retrieved much more often than it is updated. It must support browsing (give me a list of people in Topeka born in January 1995) and searching (what's the phone number of Janice Doe on Broad Street in Austin?).
- The information is not updated very often. Janice doesn't move or change her phone number frequently.

- The information can be a bit out of date. You don't mind too much if Janice moved last week and the directory doesn't show that, but you do mind if the bank didn't record your deposit this morning when you try to pay your utility bill this afternoon.

Each item of information describing an object in a directory is called an *attribute* or *property*. For instance, the telephone number and name are attributes of the person object. The list of attributes available for a particular object, with their characteristics, is called a *schema*. In the past, each organization has developed schemas to meet their own needs, even though they might describe the same thing, such as the employee of a company. Efforts to standardize key schemas such as an "organizational person" have achieved some success.

In the past, automated directories were implemented using proprietary software and technologies. This made development cumbersome because each directory had its own programs. Integration of multiple directories was nearly impossible, and you had to use those proprietary programs to access any information in the directory. Examples of proprietary directories include the Windows NT 4 domain accounts database and Microsoft Mail's Global Address List.

A directory standard called X.500 was adopted in the late 1980s that tried to provide a standard set of definitions to meet all directory needs. This complex standard continues to evolve to meet new requirements, such as supporting multiple languages at the same time (What's your department name in English? In French?). The X.500 protocol used to access and update information in a directory is called the Directory Access Protocol, or DAP. A simpler protocol, call Lightweight Directory Access Protocol, LDAP, was developed in the early 1990s. The LDAP protocol has now become the de facto standard for accessing and updating directory information.

Microsoft also realized that proprietary access methods were not cost-effective, but took a slightly different approach to use new technologies to manage their proprietary directories. The Active Directory is a Windows 2000 concept that incorporates an LDAP-accessible directory that includes users, groups, computers, share names, and all other aspects of the current Windows NT domain. It also includes the Active Directory Services Interface (ADSI), which is available now.

The ADSI provides a consistent method to access any directory regardless of its underlying technology. Microsoft and other vendors supply Service Provider Interfaces (SPIs), which translate standard ADSI requests from an application into the format required by the target directory. The standard ADSI package comes with SPIs for Windows NT 4, Novell NetWare (both Bindery and NDS directories), and LDAP. Microsoft also has an SPI for managing the configuration of the Internet Information Server 4. Providers support *namespaces*, which are the top-level items of the directory. LDAP and WinNT are examples of namespaces.

18

Windows NT 4 Domains

Every Windows NT 4 workstation or server has an accounts database, or SAM. A Windows NT 4 *domain* is simply a group of computers with a common accounts database. Users are kept in the domain SAM. *Global groups*, which can contain users in that domain, are also kept in the domain accounts database. Changes to the accounts database are always done via the *Primary Domain Controller*, or *PDC*. There can be many *Backup Domain Controllers (BDCs)*, and they receive updates to the SAM from their PDC. When you log in to the network, your computer finds a domain controller for the domain you are logging in to and validates you. Another type of server is called a *member* server. Each server has a local accounts database where you can create accounts and groups on this one computer. Member servers can belong to a domain and enable users and groups in that domain to access resources on the server. NT Workstation works in the same way as member servers.

In NT 4, domains can *trust* each other. If domain ATLANTA trusts domain ACME, an administrator on ATLANTA can give a user or group in domain ACME access to a local printer or share name. This saves a lot of work because users no longer have to have an account in domain ATLANTA to access resources there. Trusts are defined in one direction—you have to establish separate trusts from domain ACME to ATLANTA and from ATLANTA to ACME. Also, trusts are not *transitive*: If ATLANTA trusts ACME and ACME trusts UNIVERSAL, ATLANTA does *not* implicitly trust UNIVERSAL. This provides additional security but also imposes additional work in complex organizations. Trusts lead to four basic enterprise permissions models:

- **Single domain**   A small organization might have a single domain.
- **Network**   All domains in the company trust all other domains in the company. This is simplest in small organizations or where administration is completely decentralized. It becomes increasingly difficult to manage as the number of domains grows.
- **Single master**   All users and global groups are created in a *master* domain. *Resource* domains contain all the users' sharenames and printers, and each trusts the master domain. This is preferred at most medium-sized organizations. Permissions on the resource domains can be delegated, but administrative access to the master domain is usually strictly controlled.
- **Multiple master**   In very large organizations or where account management is delegated, you establish a small number of master domains that hold users and groups for their scope of operations, such as a continent or subsidiary. These master domains trust all other master domains, and each resource domain trusts all the master domains. This enables an administrator in any domain to give permissions to a user or group from any of the master domains. A variation of this model has a

third "security" domain that is trusted by all the other domains. The small number of "super administrators" in this domain can see the entire enterprise while protecting themselves from access.

Remember that trusts do not imply that permissions are granted. It simply enables the administrator to assign permissions to users and groups from the trusted domains.

Individual computers have *local groups*. You usually assign permissions on resources (printers, share names, and so on) to local groups. Local groups then contain users and global groups from the local domain or from trusted domains. There are a number of pre-configured local groups on each server and Windows NT workstation: Administrators, Server Operators or Power Users, Account Operators, Backup Operators, and Users. You can add your own. You should note that all domain controllers in a domain share the same local group. For example, adding a user to the local Administrators group on one domain controller grants them administrative rights to all the domain controllers there. This can be a blessing (no separate permissions needed) and a curse ("I didn't know they could do that there!").

There are several other directories in the Windows NT 4 environment:

- Computers in a domain
- Share names on a computer
- Printer queues
- DHCP, DNS, and WINS services, which map computer names to their TCP/IP network addresses

There are few attributes defined for the NT 4 directories. For example, groups have only their ID, description, and members.

In Windows 2000 Server, an integrated directory becomes its central component.

Windows 2000 Active Directory

There are a number of limitations to the Windows NT 4 directory. There are many proprietary directories meeting specialized needs. As enterprises become more complex, Windows NT 4 becomes more difficult to administer.

Probably the single most important component of Windows 2000 is the Active Directory. With the Active Directory, Microsoft has achieved most if not all the requirements for a directory:

- It's standards-based. The directory is accessed and updated using LDAP.
- It's extensible. You can add your own attributes to objects that are currently defined, and you can even add your own objects.

18

- It's manageable. You can grant or revoke administrative or access permissions anywhere in the directory.

- It's scalable. The directory is designed to support millions of objects.

- It's malleable. As your organization changes, as companies merge or divest, the organization of the directory can be changed.

- It's secure. Updates to all objects, including the directory, are authenticated using a secure, efficient, standard protocol called Kerberos.

The Active Directory is organized as a forest of trees. Each tree is a single Windows 2000 domain, and the collection of all domains in an enterprise is a forest. Users can search the entire forest. Permissions between trees can be assigned.

A domain is given an Internet name such as `acme.com`, and domain controllers are found using DNS.

A domain is no longer a flat structure. It can include a hierarchy of *Organizational Units*, as shown in the Figure 18.1, taken from a Windows 2000 directory management window. In this domain, march2000, you have Organizational Units Asia, EuropeAfrica, and NorthAmerica. NorthAmerica has further Organizational Units Atlanta, LosAngeles, and Ottawa. Notice that you can add users, groups, or computers anywhere in this hierarchy. You can delegate administrative permissions anywhere, too, so that you can grant the group "Atlanta Lan Administrators" permissions to manage people and computers in the Atlanta Organizational Unit. By default, having permissions at one level of the hierarchy gives permissions at all lower levels.

FIGURE 18.1

Windows 2000 directory hierarchy.

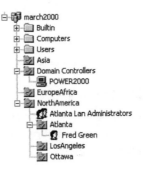

The schema is much bigger too. There are about 200 objects, called *classes* in Windows 2000, and about 1500 attributes. Figures 18.2 and 18.3 show some of the information that can be filled in for users. You can see all the Windows NT 4 fields are still there, but there are many more.

FIGURE 18.2

Windows 2000 User— General tab.

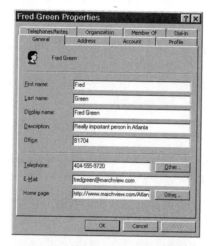

FIGURE 18.3

Windows 2000 User— Account tab.

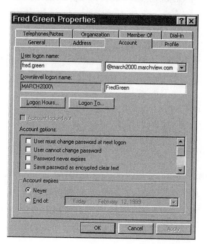

18

Active Directory Services

Active Directory services are relatively straightforward for Windows Scripting Host.

A comprehensive set of access facilities exists for C++ programmers, but the discussion here will limit itself to the Automation access methods available from Windows Scripting Host.

Retrieving Directory Objects

First, you retrieve an object using GetObject(), passing in the directory object you want or the name of the directory service provider. This establishes a session to your object with your current login credentials. Note that *the provider name is case sensitive*, whereas attributes and methods are not. For example:

```
set oProvider=GetObject("WinNT:")
set oProvider=GetObject("LDAP:")
```

In the rare case where you need to access the object using other credentials, use the DSOpenObject() method for any existing directory object, or the provider itself, as follows:

```
Set oDirEntry=oProvider.OpenDSObject(<ADSPath>,<userid>,<password>,
➥<flags>)
```

The <ADSPath> is the directory object you want to open; the <userid> and <password> are straightforward. Flags depend on what directory provider you are using and can usually be omitted.

How you name a directory object depends on its directory service provider.

ADSPath

Each directory object has a unique identifier. This is usually the namespace and each element of the directory hierarchy to the object.

For example, the ADSPath of a Windows NT user is WinNT://domain/userid.

Objects in Microsoft Exchange Server and the Windows 2000 Active Directory are accessed using LDAP. Each item in the list is the next element as you work down the tree. For example, the ADSPath to an Exchange mailbox is as follows:

```
LDAP://ExchangeServer/o=organization/ou=site/cn=container/cn=mailbox
```

A NOTE TO MICROSOFT EXCHANGE ADMINISTRATORS

ADSI is a good way to automate many administration tasks for Exchange 5.5 mailboxes and distribution lists. There are a couple of excellent articles on this topic in Microsoft Technet. Search for the keywords *exchange* and *adsi*.

If you want to go beyond those articles, you can find the LDAP name of any attribute or class. Use admin in raw mode (admin -r), and look at its definition in the schema. The *description* field of the attribute contains the LDAP name. If you are not sure what class a particular object has, open the raw properties of that object and search for the attribute Object-Class. Choose the first incomprehensible number, click Viewer, and then Choose properties.

An LDAP path can also be written with commas instead of slashes. In this case, you reverse the order of the items in the tree with the top value at the right, as follows:

```
LDAP://ExchangeServer/cn=mailbox,cn=container,ou=site,o=organization
```

The first form might be easier to use in Windows Scripting Host because you can just tack on items to the end of the ADSPath to work down the hierarchy, rather than fitting the new level into the middle of the ADSpath name.

Accessing Properties

You can refer to the properties or attributes of a directory object by using the attribute name, or the Get method:

```
Wscript.echo oDirEntry.name
Wscript.echo oDirEntry.Get "name"
```

You can explicitly load all the properties for the object into local memory using getInfo. getInfo is called "under the covers" when you access a property. Note that there are some properties that can be accessed only by using .get.

Some properties are multi-valued, and the method GetEx enables you to retrieve these properties into arrays. For example, in Windows 2000, TelephoneNumber is a multi-valued property containing all of a person's work-related phone numbers.

Updating Objects

You change values by setting the properties or using the Put method:

```
oUser.FullName = sFullName
oUser.Put "FullName",sFullName
```

18

Use putex to change values of multi-valued properties:

```
Const ADS_PROPERTY_CLEAR=1      ' Remove the property from the object
Const ADS_PROPERTY_UPDATE=2     ' Replace current value(s) with these
➥value(s)
Const ADS_PROPERTY_APPEND=3     ' Add these value(s) to existing value(s)
Const ADS_PROPERTY_DELETE=4     ' Remove all current value(s)
oUser.putex ADS_PROPERTY_UPDATE,"TelephoneNumber",aPhones
```

Finally, you update the directory by calling setInfo. *Changes are not reflected in the directory until you execute setInfo.*

```
oDirEntry.setInfo
```

Containers and Collections

Two kinds of directory objects can hold other objects. *Containers* are part of the formal directory tree and hold objects of different types. You create objects in a container using the create method and delete them using the delete method. The objects are created and destroyed using these methods:

```
oDomain.create "user",sUserid
oDomain.delete "user",sUserid
```

Think of the members of a *Collection* object as a property of that object. The objects that are added to collections already exist. Users are members of the group collection object:

```
oGroup.add(oUser.ADSPath)
oGroup.remove(oUser.ADSPath)
```

Users are identified by their directory name: WinNT://domain/userid.

The printjobs object holds a collection of printjob objects. Again, you add members to a collection using the add method and remove them using the remove method.

You can go through each object in a collection or container using the for each statement:

```
for each oItem in oCollection
    do something with oItem
next
```

You can access individual items using your familiar getobject:

```
oItem=oCollection.getobject(sName)
```

The Windows NT 4 Schema

Figure 18.4 shows the NT 4 Schema model. The directory service provider is named "WinNT:"

FIGURE 18.4

Windows NT 4 directory object model.

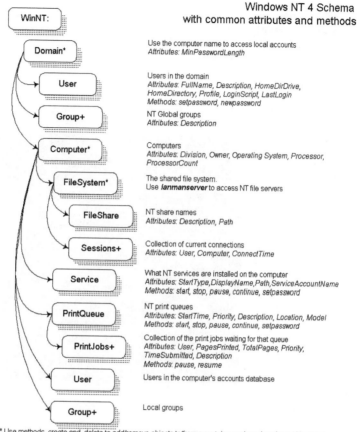

Windows NT 4 Schema
with common attributes and methods

WinNT:

Domain*
Use the computer name to access local accounts
Attributes: MinPasswordLength

User
Users in the domain
Attributes: FullName, Description, HomeDirDrive, HomeDirectory, Profile, LoginScript, LastLogin
Methods: setpassword, newpassword

Group+
NT Global groups
Attributes: Description

Computer*
Computers
Attributes: Division, Owner, Operating System, Processor, ProcessorCount

FileSystem*
The shared file system.
Use *lanmanserver* to access NT file servers

FileShare
NT share names
Attributes: Description, Path

Sessions+
Collection of current connections
Attributes: User, Computer, ConnectTime

Service
What NT services are installed on the computer
Attributes: StartType, DisplayName, Path, ServiceAccountName
Methods: start, stop, pause, continue, setpassword

PrintQueue
NT print queues
Attributes: StartTime, Priority, Description, Location, Model
Methods: start, stop, pause, continue, setpassword

PrintJobs+
Collection of the print jobs waiting for that queue
Attributes: User, PagesPrinted, TotalPages, Priority, TimeSubmitted, Description
Methods: pause, resume

User
Users in the computer's accounts database

Group+
Local groups

* Use methods .create and .delete to add/remove objects to/from a container such as domain and filesystem
  oDomain.create("user",sUserid) oDomain.delete("user",sUserid)
+ Use methods .add and .remove to add/remove objects to/from a collection, such as printjobs and group
  oGroup.add(sUserid)   oGroup.remove(sUserid)
oGroup.isMember(<ADSPath>) returns true if the object identified as ADSPath is a member of oGroup

18

The schema is an object in the directory like any other object, and it can be displayed like any other object. This script shows many of the operations you will use to browse through the directory:

```
' ShowSchemaInfo_NT4.vbs  -  Display information about the Schema
' 1998-12-13 stephen.campbell@marchview.com
option explicit
dim sDomain
dim oSchema        ' WinNT
dim oSchemaItem    ' Schema items
on error resume next
```

```
sDomain="MARCH"
set oSchema = GetObject("WinNT://" + sDomain + "/Schema")   ' WinNT is
➥case-sensitive!!
for each oSchemaItem in oSchema
  WScript.echo oSchemaItem.class + " " + oSchemaItem.name
next
WScript.quit
```

Figure 18.5 shows the first page of output from this script.

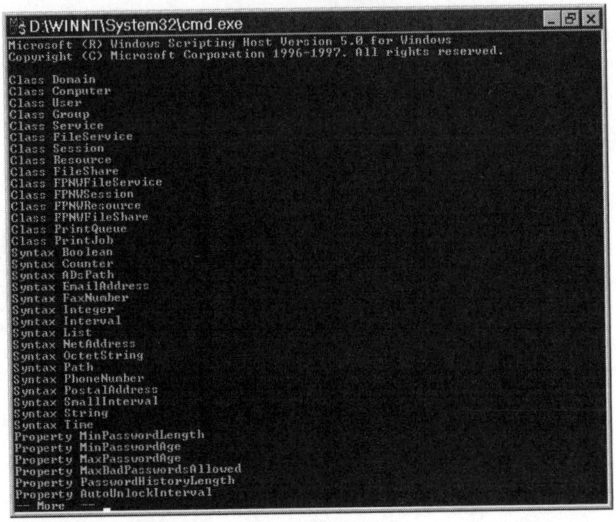

FIGURE 18.5

Output from
ShowSchema
Info_NT4.vbs.

The following line shows how you get directory objects:

```
set oSchema = GetObject("WinNT://" + sDomain + "/Schema")   ' WinNT is
➥case-sensitive!!
```

Most important is how to form the name of the directory object. Here, you are asking for the Schema object associated with the MARCH domain. For Windows NT, you find the first entry (either the domain or the computer you want to connect to) using //, then you separate each component of the directory tree with a /, and then you finish up with a command and the class of the object you are retrieving. You don't have to enter the class of the object, but if you leave it out, you might not get what you expect. For example, the first line in the following example returns the computer account for the server as a user object, whereas the second line returns the computer object:

```
set oSchema = GetObject("WinNT://MARCH/SABER")
set oSchema = GetObject("WinNT://MARCH/SABER,computer")
```

To find a particular sharename, you enter the following:

```
set oSchema =
➥GetObject("WinNT://MARCH/SABER/lanmanserver/netlogon,fileshare")
```

To go through each member of a container or collection, you can use the for each state-ment, as follows:

```
for each oSchemaItem in oSchema
  WScript.echo oSchemaItem.class + " " + oSchemaItem.name
next
```

Using WSH with Windows NT 4 Domains

Okay, enough of the blah, blah, blah. Now do something concrete. When a typical user joins the organization, he receives the following:

- An NT userid
- Access to printers and shared directories available to members of the group he joins
- A home directory where he can keep personal and configuration information
- An email mailbox

In the next few sections, you'll step through how to use Windows Scripting Host to cre-ate this information. You'll do the following:

- Create a home directory for the new user, Ted Smith, and share it with a hidden share. You'll see how to manipulate the FileShare object
- Create the userid, associate his home directory with the userid, and add him to NT groups to give him access to shared resources. This manipulates the Domain, Group, and User objects.
- Change the permissions on the home directory. This is technically outside the scope of this discussion but is required in the real world.

You'll also look at manipulating printer queues and deleting Ted when he leaves the organization.

You won't get into creating a mailbox here, but you can do this with WSH using LDAP to access an Exchange server.

18

Listing a Domain

You can modify ShowSchemaInfo_NT4.vbs slightly to show all the objects in the domain. Part of the output is shown in Figure 18.6.

```
' ShowDomainInfo_NT4.vbs  -  Display information about each object in a
➥domain
' 1998-12-13 stephen.campbell@marchview.com
set oWinNT = GetObject("WinNT:")  ' WinNT is case-sensitive!!
for each oDomain in oWinNT
  WScript.echo oDomain.name
for each oDomainItem in oDomain
    WScript.echo "  " + oDomainItem.Class + " " + oDomainItem.Name
    select case oDomainItem.Class
    case "User"
      WScript.echo "     Full Name=" + oDomainItem.FullName + _
          vbcrlf + "     Home Directory=" + oDomainItem.HomeDirectory + _
          vbcrlf + "     Login Script=" + oDomainItem.LoginScript + _
          vbcrlf + "     Profile=" + oDomainItem.Profile
      ' This may fail...
      WScript.echo "     Last Login=" +
➥formatdatetime(oDomainItem.LastLogin)
    case "Computer"
      WScript.echo "     Owner=" + oDomainItem.Owner + " Division=" + _
                oDomainItem.Division + _
          vbcrlf + "     OS=" + oDomainItem.OperatingSystem + _
                oDomainItem.OperatingSystemVersion + _
          vbcrlf + "     Processor=(" + oDomainItem.ProcessorCount + _
                ") " + oDomainItem.Processor
      for each oServerItem in oDomainItem
        WScript.echo "       " + oServerItem.Class + " " + oServerItem.Name
      next
    case "Group"
      WScript.echo "     Description=" + oDomainItem.Description
    end select
  next
next
```

Look at this script a little more carefully, starting with the first line:

```
set oWinNT = GetObject("WinNT:")  ' WinNT is case-sensitive!!
```

This connects you to the WinNT directory object. Note that you haven't specified a domain. The WinNT object is a container object that holds each domain it can find using the NT or Windows 95/98 browser service.

The following line will therefore go through this collection and return each available domain:

```
for each oDomain in oWinNT
```

The following line returns each item in the domain:

```
for each oDomainItem in oDomain
```

This includes all the userids, groups, computers, and the schema again.

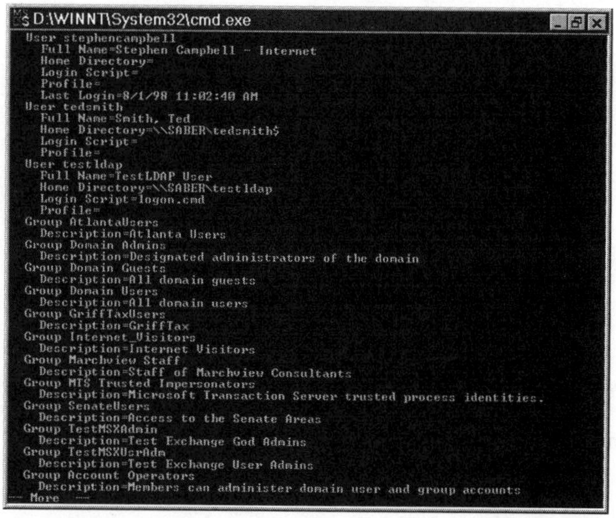

FIGURE 18.6

Partial output from
ShowDomainInfo_
NT4.vbs.

You use a select case statement with oDomainItem.class to determine how you should interpret the object. If it is a user, you display selected information about the userid. Computers contain further objects, so if the class is a computer, you display each object associated with that computer. This will include users and groups (local users and groups this time), print queues, services, and so on.

This can be easily extended to other reports using the information from Figure 18.4, as in this example, which displays information about the jobs in a print queue:

```
' ShowPrintQueueInfo_NT4.vbs  -  Display information about all Print
'                                 Queues on a server
' 1998-12-13 stephen.campbell@marchview.com
option explicit
dim sDomain        ' Domain
dim sServer        ' Server
dim oServer        ' Server to find all the printqueues
dim oServerItem    ' Items in the Server object
dim oPrintJobs     ' Jobs in the print queue
dim oPrintJob      ' Print job
sDomain="MARCH"
sServer="SABER"
' If you omit the ",computer" you will get the Machine account
set oServer = GetObject("WinNT://" + sDomain + "/" + sServer +
```

```
➥",computer")
for each oServerItem in oServer
  if oServerItem.Class = "PrintQueue" then
    WScript.echo oServerItem.class + " " + oServerItem.name
    WScript.echo "  Description=" + oServerItem.description + _
                  vbcrlf + "  Location=" + oServerItem.location + _
                  vbcrlf + "  PrintProcessor=" + oServerItem.PrintProcessor
➥+ _
                  vbcrlf + "  StartTime=" + _
                               FormatDateTime(oServerItem.StartTime) + _
                  vbcrlf + "  UntilTime=" + _
                               FormatDateTime(oServerItem.UntilTime)
    set oPrintJobs = oServerItem.PrintJobs
    for each oPrintJob in oPrintJobs
      WScript.echo "  " + oPrintJob.class + " Name=" + oPrintJob.name + _
                        " User=" + oPrintJob.user
      WScript.echo "    Description=" + oPrintJob.Description
      WScript.echo "    TimeSubmitted=" + _
                             formatdatetime(oPrintJob.TimeSubmitted)
      WScript.echo "    TotalPages=" +
➥formatnumber(oPrintJob.TotalPages,0)
      WScript.echo "    Priority=" + formatnumber(oPrintJob.Priority,0)
    next
  end if
next
WScript.quit
```

The output is shown in Figure 18.7.

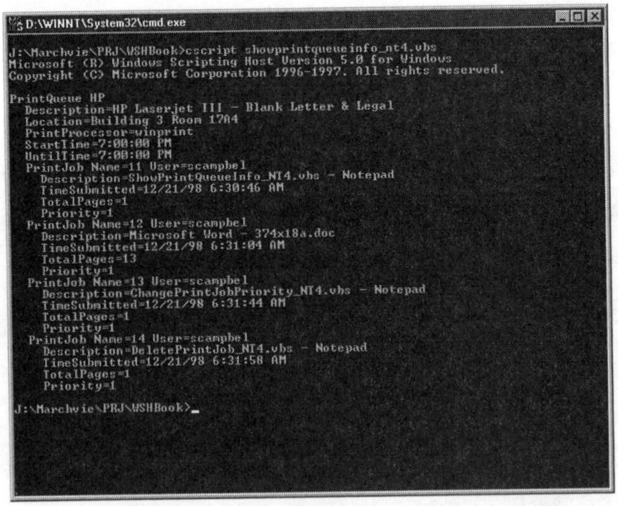

FIGURE 18.7

Output from
ShowPrintQueueInfo_
NT4.vbs.

This is discussed in a bit more detail later in this chapter.

Creating and Modifying Sharenames

At most organizations, each user has a home directory where she can keep her own set-tings and personal files. In this section, you'll create a directory on a file/print server, and then you'll share that directory with the user's sharename. The sharename will be the same as the userid, although this is not necessary. Also, the sharename will end with a $ so that it is hidden from the sharename browse list. This makes it much easier to find the sharenames people use every day.

Here is the script to do that, although all the declaration statements are taken out.

```
' CreateUserShare_NT4.vbs  -  Create a User's Sharename
' 1998-12-13 stephen.campbell@marchview.com
sDomain="MARCH"
sServer="SABER"
sDrive="D"
sUserid="TedSmith"

' First we create the user's directory
set oFileSystem = CreateObject("Scripting.FileSystemObject")
set oUsersFolder = oFileSystem.getFolder("\\" + sServer + "\" + sDrive +
➥"$\users")
set oUsersSubFolders = oUsersFolder.SubFolders
set oUserHome = oUsersSubFolders.add(sUserId)

' Get the LAN Manager (aka Windows NT) File sharing Service
set oLANMAN = GetObject("WinNT://" + sDomain + "/" + sServer +
➥"/lanmanserver")

set oShare = oLANMAN.Create("fileshare", sUserid + "$")
oShare.Path = "D:\Users\" + sUserid
oShare.Description = "Home Directory - " & sUserid
oShare.SetInfo
```

Normally, you would accept the input using the inputbox function or from command line parameters.

You use the techniques described in Chapter 3, "The Scripting Object Model," and Chapter 9, "Handling WSH Script Arguments and Reading/Writing Files," to create the user's home directory:

```
set oFileSystem = CreateObject("Scripting.FileSystemObject")
set oUsersFolder = oFileSystem.getFolder("\\" + sServer + "\" + sDrive +
➥"$\users")
set oUsersSubFolders = oUsersFolder.SubFolders
set oUserHome = oUsersSubFolders.add(sUserId)
```

18

Sharenames are objects contained in a file system container object. For Windows NT environments, this object is retrieved using the following:

```
set oLANMAN = GetObject("WinNT://" + sDomain + "/" + sServer +
➥"/lanmanserver")
```

Note that the `filesystem` container also contains objects for active user sessions and Windows NT services, such as the scheduler. When retrieving the objects in `lan-manserver`, don't assume they all refer to sharenames.

To add an object to a container, you use the `.create` method on the container object and provide the object class and name. Here you are creating a `fileshare` object with the name TedSmith$.

```
set oShare = oLANMAN.Create("fileshare", sUserid + "$")
```

Now that you have the `sharename` object, you can set the rest of its properties: what directory it refers to, its description, and so on.

```
oShare.Path = "D:\Users\" + sUserid
oShare.Description = "Home Directory - " & sUserid
```

Finally, none of these changes are applied until you do the following:

```
oShare.SetInfo
```

You can use this technique to create any file sharename.

Creating and Modifying Groups

Windows NT 4 contains global and local groups. Global groups contain only userids in the same domain as the global group, and they usually define people by the organization of the company (Atlanta division), by the projects they are working on (Ultimate/2000 development team), or the kinds of jobs they do (Engineers).

Local groups are usually used to assign permissions to resources, such as people who can use the Atlanta printers or sharenames. Local groups contain global groups or userids from their own or any trusted domain.

Local and global groups are created using the same method, but the location is different.

Global groups are created under the `domain` object:

```
set oDomain = GetObject("WinNT://" + sDomain)     ' Get the domain
set oGroup = oDomain.Create("group",sGroup)
oGroup.Description = sDescription
oGroup.SetInfo
```

Local groups are created under the `computer` object:

```
set oServer = GetObject("WinNT://" + sDomain + "/" + sServer +
➥",computer")
set oGroup = oServer.Create("group",sGroup)
oGroup.Description = sDescription
oGroup.SetInfo
```

Again, changes are not made until you call `SetInfo`.

What good are groups if you can't add things to them? A group is a collection (not a container), so you add items to the collection using the `.add` method and remove them using the `remove` method. You use the ADSPath to add and delete users and other groups:

```
oGroup.add("WinNT://" + sDomain + "/" + sMember)
```

Figure 18.8 shows the output from User Manager for Domains after running this sample script, which creates a local group and adds the global group (The `dim` statements have been removed.):

```
' CreateLocalGroup_NT4.vbs - Create an NT Local Group
' 1999-01-10 stephen.campbell@marchview.com
sDomain="MARCH"
sServer="SABER"
sGroup="AtlantaShares"
sDescription="Access to Atlanta Sharename"
aMembers=array("AtlantaUsers","FredGreen")   ' Groups this group should
➥contain

set oServer = GetObject("WinNT://" + sDomain + "/" + sServer +
➥",computer")
set oGroup = oServer.Create("group",sGroup)
oGroup.Description = sDescription
oGroup.SetInfo

WScript.echo "Created local group " + sGroup
' Now add the members to this group
for each sMember in aMembers
  oGroup.add("WinNT://" + sDomain + "/" + sMember)
  WScript.echo "Added " + sMember + " to group " + sGroup
next
WScript.quit
```

18

FIGURE 18.8

User Manager for Domains screen showing AtlantaUsers Local Group.

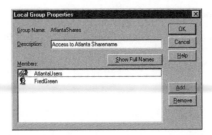

Local groups can also be created and managed on NT Workstations by referring to the workstation object `WinNT://domain/workstation`. They can include local userids and domain userids or groups.

Creating and Modifying Userids

Are you ready to create Ted Smith's userid?

Here is the full script, which you will take apart (again, the `dim` statements have been removed in the interest of space):

```
' CreateNTUser_NT4.vbs - Create an NT Userid
' 1998-12-13 stephen.campbell@marchview.com
' The following properties require ADSI 2.5
'    .HomeDirDrive

' We use this to create a user-friendly initial password
aWords=split("dog,cat,mouse,child,field,desk,pen,house,barn,shed," + _
    "glass,plate,fork,spoon,cup,fence,yard,bird,desk,tree",",")
Randomize

sDomain="MARCH"      ' Domain where user id created
sServer="SABER"      ' Server containing home share
sUserid="tedsmith"
sFullName="Smith, Ted"
sDescription="LAN Admin - Atlanta"
sPassword=makePassword()
aGroups=array("AtlantaUsers","Administrators")  ' Groups this user should
➥be part of
' We get the domain
set oDomain = GetObject("WinNT://" + sDomain)
set oUser = oDomain.Create("user",sUserid)
oUser.FullName = sFullName
oUser.Description = sDescription
oUser.put "HomeDirDrive","H:"  ' oUser.HomeDirectory="H:" does not work
oUser.HomeDirectory = "\\" + sServer + "\" + sUserid + "$"
oUser.setInfo  ' changes are not applied until we do setInfo
' Set the password
oUser.setPassword(sPassword)
```

```
' Set the group membership
for each sGroup in aGroups
  set oGroup = GetObject("WinNT://" + sDomain + "/" + sGroup)
  oGroup.add(oUser.ADSPath)
next

WScript.echo "Created user " + sUserid + " in domain " + sDomain + _
             " with password " + sPassword
WScript.quit

function makePassword
dim iWords,sPass
iWords = UBound(aWords)
makePassword=aWords(INT(iWords*Rnd())) & "+" & int(2+(8.*rnd())) & "+"
➥& aWords(INT(iWords*Rnd()))
end function
```

Often, you need to create userids with initial passwords that can't be easily guessed or known, but which are easy for the user to remember. The function makePassword makes a password of the form: *word+number+word*. The words are short and chosen randomly, and the number is chosen randomly between 2 and 9 to avoid confusion with the letters "O" and "l". Even with this simple list of 20 words, hackers have only a 1 in 3200 chance of guessing the password, and that is only if they have the words list. You use the function split to make an array from a string, just to make it easier to type in the word list. Randomize generates a random starting number, and rnd returns real numbers chosen at random between 0 and 1, but always excluding 1 itself, as follows:

```
aWords=split("dog,cat,mouse,child,field,desk,pen,house,barn,shed," + _
    "glass,plate,fork,spoon,cup,fence,yard,bird,desk,tree",",")
Randomize
function makePassword
dim iWords,sPass
iWords = UBound(aWords)
makePassword=aWords(INT(iWords*Rnd())) & "+" & int(2+(8.*rnd())) & "+" &
➥aWords(INT(iWords*Rnd()))
end function
```

To create the user, you use the .create method of a domain object:

```
set oDomain = GetObject("WinNT://" + sDomain)
set oUser = oDomain.Create("user",sUserid)
```

Now, you set all its properties. The FullName and Description help to identify the user. You set the home directory drive letter and sharename using the remaining parameters. Note that HomeDirDrive was only added in ADSI 2.5, and using the alternative method to set the value does not work in this case:

```
oUser.FullName = sFullName
oUser.Description = sDescription
```

```
oUser.put "HomeDirDrive","H:"   ' oUser.HomeDirectory="H:" does not work
oUser.HomeDirectory = "\\" + sServer + "\" + sUserid + "$"
```

The setPassword doesn't work until after setInfo is run because the object hasn't yet been updated in the domain, so you use the following:

```
oUser.setInfo
```

To set the password for this user, you use the following:

```
oUser.setPassword(sPassword)
```

Note that a user can change his own password in a script by using the method oUser.ChangePassword(*oldpassword*,*newpassword*). setPassword doesn't work unless the user is a member of the account operators, administrators, or domain administrators group.

Finally, you use the same methods as in the previous section to add Ted to the Atlanta Users global group and the Administrators local group:

```
WinNT://ATLANTA/WATLAN01/Administrators (Group on a workstation)
WinNT://ACME/AtlantaUsers (Global Group in a domain)
WinNT://ATLANTA/Administrators (Local group in a domain)
```

If Ted is a member of local or global groups in other workstations or domains, the groups' getObject method should identify the entire, correct path.

Now, you have created Ted and set up his home directory, but you haven't given Ted permissions to use it yet. ADSI is only just emerging with methods to change security. The following example works with ADSI 2.0 and uses the free tool, xcacls, from the NT Resource Kit to make the change. Note that you are leaving the permissions on the sharename unchanged, but you are changing the underlying NTFS directory permissions. This is usually a better way to control security because it also protects the information from someone accessing the directory from another sharename, such as \\Server\Users, or from the server console. This uses the techniques described in Chapter 4, "The WSH Object Model," to run a program using the .run method of the Wscript.Shell object:

```
' GrantUserPermissions_NT4.vbs  -  Change NTFS permissions to grant
'                                  use full control over their home directory
' 1998-12-14 stephen.campbell@marchview.com

' Notes
' When you created d:\users\tedsmith, it inherited permissions from
'    d:\users
' At most organizations, you would set this to:
'    Administrators:Full Control
' XCACLS IS A POWERFUL TOOL.  USE WITH EXTREME CAUTION!!!
sDomain="MARCH"
```

```
sServer="SABER"
sDrive="D"
sUserid="TedSmith"
sProgram="xcacls.exe"
sPath="\\" + sServer + "\" + sDrive + "$\users\" + sUserid
' For more information on the xcacls program see the NT4 Resource Kit
' Type xcacls /? for full syntax
'        /E Add this to permissions
'                   ' domain\user:Permissions
'                              F-Full permissions
sParms="/E /G " + sDomain + "\" + sUserid + ":F"

' Open a shell object
set oShell=CreateObject("WScript.Shell")
sCmd=sProgram + " " + sPath+ " " + sParms
WScript.echo "Running " + sCmd
'                   1->normal window, true->wait until finished
iRet = oShell.run(sCmd,1,true)
WScript.echo "Full permissions on " + sPath +" granted to " + _
   sUserid + ". Return code=" + formatnumber(iRet,0)
WScript.quit
```

The command run by this program is the following:

```
xcacls.exe \\SABER\D$\users\TedSmith /E /G MARCH\TedSmith:F
```

Figure 18.9 shows selected parts of the User Manager for Domains output for Ted.

18

FIGURE 18.9

User Manager for Domains screen showing user Ted Smith.

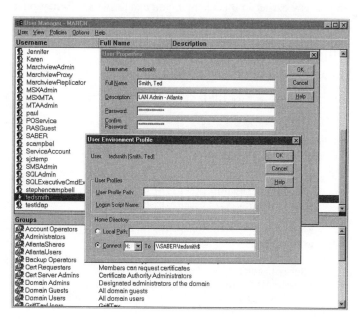

Deleting a Userid

When Ted leaves, you want to delete his userid but perhaps save his personal files to determine whether anything should be archived permanently.

Its as simple as this:

```
' DeleteNTUser_NT4.vbs - Create an NT Userid
' 1998-12-20 stephen.campbell@marchview.com
sDomain="MARCH"      ' Domain where user id created
sUserid="tedsmith"

' We get the domain
set oDomain = GetObject("WinNT://" + sDomain)
oDomain.delete "user",sUserid

WScript.echo "Deleted user " + sUserid + " from domain " + sDomain
WScript.quit
```

Note that you use the delete method, which destroys the object and removes it from the domain container object. You specify the object class (user) to delete the correct object. As mentioned earlier, you can have two objects with the same name, such as the computer and the computer account, which is a user object.

Managing NT Resources Using ADSI

As you saw earlier in this chapter, you can retrieve information about printer queues and print jobs using ADSI.

Print Queues

The printqueue object lies within the computer object. It is defined in the following:

```
set oPrintQueue = GetObject("WinNT://" + sDomain + "/" + sServer + "/" +
➥sPrintQueue)
```

The list of print jobs in a queue can be examined using the collection oPrintQueue.PrintJobs:

```
    set oPrintJobs = oServerItem.PrintJobs
    for each oPrintJob in oPrintJobs
      WScript.echo "   " + oPrintJob.class + " Name=" + oPrintJob.name + _
                      " User=" + oPrintJob.user
      WScript.echo "     Description=" + oPrintJob.Description
      WScript.echo "     TimeSubmitted=" + _
                      formatdatetime(oPrintJob.TimeSubmitted)
      WScript.echo "     TotalPages=" +
➥formatnumber(oPrintJob.TotalPages,0)
      WScript.echo "     Priority=" + formatnumber(oPrintJob.Priority,0)
    Next
```

You can increase the priority of a print job using the following sample as a guide:

```
' ChangePrintJobPriority_NT4.vbs  -  Change the priority of a job in the
➥print queue
' 1998-12-13 stephen.campbell@marchview.com
sDomain="MARCH"
sServer="SABER"
sPrintQueue="HP"
sPrintJob="84"
set oPrintQueue = GetObject("WinNT://" + sDomain + "/" + sServer + "/" +
➥sPrintQueue)
set oPrintJobs=oPrintQueue.PrintJobs
set oPrintJob = oPrintJobs.GetObject(sPrintJob)
WScript.echo "Job=" + oPrintJob.Name
iPriority = oPrintJob.Priority + 1
oPrintJob.Priority = iPriority
oPrintJob.SetInfo
```

Jobs with the highest priority print first, although they don't interrupt jobs that are already printing.

Sessions

When a user connects to a server, a session is established. Connect and idle time for sessions can be tracked. Sessions are a collection under the FileSystem object, which is lanmanserver in the Windows NT world:

```
set oLANMAN = GetObject("WinNT://" + sDomain + "/" + sServer +
➥"/lanmanserver")
set oSessions = oLANMan.Sessions
for each oSession in oSessions
  WScript.echo oSession.User + " connected to " + oSession.Computer
  WScript.echo "Connected " + FormatNumber(oSession.ConnectTime,0) + "
➥minutes. " + _
              " Idle for " + FormatNumber(oSession.IdleTime,0) + "
➥minutes."
next
```

Using ADSI with Windows NT 2000

Many of the concepts discussed in earlier sections can be applied now to manage your Windows NT 2000 environment. You might want to go back and review the discussion of Windows 2000 domains at the beginning of this section before you move into this.

Remember that you use the ADSI LDAP interface to interact with the Windows 2000 domain. To manipulate LDAP objects, you need their path and attribute names.

In Windows NT 4, separate tools were used to manage users (User Manager for Domains), computers (Server Manager), and so on. In Windows 2000, all administrative tasks are now performed using the Microsoft Management Console, or MMC, and you have seen this trend emerging with Internet Information Server 4.

Figure 18.10 shows this console.

FIGURE 18.10

MMC Console showing schema and directory tree and attribute definitions.

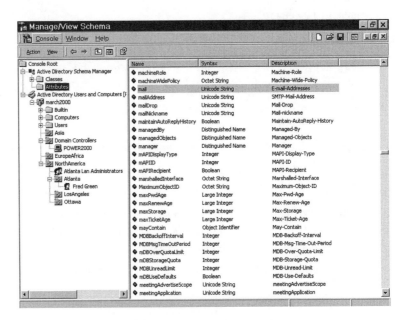

In the left panel, you can see the schema and domain hierarchy. You have selected the Attributes container, which lists all the attributes defined in the Schema, with their data type and description. You should use the Name column to identify the attribute using LDAP. For example, to access the highlighted Email-Addresses field, use the following:

```
SMail = oUser.get("mail")
```

Although most attributes are single-valued, some are multi-valued, and you must use the `getex` method. Double-click on the line in the attribute list to see all properties of the schema, including whether it is multi-valued.

To see the objects defined in the schema, expand Classes in the left panel. When you choose a class, you see a list of the attributes that class can contain, as shown in Figure 18.11

FIGURE 18.11

MMC Console showing attributes associated with a class.

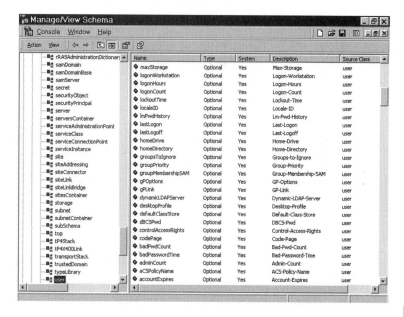

18

Caution Do not modify the Schema without knowing what you are doing. Like Registry changes in Windows NT 4, you can do irreversible damage to your configuration.

Accessing the Windows 2000 Domain

Now, look at this script, which shows the information about a Windows 2000 domain:

```
' ShowDomainInfo_W2000.vbs  -  Show info about objects in a Windows 2000
➡Tree
' 1999-01-17 stephen.campbell@marchview.com
option explicit
sDomain="LDAP://power2000/DC=COM/DC=marchview/DC=march2000"
sDomain="LDAP://power2000/DC=march2000,DC=marchview,DC=com"
sDomain="LDAP://power2000"

set oLDAP = GetObject(sDomain)  ' Top of the Domain tree
if Err.number > 0 then Call Err_EnumTrees
for each oTopItem in oLDAP
  showTree oTopItem, ""
next
WScript.quit

sub showTree(oTop,sIndent)
```

```
dim oItem    ' Users, Groups, Computers, Schema
dim oServerItem    ' Server Items
WScript.echo sIndent + "Showing Tree=" + oTop.ADSPath
for each oItem in oTop
  WScript.echo "   " + oItem.Class + "=" + oItem.Name
  select case oItem.Class
  case "user"
    WScript.echo "     Full Name=" + oItem.get("cn")
    WScript.echo "     Full Name=" + oItem.get("givenName")
    WScript.echo "     Home Directory=" + oItem.get("homeDirectory")
    WScript.echo "     Login Script=" + oItem.get("loginScript")
    WScript.echo "     Profile=" + oItem.get("profilePath")
    WScript.echo "     Last Login=" + formatdatetime(oItem.LastLogin)
  case "computer"
    WScript.echo "     Owner=" + oItem.Owner + " Division=" +
➥oItem.Division
    WScript.echo "     OS=" + oItem.OperatingSystem +
➥oItem.OperatingSystemVersion
    WScript.echo "     Processor=(" + oItem.ProcessorCount + ") " +
➥oItem.Processor
    for each oServerItem in oItem
      WScript.echo "       " + oServerItem.Class + " " + oServerItem.Name
    next
  case "group"
    WScript.echo "     Description=" + oItem.Description
  case "organizationalUnit"
    WScript.echo "     Description=" + oItem.Description
    showTree oItem, sIndent+"   "
  case "container"
    WScript.echo "     Description=" + oItem.Description
    showTree oItem, sIndent+"    "
  end select
next
end sub

sub Err_EnumTrees
  WScript.echo "Error=" + err.number + "-" + err.description
end sub
```

There are three ways to name a domain in Windows 2000:

```
sDomain="LDAP://power2000/DC=COM/DC=marchview/DC=march2000"
sDomain="LDAP://power2000/DC=march2000,DC=marchview,DC=com"
sDomain="LDAP://power2000"
```

The first returns LDAP objects named from left to right as you work down the tree. The second and third return the same information. Note that a domain path is identified using all the components of the domain's dns name. The domain, March2000, has the dns name march2000.marchview.com, and therefore the LDAP name DC=march2000,DC=marchview,DC=com.

Unlike Windows NT 4 domains, you now have a hierarchy of Organizational Units. To handle your view, you rewrote the main display loop to run as a recursive procedure (a procedure that calls itself) called showTree. You will now work down the tree of organizational units.

Figure 18.12 shows a sample of the output from this script.

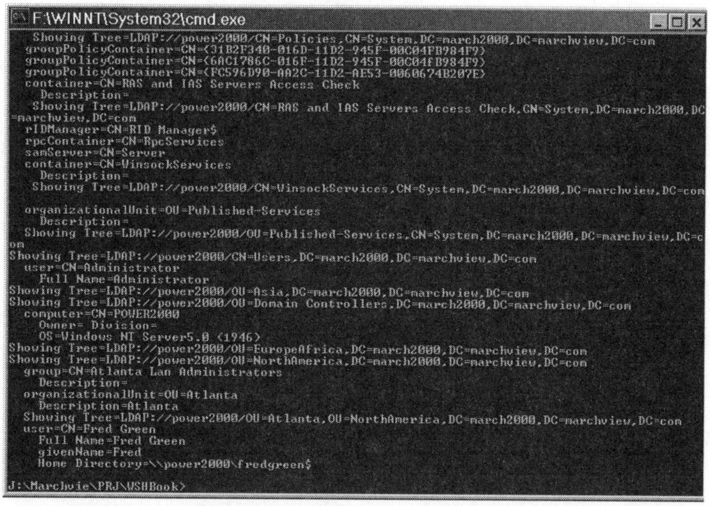

FIGURE 18.12

Partial Output from
ShowDomainInfo_
W2000.vbs.

Creating a Windows 2000 User

There are a number of differences between the NT 4 and Windows 2000 create user script, which apply equally to other Windows 2000 objects. Look at the whole script to create Ted Smith in Atlanta, and then take it apart:

```
' CreateNTUser_W2000.vbs - Create a Windows 2000 Userid
' 1999-01-17 stephen.campbell@marchview.com
sOrg="ou=Atlanta,ou=NorthAmerica"
sUserid="tedsmith"
sServer="POWER2000"
sGiven="Ted"
sSurname="Smith"
sFullName=sGiven & " " & sSurname
sUserPrinc = sGiven & "." & sSurname & "@march2000.marchview.com"
sDescription="LAN Admin - Atlanta"
sPassword=makePassword()
aGroups=array("cn=Atlanta LAN Administrators,ou=NorthAmerica", _
  "cn=Domain Admins,cn=Users")

'Get the domain and organizational unit
Set oDir = GetObject("LDAP://RootDSE")
```

```
Set oDomain = GetObject( "LDAP://" & oDir.Get("defaultNamingContext"))
set oOrg = oDomain.GetObject("organizationalUnit",sOrg)

set oUser = oOrg.Create("user","cn=" & sFullName)
oUser.samAccountName=sUserid           ' Allows NT4 connections
oUser.userPrincipalName=sUserPrinc  ' Windows 2000 login
oUser.description = sDescription
oUser.givenName=sGiven
oUser.sn=sSurname
oUser.displayName=sFullName
oUser.mail=sUserPrinc
oUser.homeDrive="H:"
oUser.homeDirectory = "\\" + sServer + "\" + sUserid + "$"
oUser.AccountDisabled=FALSE ' Use ADSI to enable the account
                           ' This actually changes bit 2 of
➥userAccountControl
oUser.SetInfo  ' changes are not applied until we do setinfo

' Set the password
oUser.setPassword(sPassword)

' Set the group membership
for each sGroup in aGroups
  set oGroup = oDomain.GetObject("group",sGroup)
  WScript.echo "Adding to group " & oGroup.ADSPath
  oGroup.add(oUser.ADSPath)
next
WScript.quit
```

In the previous section, you used the explicit LDAP path to find the domain. These statements find the domain that the current workstation is running in and then switch to the Atlanta organizational unit. Note that these return the names using the comma syntax (dc=march2000,dc=marchview,dc=com):

```
Set oDir = GetObject("LDAP://RootDSE")
Set oDomain = GetObject( "LDAP://" & oDir.Get("defaultNamingContext"))
set oOrg = oDomain.GetObject("organizationalUnit",sOrg)
```

You create the user object the same way as for NT 4, but using cn=:

```
set oUser = oOrg.Create("user","cn=" & sFullName)
```

Look at all the properties you can set now! You *must* set the sAMAccountName, which is the name users at non-Windows 2000 workstations use to login. The userPrincipalName is the Windows 2000 userid, which can look remarkably like the user's email address.

Group names also follow the LDAP naming convention. Notice that the old NT4 domains still exist in a special container under the domain, called cn=Users (not ou=Users):

```
aGroups=array("cn=Atlanta LAN Administrators,ou=NorthAmerica","cn=Domain
➥Admins,cn=Users")
```

Figure 18.13 shows the results of running this script. It has the DOS screen and a screen from the Domain Manager MMC console showing Ted's properties.

FIGURE 18.13

Screen showing the results of running CreateNTUser_W2000. vbs.

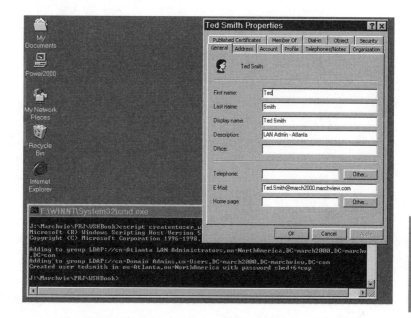

This is just one flavor of the Windows 2000 directory. The Microsoft Web site has many more details and examples than there is space for here.

Using ADO to Retrieve Directory Information

In Chapter 16, "Using WSH to Access Databases Through Microsoft Active Data Objects (ADO)," you used Active Data Objects, ADO, to retrieve and update information in databases. The first section mentioned that directories are very much like databases, and sure enough, you can use ADO to retrieve information from directories.

The current version of ADSI and its ADO driver do not support updates. Also, ADO cannot be used to access WinNT objects, but LDAP works and can be used to access Microsoft Exchange, Windows 2000, or any other LDAP service.

You use the same procedure to access a directory as any other object: Establish a connection, create a recordset, and then read through the recordset.

Establishing a Connection

The following shows the statements you include to set up an ADO connection to ADSI.
The Provider name must be entered as specified:

```
set oADOConn=CreateObject("ADODB.Connection")
oADOConn.Provider = "ADsDSOObject"  ' This is the ADSI ADO provider
oADOConn.Open "My ADS Provider"
```

Specifying the Selection

The query consists of four parts, each separated by a semicolon:

- The starting point in the directory where the search is to begin. This is a standard
  LDAP path, enclosed in angle brackets <>.
- The search filter, following RFC-1960. It must always be enclosed in parentheses
  () and uses "prefix" notation to combine elements. In its most basic form, it uses
  attribute=value. The value can include an *, which means match everything, in
  a manner similar to the SQL LIKE operator.
- The LDAP attributes to return as columns in the query.
- The scope of the query. This can have three values: Base looks only at the starting
  point object. OneLevel looks at the starting point and all objects at the next level.
  Subtree looks at the entire tree under the starting point.

This script returns some information for all users in your Windows 2000 domain:

```
' ShowUserswithADO.vbs  -  Display information about all users in a domain
' 1999-01-17 stephen.campbell@marchview.com
sFilter="<LDAP://POWER2000>;(objectClass=user);cn,sAMAccountName,ADSPath;
➥Subtree"
' Syntax of Filter
'    <base>;filter;attributes;options
'    base:       Distingushed Name of the starting point, e.g.,
'                LDAP://Server[/o=<org>/ou=<site>/...]
'                LDAP://Server[cn=,ou=,dc=]
'    filter:     selection criteria (RFC-1960)
'                (objectClass=*)
'                (&(objectClass=user)(cn=D*))
'                    () around everything.  Above finds all users
'                        which start with "D"
'    attributes: comma-delimited list of attributes to return
'    options:    Base - base only,
'                OneLevel - all matching objects at the base's level
'                Subtree - all matching objects at this and lower levels
set oADOConn=CreateObject("ADODB.Connection")
oADOConn.Provider = "ADsDSOObject"  ' This is the ADSI ADO provider
oADOConn.Open "My ADS Provider"
```

```
set oRSet=oADOConn.Execute(sFilter)
do while not oRSet.EOF
  WScript.echo "cn=" + oRSet.Fields(0).Value
  WScript.echo "  NT4Id=" + oRSet.Fields(1).Value
  WScript.echo "  " + oRSet.Fields(2).Value
  oRSet.movenext
loop
oRSet.close
oADOConn.close
```

The sFilter variable contains a sample of the query line. Figure 18.14 shows the output of this script.

FIGURE 18.14

Screen showing results of running ShowUserswithADO.vbs.

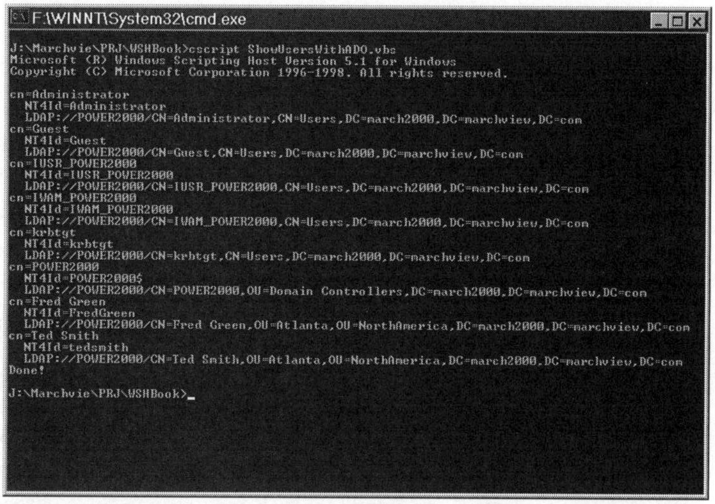

LDAP SEARCH FILTERS (RFC-1960)

Internet standards are established using a process called "Request for Comment" or RFC. These are discussed in an open forum and eventually "ratified". RFC-1960 is the standard defined for LDAP standard search filters or search expressions. A good source for the RFC texts is http://www.rfc-editor.org/

You can also use a SQL-like syntax for the query. Check out the Microsoft Web site for more information about this syntax.

Often, LDAP servers limit the number of rows they return in a query. Watch for this if you are creating recordsets with many rows.

Summary

Tired? It's a lot to cover, and it could easily take an entire book to discuss the Active Directory thoroughly. In this chapter, you have seen how you can use WSH to create and delete users and their sharenames and how you can manage group membership. You also learned to use WSH to manage more complicated configuration items, such as Windows NT and Windows 2000 services. In addition, you saw that ADSI, and especially its documentation, is evolving quickly as Windows 2000 approaches and is delivered. The Microsoft Web site (`http://www.microsoft.com/ntserver/adsi`) should be your constant companion.

Q&A

Q How will Windows 2000 permissions differ from NT Security?

A As you saw, the Windows 2000 directory is truly hierarchical. You can assign administrative and operations privileges anywhere in the directory tree. You can enable the local LAN administrator and the corporate support group to create users in a branch office while preventing the local LAN admin from changing anything else. You can assign permissions from any branch of the tree to anywhere else and include all lower branches if you choose.

Q How do I find out the meanings of the error codes and messages that I receive?

A At the time of this writing, documentation of ADSI is "evolving" (in other words, bad), especially in the area of error messages. Most of ADSI debugging these days involves going back to something that works and trying one new thing at a time. Often the errors are inexplicable. Keep going to the Microsoft Web site.

DAY 19

Using Scripting for Messaging

By Stephen Campbell

Day 19: Chapter Overview

Electronic messaging forms a vital part of any enterprise, and it is easy to integrate messaging into your scripting files using Microsoft's Collaborative Data Objects (CDO).

Today you will learn the following:

- The flavors of Collaborative Data Objects
- Using CDO for NT Server to send and receive messages at a mail server
- Using CDO to send and receive messages at any server or workstation

Before You Get Started

There are two messaging libraries provided by Microsoft.

CDONTS version 1.2 is installed as part of Internet Information Server (IIS) version 4.0, which is free if you own Windows NT Server version 4.0. IIS4 is located on the Windows NT 4 Option Pack. CDONTS works with the SMTP service that comes with IIS. CDONTS is also installed as part of Microsoft Exchange Server version 5.5 where it interacts with the Internet Mail Service. In the second case, Internet Explorer 4 or IIS4 must also be installed on the Exchange Server. If you plan to use CDONTS, I recommend that you update your server to Windows NT Service Pack 4 or later.

Microsoft's CDO version 1.2.1 is included with Outlook 98 and Outlook 2000. If you have Inbox, Exchange client, or an earlier version of Outlook, you can download CDO 1.2.1 free from the Microsoft Web site (`http://www.microsoft.com/Exchange/55/downloads/CDO.htm`). Although some parts of the CDO environment *might* work with other Microsoft messaging clients such as Windows Inbox, Microsoft Exchange Client, and so on, it is not supported by Microsoft. The examples in this chapter were tested with the Windows Messaging Inbox and CDO 1.2.1 installed.

To determine whether the libraries are installed and what version they are, run the following script from a command prompt:

```
cscript CDOVersion.vbs
```

By now, you are familiar enough with WSH and objects to see that you are just creating the CDO objects and looking at the property Version as shown in this listing. Figure 19.1 shows a sample output with the version the samples were created with.

LISTING **19.1**   CDOVersion.vbs—DETERMINE THE VERSION OF **CDO** AND **CDONTS**

```
' CDOVersion.vbs - Determine the version of CDO and CDONTS
' 1999-04-24 stephen.campbell@marchview.com
option explicit
dim oCDONTS, oCDO
on error resume next
Err.Clear
set oCDONTS=CreateObject("CDONTS.Session")
if Err.Number <> 0 then
    WScript.echo "CDONTS not available. Error was " & Err.Description
else
    WScript.echo "CDONTS Version " & oCDONTS.Version
    set oCDONTS=Nothing
end if
set oCDO=CreateObject("MAPI.Session")
```

```
if Err.Number <> 0 then
    WScript.echo "CDO not available. Error was " & Err.Description
else
    WScript.echo "CDO Version " & oCDO.Version
    set oCDO=Nothing
end if
WScript.echo "Done."
WScript.quit
```

FIGURE 19.1

CDO library versions.

To install CDO, run the `.exe` file, which extracts files into a location you specify. Follow the instructions in the extracted `readme` file to install it.

Overview of Collaborative Data Objects

Collaborative Data Objects are Microsoft's objects to access messaging environments.

What Is Messaging?

Now there's a loaded question! Messaging could be thought of as any automated process to get information from one place to another via an intermediary. For example, mouse movements and clicks are sent as messages within your Windows environment.

For your purposes, however, I'll limit the discussion of messaging to email. Email messages include the following:

- The sender (you).
- Recipients. These are the people who should receive the message. There are three common types that closely follow their paper counterparts. "To" are the primary recipients, "CC" (Carbon-Copy) receive the email primarily for informational purposes. Managers receive a lot of CC mail. "BCC" (Blind Carbon Copy) receive the email but no one else knows, not even other BCC recipients.
- Flags, which include Importance (how urgent), Sensitivity (how confidential), when it should be delivered (not before, not after), and requests for delivery and read receipts.

19

- The subject is the topic of the email.
- A message body includes the text and might also include proprietary formatting codes, HTML documents, and related links or arbitrary information in the form of attachments.

The Internet has become the de facto method for sending email, so I'll define a few terms that will be used in this chapter.

Clients send messages to a mail server using a protocol called Simple Mail Transfer Protocol (SMTP). Most Internet service providers offer an SMTP service. Messages are delivered from server to server to the destination using SMTP.

Although SMTP servers store messages during the delivery process, they have no "persistent" storage and typically throw a message away if it hasn't been delivered within a few days. The Post Office Protocol version 3, POP3, was the first widely accepted method for getting your email from a mail server. This limited protocol holds mail until you are ready to download it to your client where it is usually stored in a proprietary format. In the 1990s, a more powerful protocol, Internet Mail Access Protocol (IMAP) version 4, emerged. This enables you to organize your mail into folders on the messaging server and to share those folders with others.

Almost all computers work with 8-bit characters. This enables you to use any one of 256 possible values in each storage location on disk or in memory. However, most communications over the Internet use a 7-bit protocol. To send files stored using the 8-bit format over the Internet, they must be converted to a form that uses normal printing characters and returned to their original format at the other end. There are two standard methods of converting: UUENCODE and Base64. Base64 is the more common method today.

SMTP, POP3, and IMAP have no notion of attachments. They see a single message stream and deliver that. In the past, people (or their mail programs) just stuck streams of UUENCODE onto the end of the message to send attachments. Again, in the mid-1990s, a standard called MIME (Multipurpose Internet Mail Extensions) emerged, which provided a more rigorous definition for parts of a message. The uses for MIME have expanded, and now MIME is the protocol used most commonly to transfer any document over the Internet.

People weren't happy with boring old text messages and attachments when their Web sites exploded with sounds and lights (many, many useless sounds and lights). Most proprietary email systems have provided for some formatting of messages. A new standard has evolved to provide for messages formatted as HTML to be recognized. These messages, in MHTML format, also enable embedded graphics and other Web elements to be included seamlessly within the message.

What Is CDO?

In the days of Windows 3.1, Microsoft established a Messaging Application Programming Interface (MAPI) version 0, sometimes called Simple MAPI. This enabled clients such as the MS Mail client to access different mail services without making significant changes for each mail service while enabling people to write mail delivery and addressing systems without worrying about client details. At the same time, it was reasonably easy to write simple programs in Visual Basic and other languages to read and send messages.

MAPI 1, or Extended MAPI, was released at the same time as Windows 95. This API was much richer. It defined MAPI calls to enable a client to manipulate any messaging, addressing, or scheduling service. It also provided many more functions for the service providers. With MAPI 1, Microsoft shipped providers for MS Mail, Personal Folders, Personal Address Book, CompuServe, Internet Mail, At Work Fax, and Microsoft Exchange Server. Third-party messaging vendors followed quickly; for example, Lotus (now IBM) wrote a provider for Lotus Notes.

Providers support one or more of these three major functions:

- *Message Delivery* provides services that control the flow of mail into and/or out of your environment. Examples include Microsoft At Work Fax, Microsoft Internet Service (using SMTP to send messages and POP3 to retrieve them), Microsoft Mail, and Microsoft Exchange Server.

- *Message Store* provides a place to keep messages and other "items" where you can access them. Microsoft Exchange Server and Personal Folders are examples from Microsoft.

- *Address Book* provides a place to keep and access personal and/or centrally managed email addresses and groups of addresses (Distribution Lists). Microsoft Exchange Server, Personal Address Book, and Microsoft Mail are examples.

MAPI 1 enables the user to define separate *profiles*. A profile holds a combination of services with specific configuration information for each service. For example, your primary profile at the office might connect to your Exchange Server, Personal Address Book, and a Fax service. You might have a second profile connecting to your home Internet account, Personal Folders to keep those messages, and that same Personal Address Book mentioned previously.

When MAPI 1 was released, Microsoft also provided a simple set of objects called OLE Messaging. You will remember from earlier chapters that OLE stands for object linking and embedding. This provided a method for applications to access simple messaging services without worrying about the details of the now complicated MAPI interfaces. OLE

19

Messaging provided easy-to-use methods for sending and receiving messages and reading information from Address Books.

In the ActiveX frenzy, Microsoft renamed OLE Messaging to Active Messaging. Active Messaging shipped with Outlook 97 and had about the same functionality as OLE Messaging.

Outlook 98 and now Outlook 2000 include Collaborative Data Objects, or CDO. CDO extends the Active Messaging objects and provides more functionality in the messaging and addressing areas. CDO adds appointment and meeting objects (an appointment is for yourself while a meeting involves other people). Finally, it includes a *rendering library* of objects that render messaging objects in HTML format so they can be seen from a Web browser. Microsoft Exchange's Outlook Web Client makes extensive use of CDO and its rendering library, and many others are developing Web pages using these objects. At this writing, the most recent version of CDO is 1.2.1.

To use CDO, you must install Outlook 97, Outlook 98, or Outlook 2000 in workgroup mode. If you installed Outlook 97, you can upgrade Active Messaging to the most recent version of CDO by running the procedure described in the section "Before You Get Started." Depending on the task you want to perform, you might be able to use CDO with the Inbox (Windows Messaging) that comes with Windows 9x and Windows NT 4 Server and Workstation.

What Is CDONTS?

In the mid-1990s, Microsoft realized that the Internet was not just a passing fad. They quickly released a series of browsers called Internet Explorer (IE). With IE came a mail program called Internet Mail and News that accessed mail using SMTP and POP3 without using MAPI. IE 4 included Outlook Express, which extended Internet Mail and News to include the new IMAP mail store protocol.

In 1998, Outlook 98 was released and provided many more features than Outlook Express, such as contacts, mail handling rules, and calendars. Outlook 98 can run in one of two distinct modes. In Internet mode it takes over the functions of Outlook Express and enables you to send messages using SMTP, access your mail using POP3 or IMAP, and access shared addressing using LDAP, which is a protocol that was discussed in Chapter 17, "Using ADO for WSH Scripting Tasks." In Workgroup mode, it uses MAPI and MAPI Profiles.

Microsoft made similar advances on the server side. Internet Information Server (IIS) allows Windows NT Servers to act as Web and FTP hosts. Microsoft included an SMTP server with IIS version 4 to enable users to send Internet mail through an IIS server. It also provides a limited mechanism to enable administrators and server processes to handle inbound messages.

It has provided access to these SMTP services using CDONTS, or Collaborative Data Objects for NT Server. CDONTS provides a simple tool to allow server processes (and WSH scripts!) to send messages using SMTP and read messages.

If Microsoft Exchange Server is installed on the IIS server, CDONTS talks to the Internet Mail Service on the Exchange Server, not the IIS SMTP service.

> **Caution** Note that CDONTS objects can only be used on a Windows NT Server with IIS version 4 or higher installed. If you are running on a server without IIS or on a workstation, you must use CDO.

What Is CDO Version 2?

The next version of CDO will ship with Windows 2000 and the next version of Exchange Server. It combines features from CDO and CDONTS and is available for use in both client and server environments. There is a clear Internet flavor to CDO 2.0.

Using CDONTS with WSH

CDONTS provides a simple way for server processes to communicate with administrators and users using mail. A common use is to notify administrators when a scheduled job succeeds (or fails) or to send bulk mail very efficiently.

CDONTS can also be used for applications to send messages to each other. However, Microsoft recommends using Microsoft Message Queue (MSMQ) for application-to-application communications because it incorporates important concepts such as guaranteed delivery.

The CDONTS Object Model

Figure 19.2 shows the object model for CDONTS with the most commonly used properties and methods. You will see later that there are many similarities between this and CDO.

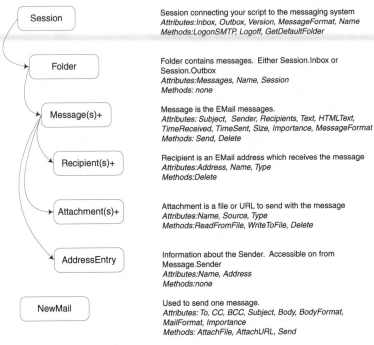

FIGURE **19.2**

The CDONTS object model.

Sending Messages Using the NewMail Object

The NewMail object stands alone and can be used to quickly send an email message with only a few lines of code. Listing 19.2 shows a simple example.

LISTING **19.2**   NewMail.vbs—USING newmail TO SEND A MESSAGE

```
' CDONTS_NewMail.vbs - Use the newmail function to send a message
' 1999-04-21 stephen.campbell@marchview.com
dim oNewMail
sTo="stephen.campbell@marchview.com"
set oNewMail=CreateObject("CDONTS.NewMail")
oNewMail.AttachFile "CDONTS_NewMail.vbs"
oNewMail.Send "webmaster@marchview.com", _
    sTo, "NewMAIL VBS File", "Here is your file."
set oNewMail=Nothing
WScript.echo "Sent message."
WScript.quit
```

First, you obtain an instance of the NewMail object by including the following statement:

```
set oNewMail=CreateObject("CDONTS.NewMail")
```

AttachFile(*Source*,[*FileName*],[*EncodingMethod*]) attaches the specified file to the message. The string field Source identifies the file to be attached. The optional string FileName is the name that the person reading the message will see. Leaving this field blank uses the filename. Finally, the optional long EncodingMethod specifies the way the attachment should be converted for the message. It has values CdoEncodingUUencode (0) and CdoEncodingBase64 (1). The default is UUEncode for text messages and Base64 for MIME messages. Here is an example of AttachFile:

```
oNewMail.AttachFile "CDONTS_NewMail.vbs"
```

Send([*From*],[*To*],[*Subject*],[*Body*],[*Importance*]) sends the message. You can use the optional fields to define the sender, recipients, subject, text of the message, and the importance, or you can use the individual properties, as you will see in the next example. Importance has values CdoLow (0), CdoNormal (1), and CdoHigh (2), where the default is 1. An example follows:

```
oNewMail.Send "webmaster@marchview.com", _
    sTo, "NewMAIL VBS File", "Here is your file."
```

 Caution

> The NewMail object can only be used once. As soon as you send the message, you should set its value to Nothing. If you want to send more than one message, use the Session object or create another NewMail object.

19

Figure 19.3 shows my mail client (Outlook 2000) with the message I sent.

FIGURE 19.3

Simple text message with attachment.

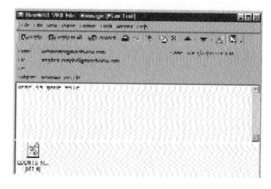

It's almost as easy to send a message with HTML formatting and embedded images or other items. You can use any modern word processor or Web page editor to create HTML files. Listing 19.3 shows the code for this. Figure 19.4 shows the message as I received it.

LISTING 19.3   CDONTS_NewMail_HTML.vbs—USING newmail TO SEND A MESSAGE WITH HTML FORMATTING

```
' CDONTS_NewMail_HTML.vbs - Use newmail to send a message with HTML
➥formatting
' 1999-04-27 stephen.campbell@marchview.com
const CdoMailFormatMime = 0
const CdoMailFormatText = 1
const CdoBodyFormatHTML = 0
const CdoBodyFormatText = 1
sTo="stephen.campbell@marchview.com;postmaster@marchview.com"
sBody="<HTML><HEAD><TITLE>Test HTML Message using NewMail</TITLE></HEAD>"
➥& vbcrlf & _
        "<BODY>" & vbcrlf & _
        "<H1><CENTER>Testing CDONTS.NewMail with HTML</CENTER></H1>" &
➥vbcrlf & _
        "<P><IMG SRC=office.jpg ALIGN=LEFT WIDTH=230 HEIGHT=125 >" &
➥vbcrlf & _
    "This is a test message with an imbedded image." & vbcrlf & _
    "<P>(<B>Note to self.</B>" & _
    " <FONT COLOR=RED SIZE=+1>Time to clean up the office!</FONT>)" & _
        "</BODY></HTML>"
set oNewMail=CreateObject("CDONTS.NewMail")
oNewMail.From = "webmaster@marchview.com"
oNewMail.To = sTo
oNewMail.CC = "webmaster@marchview.com"
oNewMail.Subject = "Sample HTML message"
oNewMail.Body = sBody
oNewMail.BodyFormat = CdoBodyFormatHTML
oNewMail.MailFormat = CdoMailFormatMime
oNewMail.AttachURL "Office.jpg", "office.jpg"
oNewMail.Send
set oNewMail=Nothing
WScript.echo "Sent message."
WScript.quit
```

Rather than filling all the fields in with .Send, you use the individual properties: .From, .To, .Subject, and .Body. Note that you can separate multiple addresses in the .To field with semicolons. Also, you can use the properties .CC and .BCC to include carbon-copy and blind carbon-copy recipients, as follows:

```
oNewMail.From = "webmaster@marchview.com"
oNewMail.To = sTo
oNewMail.CC = "webmaster@marchview.com"
oNewMail.Subject = "Sample HTML message"
oNewMail.Body = sBody
```

To send HTML-format messages, you must set the property .MailFormat to CdoMailFormatMime (0) rather than the default of CdoMailFormatText (1). You mark the HTML body using .BodyFormat CdoBodyFormatHTML (0) instead of its default of CdoBodyFormatText (1). Setting attachment encoding to Base64 or the body to HTML automatically sets .MailFormat to MIME, as follows:

```
const CdoMailFormatMime = 0
const CdoMailFormatText = 1
const CdoBodyFormatHTML = 0
const CdoBodyFormatText = 1
oNewMail.BodyFormat = CdoBodyFormatHTML
oNewMail.MailFormat = CdoMailFormatMime
```

AttachURL(Source, ContentLocation, [ContentBase], [EncodingMethod]) attaches an embedded or attached URL to the message. Use this function to ensure the GIF file or other referenced item is included in the message. The string field Source identifies the file to be attached. The string ContentLocation is the name that the person reading the message will see and that is used inside the message body's HTML. The optional string ContentBase overrides the analogous .ContentBase for the message. The optional long EncodingMethod specifies the way the attachment should be converted for the message. It has values CdoEncodingUUencode (0) and CdoEncodingBase64 (1). If the MailFormat is Text, UUEncode is the default. If the MailFormat is MIME, Base64 is used. Following is an example of AttachURL:

```
oNewMail.AttachURL "Office.jpg", "office.jpg"
```

Caution

The second parameter of AttachURL must match exactly the reference in the HTML to properly detect the inline image or other item.

NewMail has a special property .Value. This can be used to set an additional SMTP header. The most common use is to set a separate SMTP Reply-To heading so replies are directed to a different address than the sender. You can include more than one header. Following is an example of setting a header:

```
oNewMail("Reply-To")="webmaster@marchview.com"
```

19

FIGURE 19.4

An HTML-formatted message.

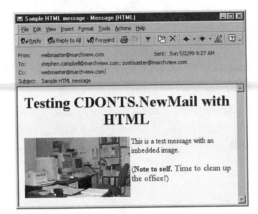

Sending Messages Using CDONTS Sessions

You have seen how easy it is to send a single message using the CDONTS.NewMail object. It's pretty easy to accomplish the same thing with the Session object, as shown in Listing 19.4.

LISTING 19.4 CDONTS_Session_Send.vbs—USING THE SESSION OBJECT TO SEND A MESSAGE

```
' CDONTS_Session_Send.vbs - Use the session object to send a message
' 1999-04-27 stephen.campbell@marchview.com
option explicit
dim oSession, oMessage, oAttachment, oRecipient
dim sTo
sTo="stephen.campbell@marchview.com"
set oSession=CreateObject("CDONTS.Session")
oSession.LogonSMTP "Marchview WebMaster","webmaster@marchview.com"
set oMessage=oSession.Outbox.Messages.Add("Session VBS File", "Here is
➥your file.")
set oAttachment=oMessage.Attachments.Add(,,"CDONTS_Session_Send.vbs")
set oRecipient=oMessage.Recipients.Add(,sTo)
oMessage.Send
oSession.Logoff
set oSession=nothing
WScript.echo "Sent message."
WScript.quit
```

You now have much more control over the individual objects, and more importantly, if you are sending many messages, you can save the overhead of setting up the session for each message.

You open the session and log on using these statements.

`.LogonSMTP(DisplayName,Address)` takes two mandatory arguments, the Display Name and email address of the sender, as shown in the following example:

```
set oSession=CreateObject("CDONTS.Session")
oSession.LogonSMTP "Marchview WebMaster","webmaster@marchview.com"
```

The CDONTS session has two folders. Inbox is used to read messages, and Outbox is used to send messages. Each folder includes a collection, `.Messages`, which holds all the messages waiting to be read or messages waiting to be sent. With CDONTS, you can only access the one message you are working on in the Outbox.

You use the method `.Add([Subject],[Text],[Importance])` of the `Folders` object to add a new message to the Outbox, optionally set the properties, and return the new `Message` object:

```
set oMessage=oSession.Outbox.Messages.Add("Session VBS File", "Here is
➥your file.")
```

The `Message` property `.Text` corresponds to `NewMail.Body` with an important exception. In the `Message` object, another property, `.HTMLText`, holds the message body in HTML format. CDONTS keeps these two properties synchronized; if you set one of these properties, the other will also be set.

Like `NewMail`, the `Message` object has the property `.MailFormat` (CdoMime=0 or CdoText=1) to define the format of the message.

The `Message` object has an `.Attachments` collection that contains each of the message attachments. To add an attachment, you use the `Attachments` method `.Add([Name]`, `[Source]`, `[Type]`, `[ContentBase]`, `[ContentLocation]`). This method returns an `Attachment` object with any parameters you have included set in the `Attachment` object.

The `Attachment` object has the following properties. *Name* is the name the recipients see on the message. *Source* is the name of the file or URL. *Type* indicates the type of the attachment (CdoFileData=1 (Default), CdoEmbeddedMessage=4 means the attachment is a message object.) Methods `.ReadFromFile([FileName])` and `.WriteToFile([FileName])` are used to load the content of the attachment into the message or save an existing attachment to a file. The method `.Delete()` deletes the `Attachment` object from its `Attachments` collection. You can set attachments as follows:

Caution

Use an object's `.Delete` method to remove an item from a collection. Use a collection's `.Delete` method to empty the entire collection.

19

```
set oAttachment=oMessage.Attachments.Add(,,"CDONTS_Session_Send.vbs")
```

The message also has a `.Recipients` collection. Like `Attachments`, you use the `Recipients`' `.Add([Name],[Address],[Type])` method to create a `Recipient` object and add it to the message.

The Recipient object has properties `.Name`, which holds the recipient's display name, `.Address` for his Internet address, and `.Type` (CdoTo=1, CdoCC=2, CdoBcc=3). Like Attachment, the `.Delete` method removes this recipient from the `Recipients` collection.

Now you can manipulate the message to add your attachment to the `Attachments` collection and your recipient to the `Recipients` collection or any other properties:

```
set oRecipient=oMessage.Recipients.Add(,sTo)
```

You send the message using the `.Send()` method of the message object:

```
oMessage.Send
```

You close the session using the following:

```
oSession.Logoff
set oSession=nothing
```

The following example is slightly more complicated and shows how you might use this for sending bulletins, and so on. As you'll see later in this chapter, you can use Active Data Objects from Chapter 17 to get the mailing list from an Access or SQL database or even a spreadsheet. In the interest of brevity, here you'll just use an array:

```
' CDONTS_Session_Broadcast.vbs - Send broadcast messages
' 1999-04-27 stephen.campbell@marchview.com
option explicit
dim oSession, oMessage, oAttachment, oRecipient
dim sCC, sTo, sToList(1,2), iToMax, i
const CdoTo=1
const CdoCc=2
const CdoBcc=3
sCC="stephen.campbell@marchview.com"
const gDocument=0
const gAddress=1
iToMax=2
```

Each row of this array is a recipient. There is a column for the address and one for the bulletin document each should receive.

```
sToList(0,0) = "bulletin1.txt"
sToList(1,0) = "john.doe@marchview.com"
sToList(0,1) = "bulletin1.txt"
sToList(1,1) = "jane.doe@marchview.com"
sToList(0,2) = "bulletin2.txt"
```

```
sToList(1,2) = "ted.smith@marchview.com"
set oSession=CreateObject("CDONTS.Session")
oSession.LogonSMTP "Marchview WebMaster","webmaster@marchview.com"
for i = 0 to iToMax
```

You go through each row of the array, create a new message with a short subject and message, and add the attachments. Note that you also add a carbon-copy recipient (me) to make sure everyone received the bulletin—not something you would normally do. Finally, you send the message and move on to the next recipient:

```
  set oMessage=oSession.Outbox.Messages.Add("Bulletin!!", _
        "Please read the attached bulletin.")
  set oAttachment=oMessage.Attachments.Add(sToList(gDocument,i),,sToList
➥(gDocument,i))
  set oRecipient=oMessage.Recipients.Add
  oRecipient.Address=sToList(gAddress,i)
  set oRecipient=oMessage.Recipients.Add
  oRecipient.Address=sCC   '
  oRecipient.Type=CDOBcc   ' We want the messages to make sure its OK, but
➥Blind CC
  oMessage.Send
next
oSession.Logoff
set oSession=nothing
WScript.echo "Sent messages"
WScript.quit
```

Reading Messages—A Simple List Server

This rather long example collects many of the concepts you have learned throughout this book to implement a simple mailing list server. A list server enables people to subscribe to and leave the list. When someone sends a message to the list address, the list server forwards it to each subscribed member of the list.

To subscribe to the list, the user sends a message to the list's email address with subject SUBSCRIBE. To leave the list, she uses the subject UNSUBSCRIBE. To contribute, she sends a message to the list without one of those subject lines, and the message is sent to all list subscribers.

The mailing list is maintained using a Microsoft Access database called ListServer.MDB, which can support many lists. The list owner can use Microsoft Access to manage the list, or he can use the very basic scripts CDONTS_ListServer_AddList.vbs and CDONTS_ListServer_DeleteList.vbs, which are available at www.fredell.com.

19

The database consists of two tables: List and Subscribers. The table List includes these fields:

- **Id**—A unique number for each list. It is this number that ties the subscribers to a specific list.
- **Name**—Name of list.
- **Address**—Email address of list.
- **Moderator**—Email address of moderator. The moderator receives a copy of all notices, such as subscriptions, and rejected messages.
- **Footer**—This is attached to the bottom of each message.
- **Maximum Size**—Forward if size is less than the limit.
- **Allow Attachments**—If unchecked, forward only if there are no attachments.
- **Members Only**—If checked, forward if sender is a subscriber.

The table Subscribers contain the fields:

- **Id**—A unique number for each record.
- **ListId**—What list this subscriber is a member of. There would be several records if the person subscribed to multiple lists.
- **Name**—Name of the subscriber, taken from his email.
- **Address**—Email address of subscriber.
- **Subscribed**—Rather than deleting subscribers, adding and removing subscriptions changes this true or false value.
- **SubscribedDate**—The date this person last subscribed to this list (for statistical and pruning purposes).
- **UnsubscribedDate**—The date this person last unsubscribed to this list.

You will go through this script in pieces, picking out the interesting bits (the full script is on www.fredell.com):

```
' CDONTS_ListServer.vbs - A Simple List Server
' 1999-05-01 stephen.campbell@marchview.com
'
' Arguments
'   (1) Address of the list to manage
'   (2) (Optional) Location of List database
'     (Default LISTSERVER.MDB in current directory)
option explicit
const gbDebug = false    ' Set this to true to see more output
```

This script takes the SMTP address of the list as its command line argument. It can also get the name of the database file from the command line. This is where you extract the information from the command line using the Wscript.Arguments object described in Chapter 4, "The WSH Object Model":

```
' Get Arguments
set oArgs=WScript.Arguments
if oArgs.Count >= 1 then
  sListAddress = oArgs(0)
else
  WScript.echo "Must pass the List Address on the command line"
  WScript.quit
end if
if oArgs.Count >= 2 then
  sDatabase = oArgs(1)
else
  sDatabase="LISTSERVER.MDB"
end if
```

Now you open up the database and get the information for your mailing list. You just save these in variables for use later. You're using the ADO Connection to an Access database and creating a record set to read the item:

```
set oADOConn = WScript.CreateObject("ADODB.Connection")
oADOConn.Open "driver={Microsoft Access Driver (*.MDB)};" & _
    "DBQ=" & sDatabase & ";UID=Admin"
set oRSList = WScript.CreateObject("ADODB.Recordset")
sSQL = "SELECT * FROM List WHERE Address='" & sListAddress & "'"
oRSList.Open sSQL,oADOConn
if oRSList.EOF then
  WScript.echo "Error!! Mailing List address not found (" & _
    sListAddress & ")"
  WScript.quit
end if
lListID=oRSList("ID")
sListName=oRSList("Name")
sModerator=oRSList("Moderator")
sFooter=oRSList("Footer")
lListMax=oRSList("MaxSize")
bAttach=oRSList("AllowAttach")
bMembersOnly=oRSList("MembersOnly")
oRSList.Close
set oRSList=nothing
set oRSSubscribers = WScript.CreateObject("ADODB.Recordset")
oRSSubscribers.ActiveConnection = oADOConn
```

Now you are ready to actually do some work. You open the CDONTS session, log on with the name and address, and get the Messages in the Inbox folder.

```
' Start a processing Cycle
set oSession=CreateObject("CDONTS.Session")
oSession.LogonSMTP sListName, sListAddress
set oInbox=oSession.Inbox.Messages
```

19

> **Caution**
>
> An IIS SMTP server keeps all the messages it receives in a single file directory. However, the Inbox folder will only contain those messages sent to the LogonSMTP address.
>
> Exchange Server behaves slightly differently. You are connected to the Exchange mailbox whose `Alias` field is the same as the Windows NT account the script is running from, and you receive all messages sent to that mailbox regardless of which of the mailbox's addresses you used on the message.
>
> As a result, this script can support multiple mailing lists running on the same server. To use the script with Exchange to support multiple mailing lists, you need to log on with separate NT accounts.

```
for each oMessage in oInbox
  ' Is it a subscription message?
```

An existing `Message` object contains the same properties as a new message, but they are all read-only. The only thing you can do to an existing message is `.Delete()` it.

The `.Sender` property returns an `AddressEntry` object. This object is used only for the sender and contains the properties `.Address`, the SMTP address, and `.Name`, the Display Name.

```
sSubject = oMessage.Subject
set oSender=oMessage.Sender
sSender=oSender.Address
WScript.echo "Found message " & sSubject & " from " & sSender
```

This section deals with subjects containing the string `SUBSCRIBE` or `UNSUBSCRIBE`. It first tries to find the subscriber in the Subscribers table:

```
if 0<>instr(UCase(sSubject),"SUBSCRIBE") then
  ' Find the subscriber
  sSQL = "SELECT * from Subscribers WHERE ListID=" & CStr(lListID) & _
      " AND Address='" & sSender & "'"
  oRSSubscribers.Open sSQL, ,adOpenDynamic,adLockOptimistic
```

If it can't find the subscriber (`.EOF` is set), it adds a new Subscriber record:

```
if oRSSubscribers.EOF then
  oRSSubscribers.AddNew
  oRSSubscribers("ListID") = lListID
  oRSSubscribers("Name") = oSender.Name
  oRSSubscribers("Address") = sSender
end if
```

Now, it updates the database and sets the subscribed flag and the date and time the change was made:

```
if 0 <> instr(UCase(sSubject),"UNSUBSCRIBE") then
  oRSSubscribers("UnsubscribedDate")=Now
  oRSSubscribers("Subscribed")=false
  sBody = "You have been unsubscribed from the list"
else
  oRSSubscribers("SubscribedDate")=Now
  oRSSubscribers("Subscribed")=true
  sBody = "You have been subscribed to this list"
end if
```

Now, it commits the change to the database. sendNotice is a subroutine that you will learn about at the end of this section. It sends a notification message to the sender with a blind carbon-copy to the moderator:

```
oRSSubscribers.Update
WScript.echo "  Subscription Updated"
oRSSubscribers.Close
sendNotice sSubject,sBody,sSender,sModerator
else
```

This section deals with messages that are sent to the list members. First, you check to make sure the message obeys the rules of this list. The Message object contains the same Attachments collection as with sending messages, and its .Count property indicates how many attachments there are:

```
bMessageOK = true
if (oMessage.Attachments.Count > 0) and (NOT bAttach) then
   sBody = "The message you sent to this list had attachments." &
➥vbcrlf & _
      "Attachments are not allowed on this list" & vbcrlf & _
      "The message was not distributed."
   sendNotice "(No Attachments) " & sSubject,sBody,oSender.Address,
➥sModerator
   bMessageOK=false
end if
```

The .Size property is the total size of the message, including all attachments:

```
if bMessageOK and oMessage.Size > lListMax then
   sBody = "The message you sent to this list was too big." & vbcrlf &
➥_
      "The limit is " & CStr(lListMax) & " characters." & vbcrlf & _
      "The message was not distributed."
   sendNotice "(Message Size Exceeded) " & sSubject,sBody,oSender.
➥Address,sModerator
   bMessageOK=false
end if
```

19

If the list is restricted to members only, you query the Subscribers table for the sender's address. If it is not found (.EOF is set), the sender is not a member of the list, and the message is not forwarded:

```
if bMessageOK and bMembersOnly then
    sSQL = "SELECT Address from Subscribers WHERE ListID=" &
➥CStr(lListID) & _
        " AND Address='" & sSender & "' AND Subscribed"
    oRSSubscribers.Open sSQL
    if oRSSubscribers.EOF then
        sBody = "You must be a subscriber to send to this list." & vbcrlf
➥& _
            "To join send, a message to the list with Subject SUBSCRIBE" &
➥vbcrlf & _
            "The message was not distributed."
        sendNotice "(Not Member) " & sSubject,sBody,oSender.Address,
➥sModerator
        bMessageOK=false
    end if
    oRSSubscribers.Close
end if
```

Now you can finally send the message! Open a recordset containing all members of the list:

```
' Now we can send the message!!
if bMessageOK then
    WScript.echo "  Forwarding"
    sSQL = "SELECT Name,Address from Subscribers WHERE ListID=" &
➥CStr(lListID) & _
        " AND Subscribed"
    oRSSubscribers.Open sSQL
    while not oRSSubscribers.EOF
```

You have seen the process of creating messages before, but there are two points that should be mentioned where you have cheated.

For a real mailing list, you usually want to set the Sender to the person who contributed the message and set a separate SMTP Reply-To field to the address of the mailing list. Readers can then see the contributor's name, but when they reply, their reply will be sent to all list members. The NewMail object enables you to do this by specifying the Sender property and adding a separate Reply-To value. The Session object restricts the Sender to the LogonSMTP user and does not support the Value property that is used to set the Reply-To. To work around this problem, you put the sender's email address into the body of the message. I leave it as an exercise for you to implement this functionality by replacing the set oNewMessage=oSession.Outbox.Messages.Add with set oNewMessage=CreateObject("CDONTS.NewMail"). (Don't forget to set oMessage= nothing after each message is sent.)

For proper operation of the list, you should open each attachment in the old message, use its `.WriteToFile` method to save the attachment to a file, and then use `oNewMessage.Attachments.Add` to add the attachment. In your case, you simply attach the existing message, and it will then carry all its attachments.

After assembling the message, you send it off to the subscriber and continue with the next subscriber:

```
        set oNewMessage=oSession.Outbox.Messages.Add
        oNewMessage.Subject=sSubject
        oNewMessage.Text="From: mailto:" & sSender & " ("& oSender.Name &
➥")" & _
            vbcrlf & "——-" & vbcrlf & oMessage.Text & vbcrlf & sFooter
            ' We should really save each attachment and re-add them rather
            ' than "cheat" and just forward the original message
        oNewMessage.Attachments.Add ,CdoEmbeddedMessage,oMessage
        set oRecipients = oNewMessage.Recipients.Add(oRSSubscribers
➥("Name"), _
            oRSSubscribers("Address"),CDOTo)
        oNewMessage.Send
        oRSSubscribers.MoveNext
      wend
      oRSSubscribers.close
    end if
  end if   ' Subscription Message?
```

If you don't delete the message, it will be there the next time. CDONTS has no notion of read and unread messages:

```
  ' Delete this message from the inbox
  oMessage.Delete
next
```

Finally, you clean up:

```
oSession.Logoff
set oSession=nothing
oADOConn.Close
set oADOConn=nothing
WScript.echo "ListServer exiting"
WScript.quit
```

The `sendNotice` function sends a notification message as a reply to the sender. It reports on subscription status or the reason why the message was not sent out. It follows the standard method to send a message. Note that it includes the moderator as a Bcc recipient so she is aware of these notifications.

```
function sendNotice(sSubject, sBody, sTo, sModerator)
  ' This sends a notice to the sender and the moderator
  set oNewMessage=oSession.Outbox.Messages.Add("Re: " & sSubject,sBody)
  oNewMessage.Recipients.Add ,sTo,CDOTo
```

19

```
oNewMessage.Recipients.Add ,sModerator,CDOBcc
oNewMessage.Send
set oNewMessage=nothing
WScript.echo "  Sending Notice: " & sSubject
sendNotice = true  ' This should really check for errors
end function
```

Figure 19.5 shows a sample of the script running. Figure 19.6 shows the message I received from the list. Note the message attachment.

FIGURE 19.5

Output of list server script.

FIGURE 19.6

Message received from the list server.

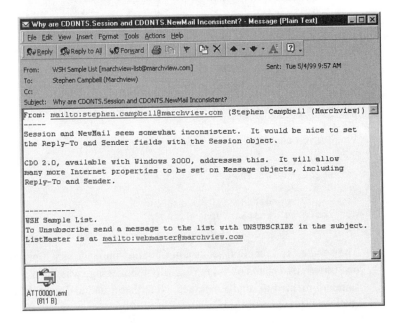

Using CDO 1.2 with WSH

Most of the concepts you have learned with CDONTS apply equally to CDO itself. You still have Sessions, Folders, Message collections and objects, Attachment collections and objects, and Recipient collections and objects.

CDO supports special types of Message objects for meetings and appointments.

CDO also introduces these new concepts:

- `Profiles`—Each profile holds a separate configuration of the available messaging services on the system.

- `Information Stores`—An Information Store holds messages in a persistent manner. You can have several information stores in one profile.

- `Address Lists`—An address list holds addresses in a persistent manner. Like Information Stores, you can have several address lists in a profile.

- `Rendering`—These routines enable you to convert messaging objects into an HTML presentation format. I will not discuss this here because it is more applicable to a Web development environment.

Creating a Profile

As discussed at the beginning of this chapter, you need to have a MAPI client, such as Inbox or Outlook, installed to use CDO. All the examples in this chapter were tested with Inbox and did not require Outlook.

You must create a profile to use with the sample scripts. You will create a profile called "WSH" that connects to a Personal Folders service, a Personal Address Book service, and an Internet service.

Service	Name	Other Settings
Personal Folders	My Inbox	Use `MyInbox.pst` from the Web site, or use your own file.
Personal Folders	My Backup	Use `MyBackup.pst` from the Web site, or use your own file.
Personal Addresses	My Addresses	Use `MyAddresses.pab` from the Web site, or use your own file.

continues

19

Service	Name	Other Settings
Internet Mail *or* some other Delivery Service such as Exchange Server		To use the Outbox and .Send commands you must have a delivery service configured that works with Internet addresses. You can use your existing Internet account.

I assume you know how to use the Mail icon in the Control Panel to create the profile. Figure 16.7 is a display of my profile.

FIGURE 19.7

Profile display.

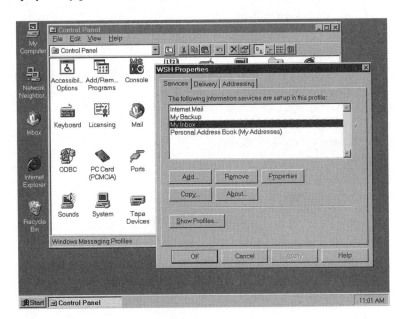

The CDO Object Model

Figure 19.8 shows the object model for CDO with the most commonly used properties and methods. Figure 19.8 shows the CDO object model. You can see it is much more complex, and you have only touched on the properties and methods that are available.

FIGURE 19.8

CDO Object Model

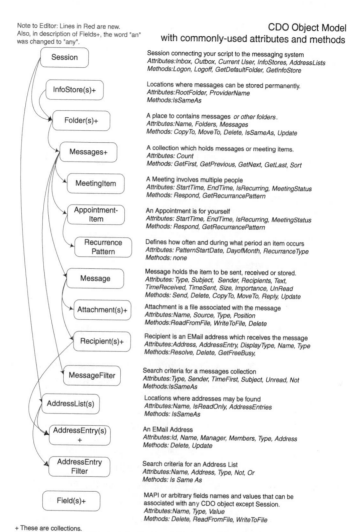

Note to Editor: Lines in Red are new.
Also, in description of Fields+, the word "an"
was changed to "any".

CDO Object Model
with commonly-used attributes and methods

Session — Session connecting your script to the messaging system
Attributes:Inbox, Outbox, Current User, InfoStores, AddressLists
Methods:Logon, Logoff, GetDefaultFolder, GetInfoStore

InfoStore(s)+ — Locations where messages can be stored permanently.
Attributes:RootFolder, ProviderName
Methods:IsSameAs

Folder(s)+ — A place to contains messages *or other folders*.
Attributes:Name, Folders, Messages
Methods: CopyTo, MoveTo, Delete, IsSameAs, Update

Messages+ — A collection which holds messages or meeting items.
Attributes: Count
Methods: GetFirst, GetPrevious, GetNext, GetLast, Sort

MeetingItem — A Meeting involves multiple people
Attributes: StartTime, EndTime, IsRecurring, MeetingStatus
Methods: Respond, GetRecurrancePattern

Appointment-Item — An Appointment is for yourself
Attributes: StartTime, EndTime, IsRecurring, MeetingStatus
Methods: Respond, GetRecurrancePattern

Recurrence Pattern — Defines how often and during what period an item occurs
Attributes: PatternStartDate, DayofMonth, RecurranceType
Methods: none

Message — Message holds the item to be sent, received or stored.
Attributes: Type, Subject, Sender, Recipients, Text,
TimeReceived, TimeSent, Size, Importance, UnRead
Methods: Send, Delete, CopyTo, MoveTo, Reply, Update

Attachment(s)+ — Attachment is a file associated with the message
Attributes:Name, Source, Type, Position
Methods:ReadFromFile, WriteToFile, Delete

Recipient(s)+ — Recipient is an EMail address which receives the message
Attributes:Address, AddressEntry, DisplayType, Name, Type
Methods:Resolve, Delete, GetFreeBusy,

MessageFilter — Search criteria for a messages collection
Attributes:Type, Sender, TimeFirst, Subject, Unread, Not
Methods:IsSameAs

AddressList(s) — Locations where addresses may be found
Attributes:Name, IsReadOnly, AddressEntries
Methods: IsSameAs

AddressEntry(s)+ — An EMail Address
Attributes:Id, Name, Manager, Members, Type, Address
Methods: Delete, Update

AddressEntry Filter — Search criteria for an Address List
Attributes:Name, Address, Type, Not, Or
Methods: Is Same As

Field(s)+ — MAPI or arbitrary fields names and values that can be
associated with any CDO object except Session.
Attributes:Name, Type, Value
Methods: Delete, ReadFromFile, WriteToFile

+ These are collections.
Use method .add to add an item to a collection. Use the .delete method to remove **all** items from the collection.
Large collections Messages and AddressLists also include GetFirst, GetPrevious, GetNext and GetLast. As
filters are applied to the Messages and AddressEntries collections, they are applied immediately.
The Recipients collection also includes .AddMultiple.
e..g, oAttachments.add(<filename>) oAttachments.Delete

19

Sending Messages using CDO

Take your earlier CDO example, and make it work with CDO, as shown in Listing 19.5.

LISTING 19.5   CDO_Session_Send.vbs—USING THE Session OBJECT TO SEND A MESSAGE

```
' CDO_Session_Send.vbs - Use the session object to send a message
' 1999-05-03 stephen.campbell@marchview.com
option explicit
dim oSession, oMessage, oAttachment, oRecipient
dim sTo
sTo="SMTP:stephen.campbell@marchview.com"  ' Added SMTP:
set oSession=CreateObject("MAPI.Session")
oSession.Logon "WSH" ' Replaced LogonSMTP with Logon
set oMessage=oSession.Outbox.Messages.Add("Session VBS File", "Here is
➥your file.")
set oAttachment=oMessage.Attachments.Add(,,,"CDONTS_Session_Send.vbs") '
➥Added Comma
set oRecipient=oMessage.Recipients.Add(,sTo)
oRecipient.Resolve
oMessage.Send
oSession.Logoff
set oSession=nothing
WScript.echo "Sent message."
WScript.quit
```

Where CDONTS deals with Internet addresses, CDO can use addresses in Internet, MS
Mail, Fax, Exchange, X.400 or any proprietary format accepted by an installed MAPI
Service provider. You must now indicate the address type by using SMTP: before your
addresses. Other common address types are EX: (Exchange), MS: (MS Mail), X400:
(X.400), and FAX: (Fax addresses).

```
sTo="SMTP:stephen.campbell@marchview.com"  ' Added SMTP:
```

The method .Logon([ProfileName], [ProfilePassword], [showDialog],
[newSession], [parentWindow], [NoMail], [ProfileInfo]) is quite different.
Because you must log on to a profile, you give the ProfileName and ProfilePassword.
Set showDialog to True if you want a dialog box to be shown to help the user to select a
profile. By default, Logon will attach to an existing session if one is already running from
Outlook or another program. Set newSession to True to always establish a new session.
Here is an example of the Logon method:

```
oSession.Logon "WSH" ' Replaced LogonSMTP with Logon
```

Caution

The profile password protects the profile and has nothing to do with your
email password. The profile password is almost always empty.

You can avoid creating a profile in advance if you want to connect only to an Exchange Server mailbox. Leave the `ProfileName` field blank and pass the Exchange Server, a line-feed, and the mailbox name using the `ProfileInfo` parameter. This creates a temporary profile for the session and deletes it when you call the `.Logoff` method.

```
oSession.Logon ,,,,,, "POWER" & vbLF & "scampbel"
```

You get a new message object the same way as before:

```
set oMessage=oSession.Outbox.Messages.Add("Session VBS File", "Here is
➥your file.")
```

The Attachments' `.Add([Name], [Position], [Type], [Source])` method has a new parameter, *Position*, which identifies where the attachment should be placed in the message. It is a byte location and is the first character of the message. Note that the attachment overwrites the specified character position in the message. The *Type* property now has values `CdoFileData=1`, `CdoFileLink=2` (a Windows NT/9x shortcut), `CdoOLE=3`, or `CdoEmbeddedMessage=4`.

The `Recipient`'s `.Add([Name],[Address],[Type],[EntryId])` now enables you to specify an Entry from an Address Book using that Entry's ID property, which is a unique identifier for an address in an Address Book (Personal Address Book, Contacts, Exchange Global Address List, and so on). You must also `.Resolve([showDialog])` each `Recipient` or the `Recipient`'s collection. This goes through each `Recipient` with no `EntryId` and creates an AddressEntry object, or attempts to find the `AddressEntry` in an `AddressList` whose name or address matches the text specified. Set `showDialog` to `True` if you want the user to see a dialog box if the address cannot be resolved. This is the same process as you are familiar with in Outlook or Inbox when you use the `Check Names` function to change an entry you typed into the `To:` line to `underline`.

Reading Messages Using CDO

Reading messages from the Inbox using CDO is very similar to CDONTS, except you are dealing with `AddressEntry` objects for the sender and other recipients, not just text strings.

This example just shows all messages in the Inbox.

LISTING 19.6   `CDO_Read_Inbox.vbs`—READ ALL MESSAGES IN THE INBOX

```
' CDO_Read_Inbox.vbs - Read all messages in the Inbox
' 1999-05-03 stephen.campbell@marchview.com
option explicit
const MAPI_E_NOT_FOUND = &H8004010F
```

continues

LISTING 19.6 CONTINUED

```
const MAPI_E_TOO_COMPLEX = &H80040117
const CdoPR_SUBJECT=&H0037001E
const CdoPR_SENDER_NAME=&H0C1A001E
const CdoPR_MESSAGE_SIZE=&H0E080003
const CdoPR_CLIENT_SUBMIT_TIME=&H00390040
const CdoPR_MESSAGE_DELIVERY_TIME=&H0E060040const CdoNone=0
const CdoAscending=1
const CdoDescending=2
const CdoTo=1
const CdoCc=2
const CdoBcc=3

dim oSession, oInbox, oMessage, oSender, sMsg
dim oRecipients, oRecipient, oAddress

set oSession=CreateObject("MAPI.Session")
oSession.Logon "WSH"
set oInbox=oSession.Inbox.Messages
oInbox.Sort CdoAscending,CdoPR_SUBJECT

on error resume next
Err.Clear
for each oMessage in oInbox
  sMsg=""
  if oMessage.UnRead then sMsg="(NEW) "
  WScript.echo "Message " & sMsg & oMessage.Subject
  WScript.echo "  Type: " & oMessage.Type
  ' Unlike CDONTS, not every message has sender
  set oSender=oMessage.Sender
  if Err.Number = MAPI_E_NOT_FOUND then
    WScript.echo "  (No Sender)"
  else
    WScript.echo "  Sender=" & oSender.Name & " (" & _
      oSender.Type & ":" & oSender.Address & ")"
  end if
  ' ...or recipients.
  set oRecipients=oMessage.Recipients
  if Err.Number = MAPI_E_NOT_FOUND then
    WScript.echo "  (No Recipients)"
  else
    for each oRecipient in oRecipients
      set oAddress = oRecipient.AddressEntry
      WScript.echo "  " & showType(oRecipient.Type) & _
    oAddress.Name & " (" & _
        oAddress.Type & ":" & oAddress.Address & ")"
    next
  end if
next
oSession.Logoff
```

```
set oSession=nothing
WScript.echo "Done."
WScript.quit

function showType(iType)
  dim sType
  select case iType
  case CdoTo
    sType="To: "
  case CdoCc
    sType="CC: "
  case CdoBcc
    sType="Bcc: "
  case else
    sType="??"
  end select
  showType=sType
end function
```

You connect to the profile as usual and get the `Folder` object. The `Messages` collection contains all the messages in the Inbox. You sort the collection using `.Sort([direction],[property])`. *Property* is a string naming the MAPI property being sorted, or it is the unique binary identifier for that property. Some information stores do not support passing string property names or descending sorts. They will return the error code `MAPI_E_TOO_COMPLEX`. You use `Sort` as follows:

```
oSession.Logon "WSH"
set oInbox=oSession.Inbox.Messages
oInbox.Sort CdoAscending,CdoPR_SUBJECT
for each oMessage in oInbox
```

Messages in CDO don't have to be emails. As a result, there might be no sender or recipient. For this reason, you have to trap errors and check the error code `MAPI_E_NOT_FOUND`:

```
set oSender=oMessage.Sender
if Err.Number = MAPI_E_NOT_FOUND then
  WScript.echo "  (No Sender)"
else
  WScript.echo "  Sender=" & oSender.Name & " (" & _
    oSender.Type & ":" & oSender.Address & ")"
end if
```

In CDONTS, each `Recipient` contains the `Name` and `Address` of the recipient. In CDO, the address information is found in an `AddressEntry` object. `oRecipient.Type` indicates whether they were a "To", "Cc" or "Bcc" recipient. `oAddressEntry.Type` is the address type, such as SMTP:

```
for each oRecipient in oRecipients
  set oAddress = oRecipient.AddressEntry
```

19

```
    WScript.echo "  " & showType(oRecipient.Type) & _
oAddress.Name & " (" & _
    oAddress.Type & ":" & oAddress.Address & ")"
next
```

Figure 19.9 shows the output from running this script with the Inbox client showing the same messages.

FIGURE 19.9

Output from
CDO_Read_Inbox.

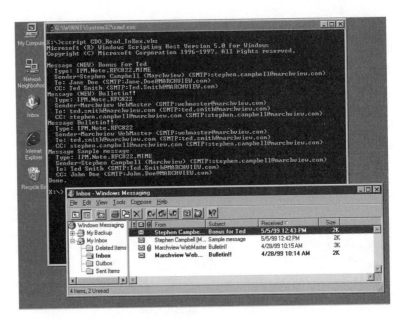

Manipulating Folders and Information Stores

CDO enables you to have many Information stores in one profile. An example is to have a primary and a backup PST file, as you have, or an Exchange mailbox and an Archive PST. This is what Outlook's Autoarchive process does, more or less.

In this example, you copy all folders in a source store to a subfolder in a target store. In the image shown in Figure 19.10, I copied the My Inbox store to a folder in the My Backups store.

FIGURE 19.10

Output from
CDO_Copy_Folders.

You follow your standard practice of opening the session. Here, you haven't specified a profile name, so a prompt will be displayed:

```
' CDO_Copy_Folders.vbs  Copy folders from one store to another
' 1999-05-05 stephen.campbell@marchview.com
option explicit
set oSession=CreateObject("MAPI.Session")
oSession.Logon  ' This will prompt
```

You open the InfoStores collection and then go through each InfoStore saving its .Name. You prompt the user for the source and target information stores:

```
set oStores=oSession.InfoStores
sMsg=""
i=1
for each oStoreOut in oStores
  WScript.echo "Store(" & i & ")=" & oStoreOut.Name
  sMsg=sMsg & vbcrlf & "(" & i & ") " & oStoreOut.Name
  i = i + 1
next
iIndexIn=CInt(inputbox("Enter input index: " & vbcrlf & sMsg))
iIndexOut=CInt(inputbox("Enter output index: " & vbcrlf & sMsg))
if (iIndexIn > oStores.Count) or (iIndexOut > oStores.Count) then
  WScript.echo "Index value is invalid.  Quitting"
  WScript.quit
end if
```

19

Now, you save the source and target stores. Note that the folders actually sit under the .RootFolder property. You will use a Folder's .Id property extensively. .Id is an identifier that can be used to identify uniquely a messaging object: Folder, Message, AddressEntry, and so on:

```
set oStoreIn = oStores(iIndexIn)
set oRootIn = oStoreIn.RootFolder
set oStoreOut = oStores(iIndexOut)
sStoreID = oStoreOut.ID
set oRootOut = oStoreOut.RootFolder
```

You want to create a new folder for each backup. This goes through all the top-level folders in the target store to determine whether your folder exists. If it already exists, you simply add 1 and try again:

```
' Find and create a new root backup folder
sFolder="BACKUP " & FormatDateTime(Now(),vbShortDate)
i=0
bLooking=true
do while bLooking
  WScript.echo "Does " & sFolder & " exist?"
  bNew=true
  for each oFolder in oRootOut.Folders
    WScript.echo "Looking at " & oFolder.name
    if ucase(oFolder.Name)=sFolder then
      bNew=false
    end if
  next
  if bNew then
    bLooking=false
  else
    i = i + 1
    sFolder=sFolder="BACKUP " & _
      FormatDateTime(Now(),vbShortDate) & "-" & CStr(i)
  end if
loop
WScript.echo "Creating subfolder=" & sFolder
```

You create the new folder by using the Folders .Add([name]) method. You save the Id of this new folder because you will be adding all your copied folders here:

```
set oFolders=oRootOut.Folders
set oFolderOut=oFolders.Add(sFolder)
WScript.echo "Created subfolder=" & sFolder
oRootOut.Update
WScript.echo "Committed."
sFolderID = oFolderOut.ID
WScript.echo "Got output folder Id=" & sFolderID
```

Now, you use the method oFolder.CopyTo(*DestinationId*, [*storeId*], [*name*], [*subfolders*]). This copies the oFolder object to the destination folder that is identified by its storeId. Subfolders=True means to also copy any subfolders. Note that Folder.MoveTo, Message.CopyTo, and Message.MoveTo work in a very similar manner:

```
on error resume next
for each oFolder in oRootIn.Folders
  WScript.echo "Copying folder " & oFolder.Name
  oFolder.copyto sFolderID,sStoreID,,true
  if err.number > 0 then
    WScript.echo "    ***Problem copying folder. " & err.number & "-" &
➥err.description
  end if
next
```

Changes to Folder and Message objects are not committed until you execute the .Update method:

```
WScript.echo "Copying done. Commit change to " & sFolder
oFolderOut.Update
oSession.logout
WScript.quit
```

If you don't do this, all changes are lost.

Summary

You have covered a lot of material again today. Hopefully, you have now thought of neat ways to use CDONTS to send messages to users or other programs from your servers, and to use CDO to make your users' and applications experience better.

You have only scratched the surface of CDONTS and especially CDO, leaving Address Lists, Appointments, and other Calendar items for another time.

Microsoft's MSDN Web site http://msdn.microsoft.com is the definitive source for the CDO and CDONTS documentation. The information is also available on the MSDN Library CD, an excellent investment for its reasonable cost.

Workshop

Q&A

Q What is the difference between CDO and CDONTS?

A CDONTS is a very simple interface that works with Internet addresses. It runs only on messaging servers running Internet Information Server. CDO works with any server or client with Outlook installed. CDONTS supports MHTML, a standard

19

that enables multiple HTML components in an email message. The current version of CDO does not.

Q How do `Recipients` differ in CDO and CDONTS?

A `Recipients` in both environments include the address, the address type, To, Carbon-copy, and Blind-carbon-copy. Where they differ is that a CDONTS `Recipient` includes the address information, whereas the CDO `Recipient` includes an `AddressEntry` object that contains the addressing information. The reason is that an `AddressList` contains lists of `AddressEntry` objects. You can search through `AddressLists` to find `AddressEntrys` and add these to output `Recipient` objects.

Q What's in CDO 2.0?

A CDO 2.0 will be available in all Windows 2000 workstations and servers and will co-exist with both CDO and CDONTS. CDO 2.0 provides access to SMTP and NNTP services with or without MIME support. It provides a comprehensive mechanism to form and manipulate MHTML messages. CDO 1.2 will continue to play a key role in accessing Exchange version 5.x servers.

DAY 20

Using WSH with Custom VB and Java Objects

By now, you've seen how powerful the Windows Scripting Host can be. The scripting languages themselves provide useful functionality. Coupled with the built-in Windows scripting host objects, you can perform an infinite variety of useful automated tasks. If the WSH objects aren't enough, you can always use objects provided by other software programs, such as the ADO objects for database access or the Microsoft Office objects.

The Windows Scripting Host has one major limitation. It provides minimal user interface capabilities. You can use it to echo output to the command console, or you can use the WshShell object (described in Day 3, "The Scripting Object Model") to display basic input dialog boxes. This chapter shows you how to create objects using Visual Basic and Java that allow you to supplement your WSH script with a real user interface.

On the 20th day of your introduction to WSH, you'll

- Learn how Visual Basic and Java can be used to supplement WSH scripts
- Construct examples that show you how to use Visual Basic and Java with WSH
- Explore ways that you can create your own objects

WSH and Custom Objects

The Windows Scripting Host is an extremely powerful scripting language. It leverages languages such as VBScript and JScript that people may have already used for coding in, for example, Active Server Pages. However, it does have limitations. For example, it has no inherent support for database access. But it can leverage other ActiveX components that provide database access; for example, you saw in Day 16, "Using WSH to Access Databases Through Microsoft Active Data Objects (ADO)" and Day 17, "Using ADO for WSH Scripting Tasks," how it can be used to call Microsoft Active Data Objects (ADO) to access database systems.

The biggest and most problematic limitations of WSH are perhaps the user interface (UI) limitations. WSH has limited UI capabilities as illustrated in Figure 20.1. Your choice is either the VBScript InputBox() function or the WshShell object, which only allows you to display a basic window using its Popup() method. If you need to display a more complex type of dialog box, WSH won't help you out.

FIGURE 20.1

The limited UI provided by WSH.

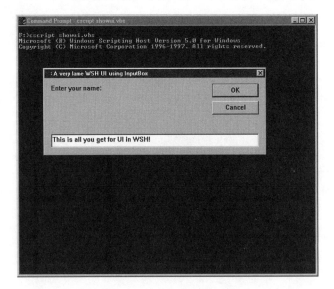

Thankfully, the Windows Scripting Host can leverage any ActiveX objects that provide OLE automation capabilities. It's easy for a script to access any OLE automation object; all the script needs to do is call the `CreateObject()` function and then access any methods or properties as appropriate.

In this chapter, you're going to develop ActiveX objects using Visual Basic 6.0 and Visual J++ 6.0. For each object, we'll go through all the steps involved in creating the object and then we'll show a sample script that uses the object. You can use this technique with Visual Basic, Visual J++, or any other development tool that creates ActiveX objects, to create objects that allow you to extend and enhance your WSH scripts.

Creating a Visual Basic Password Dialog

For the first example, you're going to develop a Visual Basic object that allows you to display an Enter Password dialog box. The object that you create will be basic. It will provide methods that can be used to set or get `username` and `password` properties, and it will provide one function, `GetUserDetails()`, which will display the dialog and return true if the user clicks OK or false if the user decides to cancel.

The Visual Basic object will be implemented using two pieces. A Visual Basic class will provide the object interface and will implement `Username` and `Password` properties, and the `GetUserDetails()` function. The second piece is a Visual Basic form that provides space to enter a username and password, and to click an OK or Cancel button. The Visual Basic class is what you will access from your WSH script; it hides the implementation details of the form that you use to display the input dialog. When you execute the `GetUserDetails()` function, the Visual Basic class loads and displays the form, and then saves the results of the form input in the public `Username` and `Password` properties. As far as the sample script is concerned, it has no idea that the form exists.

This example assumes some familiarity with Visual Basic. We are going to cover the steps involved in assembling the object, but we aren't going to discuss the details of coding using Visual Basic.

Coding the Password Dialog

To begin coding the password dialog, start Visual Basic 6.0 from your Windows Programs menu. You should see a dialog, as illustrated in Figure 20.2, which prompts you for the type of project that you want to create. Next, follow these steps:

20

FIGURE 20.2

*Visual Basic New
Project dialog.*

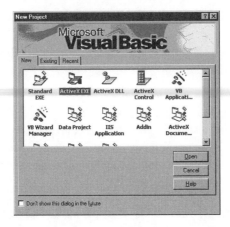

1. For the project type, select ActiveX DLL and click the Open button. You should see a new project with a single class file, as depicted in Figure 20.3.

FIGURE 20.3

*New Visual Basic
project.*

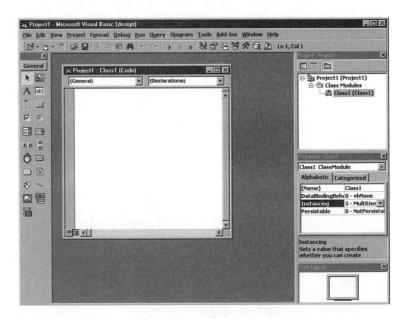

2. Choose Project, Add Form on the main menu. You should see the dialog shown in Figure 20.4. Select Form for the form type and then click the Open button. A new form will be added to your project as shown in Figure 20.5.

FIGURE 20.4

Visual Basic Add Form dialog.

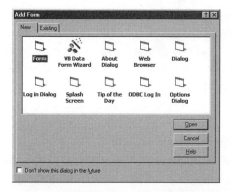

FIGURE 20.5

New form added to Visual Basic project.

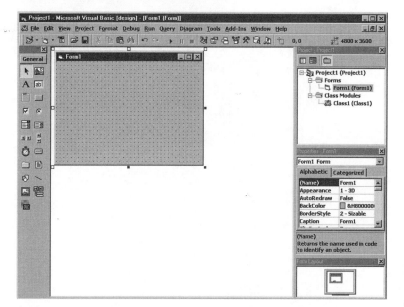

3. Now you need to configure the form. Select the form's (Name) property and change it to frmLogin; change Caption to Enter User Name and Password; change MaxButton to False; change MinButton to False; then change the StartUpPosition to 2-CenterScreen. Next, add controls to the form.

   • Add a frame control and set the Caption property to Login Details. Add a label and change the Caption to User &Name:. Add another label and change the Caption to &Password:.

20

- Next you need to add text boxes that allow the user to enter his name and password. Add a text box next to the User Name: label; change the Text property to "" and change (Name) to txtName. Add another text box for the password, set Text to "", change (Name) to txtPassword, and set PasswordChar to *.

- All that's left is to add OK and Cancel buttons. At the bottom of the form, add a button and set the Caption to &OK, the (Name) to cmdOk, and Default to true. Add another button next to the OK button, and set the Caption to &Cancel, the (Name) to cmdCancel, and the Cancel property to true.

- After you've completed those steps, your form should look like Figure 20.6.

FIGURE 20.6

*The fully configured
VB login form.*

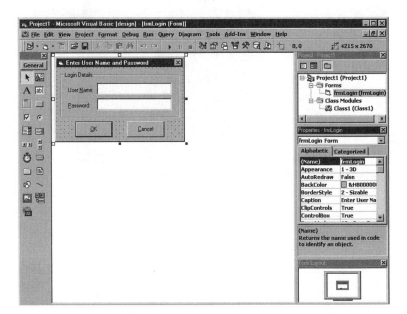

4. Now you need to add some code to the Login form. Select frmLogin in the project explorer, and choose View, Code on menu to see code for frmLogin. Add the following. After you're finished, your screen should look similar to Figure 20.7.

```
' The following property will be used to indicate
' whether or not the form was cancelled
Public Cancelled As Boolean

Private Sub cmdCancel_Click()
    ' This sets Cancelled to True then hides the
    ' form.
    Me.Cancelled = True
    Me.Hide
End Sub
```

```
Private Sub cmdOk_Click()
    ' This sets Cancelled to False then hides the
    ' form.
    Me.Cancelled = False
    Me.Hide
End Sub
```

FIGURE 20.7

Code in the login form.

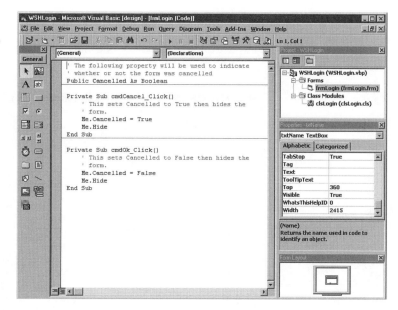

5. Now you need to add code to the VB class file. Select Class1.cls in the project explorer. Change the (Name) property to clsLogin. In the code window for the class, add the following code:

```
' These properties hold the User name and password
' respectively.
Public Username As String
Public Password As String

Public Function GetLoginDetails() As Boolean
    ' Load the login form
    Load frmLogin

    ' Set control attributes and show the form
    frmLogin.txtName.Text = Username
    frmLogin.txtPassword.Text = Password
    frmLogin.Show vbModal

    ' Check if form was cancelled
    If frmLogin.Cancelled Then
        GetLoginDetails = False
```

20

```
    Else
        GetLoginDetails = True
        Username = frmLogin.txtName.Text
        Password = frmLogin.txtPassword.Text
    End If

    ' Unload the form
    Unload frmLogin
End Function
```

After you've finished adding the code to the class, your screen should look like Figure 20.8.

FIGURE 20.8

Code in the login class.

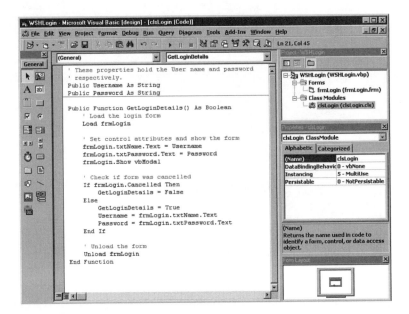

6. Select Project1 in the project explorer. Change the (Name) property to WSHLogin. Change the project properties by choosing Project, WSH Login Properties from the menu. Set Project Type to ActiveX DLL and then click OK. Save the project by choosing File, Save Project. You can save the parts of the project using the default names (frmLogin.frm, clsLogin.cls, and WSHLogin.vbp). After you've saved the project, switch to the Login form. Your screen should look like Figure 20.9.

FIGURE 20.9

The saved project.

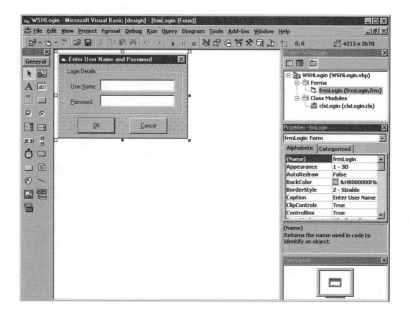

7. Now you need to make the ActiveX DLL that will contain the compiled Visual Basic form and class. Make the DLL by choosing File, Make WSHLogin.dll. A dialog will appear prompting you for the DLL filename. Click OK to select the default.

8. Verify that the WSHLogin object was successfully registered by going to the OLE/COM viewer tool that comes with Visual Studio 6. Choose View, Expert Mode to make sure that setting is on. Expand the tree under Object Classes, Grouped by Component Category, Automation Objects. You should find WSHLogin.clsLogin in the list. Figure 20.10 shows the OLE viewer with the WSHLogin object details. Choose Object, View Type Information to see the OLE automation type description for the class. The type information is cryptic, but you might be able to decipher the fact that there are two properties, Username and Password, and one function, GetLoginDetails, which are exposed by the class.

That's it! Eight easy steps, and your login object is ready to use.

20

Note

If you want to add more fields to the dialog, you can follow the example. First add a label and a text box to the form. Then add a public property to the Visual Basic class. The new public properties will be available the next time that you build the WSHLogin DLL.

FIGURE 20.10

*The OLE viewer
displaying the*
WSHLogin *object.*

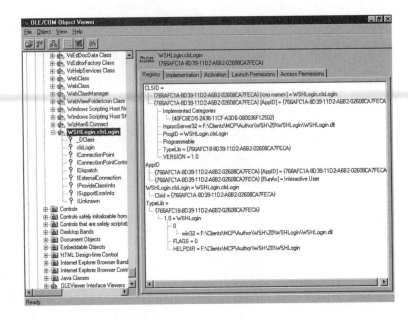

Using the Visual Basic Password Dialog from WSH

Using the Login Details dialog from WSH is simple. All you need to do is create an
instance of the WSHLogin object using the CreateObject() function with the string
WSHLogin.clsLogin, which represents the object. Then you can call the
GetLoginDetails() function to display the dialog shown in Figure 20.11.

FIGURE 20.11

*The WSHLogin dialog
box.*

After the GetLoginDetails() function returns, you'll see the values entered in the dialog
logged to the screen, as shown in Figure 20.12.

You can use the script from Listing 20.1, UseVBobj.vbs, to test the login object.

FIGURE 20.12

The results from the
WSHLogin *object.*

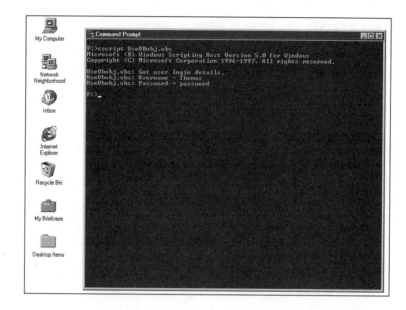

LISTING 20.1   UseVBobj.vbs

```
' FILE: UseVBobj.vbs
' DESC: This WSH script demonstrates how you can use the custom
'       Visual Basic login object.
' AUTH: Thomas L. Fredell
' DATE: 12/4/1998
'
' Copyright 1998 Macmillan Publishing
'

Dim login

'
' Instantiate the login object
'
Set login = Wscript.CreateObject("WSHLogin.clsLogin")

'
' Now call the GetLoginDetails() function to display the
' user login details dialog
'
If login.GetLoginDetails Then
    Wscript.Echo "UseVbobj.vbs: Got user login details."
    Wscript.Echo "UseVbobj.vbs: Username = " & login.Username
    Wscript.Echo "UseVbobj.vbs: Password = " & login.Password
Else
    Wscript.Echo "UseVbobj.vbs: User cancelled login dialog."
End If
```

20

Creating a Java Password Dialog

For the next example, you're going to develop a Java object using Microsoft Visual J++ 6.0 that allows you to display an Enter Password dialog box that is identical to the dialog box in the preceding Visual Basic example. Like the Visual Basic object, it will provide username and password properties and the getUserDetails() function.

Also like the Visual Basic example, the Java example will be implemented using two pieces. The Login class will provide the object interface for the object, and the LoginForm class will provide the user interface.

Before you go through the example, be forewarned that the ActiveX/Java integration is a capability provided specifically by the Microsoft Java Virtual Machine. You can't use these techniques with the standard Java VM provided with the Sun JDK.

This example assumes some familiarity with Visual J++. You are going to cover the steps involved in assembling the object, but you aren't going to discuss the details of coding using Visual J++.

Coding the Password Dialog

To begin coding the password dialog, follow these steps:

1. Run Microsoft Visual J++. Select the Components category, and then the COM DLL project type. Enter VJLogin for the name of the project. Figure 20.13 illustrates the new project dialog. Figure 20.14 shows the empty project that is created.

FIGURE 20.13

Visual J++ New Project dialog.

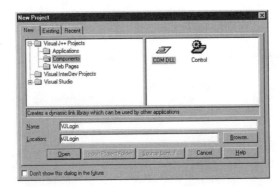

FIGURE 20.14

*Visual J++ New
VJLogin project.*

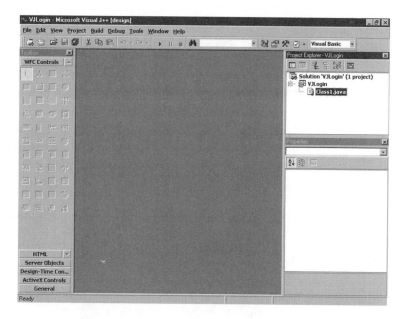

2. Add a new form by selecting Project, Add Form from the menu. In the dialog that appears, select the Form icon and enter LoginForm.java for the name, as illustrated in Figure 20.15.

FIGURE 20.15

Add new form dialog.

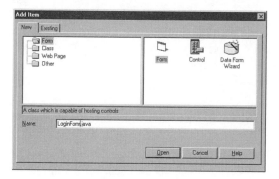

3. You should now see a blank form. First, configure the form. Select the form's text property and change the value to Enter User Name and Password. Change the startPosition property to Center Screen. Set the minimizeBox and maximizeBox properties to false. Finally, change the borderStyle to Fixed Dialog.

   • Next, add a bunch of controls to the form. First, add a Group Box control. Change the text property to Login Details. Add a label and change the text property to User &Name. Add another label and change the text property to &Password.

20

- Now add edit boxes for the username and password. Add a new edit box next to the User Name label. Change the `text` property to `""` and the `name` property to editName. Next, add an edit box next to the Password label. Change the `text` property to `""`, the `name` property to editPassword, and the `passwordChar` property to `*`.

- You're almost done! You need to add OK and Cancel buttons. Add a button at the bottom of the form, and then change the `text` property to &OK and change the `name` to btnOk. Add a button next to that button and change the `text` property to &Cancel and the `name` to btnCancel.

- That's it; your form should look like the form depicted in Figure 20.16.

FIGURE 20.16

The fully configured Login form.

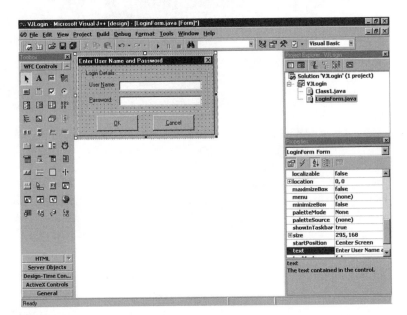

4. Now you'll add some code to the LoginForm. Right-click on LoginForm.java in the project explorer and select view code. You should see code that looks like the code in Figure 20.17.

FIGURE 20.17

Default Login form code before modifications.

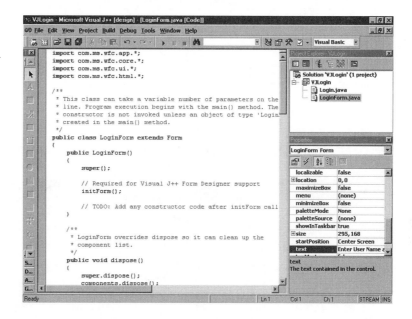

Go to the bottom of the LoginForm class. Just before the code in gray (which is managed by Visual J++), add the following code:

```
public boolean cancelled = true;

public void setName(String name)
{
    editName.setText(name);
}

public String getName()
{
    return editName.getText();
}

public void setPassword(String password)
{
    editPassword.setText(password);
}

public String getPassword()
{
    return editPassword.getText();
}

private void btnOk_click(Object source, Event e)
{
```

20

```
        cancelled = false;
        this.close();
    }

    private void btnCancel_click(Object source, Event e)
    {
        cancelled = true;
        this.close();
    }
}
```

After you've done that, the code for the form should look like Figure 20.18.

FIGURE 20.18

*Login form code after
modifications.*

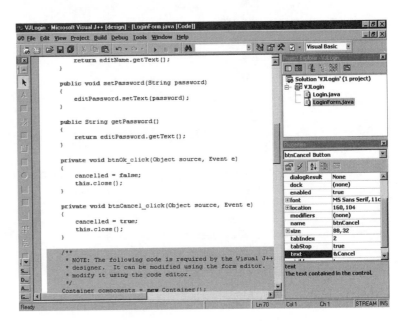

5. Double-click on Class1 in the project explorer. You should see a class with some
   comments as depicted in Figure 20.19.

FIGURE 20.19

Default class code before modifications.

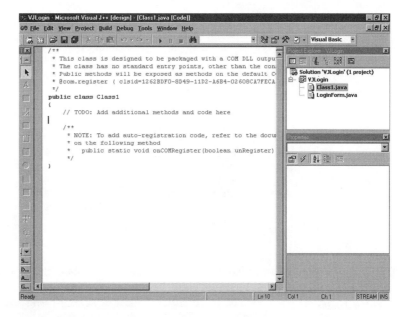

Change the class name to Login; then right-click on the Class1.java file in the project explorer, select Rename, and then change the filename to Login.java. Next, add the following code:

```java
String username = "";
String password = "";

public void setUsername(String username)
{
    this.username = username;
}

public String getUsername()
{
    return this.username;
}

public void setPassword(String password)
{
    this.password = password;
}

public String getPassword()
{
    return this.password;
}
```

20

```
public boolean getLoginDetails() {
        // Instantiate the LoginForm
        LoginForm loginForm = new LoginForm();

        // Set form parameters
        loginForm.setName(username);
        loginForm.setPassword(password);

        // Display the form
        loginForm.showDialog();
        if (loginForm.cancelled) {
            return false;
        } else {
            this.username = loginForm.getName();
            this.password = loginForm.getPassword();
            return true;
        }
}
```

After you've added the code, your class should look like Figure 20.20.

FIGURE 20.20

Class code after modifications.

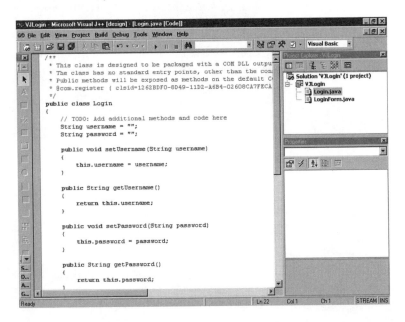

6. Save your project. Then select Build, Build from the menu. Your classes should compile, and you should see a new file, VJLogin.tlb, in the project files list. The file VJLogin.dll should also have been created in your project directory.

7. Register your new DLL by running the regsvr32 program from the command line. You can do so using the following command:

```
regsvr32 VJLogin.dll
```

After you run the command, a dialog should appear indicating that the registration was completed successfully.

8. Verify that the VJLogin object is registered by going to the OLE/COM viewer tool. Choose View, Expert Mode to make sure that setting is on. Expand the tree under Object Classes, Grouped by Component Category, Java Classes. You should find VJLogin.Login in the list; Figure 20.21 illustrates how it shows up.

FIGURE 20.21

The VJLogin *object in the OLE/COM viewer.*

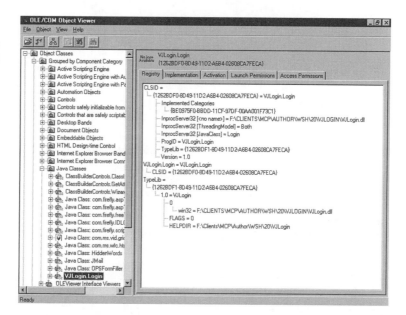

Choose Object, View Type Information to see the OLE automation type description for the class. As you can tell from Figure 20.22, the type information is cryptic, but you may be able to decipher the fact that there are two properties, username and password, some get/set helper functions, and a getLoginDetails() function.

20

FIGURE 20.22

Viewing type library information for the VJLogin *object.*

You're finished! Now you have a Java object that you can use from within your WSH scripts.

> **Note**
>
> Like the previous example, you can easily add more fields to the dialog. For each field, simply add a label and an edit box. As you get more experienced, you can use other more exotic UI objects such as tree controls.
>
> Next, add a property to the Java class, and add appropriate set/get methods. The new public properties will be available the next time that you build the DLL.

Using the Java Password Dialog from WSH

Using the Java dialog object is just like using the Visual Basic dialog object. That's part of the magic of ActiveX and COM; as long as something provides a valid COM interface, no matter the language, it can be used just the same as any other COM object.

To use the Login Details dialog, you need to create an instance of the VJLogin object using the CreateObject() function with the string VJLogin.Login. Then you can call the getLoginDetails() function to display the dialog shown in Figure 20.23.

FIGURE 20.23

The VJLogin dialog.

Looks similar to the Visual Basic dialog, eh? The Microsoft WFC classes ensure that the Java interface will be consistent with the look and feel of standard Windows programs.

After the `getLoginDetails()` function returns, you'll see the values entered in the dialog logged to the screen, as shown in Figure 20.24.

FIGURE 20.24

The results from the VJLogin *object.*

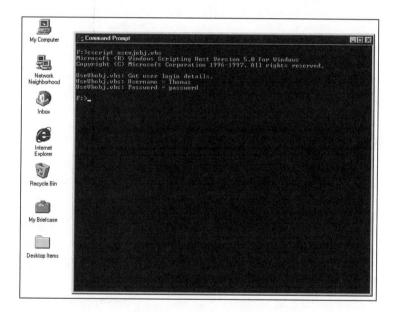

You can use the script from Listing 20.2, UseVJobj.vbs, to test the login object.

20

LISTING 20.2 UseVJobj.vbs

```
' FILE: UseVJobj.vbs
' DESC: This WSH script demonstrates how you can use the custom
'       Visual J++ Java login object.
' AUTH: Thomas L. Fredell
' DATE: 12/4/1998
'
' Copyright 1998 Macmillan Publishing
'
```

continues

LISTING 20.2   CONTINUED

```
Dim login

'
' Instantiate the login object
'
Set login = Wscript.CreateObject("VJLogin.Login")

'
' Now call the GetLoginDetails() function to display the
' user login details dialog
'
If login.getLoginDetails Then
    Wscript.Echo "UseVJobj.vbs: Got user login details."
    Wscript.Echo "UseVJobj.vbs: Username = " & login.username
    Wscript.Echo "UseVJobj.vbs: Password = " & login.password
Else
    Wscript.Echo "UseVJobj.vbs: User cancelled login dialog."
End If
```

Summary

The Windows Scripting Host provides terrific scripting and automation capabilities, but it doesn't provide any inherent user interface beyond a trivial Windows input box.

You can extend the Windows Scripting Host using any language that provides the capability to create COM objects. In this chapter, you used Visual Basic and Visual J++ to create objects that you can use from within WSH scripts. The custom objects allow you to present a better, more functional user interface than you can present using the standard WSH capabilities.

You can take the examples from here and add more fields or validation logic, or you can develop your own entirely new objects. Thanks to the support for COM/ActiveX objects in the Windows Scripting Host, the capabilities are wide open!

Q&A

Q Can I use Visual C++ to build an object that I use from WSH?

A Yes. You can use any language that allows you to build ActiveX objects.

Q Why isn't there any validation logic in the Visual Basic or Java forms?

A For the example, you decided to allow the script to control validation logic. The script could take the username and password, attempt to verify them, and then redisplay the username and password dialog.

Q **How can I distribute scripts that use custom Visual Basic or Visual J++ objects?**

A If you want to distribute scripts that use the custom objects that you've built, you need to create an installation program for the custom objects. The installation program ensures that the object is registered on the user's machine with all the correct DLL dependencies.

20

DAY 21

Deploying Script Solutions

Day 21: Chapter Overview

In the last several chapters, you taught yourself a variety of advanced scripting tasks. Those tasks include the following: scripting databases; scripting the Microsoft Active Directory; sending and receiving messages with collaborative Data Objects; and creating custom objects, which you learned in the previous chapter.

Now you're down to Day 21 and you're almost finished. This is where everything you've learned culminates, and you start planning how to distribute your new scripts to the rest of the organization. Do the computers in your organization meet the hardware and software requirements for Microsoft Windows Script Host? Do you know how to deploy Windows Script Host to users who don't already have it? What about scripts; do you know the best way to run scripts on users' computers? On this, the 21st day of this book, you will

- Consider the hardware and software requirements for running scripts on users' computers.

- Learn when installing Windows Script Host is necessary and how to install it on large numbers of computers with relative ease.

- Deploy scripts to users and run scripts on their computers using a variety of easy, proven methods.

Planning WSH Deployment

If you were planning to deploy a new operating system to hundreds or thousands of seats, you would plan and test carefully. You should. Don't take deploying Windows Script Host or your scripts quite that seriously. First, treating this process as a major deployment costs a lot of loot and, beyond cost, you're unlikely to convince management that you need a team to help you write specifications and deploy a handful of somewhat innocuous files to each seat in the organization.

That doesn't mean that you shouldn't be smart about deploying Windows Script Host and scripts. With a bit of forethought, deploying the required files can be a process that is *business as usual*. In all cases, while sitting at your own desk, here are some steps to take before deploying Windows Script Host and before deploying your scripts:

- **Determine what you need to deploy**—Do you need to deploy a new version of Windows Script Host? Do you need to deploy a script? Make sure you have a handle on which versions of which files you need to deploy (a topic you learn more about in this chapter).

- **Determine to whom you need to deploy**—Are you deploying to all users in the organization or just some groups or some users? Who are they? For example, if accounting is using an outdated version of Windows Script Host but you want to use the new features of version 5.0, target that particular group.

- **Determine how you're going to deploy**—This chapter presents a number of alternatives for deploying Windows Script Host and scripts. Choose the alternative that is best for the files you're deploying and your target. Don't go overboard, however. For instance, using Microsoft Systems Management Server to deploy a script to 10 users is overkill. You would be better off walking around with a floppy disk.

If you have an aptitude for journalism, you might be asking yourself what happened to the *when* and *where* part of who, what, when, where, and how. Considering the deployment advice you learn in this chapter, timing doesn't mean much. You're not going to bog the network down with this deployment and, in most cases, you're going to deploy as part of users' logon scripts. That leaves the *where*. Part of the process you learn in this chapter is creating network shares from which users' logon scripts install files. You also learn, later in this chapter, about directory conventions that make sure scripts are in the same place on every machine in the organization.

 Caution

Part of your deployment planning should be testing your scripts. In many organizations, network administrators get a reputation for shutting down the server at the wrong times and breaking computers with faulty software, among other things. Don't let a buggy script add fuel to the fire.

Hardware and Software Requirements

Windows Script Host, and thus your scripts, will run anywhere a suitable (32-bit Windows) operating system will run. Thus, if a computer runs Microsoft Windows 98 well, the host will run well on that same computer. If a computer runs Microsoft Windows 95 with Microsoft Internet Explorer 4 well, the host will also run well.

To clarify the requirements for Windows Script Host, examine the hardware requirements for each Microsoft operating system. Windows 95, Windows 98, Windows NT Workstation 4.0, and Windows 2000 Professional have many requirements in common. They all require a VGA or better resolution monitor and a mouse or similar pointing device. None require a CD-ROM drive, but all are less cantankerous if one is available. Processors and memory are different stories, however. No version of 32-bit Windows runs well on anything less than a Pentium or compatible processor. Windows 95 and Windows 98 require at least 32MB of memory to avoid tapping the user's patience, but 64MB makes for a better experience. Windows NT Workstation 4.0 and Windows 2000 Professional are nothing short of doggish on a computer that doesn't have at least 64MB of memory, but you'll go from ho-hum to wow on a computer with at least 96MB.

As far as disk space is concerned, Windows Script Host requires about 2MB beyond the disk space that the operating system normally requires. Obviously, scripts require additional space. The disk space requirements for the host and your scripts should never really be an issue, however, because a healthy computer always has far more than 2MB of disk space available.

All 32-bit versions of Windows, except Windows 95, meet the minimum software requirements for Windows Script Host. To install Windows Script Host in Windows 95, however, you must install OSR2 or install Internet Explorer 4 or better. On computers without either, you can still install Windows Script Host version 5.0, the latest version, if you install DCOM. DCOM, which stands for *Distributed Component Object Model*, allows COM components (ActiveX controls, scripts, and so on) to communicate across networks.

21

To recap, there are three different ways to bring Windows 95 up-to-par with Windows Script Host:

- Download OSR2 for Windows 95 from the following URL, and deploy it as necessary:

  `http://www.microsoft.com/windows95/downloads/default.asp`

- Download DCOM for Windows 95 from the following URL, and deploy it as necessary:

  `http://www.microsoft.com/com/dcom/dcom95/dcom1_3.asp`

- Install the latest version of Internet Explorer from the following URL:

  `http://www.microsoft.com/windows/ie/default.htm.`

Note Even if international users are using Windows 95 with OSR2 or Internet Explorer 3, they must still install DCOM before installing version 5.0 of Windows Script Host. The DCOM download described in this section works on localized versions of Windows 95.

Scripting Versions and Compatibility

Version 5.0 is the latest version of Windows Script Host. If your organization uses recent Microsoft operating systems throughout—a homogeneous organization—you don't have to worry about deploying Windows Script Host. That's because Microsoft's recent product offerings already include the latest version of the host. Computers running Windows 2000 or Windows 98 Second Edition have version 5.0. And Internet Explorer 5 installs Windows Script Host version 5.0 on any version of 32-bit Windows. The following combinations of products provide the latest version of Windows Script Host:

- Windows 2000
- Windows 98 Second Edition
- Internet Explorer 5 with any 32-bit Windows

With potentially so many versions of Windows Script Host floating around your organization, how do you know who is using what version? The answer is in the files themselves. Table 21.1 describes the most important files that make up each part of Windows Script Host: host, language, object library, and runtime. To refresh your memory about the different parts of Windows Script Host, see Chapter 1, "Introduction to the Windows Script Host (WSH)." I've left unimportant files, such as Advpack.dll and Regsvr32.dll, out of the table.

Microsoft delivers the same versions of these files as described in the table with Windows 2000, Windows 98 Second Edition, Internet Explorer 5, and with the scripting download that you learn about later in this chapter. Most of the files are in *WinDir*\System or *WinDir*\System32, depending on the program that installed them. Wscript.exe is usually in *WinDir*, and Cscript.exe is usually in *WinDir*\Command. Use these steps to check a file's size, date, and version:

1. On the file's shortcut menu, click Properties to display its Properties dialog box.

2. On the General tab of the file's Properties dialog box, note the file's creation file size in bytes and its creation date. When noting the file's size, make sure you use the size in parentheses, which is the exact number of bytes used by the file, not the number next to it that indicates the number of bytes used.

3. On the Version tab of the file's Properties dialog box, note the file's version, which you see at the top of the dialog box as shown in Figure 21.1.

4. Close the Properties dialog box.

FIGURE 21.1

The file's version is at the top of the Version tab and is available in the Other Version Information area, too.

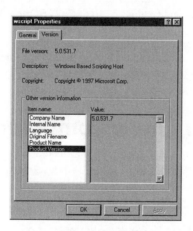

Compare the versions of the installed files to versions in Table 21.1. If the installed files are older, consider deploying an update to Windows Script Host. Keep in mind, however, that your scripts might work with Windows Script Host version 3.1, the version that most users had prior to version 5.0, so don't automatically assume that you need to deploy the latest and greatest. To make sure, test them.

21

TABLE 21.1   FILE VERSIONS

Component	File	Size	Date	Version
Host	Cscript.exe	122,128	9/29/97	5.0.531.7
Host	Dispex.dll	26,896	1/15/99	5.0.0.3715
Host	Wscript.exe	130,320	9/29/97	5.0.531.7
Host	Wshext.dll	61,712	9/29/97	5.0.531.7
Language	Jscript.dll	487,696	1/15/99	5.0.0.3715
Language	Vbscript.dll	426,256	1/15/99	5.0.0.3715
Library	Scrobj.dll	165,824	1/15/99	1.0.0.3715
Library	Wshom.ocx	132,368	9/29/97	5.0.531.7
Runtime	Scrrun.dll	151,824	1/15/99	5.0.0.3715

Caution

Armed with knowledge about which files comprise each part of Windows Script Host, you might be tempted to deploy just those files comprising a particular part. Don't. All parts of Windows Script Host interrelate and upgrading one part without upgrading the others might cripple the host. As well, you should always install Windows Script Host using the proper installer, because the installer's INF file changes a variety of Registry settings.

Installing WSH on Client Computers

Having covered the situations in which you'll need to install Windows Script Host, this section shows you how to do it. If you must install Windows Script Host on but a handful of computers, the manual installation described in the next section, "Installing WSH on a Single Computer," is the best approach.

If, on the other hand, you must install Windows Script Host on a large number of computers, deploy it using what you learn in "Deploying WSH to Numerous Computers." This section shows you how to *push* the installation so that users have no choice but to install the files or *pull* the installation so that users have to make a choice and put forth some effort to do so. The choice depends on the types of users with which you're dealing. In most cases, pushing the installation via users' logon scripts is the best approach, particularly if you're relying on Windows Script Host as a management tool.

> **Note** Before you go any further, be warned that all the deployment examples in this chapter rely on Windows NT Server 4.0. The examples are still valid even if you're using a different server platform in your organization. You'll certainly have to adjust the logon scripts and instructions you see in this chapter, but the concepts are the same.

Installing WSH on a Single Computer

The Windows Script Host version 5.0 setup file is available on Microsoft's Web site. In addition to the English language version, Microsoft offers localized versions for many languages. The setup file contains the host, language, object library, and runtime components. At the time of this writing, the filename is Ste50en.exe and the file's size is about 900KB. Download the installation file from the following URL, and either install it now or save it for later:

```
http://www.microsoft.com/msdownload/vbscript/scripting.asp
```

To install Windows Script Host, run the setup file you downloaded from Microsoft's Web site. You can double-click the file in Windows Explorer; or, click **Run** on the Start menu, type the file's path and filename, and click OK. After the setup program starts, follow the instructions you see on the screen to finish installing the host.

The setup program has additional command-line options that you can specify in the Run dialog box or at the MS-DOS command prompt (see Table 21.2). These options aren't useful when manually installing Windows Script Host on a single machine, but they are useful if you want to deploy Windows Script Host automatically whether via a logon script or custom installation package (more on these topics later in this chapter).

TABLE 21.2   COMMAND-LINE OPTIONS FOR Ste50en.exe

Option	Description
/q	Asks no questions and displays nothing during installation; also known as quiet mode.
/t:path	Specifies a temporary working folder.
/c	Extracts files without installing them, which is useful if you want to examine the files or repackage them for alternative installation methods such as Systems Management Server.
/c:cmd	Overrides the installation command defined by the author of the package; not useful in this case.

21

> **Note**   Although it's recommended that you install Windows Script Host by execut-
> ing the setup file you download from the Microsoft Web site, there is an
> alternative. Using the /c command-line options, unpack the contents of the
> installation file into a folder; then, in Windows Explorer, click Install on the
> Ste50en.inf file's shortcut menu. Also, within a batch file, you can automat-
> ically install Windows Script Host using the files you unpacked by executing
> the following command:
>
> ```
> rundll.exe setupx.dll,InstallHinfSection DefaultInstall 132
> ➥ste50en.inf
> ```
>
> If Ste50en.inf isn't in the current path, make sure you add the file's path to
> the command line. If you want to learn more about this command line, refer
> to Microsoft's developer Web site, http://msdn.microsoft.com.

Deploying WSH to Numerous Computers

Since the early days of MS-DOS, the command shell (Command.com) supported batch
files. Even now, support for batch files hasn't changed much—with the exception of a
few new commands, it's still rudimentary.

Throughout the remainder of this chapter, you will learn how to use batch files to ease
deploying Windows Script Host and your scripts. For example, Windows NT Server 4.0
uses batch files as logon scripts, and logon scripts present a terrific opportunity to install
the host on a large number of computers. So don't count out batch files just yet. Just consider them the host's older, dumber brother.

Many different methods are available for deploying Windows Script Host. Internet
Explorer Administration Kit and Systems Management Server are examples, although
both are overkill. The following are the most practical methods for deploying Windows
Script Host, considering the limited magnitude of what you're trying to accomplish:

- Push (mandatory) via Logon scripts or policies.
- Pull (voluntary) installation via mail, intranet, or other methods for distributing the
  setup file. Because this involves little more than making the setup file available so
  that users can run it on their own—whether via email, the intranet, or a network
  share—there's no need to waste space discussing it.

Sharing the Setup File

In most cases, you'll want to store the setup file on the network and share that file with
users who need to install it. The following instructions describe how to share the setup
file on a Microsoft network running Windows NT Server 4.0, but sharing the setup file
on other networks is similar:

1. Create a folder on the network, copy the setup file to that folder, and set the folder's permissions so that the users can access it. When setting local and network permissions, make sure you give users who need access to the setup file no less than Read and Execute (RX) permissions.

2. In Windows Explorer, click Sharing on the folder's shortcut menu to display the Sharing tab of the Properties dialog box shown in Figure 21.2.

3. Do one of the following:

   - If you've already shared the folder or it has an administrative share, which you would know if the folder already has a share whose name ends with a dollar sign ($), click New Share to create a new share and set permissions for it. Make sure you give users who require access to the setup file no less than Read access.

   - If you haven't shared the folder and it doesn't have any administrative share, click Shared As, type the name of the share in Share Name, and click Permissions to determine which users have access to the folder. Make sure you give users who require access to the setup file no less than Read access.

4. Click OK to make the new share immediately available.

FIGURE 21.2

If you are concerned about resource usage, click Allow N Users and specify the maximum number of users that can install Windows Script Host simultaneously.

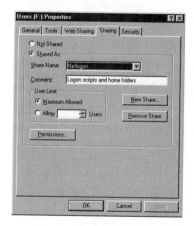

Installing WSH from a Logon Script

After sharing the setup file, you have many options for actually running it on users' computers. The option that requires no interaction with users is running it from their setup scripts. To associate a logon script with a user's domain account in Windows NT Server 4.0, use the following steps:

1. On the Start menu, point to Programs, followed by Administrator Tools (Common), and then click User Manager for Domains.

21

2. Select one or more users from the list and choose Properties from the User menu. You'll see the User Properties dialog box.

3. Click Profile, and you'll see the User Environment Profile dialog box shown in Figure 21.3.

4. Type the filename of the logon script in Logon Script Name. Note that you configure the root path of the server's logon scripts using the Directory Replication dialog box in Server Manager, which you open by double-clicking the Server Manager icon in Control Panel. The operating system appends the path and filename you specify in Logon Script Name to the logon script path, which is shared as Netlogon and is usually *WinDir*\System32\Rep\Nmport\Scripts.

5. Click OK to close the User Environment Profile dialog box, and click OK again to close the User Properties dialog box.

FIGURE 21.3

For more information about configuring user accounts in Windows NT Server 4.0, see the online documentation.

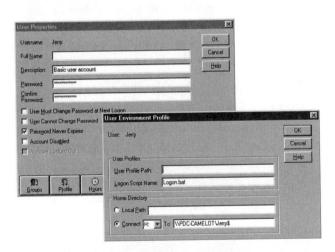

The logon script itself should be a .bat file, especially because you want Windows 95 clients to run it and those clients don't understand .cmd files. The contents of the logon script should look something like Listing 21.1.

LISTING 21.1 INSTALLING WSH IN A LOGON SCRIPT

```
If Exist %WinDir%\Wscript.exe Goto Installed
If Exist %WinDir%\System32\Wscript.exe Goto Installed

\\pdc-camelot\wsh\st50en.exe

:Installed
```

Here's how this logon script works:

1. The logon script tests for the existence of the scripting console, `Wscript.exe`.

2. Because you expect this script to run on any version of Windows, it checks for `Wscript.exe` in the two most likely locations.

3. If the logon script finds `Wscript.exe` in either place, it skips to the end of the script.

4. If the logon script doesn't find `Wscript.exe` in either place, it runs the setup program. Note that in your script, you should substitute the server name for `pdc-camelot`, your share name for `wsh`, and the appropriate filename for `st50en.exe`.

Saving Time and Bandwidth

By now, you get the basic idea behind installing Windows Script Host via logon scripts. There are a few more things to consider, however:

- If you don't want to bother with configuring each user's account to use a logon script, consider creating a single account, call it whatever you like, and configure that account to use the logon script. Then, you can instruct users to log on to the network using that particular account. After the logon script installs Windows Script Host, the script can forcefully log the user off using `Net.exe`: **net logoff /yes**.

- If bandwidth is a problem, you can limit the number of users that have access to the share. You can also create multiple accounts, schedule the times when each account can log on to the server, and then instruct different groups of users to use different accounts. Windows NT Server 4.0 and other network servers provide a plethora of ways you can balance the load on your network. Installing Windows Script Host is a menial task for most network servers, however, and you shouldn't fear stressing the network.

Using System Policies to Install WSH

Okay, enough is enough, but you have one more alternative for pushing the installation of Windows Script Host to users on the network: system policies. Windows 95 comes with System Policy Editor, which you use to create a policy file that Windows 95 downloads from the Netlogon share on the network each time it starts. In that policy file, you can specify one or more programs that Windows 95 will run each time it starts. You can also specify one or more programs that Windows 95 will run one time, the next time it starts. For more information about System Policy Editor and system policies in general, refer to *Windows 98 Registry Handbook* (Que, 1999) or *Windows 2000 Registry Handbook* (Que, 1999). This particular policy affects the following Registry key:

`HKEY_LOCAL_MACHINE\Software\Microsoft\Windows\CurrentVersion\RunOnce`

21

Deploying Your WSH Scripts

Deploying your scripts to users is not any more complicated than deploying Windows Script Host to them. And, like deploying Windows Script Host, you can use Internet Explorer Administration Kit or Systems Management Server; however doing so is senseless. Options for deploying scripts include the following:

- Push (mandatory) via logon scripts, replication, policies, and so on.
- Pull (voluntary) via email, Web site, floppy disk, and so on. This involves little more than making the script available so users can run it. Although you won't learn how to distribute files via email, Web, or floppy disk, you will learn how to package a script file with an INF file so that installation is easy and the file goes into the folder you intend.

Using Cscript.exe and Wscript.exe

Windows Script Host provides two different consoles for running scripts: Cscript.exe for running scripts at the MS-DOS command prompt and Wscript.exe for running scripts in Windows. Both Cscript.exe and Wscript.exe have similar command lines and, for the sake of completeness, here they are:

```
Cscript.exe scriptname.ext options arguments
Wscript.exe scriptname.ext options arguments
```

Options are flags that Cscript.exe and Wscript.exe interpret. You start options with two slashes (//). Cscript.exe and Wscript.exe pass arguments, which start with a single slash (/), directly to the script. The following table describes the options that control how Cscript.exe and Wscript.exe run a script:

Option	Description
//i	Allows the script to interact with the user.
//t	Specifies the amount of time in seconds that the script can run, a feature that is really just a watchdog timer that catches runaway scripts.
//logo	Causes Cscript.exe and Wscript.exe to display a banner each time they start.
//nologo	Causes Cscript.exe and Wscript.exe not to display a banner each time they start.
//h:cscript	Makes Cscript.exe the default console.
//h:wscript	Makes Wscript.exe the default console.

//s	Saves the current command-line options as the defaults for future sessions.
//?	Displays the available command-line options.
//b	Prevents scripts from displaying errors; the *b* is for *batch mode*.

An alternative to specifying all these command-line options when you run a script is creating .wsh files and launching those files instead. The .wsh files are to scripts what .pif files are to MS-DOS programs. A .wsh file looks much like an .ini file; it has sections and items. In Listing 21.2, which shows a typical .wsh file, you see two sections, [ScriptFile] and [Options]. The [ScriptFile] section contains a single item path, which indicates the path and filename of the script. The [Options] section contains a few self-explanatory items that set the options you learned about earlier in this section. To launch a script using a .wsh file, you use a command line similar to this:

```
Wscript.exe myscript.wsh
```

LISTING 21.2   A SAMPLE .WSH FILE

```
[ScriptFile]
path=%WinDir%\Scripts\Logon.js

[Options]
timeout=30
displaylogo=0
batchmode=1
```

A better alternative to create a .wsh file by hand is using the script's Properties dialog box. Follow these steps:

1. Click Properties on the script's shortcut menu.

2. On the Script tab of the script's Properties dialog box (see Figure 21.4), click the Stop Script After Specified Number of Seconds check box to select it if you want to enable the watchdog timer for the script; otherwise, click the check box to clear it.

3. On the same tab, click the Display Logo When Script Executed in MS-DOS Prompt check box to select it if you want to display the logo; otherwise, click the check box to clear it.

4. Click OK to save your changes. Windows stores the .wsh file in the same folder as the original script file.

21

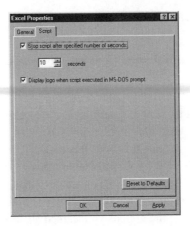

FIGURE 21.4

*Administrators can't
avoid editing .wsh
files by hand; because
of this, most useful
options aren't avail-
able on this dialog
box.*

Maintaining Directory Conventions

Deploying scripts to numerous computers is going to be significantly easier if you maintain some sort of directory conventions. These conventions can be as simple (all scripts
go in *WinDir*\Scripts) or as complex (accounting scripts go in *\\server\scripts\
accounting*) as you require. The important thing is that you can rely on the scripts resid-
ing in the exact same location relative to every computer in the organization.

One environment variable helps you better generalize the location of scripts. WinDir
expands to the drive and path of the folder in which the user installed Windows. This is
typically C:\Windows for Windows 98 users and C:\Winnt for Windows NT Workstation
4.0 users. In a batch file or on the command line, you expand this environment variable
by placing a percent sign (%) on either side, like this: %WinDir%\Scripts.

As noted, pick any directory and stick to it. I prefer to pick a share on the network so
that all network users can access the scripts. Users would tend to access these scripts
from \\pdc-camelot\scripts. Examples of local storage for scripts include

- C:\Script Files
- *WinDir*\Scripts
- *WinDir*\WSH
- *WinDir*\Profiles*Username*\Scripts
- C:\Program Files\My Scripts

Installing Scripts with `.inf` Files

You might have noticed that `.inf` files are increasing in use. Developers use these files in lieu of actual setup programs, particularly when installation is so easy that writing a full-blown setup program is senseless. Take Microsoft PowerToys, a popular set of utilities for Windows and Windows NT users. After unpacking the `.zip` file, you find several `.inf` files, one to install each of the different utilities. Unpack the setup file for Windows Script Host and you find an `.inf` file that installs the host's files. Even though the script you're distributing is simple by comparison, you too can enjoy the benefits of installing it as though it were a real application.

Listing 21.3 shows you an `.inf` file that creates a new folder under *WinDir* called Scripts. It then copies three script files—`logon.js`, `logoff.js`, and `backup.js`—to C:\Windows\Scripts. To try out this file, type this text in a plain text file with the `.inf` file extension. Create three scripts using the three filenames mentioned and put them in the same folder as the `.inf` file. To install the scripts, click Install on the `.inf` file's shortcut menu.

LISTING 21.3   A SAMPLE `.inf` FILE FOR INSTALLING A SCRIPT

```
[version]
signature="$CHICAGO$"
provider="Jerry Honeycutt"

[DefaultInstall]
CopyFiles=script.copy.js

[script.copy.js]
logon.js
logoff.js
backup.js

[DestinationDirs]
script.copy.js=10,"Scripts"

[SourceDisksNames]
1="Scripts","",1

[SourceDisksFiles]
logon.js=1
logoff.js=1
backup.js=1
```

21

As you examine an `.inf` file, keep in mind that it's not procedural. That means that you don't read it top to bottom like you do a program written in BASIC or C++. Instead, it's declarative, which means that you look at the declarations the source makes in different sections. Note, too, that the order in which each section appears isn't important. With that said, here's a section by section description of what's going on in Listing 21.3:

- **[Version]**—This section is required in all `.inf` files. Essentially, it identifies the file as a proper `.inf` file. You can set `signature` to `$CHICAGO$`, `$Windows 95$`, or `$Windows NT$`. It must be one of these values, however, or the operating system will not attempt to install the file. The `provider` item is optional, and it identifies who created or distributed the `.inf` file. Being a good administrator, you'll no doubt want to take responsibility for the `.inf` file and scripts.

- **[DefaultInstall]**—When users click Install on an `.inf` file's shortcut menu, the operating system automatically looks for a section called `[DefaultInstall]`. This section identifies the tasks that the `.inf` file performs. In this case, I have an item called `CopyFiles`, and I've assigned to it the name of another section that contains the files I want copied. The name of the item, `CopyFiles`, must appear exactly as I show you in Listing 21.3; otherwise, the operating system won't know what to do with it. Note that Windows supports a variety of other items that perform different tasks: `RenFiles`, `DelFiles`, `UpdateInis`, `AddReg`, `DelReg`, and so on.

- **[script.copy.js]**—This is the section that `CopyFiles` identified in the previous section. It contains a list of files that the operating system will copy. It's just a plain list, one filename after another. The name of the section, `[script.copy.js]`, is arbitrary, but it has to be the same name that's referenced by `CopyFiles` in the previous section. Note that you can have more than one of these sections, each with a unique name, allowing you to copy files to different destinations. In the `[DefaultInstall]` section, you would specify multiple sections like this, `CopyFiles=section1,section2`.

- **[DestinationDirs]**—If you don't provide this section, the operating system always copies files to *WinDir*\System32. This is probably not what you have in mind. This section, which must appear exactly as shown in Listing 21.3, has one item for each list of files in the `.inf` file. In the listing, you see `script.copy.js=10,"Scripts"`. This means that the operating system should copy all the files in the `[script.copy.js]` section to a *WinDir*\Scripts. The *logical disk identifier* (LDID) `10` represents *WinDir*. If you wanted put your scripts in C:\Script Files, you would have an item like `script.copy.js=30,"Script Files"`. The LDID `30` represents the root of the boot drive. Table 21.3 describes other ordinals that you can use in your `.inf` files.

- **[SourceDisksNames]**—This section identifies the name of each source disk. Because, presumably, you're distributing scripts from the network or a single floppy disk, you'll have a single entry. In most cases, you can just use what you see in Listing 21.3. The 1 on the left side of the equal sign refers to disk 1. If you had two disks, you would also have an item called 2. `"Scripts","",1` means that the disk is called `Scripts` and that the disk's serial number is 1. You can use any serial number. Useless as this section is, you must include it in your `.inf` files or the operating system won't copy any files.

- **[SourceDisksFiles]**—The files you see under this section are the same as those you saw in the `CopyFiles` section. You assign to each filename the disk number containing that file. For example, `logon.js=1` means that the file Logon.js is on disk one. Disk one is defined in `[SourceDisksNames]` as being called `Scripts` with a serial number of 1. Again, while this seems like an exercise in futility, you must associate each filename with a source disk if you want the operating system to copy your files.

TABLE 21.3 LOGICAL DISK IDENTIFIERS

LDID	Description
−1	Absolute path
00	Null LDID
01	Source drive:\path
10	Windows directory
11	System directory
12	Drivers directory
17	Inf directory
18	Help directory
20	Fonts
21	Viewers
23	Color directory
25	Shared directory
30	Root directory of the boot drive
31	Root directory for host of a virtual book drive
32	Old Windows directory
33	Old MS-DOS directory

21

The .inf file in Listing 21.3 is simple compared to the possibilities. With .inf files you can also delete and rename files. You can add, remove, and change values in the Registry. One feature common to many .inf files used this way is to copy a second .inf file to *WinDir*\Inf that removes the program from the user's computer. Then, the original .inf file adds the program to the Add/Remove Programs dialog box's list of programs that users can automatically remove. Add this capability to your script installations and you are well on your way to a promotion. There isn't room to cover all these capabilities in these few pages, but you can refer to a couple of sources to learn more. First, Microsoft's developer site, http://msdn.microsoft.com, has plenty of information about writing .inf files. If the information at this site is a bit too heady for your taste, *Windows 2000 Registry Handbook* (Que, 1999) contains a tutorial that shows you how to write advanced .inf files.

Replicating Scripts on a Network

Most network servers support some method of replicating files across a network. Windows NT Server 4.0 has a relatively simple method for doing so. Unfortunately, this feature only works with Windows NT Server 4.0 (importing and exporting) and Windows NT Workstation 4.0 (importing only). Still, if you want to replicate scripts across different servers on the domain, this is a great way to do it. As well, if your organization uses Windows NT Workstation 4.0, you can automatically replicate scripts across all the computers on the network with little effort.

An *export server* contains the source files that you want replicated across the network. Windows NT Server 4.0 can be an export server, although Windows NT Workstation 4.0 can't. You must explicitly configure an export server:

1. In Control Panel, double-click the Server icon to open the Server dialog box; then, click Replication and you see the Directory Replication dialog box.

2. Click Export Directories to enable directory replication.

3. In From Path, accept the default or type the full path of the directory that you want to replicate.

4. Click Add and specify the domain or computers to which you want to export the directory. If you specify a domain, the server exports the directory to all other servers and workstations in the domain. If you specify one or more computer names, the server exports only to those computers.

5. Click OK to close the Directory Replication dialog box. The server creates a share called Repl$ if it doesn't already exist.

Configure Import Computers

An *import computer* is the target of an export server. Both servers and workstations can be import computers. Windows 98 doesn't support replication, however, so it can't be an import computer. Follow these steps to configure Windows NT 4.0 (Server and Workstation) as an import computer:

1. In Control Panel, double-click the Server icon to open the Server dialog box; then, click Replication and you see the Directory Replication dialog box.

2. Click Import Directories to enable directory replication on the computer.

3. In To Path, accept the default or type the full path of the directory in which you want to store replicated files.

4. Click Add and specify the domain or computers from which you want to import directories. If you specify a domain, the import computer imports from all replication servers in that domain. If you specify one or more computers, the import computer imports from those export servers only.

5. Click OK to close the Directory Replication dialog box. The server creates a share called Repl$ if it doesn't already exist.

Storing and Running Scripts

Now that you've configured the export servers and import computers, you have to wonder where to put the files on the server and where you're going to find them on the import computers. By default, Windows NT Server 4.0 exports *WinDir*\System32\Repl\Export and Windows NT 4.0 imports directories to *WinDir*\System32\Repl\Import. You can certainly change these locations—but why?

Under both import and export directories, you usually find a subdirectory called Scripts. Store your scripts here. To replicate scripts across the domain, copy them into *WinDir*\System32\Repl\Export\Scripts on the server. Then, users whose computers you've configured as import computers can run them from *WinDir*\System32\Repl\ Import\Scripts. If you have users whose computers you haven't configured as import computers, they can still access the scripts through the server's Netlogon share. This share usually maps to *WinDir*\System32\Repl\Import\Scripts on the server. To recap, after setting up directory replication on your network:

- Put scripts in *WinDir*\System32\Repl\Export\Scripts
- Run scripts in *WinDir*\System32\Repl\Import\Scripts

21

Tip

> Just because Windows 98 doesn't support replication doesn't mean that you can't use replication to make scripts available to Windows 98 users. The Netlogon share, which is available to all Windows 98 users, maps to the Scripts subdirectory of server's export directory. Thus, you can copy your scripts to this directory, replicating them across all the servers in your domain and allowing users to access them through the Netlogon share.

Running Scripts from the Network

To run scripts from the network, you have to make those scripts available to users who need them. To do so, copy the files to a folder and share the folder, giving users appropriate permissions. One example of a share is \\pdc-camelot\scripts. On my network, however, I put scripts in the Netlogon share for easy replication and because this share is already available to everyone on the network. In that case, users access scripts through \\pdc-camelot\Netlogon. So that you don't have to flip back 20 pages to the last time you read about sharing folders, here's a quick refresher on how to share your scripts:

1. Create a folder on the network, copy your scripts to it, and set its permissions so that the users who require the scripts can access them. Make sure you give users Read and Execute (RX) permissions.

2. In Windows Explorer, click Sharing on the folder's shortcut menu to display the Sharing tab of the Properties dialog box shown earlier in Figure 21.2.

3. Click Shared As, type the name of the share in Share Name, and click Permissions to determine which users have access to the folder. Give users no less than Read permissions on the share.

4. Click OK to make the new share immediately available.

Note

> When sharing scripts on an NTFS volume, you set permissions in two different places. First, you set permissions on the Security tab of the folder's Properties dialog box. The operating system enforces these permissions for local and network users. Second, you set permissions by clicking Permissions on the Sharing tab of the folder's Properties dialog box. The operating system enforces these permissions for network users only. If you restrict local and network access to the folder, you can usually allow everyone access to the share. If you're using FAT or haven't restricted local and network access to the folder, make sure you set stronger restrictions on who can access the share on the network.

Running WSH Scripts from Logon Scripts

One of the most common uses for WSH scripts is as a more advanced logon script. NetWare has a reasonable logon script capability; Windows NT Server 4.0 did not—until now. To learn about the networking tasks you can do with Windows Script Host, see Chapter 10, "Replacing Batch Files with WSH," and Chapter 11, "Administering User Logins, Program Settings, Folders, and File Shortcuts Using WSH Scripts."

In Windows NT Server 4.0, logon scripts are nothing more than batch files. Although Windows NT 4.0 allows you to use the .bat or .cmd file extensions for batch files, stick to .bat for those souls using Windows 95 and Windows 98. You've already learned how to configure a logon script but that was 20 pages ago. Here's a brief summary of the process:

1. On the Start menu, point to Programs, Administrator Tools (Common), and click User Manager for Domains.

2. Select one or more users from the list and choose Properties from the User menu. You'll see the User Properties dialog box.

3. Click Profile, and you'll see the User Environment Profile dialog box shown earlier in Figure 21.3.

3. Type the filename of the logon script in Logon Script Name. Remember that this path is appended to the logon script path configured in the Directory Replication dialog box.

4. Click OK to close the User Environment Profile dialog box, and click OK again to close the User Properties dialog box.

Windows NT 4.0 wouldn't know what to do if you tried to specify a WSH script as a logon script; therefore, you must specify a batch file as the logon script and then launch the WSH script from within the batch file. Listing 21.3 shows you an example of such a logon script that checks for the installation of Windows Script Host and, if not found, installs it. Regardless, it launches the WSH script. Put this script in the appropriate place, log on to a workstation, and watch it do its magic. If you've accepted the default path for logon scripts and you specified to User Manager for Domains that the logon script is called Logon.bat, you would put Listing 21.4 in a text file called Logon.bat and store it on the server in *WinDir*\System32\Repl\Import\Scripts.

21

LISTING 21.4 A SAMPLE LOGON SCRIPT

```
If Exist %WinDir%\Wscript.exe Goto doit
If Exist %WinDir%\System32\Wscript.exe Goto doit

Echo Installing Windows Script Host
\\pdc-camelot\wsh\st50en.exe

:doit
Wscript \\pdc-camelot\Netlogon\login.wsh
```

Here's a description of how this logon script works:

1. The first thing this logon script does is make sure that Windows Script Host is installed on the computer. Because the host might be installed in one of two places, *WinDir* or *WinDir*\System32, both are checked.

2. If Windows Script Host is installed, the logon script launches the WSH script. Note two things: First, the script is executed from the Netlogon share of the server. Second, the script is launched from a .wsh file, which enables setting options separately from the logon script.

3. If Windows Script Host isn't installed, the logon script installs it from the network.

Summary

This chapter taught you how to deploy Windows Script Host on the network. It also taught you a few different ways to deploy scripts on the network. Although this chapter focused on Windows NT 4.0, the principles you learned here apply equally well to any network server.

Now, that just about wraps up *Sams Teach Yourself Windows Script Host in 21 Days*. At this point, you should know how to write a variety of simple and complex scripts. You should know how to test and debug your scripts. You should also know how to use Windows Script Host to perform a myriad of real-world, business tasks. And now that you've finished this last day, you know how to deploy your scripts to small and big organizations alike.

Index

Symbols

\\computername argument (Windows NT AT command), 178
/INTERACTIVE switch (Windows NT AT command), 179
//YES switch (Windows NT AT command), 179
<%...%> tags to identify script in Active Server Pages, 159-160

A

abend, 171
accessing
   databases, 406
   properties, Active Directory and WSH, 481
   variables, 195-196

Active Data Objects (ADO)
   Active Directory and
      connections, establishing, 504
      overview of, 503
      selections, specifying, 504-505
   Command object
      code sample, 426-427
      collections, 426
      creating new record, 455-456
      methods, 425
      overview of, 412, 423
      Parameters collection, 449-450
      properties, 424-425
   Connection object
      code sample, 419-423
      collections, 419
      creating instance of, 455
      methods, 416-418
      overview of, 411
      Parameters collection, 450
      properties, 412-415

Error object
   Errors collection, 451
   properties, 450
Field object
   code sample, 442-443
   collections, 442
   description of, 439
   methods, 442
   Parameters collection, 450
   properties, 439-440
object model, 410, 454
overview of, 21, 410
Parameter object
   code sample, 446-448
   collections, 446
   methods, 446
   properties, 444-446
Property object, 449
recording user logins in databases
   creating login database and tables, 457-460
   script for, 461-464
   setting up script for, 465

X-Z